Sloan Rules

SLOAN RULES

ALFRED P. SLOAN AND THE TRIUMPH OF GENERAL MOTORS

David Farber

THE UNIVERSITY OF CHICAGO PRESS
CHICAGO • LONDON

The University of Chicago Press, Chicago 60637
The University of Chicago Press, Ltd., London

Paperback edition 2004
Printed in the United States of America
11 10 09 08 07 06 05 04 2 3 4 5

ISBN: 0–226-23804–0 (cloth)
ISBN: 0-226-23805-9 (paperback)

Library of Congress Cataloging-in-Publication Data

Farber, David R.
Sloan rules : Alfred P. Sloan and the triumph of General Motors / David Farber.
p. cm.
Includes bibliographical references (p.) and index.
ISBN 0-226-23804-0 (cloth)
1. Sloan, Alfred P. (Alfred Pritchard, 1875–1966. 2. General Motors Corporation—History. 3. Automobile industry and trade—United States—History. I. Title.
HD9710.U52 S494 2002
338.7'62922'092—dc21 2002004967

♾The paper used in this publication meets the minimum requirements of the American National Standard for Information Sciences—Permanence of Paper for Printed Library Materials, ANSI Z39.48–1992.

Contents

Prologue

It was evening all afternoon.
It was snowing
And it was going to snow.
The blackbird sat
In the cedar-limbs.

—Wallace Stevens, "Thirteen Ways of Looking at a Blackbird"

Alone, Mr. Sloan watched television late into the evening. He appreciated the television. It was a technical box that incorporated clever advertising and entertaining programming. He saw the utility in that. He watched the television and then slept long hours.

In 1965, Alfred Sloan was ninety years old. His hearing was poor, as it had been for many years, but with mechanical aid he could hear most of what he desired. Earlier in the year there had been some health problems, resulting in his first overnight hospital stay, but he had recovered and was well again. He had always enjoyed excellent physical health.

For decades he had lived at 820 Fifth Avenue in a grand apartment rich with antique furnishings. His wife had arranged for the decor. When he and Mrs. Sloan had entertained—not a common occurrence—people always noted the gold bathroom fixtures. But these things—antiques and plumbing fixtures—meant little to him. He had bought the residence many years earlier as his New York City home. He had spent his nights there, with Mrs. Sloan, at least for much of the year, when he had not been on his regular bimonthly trips to Detroit, or traveling elsewhere, as he had so frequently, on company business.

Mrs. Sloan and he had been wed for just over fifty-eight years when she died in 1956, before he had been able to find the time he had always hoped to share with her. They had never had children. The few good friends he had were almost all dead, most of them for decades. As before, a large corps of servants, respectful of their employer and unfailingly treated by him with respect, looked after Sloan's personal needs.

Sloan was alone and distant but never, yet, disengaged from the world around him. He was chauffeured each weekday to his office at Rockefeller Center. Though his day did not extend nearly so long as it once did, he remained active with the work of the world. His mind remained a powerful engine of exactitude.[1]

On Sloan's ninetieth birthday the newspapers wished to commemorate his life. He was the man who had led General Motors—"the world's largest private industrial enterprise," as he himself phrased it—to greatness by virtue of the brilliance of his managerial practices. The previous year, his account of those management practices had been published under the title *My Years with General Motors.* Sloan's dispassionate account of his management decisions, written "to give an account of the progress of General Motors . . . from the logical point of view" had been widely heralded as an instant classic of managerial science.[2] And despite its complete, deliberate lack of quotable remarks and colorful anecdotes and its nearly perfect avoidance of Sloan's subjective feelings on life inside or out of the corporation, it stayed on the best-seller lists for twenty-two weeks, so compelling was its precise explanation of how Alfred Sloan made executive decisions.

That Sloan was rich—very rich—further enhanced his public profile. His shares in General Motors, steadily accumulated from his first connection with the corporation in the early years of the twentieth century, had made him one of the richest men in the world. By his ninetieth birthday, the philanthropic foundation that bore his name had achieved assets of some $305 million (about $1.7 billion in 2000 dollars). Under Sloan's direction, the foundation had already made gifts of over $130 million. Tens of millions of dollars, in addition to personal gifts of some $23 million, had gone to his alma mater, the Massachusetts Institute of Technology. Millions more went to other technical institutes of higher learning. Many additional millions had been spent creating and endowing the Sloan-Kettering Institute for Cancer Research. Despite such philanthropic munificence, Sloan still retained a personal fortune of a quarter of a billion dollars.

On the upcoming occasion of his ninetieth birthday, a reporter at the *New York Times* tried to convince Alfred Sloan that his life would be of great interest to the reading public. Sloan refused the newspaperman's request for an interview and sent instead a brief memo to the *Times:* "I would like to fade away and be forgotten. I think having lived to the present age justifies my so doing. I am sorry. I do not want to be discourteous. I cannot afford to be. But I most earnestly ask to be excused." Like much of what Sloan said for public use, he did not mean exactly what his curious words might have suggested to most people.

Only days before his birthday, Sloan had presided over the fourth annual Alfred P. Sloan Awards in Cancer Research. Without notes or assistance, before an appreciative audience of fellow philanthropists, doctors, and scientists, as well as invited members of the press, he had bestowed large cash awards to three eminent cancer researchers. Sloan had, in turn, been given an award of his own. Laurence S. Rockefeller, grandson of John D. Rockefeller and chairman of the Memorial Sloan-Kettering Cancer Center, had surprised him with the presentation of a medallion honoring his "personal leadership" in the struggle against cancer. Still speaking in perfectly formed paragraphs, Sloan had thanked all in attendance for his award and for their presence. "I'm proud to be a member of the team," he had said in conclusion, a remark perfectly in keeping with the corporate approach he had taken during his years with General Motors.[3]

Sloan, as his public leadership in the cancer fight demonstrated, did not really wish to "fade away and be forgotten." He valued publicity in service to defined goals, as he had for many decades. He would not have published his book on management in 1964 if he had not wished, in a certain respect, to be remembered. But Sloan, as always, had his own agenda. His statement to the press on the occasion of his ninetieth birthday was in accord with a life lived in pursuit of control over the flow of information. Until the end, Sloan would attempt to guide the public to the objects he desired them to approve. The people would know what he believed they needed to know to understand what he believed was in their own best interests. They certainly did not need to read about his life at the moment it was nearly over. His personal life was his business alone.

Less than a year later, Sloan was dead. He left no private papers. No letters exist, at least it appears, limning the fifty-eight years of his marriage or of his relations with his parents or siblings. Soon after Sloan's death, General Motors destroyed his corporate papers (or so archivists and researchers are told). Officials at the Sloan Foundation politely inform the diligent researcher that they have nothing to offer on the life of their founder. He would have been pleased.

Alfred Sloan, who more than any other individual created the form of consumer capitalism that characterized much of twentieth-century America, did not trust the public's ability to distinguish what was truly important without a great deal of responsible guidance. Sloan's life was not something he wished to see left in the hands of others. But his deeds he believed, he hoped—he knew—would live on long after he was dust.

The desire to guide the public had come only with need. And the need had developed and changed over time. When he had first gone into business the public had been far from his thoughts. Only later, while at the helm of General Motors, had the public become a thing to measure and manage. And only during the New Deal era, the crisis years, did Alfred Sloan begin to reappraise how his responsibilities as manager of General Motors' fortune necessitated public stewardship, a kind of corporate citizenship that he had never desired.

Sloan had never shirked his corporate duties. When economic and political crisis threatened General Motors during what he perceived to be the dark years of the New Deal, Sloan did everything in his power to preserve the corporation's freedom to act and its right to profitability. To manage General Motors's political crisis, Sloan had to think about the public and attempt to act on the democratic citizenry in ways he had never before imagined. He had been forced to stretch intellectually and to expand his interests in novel ways.

Alfred Sloan was a private man who believed the nation's good came from the private enterprise system. During his long tenure as a leader of America's greatest industrial enterprise, Sloan devoted himself to corporate profit. Private profit, he believed, created national prosperity. That national prosperity, he knew with great certainty, was the foundation on which everything else that Americans chose to value was built. Democracy, equality, liberty, and the other shibboleths of politicians and public-minded figures of one kind or another, he knew, even if they did not, depended on the economic productivity created by men like him. Alfred Sloan knew that much and he lived his life based on that knowledge. He acted on those beliefs. His America would be built on those sequential truths.

We live and still wrestle with Alfred Sloan's truths.

* * *

What follows is not a traditional biography. Alfred Sloan veiled his inner life too successfully for that kind of story. Still, this is an accounting of a unique man. I do my best to explore Sloan's vision of the United States and his attempts to make it conform to his ideal of a productive society. Alfred Sloan successfully built one of the world's great corporations. He played a major role in shaping twentieth-century American life. To understand contemporary American society one has to reckon with Mr. Sloan.

Much of this book carefully follows Sloan's development. In the first chapters, we watch Sloan learn how to manage industrial enterprises and then rise to the presidency of General Motors. At General Motors, he plays a critical role in inventing modern corporate management and mass marketing in the early twentieth century. In the 1920s, with support from the American people and the encouragement of the nation's political leaders, business corporations throughout the nation generally prosper and General Motors, in particular, is guided by Sloan to economic greatness. From his successes, Sloan develops a loose economic model in which highly rationalized corporate productivity combined with relentless marketing creates a mass consumer society that, in turn, produces the greatest good for the greatest possible number of people.

In the 1930s, with the economy in crisis and political forces—New Dealers—arguing that businessmen cannot be trusted to produce prosperity or economic justice, Sloan rushes to the defense of his free enterprise model, in which industrial leaders, not government officials, must be free to manage their businesses as they see fit. World War II, Sloan believes, vindicates his social vision. General Motors and other key industries, not politicians and bureaucrats, produced America's "arsenal of democracy" and, so, victory. When Sloan finally steps down from his executive duties at General Motors in 1946, he does so confident that the free enterprise system he helped build and has long championed has regained its primacy in American life. During the last years of his life, Sloan spends hundreds of millions of dollars to strengthen his version of a well-ordered American society. Alfred Sloan was a business genius and a great corporate manager. He thought little about social justice or morality.

Sloan, as he would be the first to state, did not act alone at General Motors nor in his political work. This book is a biographical study but it is also an assessment of one aspect of American conservatism. Historians, after focusing for many years primarily on liberal politicians and leftist social change movements, have begun to reckon with the power of conservative forces and ideas in American history. Corporate conservatives such as Alfred Sloan and many of his GM and Du Pont Corporation colleagues have long played a central role in American political life. Corporate conservatives argue that all political choices must be seen through a lens of economic rationality, which reveals that anything that hurts corporate investment and corporate profitability will hurt national prosperity. To say the obvious, they do not focus on income disparity between groups or individuals, or minimum economic standards of life, or democratic economic decision making, or any number of other economic and political measures of national health and the good life. Corporate conservatives focus attention on aggregate measures of the national economy that remove questions of distribution and decision making from the picture. Sloan helped to develop such a perspective. A study of his life will, I hope, bring corporate conservatism, as a historical and contemporary force in the United States, into clearer focus.

Finally, this book, as Sloan might have wished, tells the story of a critical part of American history with business corporations and industrial leaders at its center. Among the most important legacies of the twentieth century to our own time is the central place occupied by giant corporations in our economy, our politics, and our culture. These corporate enterprises have helped the United States and many other nations achieve unprecedented national wealth and dazzling consumer choices, even as they exert tremendous power over our economic lives. Corporations, through expertise and money, shape political debate and structure critical aspects of public policy. Everywhere we turn, from the arts to sports to education to the built environment, business corporations appear as a guiding force. The rise and consolidation of corporate power was not just a natural event. It has a history and a cast of characters. Alfred Sloan helped make this history; "Silent Sloan," as he was sometimes known, was one of its stars.

1

SLOAN'S WORK

Self-forgetfulness is what is required.

—Early twentieth-century engineer on being a corporate employee

Being a child held little interest for Alfred Sloan. Even before his youth had ended, he strained to begin his work.

The eldest of five children, Sloan was born in New Haven, Connecticut, on May 23, 1875. His father, Alfred P. Sloan Sr., was then twenty-five, his mother twenty-three. They were originally from upstate New York, where their respective families were "old" and respectable, but not well-to-do. Mrs. Sloan's father had been a Methodist Episcopal minister (the Sloans, but not their eldest son, maintained a close association with the denomination until their deaths). Sloan Sr.'s father had been a private school master. But when his father sickened, Alfred Sr. was forced to leave school early and make his way in the world. This he did; by the time Alfred Jr. was born, his father was already a successful merchant, purveying tea, cigars, and coffee. Primarily, he imported coffee beans, which he roasted, ground, and blended, and then sold them wholesale.

By the time young Alfred was eleven years of age, Bennett, Sloan, and Company was a two-story concern located at 100 Hudson Street in lower Manhattan. The success of the business founded in New Haven had brought Sloan Sr. and his partner to New York City in 1885. The company prospered and Sloan grew up in a large brownstone at 240 Garfield Place in a relatively fashionable part of Brooklyn.

Soon after moving to Brooklyn, Alfred began attending the Brooklyn Polytechnic Institute, which educated boys in what was then called "mechanics," or the practical sciences, much to young Alfred's delight. He was an outstanding student who relished book learning. Most of the boys in his neighborhood spent their afternoons out on the streets, teasing the iceman's horse or playing ball, "flipping" on and off wagons or hustling nickels selling newspapers (in 1890, two-thirds of newspapers were sold by newsboys—and a few newsgirls, as well—in the late afternoon). In his own accounts of his youth, Sloan states that he went straight home from school and spent his after-school hours avidly working through his text books.[1]

While Sloan would never display any nostalgic interest in his Brooklyn youth—or ever mention any particular feelings he may have had about moving from New Haven to New York—he did retain throughout his life a distinct Brooklyn accent, which others often found surprising on first hearing. He had a somewhat reedy, tenor voice and his speech was marked with such Brooklynese as "foist" for first and "woik" for work. Since neither of his parents were Brooklyn natives, the heaviness of Sloan's accent suggests that he spent more time than he later admitted outside his home playing with other children and exploring his neighborhood.

In the only published photograph from Alfred Sloan's boyhood he sits astride a high-wheel bicycle, probably an 1886 Columbia Light Roadster. Sloan, in later life, always carefully crafted his self-image for public consumption and it is likely that he provided the photo himself, first published in a 1938 *Fortune* magazine profile, to reveal his early interest in the wheeled technology that directly contributed to his own industrial career: the photo was captioned "Young Alfred, astride the mechanical marvel of his age, had already chosen his career." Whatever Sloan's intent, the photo of a cocksure boy high atop his spectacular bicycle—if it was a Columbia bicycle it cost upwards of $120 at a time when the U.S. per capita income was under $200—reveals that he was never as one-dimensional a figure as his own accounts, even of his boyhood, always suggested.[2]

Whether or not Alfred was a more playful child than he later wished others to know, by the time he was a teenager he was clearly eager to move forward and put childhood behind him. Sloan had decided that he wanted to be an engineer, a profession of relatively recent vintage. At age seventeen, he attempted to enroll at the Columbia University School of Mines. Despite easily passing the entrance exams, he was told he was too young to matriculate. Probably after some independent investigation, he turned to the more distant Massachusetts Institute of Technology, in Cambridge, which saw his age as no impediment. His father had the money to send Sloan to MIT and support him there.[3]

In 1891, the year before Sloan matriculated at MIT, and only thirty years after the school's establishment, the institute's president Francis Amasa Walker had told his fellow educators that "in the schools of applied science and technology is to be found the perfection of education for young men."[4]

Sloan wanted just such an education. He expected the work to be difficult and he intended to devote himself to it with a singular dedication. Further, he decided early on that he would compound the challenge of MIT's program of studies by completing the four-year program in three years. Sloan saw his university days as a training ground for professional activities, not as some adventure in self-discovery or youthful pleasures. As Sloan remembered almost a half a century later, "I had been a grind. I had worked every possible minute, so that I might be graduated a year ahead, with the class of 1895."[5] Sloan succeeded. He graduated from, arguably, the finest technology program in the nation in just three years. He had led his class in calculus, receiving a perfect score of 100 in his freshman year. He had also excelled in thermodynamics, in which he received a near perfect semester average of 98. Not all went so well for Sloan during his MIT days. In his courses in literature and history, which the school required, he did far worse; receiving three D's and two C's.[6] Many decades later, Sloan forgot, or more likely chose to ignore at least temporarily, that he had ever taken such frustrating courses. He told an associate, "When I went to M.I.T. I did not have a single course in English, to say nothing of a single course in literature. I did not have a course in economics or in sociology or in history, to say nothing of broader courses than that." Sloan concluded: "I had a very narrow technical education. . . . For that reason and probably for inherent reasons, I am a very narrow man."[7]

MIT's president in the 1890s, Francis Amasa Walker, would have been disappointed with Sloan's harsh self-assessment (and of his recollection of what courses he had actually taken). President Walker had hoped that requiring humanities courses, with "their liberalizing tendencies," would combine with "the work of the sciences in making the pupils exact and strong."[8] Undoubtedly, Sloan believed he had achieved exactitude in his studies, and even a certain kind of mental strength. Cultural interests, however, did not stem naturally from his exposure to them. To go for the moment far ahead in this unfolding story, throughout his long life Alfred Sloan nearly never read for pleasure or voluntarily attended cultural performances of any kind. The MIT curriculum, whatever Sloan chose to remember or say in retrospect, was not to blame for this antipathy to works of literature or the creative arts.[9]

Sloan received a bachelor of science in electricity, a field of study added to the curriculum at MIT only in 1882 but which was by the mid-1890s the most popular major at the school. Electrical engineering was, then, still in its infancy.[10] Sloan worked on equipment donated by Thomas Edison just before his arrival. Like Edison, Sloan did not see himself as a lone genius preparing for a lifetime of creative breakthroughs. He would be a scientifically trained technical problem solver prepared for coordinated work on practical concerns. Alfred Sloan had become an electrical engineer, like most of his cohort, to take a corporate position in America's world-leading industrial sector. The MIT classes of the 1890s were memorable ones. By the early 1920s, institute alumni ran General Motors, General Electric, Goodyear, and Du Pont. The engineering mind—disciplined, logical, and methodical—fit perfectly the needs of America's evolving business corporations.

When he graduated in 1895, Sloan expected that his training would afford him the opportunity to take a respectable place in an industrial enterprise. At the end of the nineteenth century, in the United States as elsewhere in the world that mattered to Alfred Sloan, it was in industry that opportunity for achievement lay. A position within an industrial enterprise, he believed, would allow him to demonstrate his abilities, make his way, and advance rapidly. The meaning and nature of that success were subjects about which Sloan made no internal queries; his mind, at least as he and others have revealed it, did not turn in those sorts of direction. Sloan, just twenty years of age when he left MIT, was already a man of some certainties.

* * *

The Great Depression, the era that will figure so centrally in this story, could not have been a huge shock to Alfred Sloan Jr. He had been born just after the horrendous Panic of 1873, and when he graduated from MIT in 1895, the American economy was still reeling from the 1893 depression, the worst the nation had yet suffered. As the economy contracted in 1893, some six hundred banks and more than fifteen thousand businesses dissolved. Farmers were hit especially hard, and for the first time in the nation's history tens of thousands of tramps, most of them farm laborers, wandered the countryside in search of food. In the urban industrial centers, employers had to let go as many as one quarter of all unskilled, industrial workers.

Sloan followed the effects of the struggling economy in the Boston newspapers. He knew and almost certainly disapproved of William Jennings Bryant's inflationary demands for the coinage of silver to increase the money supply and so ease farmers' perilous economic plight. And he read with interest the daily press reports tracking the progress of the so-called Coxey's Army of unemployed men, which made its way by rail and road to Washington, D.C. to wage the first national political campaign against unemployment.[11] In 1894, about ten thousand of the unemployed, most of them in small groups from the far Northwest, California, New England, the Middle West, and the Rocky Mountain states marched on the nation's capital to present a "petition in boots." They wanted Congress to provide a national public works program until private employment again became possible. The largest group, perhaps a thousand men, called themselves "Coxey's Army" after their radical leader Jacob Coxey, a successful Ohio businessman, who insisted that a humanitarian concern for the less fortunate and the new industrial order could be reconciled through government action. The marchers succeeded in capturing the nation's interest but received no hearing from Congress. Coxey was jailed for twenty days for "illegally carrying banners" and for walking on the grass. In the mid-1890s the federal government provided the general citizenry with less than $5 million a year for all social welfare, health, and security programs. The business cycle, while little analyzed, was understood by most men of the capitalist class to be an unfortunate but regular part of the workings of the modern economy.[12]

For Sloan, this downward turn was not merely a story in the newspapers. He could not find a job. He spent a few months after his graduation working with one of his professors on engineering projects but nothing developed from it. When he began looking in earnest for a regular position in late 1895, Alfred Sloan, who had graduated MIT in three years, was turned down by every employer he contacted. Many industrial firms still distrusted university-educated men—few of the older generation of industrialists had received a higher education—and engineering positions of any kind, following the 1893 downturn, were in short supply. In Sloan's understated way he once allowed that the year after he graduated college was an unhappy time for him, "the most discouraging point of my whole life."[13] He was forced to look inward and ask himself, "Where did I fit into the American economy, what could I do?"[14]

Sloan, remember, was only twenty years old when he finished with MIT, the youngest member of his graduating class. Forced leisure did not, however, encourage in him some desire to travel or to pursue adventure. Like most young, professional men of his time, he had no interest in fostering his personality through some course of self-discovery. Such emphasis on the rewards of personal development would not become commonplace for another quarter of a century. Sloan wished only to find opportunity for the talent and training he had developed at MIT. A favorite adage (like many American businessmen—from Benjamin Franklin through the present day—Sloan did produce and adhere to certain adages) expressed his outlook and goal: "Everyone of us has a certain talent in a certain direction and in other directions we may be completely devoid of talent." It is essential, he would say, to figure out your talent, for "that way work becomes a pleasure and not a drudgery."[15] That Sloan would simply assume that any talent worthy of being so described would be work-directed indicates a fundamental aspect of his social outlook. Sloan's talent, so well proven at MIT, was in mastering, and even exceeding, the demands of institutional structures.

Sloan needed a position, a place in an organization from which he could direct his immense capacity for focused work in problem solving. Without such an organization, he was without purpose. In another rare allowance of personal feeling, Sloan would note, "as I was naturally of a serious turn of mind, I suppose I was more than ordinarily troubled when I failed to find work at any of the places where I applied."[16] No evidence exists suggesting that Sloan's inability to find a position despite his superior qualifications during a time of market contraction caused him to regard the free enterprise system with any disfavor. In the account of his employment troubles, just quoted, which was written at the end of the Great Depression, Sloan managed to interject the first-person pronoun five times in one sentence to make it clear that he blames no one and nothing for his difficulties except himself, emphasizing: "I failed to find work." Whether or not Sloan accurately recalls what he felt at the time, he does admit to being deeply depressed in late 1895. The damaged economy thwarted him and he did not know what to do.

After some months of this unhappiness, his father, finally, was able to help. Sloan Sr. was well acquainted with one of Brooklyn's richest men, John E. Searles of the American Sugar Refining Company. Their friendship extended back to the beginnings of their respective business pursuits in New Haven and had been renewed at the Methodist Episcopal Church in Brooklyn, where both men played an active role. Searles agreed to meet Sloan's son and see what he could do for him.

The meeting was brief. Sloan was shy at first, as was his nature, but was soon put at ease by Searles' kind and courteous demeanor. Searles, whose business made him an experienced judge of character and ability, recognized what young Alfred had to offer. Sloan left the meeting with a position in one of Searles' smaller companies. His career was launched.

Sloan never, in later years, pretended his entrance into the business world to be anything other than it was. He was of a new breed. He was born not into great wealth, nor was he a "self-made man." His was no Horatio Alger story. (Sloan would later use the term "Alger-boy" to refer to the self-made.) He came from a respectable, upper-middle-class, white, Anglo-Saxon Protestant family. His father's connections, coupled to his excellent education and obvious talent, proved out over time. Sloan's "hardest problem," finding out where he "fit into the American economy," had been solved and his time—in retrospect, a very brief time—of great disappointment had come to a close.

Sloan's career did not, at first, seem to be on a meteoric course. The position that Searles had provided for him was the relatively humble post of draftsman. Young Alfred probably did not mention to Searles that the worst grade he had received at MIT—an F—had been in drawing.[17] Sloan was employed at a small factory, the Hyatt Roller Bearing Company, a fledgling company in which Searles had the major interest. Hyatt was, itself, a humble concern, which moved from gritty Newark to the even less glamorous Harrison, New Jersey shortly after Sloan began work. Its operations were composed of a single building: a dirty, shack-like structure. Its nearest neighbor was a sprawling junkyard filled with rusting, obsolete machinery. Indicative of its status, Hyatt was sited on low ground, so that when it rained the unpaved grounds surrounding the factory became a sea of mud.

Hyatt manufactured a new sort of antifriction roller bearing. This bearing served to increase energy efficiency and thus decrease energy expenditures by reducing the frictional pressures on the line shafting that still turned most of the industrial machines then in use in the United States—this being just prior to the use of electric motors in such machinery. (One can still view how industrial machinery was turned by line shafting at the textile factories preserved as museums in the old mill towns of Lowell and Lawrence, Massachusetts.) The bearing had been first used in Searles' sugar grinders.[18]

The Hyatt roller bearing had been invented by John Wesley Hyatt, an old-school inventor, largely self-taught and unsophisticated in scientific methods and theory. Despite his formal shortcomings, Hyatt was one of the most productive independent inventors of the nineteenth century. His breakthrough had come in 1869 when a shortage of elephant tusks had induced a New York City billiard ball manufacturer to offer a prize of ten thousand dollars for a synthetic billiard ball. Hyatt had combined pyroxylin (a volatile nitrocellulose substance) with camphor to make his plastine ball.[19] In a small shop, Hyatt churned out other ingenious materials including a much improved, hardened wood for golf club heads. The roller bearing that bore its inventor's name (developed from the same lathe that Hyatt had invented to produce the synthetic billiard balls) had a decided advantage over competitive products for one simple reason: it was made of coiled steel tubing that gave it a springy quality and thus, as Sloan wrote some years later, "yielded to irregularities caused by poor manufacture, thus making automatic adjustments between housing and bearing."[20]

It is worth emphasizing, given Sloan's subsequent career, that the Hyatt bearing was needed because machined parts in the late nineteenth century had not yet, as a matter of course, been engineered to fine tolerances. As a result, the flexibility of the Hyatt roller bearing made it an excellent product for the time. But as Sloan understood almost immediately, despite his lowly position and youth, the company was poorly run and so incapable of capitalizing its opportunities. At best, the company, with its twenty-five or so employees, was averaging two thousand dollars a month in sales. Sloan was paid fifty dollars monthly and he quickly observed that the payroll was quite often being met only because Mr. Searles subsidized it. The business was a money loser.

Sloan became friendly with the company's young bookkeeper, a Norwegian immigrant named Peter Steenstrup. Over lunches at the nearest eatery, they discussed the means by which Hyatt could be made into a profitable business. The talk was idle as no one in authority had the least interest in their viewpoint. Sloan was frustrated. His talents were being wasted and he was impatient to move forward in the world. He desired to be married to a women he had been courting since his days at MIT, Irene Jackson of Roxbury, Massachusetts (although where he found the time to meet and then court Miss Jackson remains a great mystery given his work habits both in college and on the job). In Sloan's mind, marriage was impossible until he had achieved a more respectable economic status.

In 1897, Sloan left Hyatt. In a rare but not unique move, he took a gamble on an unproven invention, an electric refrigeration unit being developed by Lieutenant Michael E. Wood of the U.S. Navy. Wood, no longer a young man, was an inveterate inventor, trained some years earlier at the Naval Academy, one of the nation's first institutions to professionally educate engineers. He was sure he had finally come up with a winning technology and his enthusiasm was contagious. Wood had started a company to manufacture and install his refrigeration units in large apartment houses and hotels. As he explained to Sloan, the main refrigeration machinery would be located in a building's basement. Cold brine would then be pumped to individual boxes lined with copper coils that in turn would chill the box's contents and, incredibly, also supply icy-cold running water. A rich Bostonian had provided the start-up capital.

Sloan was charged with designing the system's circulating system and with managing sales. That the shy Sloan, completely unsuited to backslapping and glad-handing, had been given salesman duties, indicates how shaky were the enterprise's foundations. Wood called his brainchild the Hygienic Refrigeration Company. As Sloan recalled many years later, "I was a kid, infected with Lieutenant Wood's blind faith."[21] Sloan was just twenty-two years old. From his experiences with the Hygienic Refrigeration Company, he would learn to trust even more in his dispassionate nature.

Like so many other new, technology-based companies, then and now, the business was not a success. Many were interested in the idea but the system was quite expensive. Worse, it frequently broke down. Even so, Sloan threw himself into the work. The enterprise was exciting, demanding of his talents, and provided, at first, a good income.

Based on his faulty expectations of a reasonable economic future with Hygienic, Sloan married Irene Jackson on September 28, 1898.[22] We do not know if the couple were giddy with love or as sober in private as they always appeared in their relatively rare public appearances in later years. Separated as they were for nearly three years, one assumes they corresponded, and perhaps they phoned one another despite the cost and the relatively poor quality of long distance transmissions. No record exists. Images of the courting Sloan, the young man in love, died with him.

All that remains of the Sloans from their first year of marriage is a single photograph made sometime during the spring or early summer of 1899.[23] Like so much else that Sloan left for others to ponder, it is a conventionalized image. The newlyweds are pictured with Alfred's family. Alfred Sr. is at the center of the family arrangement, holding his youngest child Raymond in his lap. He maintains the six year old's attention with a picture book. Alfred Jr. sits at his father's right hand, looking quite composed in a cane-backed rocking chair. He stares, as was his way all through life, with a fixed, unemotional gaze at the camera—a typical pose for a young man of his status at the end of the nineteenth century (the camera's slow shutter speed contributed to such stiff-looking poses). The only person standing in the family photo is Irene. She is all in white, positioned behind her husband, her arm on his chair but not touching him. Perhaps it is a not the best picture of her; she appears to have a very long nose on a small face. Her dark hair is neatly tied behind her head in a bun. Like her mother-in-law, she hints at a smile.

We know, at the very least, that Sloan did love his bride, at least in his own reserved way. In the same year of her death in 1956, Sloan would break down before the man, Warren Weaver, he wished to appoint to the presidency of the Sloan Foundation. Weaver had just told Sloan that he would seriously consider the presidency of the foundation but only if he not be asked to make extensive business travels. He explained that in his previous position with the Rockefeller Foundation he had been forced to spend too much time away from his wife. The eighty-one-year-old Sloan responded: "If I ever ask you to do anything that limits your companionship with your wife, you just tell me to go to hell. I understand completely. For many years I was too completely absorbed in my business. I always said that I would cut down on this, and spend more time with my wife. But Warren, I waited too long." At this point, Sloan, a man who, aside from the perfunctory and brief handshake, almost never physically touched anyone, at least in public, put his arm across Weaver's shoulders as tears rolled down his cheeks. Sloan undoubtedly loved Irene, even if he chose not to show that affection publicly and rarely found the time to demonstrate it privately.[24]

Sloan would remain married to Irene Jackson Sloan for the next fifty-eight years. According to one late-in-life acquaintance, Mr. and Mrs. Sloan wished to have children but they were unable to do so.[25] Whether they considered adopting a son or a daughter is unknown. No child would ever be theirs. Sloan's long life would not be colored by children or childish ways, though Sloan did have a great affection for his youngest brother, Raymond, his junior by eighteen years. Family life, as a rule, did not much touch the inner life or daily routine of Alfred Sloan. Though the available evidence indicates that he believed himself to be in love with his wife, even that union, as Sloan confessed, had little impact on his devotion to his work commitments. In 1941, Sloan dedicated his publicity driven autobiography, in which his personal life figures almost not at all, to "I.J.S. My partner in the enterprise." It was for Sloan a rare touch of the ironic that only highlighted the obvious—Irene had nothing at all to do with the enterprise that consumed Sloan's time and energies. For Sloan, work would always come first.

Soon after his marriage, the Hygienic Refrigeration Company dissolved. Wood had died. Sloan, by this time less than pleased with the company's founding genius, seems not to have been moved by his demise.[26] Luckily, even as the refrigeration enterprise went under, an opportunity had arisen. John Searles, the man who had given Sloan his start, was fed up with the Hyatt Roller Bearing Company. Facing some personal financial difficulties—he was soon to go broke, not unusual for backers of new technologies—he wished to sell the money-losing enterprise.

At the younger Alfred's urging, Alfred Sloan Sr. and an associate agreed to buy Searles out for five thousand dollars. Sloan Sr. further agreed to supply capital, at least for a period of six months, until the business was profitable. He clearly made this investment for his son: just twenty-three years old, Alfred Sloan Jr. was put in charge of the Hyatt Roller Bearing Company. Over time, he would accumulate a large equity interest in the business. His right-hand man was Peter Steenstrup. The lunchtime discussions the two had enjoyed little more than a year earlier were to be put to the test.

Within six months, the company was turned around. While Steenstrup relentlessly pursued new sales opportunities, Sloan completely reorganized production to achieve far greater cost efficiency and product reliability. Sloan spent the first four years working at least ten hours a day, six days a week, week after week after week. He took no vacations. For the next eighteen years, Sloan ran the company. Under his direction, Hyatt became an extraordinary success, quickly outgrowing its one, shacklike building to become an expansive, modern industrial complex. This success was due to Sloan's correct assessment that Hyatt should direct its efforts toward integrating its products with the nascent auto industry.

* * *

The auto industry at the end of the nineteenth century was pure flux and partial whimsy. It was hundreds of men tinkering in barns, garages, and dirt-floored machine shops. Carriage makers, buggy builders, bicycle mechanics, wagon wheel manufacturers, machine parts makers, and an exotic mélange of undercapitalized entrepreneurs wrestled with the possibilities of manufacturing an auto-mobile, a self-propelled vehicle, a machine that moved itself under the control of its human operator.

It was a time of technological and cultural free play in which a machine and basic ways of living, working, playing, and courting were on the verge of being integrated in unanticipated ways. In terms of its sociohistorical development, the United States had entered a liminal zone, a threshold between two cultural landscapes. The English language itself—with much borrowing from the French (chassis, limousine, garage, chauffeur, automobile)—would have to be squeezed and reshaped in order to build a vocabulary that could incorporate the construction of a way of being in the world—riding in an auto—anticipated by other modes of transport but fully realized by none other.[27] Given the right kind of imagination, it was a fantastic historic moment.

In the year 1900, few in the United States envisioned a mass market for the gasoline-powered road car. Only about fifteen hundred such cars were produced that year (whereas Manhattan alone had over 130,000 horses working the streets; or, put another way, more than ten times as many horses *died* in New York City as there were new autos with internal combustion engines built in the entire country). Wealthy sports, most of them urbanites, drove the tiny automobile market (though increasingly, rural doctors were buying cars as well). The high-priced machines were amusingly, if at times painfully, unreliable. Still, an aura surrounded this technological phenomena. The aura glistened green. Money, possibly a great deal of money, could be made in this new world. Few, of course, saw this opportunity. Horse manure still seemed a more likely growth industry (one more equine fact to ponder: New York City horses excreted roughly one million pounds of manure a day).[28] As a result, the industry for the most part was not developed by major corporations, which generally were unwilling to take on the high risks associated with technological experimentation unrelated to their ongoing businesses. Instead auto enthusiasts, small-time investors, and a mixed bag of mechanically gifted men willing to gamble in exchange for the main chance, struggled to make automobiles. Scores of workshops and small companies hammered out the parts and accessories that would be painstakingly assembled into a working vehicle by dozens of competing automakers, each of whom fought off creditors and cash flow problems in the furious rush to manufacture a breakthrough machine.[29]

Sloan did not in a leap of imagination picture the possibilities created by the small-time automakers. He was approached by them. At least that is how Sloan, in his self-deprecating manner, tells the story, though he alludes to the fact that he and his associate, Mr. Steenstrup, were aggressively looking for new markets for their product. They knew that roller bearings for machine line shafting, due to the increasingly common use of electric engines, were about to become technologically obsolete. Hyatt bearings, or at least some manufacturer's bearings, were needed by the automakers to make car wheels turn efficiently on their axles.

Hyatt was first approached about supplying auto wheel bearings in 1899 by Elwood Haynes, producer of Haynes Apperson cars in Kokomo, Indiana. Haynes, as Sloan described him some years later, was the quintessential rube, sophisticated about nothing but the possibilities of the automobile. Sloan also seems to have found it quite amusing that Haynes and his nascent auto works was based in the booming, alliterative metropolis of Kokomo, Indiana. In fact, Haynes was an extraordinarily accomplished American engineer, with degrees from both Worcester Polytechnic Institute and Johns Hopkins University, who had mastered German in order to follow the pathbreaking automotive work of Gottfried Daimler and Karl Benz. Sloan was a New Yorker, and despite Haynes's first-rate East Coast education, technical training, linguistic gifts, and proven talents, the Kokomo-based Haynes might well have appeared to Sloan as a provincial yokel. Or more likely, in his post–New Deal, 1941 description of Haynes and the advent of the auto industry, Sloan aimed to make a point about the low-cost entry, free-market creativity at work in those first days of the auto business.

While Sloan himself would soon enough do his best to ensure that the auto industry itself would become a very high-cost entry business, he took pains in his own account of his early years to tell his tale of Elwood Haynes of Kokomo, and other "rather simple people," to convince the democratic citizenry that the free market enables economic creativity in the most unexpected places by the most unexpected people. It was Alfred P. Sloan's firm belief, one which he wanted all Americans to fully appreciate, that no government planner could ever anticipate the vitality of individual Americans free to pursue their dreams of profitable accomplishment. Of course, such thoughts were, in the early years of the twentieth century, not yet in Sloan's ken. It would take the political turmoil of the 1930s to turn his mind in such an unwelcome direction.[30]

In the first years of the automobile age, Sloan and his Hyatt associate, Peter Steenstrup, became industry fixtures. Steenstrup was the field man. He visited every manufacturer and set up shop at every trade show. Steenstrup's mission was simple, but as any sales representative knows, not easy. His responsibility was to identify and to win the trust of the many men in the highly volatile auto business who had the responsibility for buying parts for their company's machines. Steenstrup had to be the hail-fellow-well-met who got Hyatt in the door. Sloan, then, would figure out how to design Hyatt bearings into the auto manufacturer's assemblage.

Through trade show excursions and factory visits, Sloan, too, met most everyone of significance in the auto industry. In his own recollections of those early days in the auto parts business, Sloan credited many individuals with providing him with life-long business lessons. One of the first and most important of these lessons came from Henry Leland, general manager of Cadillac, then an independent automaker. Sloan received this lesson firsthand after Leland rejected the first shipment of bearings Hyatt had sent Cadillac. The contract was vitally important to Hyatt's short-term profitability and even more essential to the company's reputation for reliability in the infant auto industry. Sloan rushed by train from New York to Detroit in an attempt to salvage the contract. In his office, Leland, a large, bearded gentleman of Old Testament rages, showed Sloan the facts. Bearings in hand and his anger still on call, Leland demonstrated that the Hyatt product, despite salesman Steenstrup's assurances, did not meet Cadillac's required parameters: accuracy within a thousandth of an inch. Sloan, though speaking "as softly" as he could, did at first attempt to explain away the difficulty. After Leland angrily interrupted him, however, Sloan stopped defending his company and listened. Leland explained the necessity of manufacturing precisely engineered interchangeable parts. "Mr. Sloan," he roared, "Cadillacs are made to run, not just to sell." Sloan understood. He agreed. He asked Leland's advice. From then on, he would do better: "I was determined to be as fanatical as he in obtaining precision in our work. An entirely different standard had been established for Hyatt Roller Bearings."[31]

One of Sloan's many strengths was his ability to hear others out dispassionately. If the facts, as he understood them, bore out he could and did shift his perspective. Given his later political difficulties, it is worth emphasizing the other side of this character trait. If Sloan did not believe the facts bore out or if facts, as he perceived them, were not being given their due, Sloan could become quite recalcitrant and even emotionally explosive. Such times were rare. Leland spoke in a language Sloan understood and Sloan's postgraduate work in manufacturing advanced significantly as a result.

One other character trait worth noting is revealed in the Leland anecdote. Sloan, as both a young man and a man of middle age, was skilled at working with men older than himself as well as with men of his own generation. This ability was amply demonstrated in his first years with Hyatt when he had sought out old John Wesley Hyatt, in his inventor's shop, and plied him with questions about roller ball bearings. Leland, too, was a man of an altogether different generation and set of experiences (including, Leland believed, a personal visitation from God), but Sloan developed a strong working relationship with him. Leland was an engineer of the old school of practical experience; he had received his start as a toolmaker for a federal arsenal during the Civil War. In Sloan's eyes, however, Leland was always "an elder, not only in age but in engineering wisdom."[32]

Sloan had a gift that is rare in young men: the ability to learn from one's elders and to seek their counsel. In establishing such relations, Sloan also bore out an old organizational adage to the effect that seeking help and counsel from those one admires generally brings support and concern from the sought after for the seeker. For Sloan, later in his life, a major problem would be the lack of anyone from whom he felt he could learn. In the world he respected, few people seemed to be his equal, let alone his superior. He would retain his gift for listening to the facts and admitting his own mistaken viewpoints, but what he lost was his ability to rethink fundamentals based on advice or instruction from others.

Sloan was a regular at the yearly auto shows which began in 1900 (five, in fact, were held that year, all claiming to be the first).[33] By the 1906 auto show, Hyatt passed out brochures advertising the "Hyatt Improved Self Oiling Self Contained Bearing with Removable Inside and Outside Casings." Sloan wrote the copy for the brochure, which reveals something of the state of advertising in the first decade of the twentieth century as well as of the directions Sloan's talents did and did not point: "The prospective purchaser of a motor car must be satisfied upon three vital points before he can possibly be induced to invest. . . . The car must have all the power that is required: it must be built so that it may easily be taken care of; and it must be constructed in such a manner that the driver may be reasonably sure of getting back home."[34] Any humor found in this ad is wholly the work of the reader, not the writer of the copy.

During the auto shows, Steenstrup would rope in the multitudes of car enthusiasts, master auto mechanics, and pioneering adventurers in the motor business and herd them over to the Hyatt booth. Sloan waited for them there. Henry Ford and Alfred Sloan first met at the Hyatt booth, probably in 1901, when Ford was working on the racing car that would soon thereafter bring him his first fame. Ford and Sloan, we only know, watched together from the gallery of Madison Square Garden as the earliest American auto manufacturers ran their cars—often one-of-a-kind models—around a track set up on the floor of the hall. As Sloan remembers it, they talked for hours. Ford—twelve years his senior, a great raconteur, and a man of endless, occasionally eccentric opinions—likely did most of the talking while Sloan listened to what the self-taught car genius had to say about the bumptious parade of vehicles that ran—at least most of them did—around and around below them.[35] Sloan would have learned more than Ford from their first meeting.

By 1905, Hyatt had become a sure success, its fortunes completely intertwined with the rapidly growing auto industry. The company had become an early supplier of the Ford Motor Company, which Henry Ford founded in 1903, though it would be several more years before it achieved mass production capacities. An even better customer at first was the Weston-Mott Company (run by Charles Mott, later a big man at General Motors), which supplied axles to many of the key car manufacturers: Cadillac, Oldsmobile, Elmore, Blomstrom, and Buick. Hyatt, between 1905 and 1915, became one of the premier auto parts suppliers.

Sloan's role in the auto industry during this time of its takeoff was significant if not central. He was one of a handful of men who built reliability into the car production process. His small parts were mechanically sound, engineered to precise specifications, and delivered on time. His primary market, the automakers, demanded these attributes and he worked energetically to supply them. The end user of the industry's product, the consumer, was still not his concern. His key money-making customers had become the shrinking number of car manufacturers. As they improved their product, drove out inefficient and undependable competitors, produced in larger numbers, and brought their prices down, Sloan's priority was to grow with them and meet their ever-escalating demands for cheaper part prices in ever larger numbers.

Sloan, whose later reputation would be made largely by his insight into the consumer side of the car business, was in the 1910s focused almost exclusively on the production side. In his factory, he worked ceaselessly for greater productivity, plowing profits back into the business in order to improve his own capacities. He expanded his factories and invested a great amount of capital in improving his own technological processes.

While production was his first priority, his responsibilities extended into other areas of the business. He met with the carmakers and the major parts manufacturers—specifically the axle makers—and worked alongside them in designing the manufacturing process so as to incorporate Hyatt roller bearings into their assemblages. In addition, then, to his responsibilities at the New Jersey plant, Sloan traveled extensively as a sales-engineering consultant for his company's product. Sloan was never wedded to his desk.

This approach to sales increased after the departure of Pete Steenstrup in 1909. Steenstrup had tired of life on the road and of the selling of auto parts. Salesmanship was already by this time a matter of increasingly cutthroat competition. Courses in sales technique and booklets on personality makeover in service to sales success were themselves being relentlessly peddled to the countless drummers and salesman flogging products, new and old, to a market in constant upheaval. Salesmen were told that salesmanship could not be treated as "a garment to be taken off and put on when required," but had to be "a part of a man's fiber and being."[36]

Steenstrup had no desire or had lost the desire to become such a being. He told his long-time partner that he wished to move to Oregon and grow apples. He also seems to have told Sloan that he believed that the auto industry had achieved a saturation point and, thus, was unlikely to provide enough future remuneration to make up for what a later generation would term the "rat race" aspect of the traveling salesman's life. While Sloan could not fully relate to such a dramatic change in one's life course, let alone to Steenstrup's corporate malaise, and while he fully disagreed with Steenstrup's economic prognosis, all indications point toward a cordial end to their decade-long business and personal relationship. Despite this cordiality, it is unlikely Sloan had much sympathy for Steenstrup's financially unwise decision to drop out of the auto industry just as it was approaching its takeoff. Unfortunately, no correspondence between the long-time friends discussing their ever diverging paths has been found and none may have ever existed. Sloan had little time for non-business-related letter writing. Within a short period of time, no relationship seems to have existed between the one-time friends.

Steenstrup's departure, as Sloan saw it, created an opportunity for Hyatt. Steenstrup had never comprehended the engineering aspects of the roller bearing nor its relationship to the overall assemblage of autos. His salesmanship had its basis in personal relationships cultivated over cocktails and bull sessions. Such methods would not be overlooked in post-Steenstrup days. Hyatt sales representatives would continue to be regulars at the Hotel Pontchartrain in Detroit, the growing industry's preferred after-work watering hole. ("Everything," said one able observer of the booming auto industry, "was shown off in the Pontchartrain bar; tire vulcanizers, rims, valves, brakes, carburetors, magnetos, and what not. There men began to talk a strange new language.")[37] Sloan, however, also opened an engineering office in Detroit, which by 1909 clearly had become the auto industry's center. Through this office, Sloan would regularize the integration of his bearings into the car manufacturing process. No longer would he be a one-man team whisking from one potential customer's office to another, designing his part into their car axles. Hyatt would from that time onward have a professional engineering staff working out the process of parts integration.[38]

Of Sloan's factory workers during this time of explosive growth, little is known and almost nothing is mentioned by Sloan in his various accounts of his Hyatt days. All that is known is that the number of workers under Sloan's direction had exploded from twenty-five or so when he took over the enterprise in 1898 to some thirty-eight hundred by 1915. Unions, seemingly, had no role to play in Sloan's manufacturing concern. How he prevented their incursion—whether through coercive means or good labor-management techniques—is, alas, a mystery. An educated guess, and it is only a guess, is that Sloan had no need of tough measures. About 95 percent of his production workers were on piecework. Those men willing to work hard and steady, given Sloan's own disciplined focus on maximizing both production and productivity through reinvestment in machinery and manufacturing process, had the organizational support to make a decent living. During a time of much labor-management conflict, no records indicate that Sloan had any troubles with his industrial work force.

During those years, few unionists had made much headway in the auto business generally. Sloan's engineering mentor, Henry Leland, had played a crucial role in preventing unionization in the industry (though that aspect of Leland's leadership is not mentioned in Sloan's glowing accounts). Leland, for several years, headed the Employers' Association of Detroit. He had personally led the way in firing legally unprotected union organizers and dismissing union rank-and-file members working in the first big auto plants that had come to cluster in southeast Michigan. Leland's group also played a major role in Michigan state politics, lobbying successfully against the passage of child labor laws, worker's compensation, and factory safety laws.

Leland was similar in nature to many of his fellow industrialists. He was a devout Christian who in his own fashion genuinely cared for his individual workers. Proudly, he told those fellow industrialists at a club meeting, "I do not believe any man can say [that] I have treated my employees with anything but justice and consideration." But as Leland's daughter-in-law recalled, "[he] would not tolerate, he would not let labor tell him how to run his business." A contemporary of Leland's, railway president George F. Baer, rather famously codified this viewpoint in a press statement issued in the midst of the memorable coal strike of 1902: "The rights and interests of the laboring man will be protected and cared for not by the labor agitators, but by the Christian men to whom God in his infinite wisdom has given the control of the property interests of the country."[39] While not every industrialist assumed that he acted on earth as direct agent of God Almighty, Baer's tone of moral certainty was not at all unusual among leading businessmen. Like most of the auto pioneers, Leland brooked no interference from others, whether they were his workers or his government, in the running of his business affairs.[40]

While some of the early, university-trained engineers and other newly minted professionals in the legal and medical fields took critical roles in the local, state, and national campaigns to reform the more brutal and pitiless aspects of the industrial age, automakers by and large stood opposed to most of the Progressive Era reforms that touched on their businesses. Like many businessmen involved in new industries in which competition remained fierce and markets uncertain, the auto industry pioneers wished for as little cost-increasing, government intervention as possible. The only government effort they approved of, as a group, was at the national level. As the early American auto industry was still forming, congressional representatives from auto-producing districts succeeded in pushing through tariffs on imported cars at the competition-reducing rate of 40 percent. They would be protected, even if their workers were not.

Alfred Sloan, seemingly, had nothing to do with these antireform or protariff efforts, neither as they affected his manufacturing customers in Michigan nor as they related to his own industrial affairs in New Jersey. Any interest in the urban political and social reforms whirling around him in New York City, often championed by men of backgrounds not unlike his own, seems to have been nonexistent. His attitude was not unusual, but it was indicative of his character. For example, his brilliant MIT classmate Gerard Swope found the time while rushing up the corporate ladder at General Electric to do volunteer work at Jane Addams's Hull House in Chicago. Not Sloan. He did his utmost simply to concentrate on growing his business.

By 1916, Sloan supplied parts to the two giants of the emergent auto industry: Ford and General Motors. What had been in 1900 an American free enterprise adventure with no sure destination had become a thriving industry. The auto, which had been a rich man's plaything in the first years of the twentieth century, was fast becoming a commonplace mode of transportation in rural and small-town America. Sloan, by this time with a major equity interest in Hyatt, had guessed right in a major way.

The auto industry was in a period of explosive growth and Alfred Sloan had put his company, Hyatt Roller Bearing, in the middle of it.

The Ford Motor Company was, by far, Sloan's biggest customer. By 1916, Ford was the auto industry leader by a wide margin, selling 577,036 units, almost half the market for new cars.[41] Henry Ford, the self-made, self-taught automobile engineer, had revolutionized the business and was reaping the rewards. "I will build a motor car," he told the world, "for the great multitude. . . . It will be constructed of the best materials, by the best men to be hired, after the simplest designs that modern engineering can devise. But it will be so low in price that no man making a good salary will be unable to own one—and enjoy with his family the blessing of hours of pleasure in God's great open spaces."[42]

Ford had begun full-out manufacturing of his own cars only in 1910 when he opened his sixty-two-acre Highland Park plant in Detroit (though his reliable and relatively inexpensive 1906 Ford Model N automobile had already begun to change the nature of the auto industry). At that time, his workers, most of them skilled craftsmen, took nearly thirteen hours to fully assemble a single Model T. Over the next three years, like many other early-twentieth-century American manufacturers, Ford and his production men worked relentlessly to reduce the amount of labor it took to assemble their product. Above all, they sped up production by introducing labor-saving machinery to the factory floor. Unlike the reigning proponent of "scientific management," Frederick Taylor, who focused employers' attention on making their workers more productive through "time and motion" studies, Ford mechanized production. He turned his men into machine tenders and machine feeders. Instead of using skilled mechanics and artisans to build carefully constructed, well-made, and expensive cars, Ford had figured out how to use machines assisted by a mainly unskilled work force to build well-made cars, to build them fast, and build them cheaply. Ford, undoubtedly with a sparkle in his eye, explained his system this way: "I have heard it said, in fact, I believe that it's quite a current thought that we have taken the skill out of work. We have not. We have put a higher skill into planning, management, and tool building, and the results are enjoyed by the man who is not skilled."[43]

By 1913, Ford had thirteen thousand men making cars, and only 2 percent of them were classified as "mechanics and sub-foreman." By the next year, he had further revolutionized the auto industry by taking his mass production methods one giant step further. Instead of having his unskilled men cluster around each individual car chassis, he adapted a technique of mass production introduced some years earlier in the meat packing business. Meat packers had hooked animal carcasses to a conveyor belt that allowed relatively unskilled men to dress meat in a controlled but rapid, "disassembly" line fashion. Ford substituted a car chassis for the cow carcass. He hooked the Model T chassis to a chain conveyor belt and, at six feet a minute, each individual car passed by workers stationed along the assembly line. As the car arrived at each worker's station, he rapidly performed his simple task, whether it was adding a part, turning a screw, or welding a piece. Ford enabled his workers to complete their simple assigned tasks rapidly by fitting his factory floor with some fifteen thousand highly specialized machines (it helped that the United States made the best machine tools in the world). By 1914, the Model T chassis went from bare chassis to completion in one hour and thirty-three minutes. "Fordism" had been invented.[44]

Ford still had one major problem to solve before his supremacy could be realized: he could not keep up the productivity promised by his assembly techniques. His labor turnover was extraordinarily high. For every hundred assembly line jobs, Ford had to hire some 963 men a year to work them. Most men put up with the monotony of the assembly line only until less mind-numbing work could be found. Rather than rethink his manufacturing process, Ford offered assembly line workers a new social contract. In exchange for the dullness of the work, he provided the unprecedented daily wage rate of five dollars for eight hours of work. This figure represented a wage roughly double that of most industrial workers and a shortening of the workday by two hours. Ford did not offer this wage inducement unconditionally. His workers had to comply with an array of rules if they were to receive the premium payment. Immigrants had to take mandatory classes in English. His men could not be divorced or indebted, and could not be guilty of "any malicious practice derogatory to good physical manhood or moral character."[45] Ford had a brigade of investigators charged with overseeing the men to make sure that neither at work nor at home were any workers deviating from Ford's prescribed respectability.

As much as any other single act, Ford's historic realignment of the wage rate in the auto industry, the industry that was to lead the nation for much of the twentieth century, helped to usher in the age of mass consumer society. In the nineteenth century most industrial workers spent most of their waking hours on the job in order to earn enough money to feed, house, and clothe themselves and their families. Ford's new contract gave his workers unprecedented leisure along with higher pay. With time and money to spare, these men and their families could participate in the new consumer society that these workers were helping to create through their assembly line productivity. New mass entertainments, like movie palaces, and then in the early 1920s, network radio programming, arose to meet their leisure-time interests and their expanding purchasing power. National brand name products, including the Model T itself, became markers in their emergent lifestyles.

"Fordism"—assembly line productivity, a stable workforce gained through decent wages, low manufacturing costs—rapidly accelerated Americans' automobile mania. In 1909, Ford sold his car for $950. By 1923, a brand new Model T sold for $295 and no one any longer saw automobiles as rich men's playthings. The auto had become an affordable everyday necessity for millions of Americans.

Henry Ford's success was also Alfred Sloan's. The Model T used Hyatt bearings. Over half of all Hyatt bearings went to the Ford Motor Company. Though Ford's demands that his parts suppliers match his price cutting kept profits low on a per part basis, volume sales produced an increasingly impressive bottom line for Hyatt. (At the end of the twentieth century, Andy Grove, the head of Intel, supplied a Sloan-like adage: "Price for volume, then work like the devil on your costs.")[46] Between 1913 and 1916, Hyatt had expanded its production facilities by some 80 percent and was capable of producing $20 million dollars worth of business. Three private sidings connected the burgeoning plant to the Pennsylvania Railroad. With sales offices in Newark, Chicago, and Detroit, sales were booming. Selling regularly to the industry leader, as well as to its second major manufacturer, General Motors, and to many of the other surviving automakers, meant that Alfred P. Sloan, just forty-one years old in 1916, was on his way to being a wealthy man. Sloan was well pleased with his enterprise.[47]

The world shifted pleasantly for Alfred Sloan that spring when William Crapo Durant wanted to discuss a business proposition with him. Durant suggested they have their conversation over a leisurely lunch. Sloan, being Sloan, had no time for a luncheon but told Durant that he would be pleased to join him at Durant's mid-Manhattan office for a late afternoon meeting.

Billy Durant was the founder of General Motors. In 1916, after a couple of years of financial difficulties, which were not uncommon for him, he had lost control of his auto empire. But now Durant was in the midst of an extraordinary stock market gamble that would put him back on top of General Motors. Even before Durant had fully played out his complex bid for control, he had also decided, ever optimistic, to integrate his beloved corporate giant more fully by creating a parts and accessories combine directly linked to General Motors. William Durant's sights were set on several manufacturers, including Hyatt Roller Bearings.

Sloan personally knew Durant only slightly. The two men had crossed paths fairly regularly on the New York–Detroit train but only to wish one another a pleasant good morning or good evening. Still, Sloan knew quite well who Durant was and how he operated. And he knew what he was likely to propose.

William Durant was an enthusiast: a world-class salesman, a risk-taker extraordinaire. In temperament, he was nothing like Alfred Sloan. He had been born in 1861 to a well-established, well-to-do Michigan family. His grandfather had been governor just after the Civil War. Durant's father, however, was another story. He was an alcoholic plunger who disappeared when Billy, as he was known, was just a boy. Perhaps because of his father's failings, Durant grew up "buried under waves of maternal cosseting."[48] Always elegantly dressed and living among luxuries bought with his grandfather's money, Billy came of age among the elite of Flint, Michigan. Eager to move forward in the world, he left high school a few weeks prior to graduation, even though he had been a good student with his best work done in his class on American history (an indicator of how differently worked the minds of Alfred Sloan and Billy Durant).[49] Still in his teens, Billy began an extraordinary upward progression. He rushed from business to business, using his extraordinary gifts of persuasion, succeeding and profiting and moving toward ever bigger enterprises. He worked endless hours, charmed everyone he met, and kept looking for the main chance that would make him not just rich but an American economic titan.

In 1904, at the age of forty-three, he entered the car business as managing director of the Buick company, shortly after the auto had made its transition from novelty to industry. In 1907 he attempted to convince the House of Morgan to capitalize his dream of an auto empire by painting them a word picture of roads filled with cars and of annual vehicle sales of half a million and more. Following conventional Wall Street wisdom, which still saw autos not as an industry but a hobby, Morgan partner George Perkins dismissed Durant with a sneer. (Morgan partners earlier had done the same to an unforgiving Henry Ford.) Undaunted, Durant preceded on his own; he established General Motors in the fall of 1908 as a giant holding company. Using money raised through speculative stock offerings, as well as Buick's revenues, and, whenever possible, using shares in General Motors itself as a means of payment, Durant beginning buying up the automotive business. Early purchases, in whole or part, included A-C Spark Plugs, Olds Motor Works, Weston-Mott (the axle company that had been an early buyer of Hyatt bearings), Oakland, Reliance Motor Truck Company, and the Cadillac Motor Company (owned by Sloan's mentor, Henry Leland). Little more than a year after establishing General Motors, Durant had brought eleven automobile companies, eight automotive parts makers, and two truck manufacturers into the fold.

Knowing little about the actual mechanics or engineering of the automobile, Durant meant to capture as many possible winning car companies as he could, even if he had to purchase a few losers in the process. He explained his strategy to a friend: "I was for getting every kind of car in sight, playing it safe all along the line." Alfred Sloan did everything in his power to make decisions based on observed facts. Billy Durant was guided by creative vision and the thrill of the chase. He had extraordinarily good business instincts.[50]

In 1916, after emerging from near financial disaster, Durant was ready for another strategic foray. Rather than directly incorporate more companies into General Motors, Durant meant to create a separate holding company made up of auto parts and accessory suppliers that could reliably provide General Motors car manufacturers with critical components. Durant may not have had formal managerial training but he understood how to grow his business. In his own unconventional style, he was, in essence, following the path laid down by industrial giants like Carnegie and Rockefeller of the previous generation. Durant was developing General Motors on both the vertical and horizontal planes—something he had already successfully done in the 1880s and 1890s when he had built the largest horse-drawn carriage business in the world. The new parts and accessories corporation was to be named United Motors. Hyatt Roller Bearing was to be its flagship enterprise.

Durant greeted Sloan cordially in his mid-town Manhattan office. Though Sloan, at six feet, had several inches over Durant, physically the two men bore some similarity. Unlike many of their seniors and many of their auto industry contemporaries, each was clean shaven. Also unlike the previous generation of businessmen, who seemed to associate a rotund figure with a high economic status, Durant and Sloan were both slender. Neither made any effort to stay slim; though exercise for men had been a passing fad at the turn of the century, both Sloan and Durant burned so much energy as a natural consequence of their physical intensity that they did not gain weight. Each man, too, took obvious pride in his appearance. Sloan undoubtedly arrived for the meeting impeccably dressed, just as he always was. He invested money in well-tailored suits that he wore well, even as their tight fit accentuated his much remarked upon angularity. Durant had his own expensively tailored suits cut to fit in a more relaxed fashion, which pointed toward a major difference between the men. Sloan radiated a nervous energy. He was a taut man, in the habit of sitting through meetings with a jiggling knee and much tapping of his fingers. He almost never appeared relaxed.[51] Durant had the gift of ease. His physical grace and welcoming disposition had reassured and charmed endless customers, business associates, and even adversaries. Durant's warm, genuine smile reflected an inner confidence given to few men.

Without much wasted motion or time, which he perhaps knew would please Sloan, Durant asked if Hyatt could be purchased and, if so, for how much. Sloan had expected such a line of inquiry. Nonetheless, he was much taken with Durant's manner, particularly the air of perfect calm with which Durant solicited him. Sloan himself did not feel nearly so cool. And despite his relative certainty over what the purpose of the meeting would be, Sloan was not prepared to negotiate on the spot the purchase price of Hyatt. Expressing an interest, Sloan told Durant that he would have to discuss such a major decision with his company's board of directors. Durant had anticipated a more direct engagement over the issue at hand but Sloan did not and would not act precipitously. Durant, in Sloan's words, acted in "the manner of a gentleman striving to be harmonious with the world" and allowed that Sloan should proceed just as he wished.[52] This first meeting between the two men would be the high point of their relationship.

Sloan wanted to sell. He discussed Durant's offer with the small board of directors—his father being the most important of these—who made up most of the shareholders of the privately held Hyatt company. Sloan told the men that if a reasonable price could be negotiated, Hyatt should accept for three reasons. First, Hyatt was locked into a difficult market position. More than half its production was sold to the Ford Motor Company, which dominated the auto business. If Ford chose to make their own bearings or give their business to one of Hyatt's competitors, then Hyatt would be in a grave situation. This problem was exacerbated by Hyatt's patent position; the original Hyatt patents for the production of the roller bearing had expired. While additional process patents still protected the business, the Hyatt roller bearing could be copied by another manufacturer or by the major car companies themselves. Second, the auto industry might very well, in the near term, replace the Hyatt roller bearing altogether with a new technologically superior product. While Hyatt might, as an independent company, be able to make that technical advance, it was only reasonable to recognize that on its own it might not. Third, because of the rapid rate of growth in the auto business, the equity partners in Hyatt (Sloan, of course, had become the largest of these equity holders) had been unable to realize much in the way of profits from the company due to the necessity of constant reinvestment of capital into the business in order to keep its productive capacity equal to that of its industrial customers. Approaching the issue with his usual impeccable logic, Sloan informed the board of his calculation that selling the company for $15 million would provide relief to the owners on all three grounds. The board seconded his decision with a minimum of discussion.[53]

In negotiating with Durant's money men, Sloan agreed to a purchase price of $13.5 million. Sloan might have gotten the full amount, as he ruefully put it twenty-five years later, "if my nerve had held out—but it was a big transaction for me." Sloan also knew that he had gotten a very good price; he had used more than basic bookkeeping to calculate his asking price. He had investigated Durant: "He was disposed to deal generously with the proprietors of any business he undertook to buy. He was not inclined to haggle over the price of something he really wanted."[54] Sloan and his father were to receive equal parts of approximately $10,125,000 of the agreed upon amount.[55] Sloan Sr.'s investment of a few thousand dollars in his son eighteen years earlier had paid off rather well. In 2000 dollars, corrected for inflation, the $10,125,000 gain works out to over $166 million. Alfred Jr. had made his father a very wealthy man. The son was well pleased.

The younger Sloan too was rich. Half the $10,125,000 was his. His wealth was not quite as liquid as it might have been, due to the exact terms of the sale specifying that much of the sale price was to be in the stock on the newly created company Hyatt was to be enfolded within, United Motors (providing payment in stock, rather than cash, was Durant's usual modus operandi). At the request of Sloan Sr. and the other smaller Hyatt investors, his son ended up with nearly all of the stock and little of the cash from the transaction. While this maneuver put his wealth in a less than perfectly secure position, by any measurement Alfred Sloan Jr., at the age of forty-one, had become a very wealthy man.

Such wealth did not change Sloan's life focus. Durant wanted him to head United Motors and Sloan accepted immediately. While he was well pleased to be an economic success, his interest was not in making money per se but in the challenge of running a business enterprise.

In light of this last point, it might be helpful to conclude this chapter with an interesting contrast: Sloan's near exact contemporary, Herbert Hoover, at nearly the same time, decided that his accumulated wealth offered him the possibility of changing his life course. Hoover, born in 1874 and orphaned soon after, was an "Alger-boy" who bootstrapped his way through Stanford (class of 1895) with a degree in geology. By the early 1900s, he had became one of the world's leading mining engineers. By 1914, he had a fortune of some $4 million, a little less than Sloan's in 1916. Hoover concluded that he was as rich as any man needed to be. While in no way renouncing the private enterprise system to which he owed his wealth, Hoover chose to spend the rest of his life in public service. His credo was "justice, self-restraint, [and] obligation to fellowmen." During and immediately after World War I, Hoover used his organizational brilliance to ship and distribute huge amounts of food supplies to Europe and so save millions of people from death by starvation.[56]

Few men had the boundless humanity—or, as it turned out, the historic bad luck—of Herbert Hoover, but it is worth pondering the different kinds of life choices available in the second decade of the twentieth century to extraordinary men of wealth who had barely entered their forties. On the one hand, Hoover fed Europe, became the nation's finest public servant in the 1920s, and then had a very promising presidency turn very sour; on the other, Sloan went on to build a world-renowned industrial giant and accumulate an immense fortune. How does one judge and memorialize such lives along the axes of American history and human development?

SLOAN THE EXECUTIVE

Oh! Blessed rage for order, pale Ramon,
The maker's rage to order words of the sea.

–Wallace Stevens, "The Idea of Order at Key West"

Alfred Sloan would work for almost five years under the loose hand of Billy Durant. During that time, he learned a great deal from Durant about how not to run a complex corporation. While he was allowed by Durant to manage his end of the business almost completely as he saw fit, the closer Sloan came to the organizational heart of General Motors the more frustrated he became. The years Sloan worked for Durant reinforced the lessons experience had taught him during his very first years in business: owners, entrepreneurs, and major investors did not always know what they were doing. Managing a business, Sloan would try to prove, took more than inspiration, charm, and financial wizardry.

In short order, Durant's failures provided Sloan with the opportunity he needed to reveal his organizational and managerial genius. Sloan's plan to restructure the management of General Motors not only resuscitated the corporation, it changed the course of corporate management in the twentieth century. However, Sloan's intense fight to resurrect and restructure General Motors through rational management further occluded his already narrow social vision. Corporate rationality, with its clear goals of increasing market share, productivity, and, above all, corporate profitability became Sloan's moral universe, not just a business strategy. This corporate wisdom would be the foundation on which Sloan would build his model of corporate citizenship in the years that followed.

* * *

Sloan ran the quasi-independent United Motors from 1916 to 1918. Though Billy Durant was the nominal overseer of United Motors, he gave Sloan a completely free hand in running the company. In its first year, the new combine had net sales of $33,638,956. Sloan had done very well indeed (again).

In 1918, Durant merged United Motors into General Motors in a stock swap. The reorganization was prompted, in large part, by pressure imposed on Durant by Du Pont. In 1917, Du Pont's board of directors had taken $25 million of its immense wartime profits made on the sale of gun powder and other explosives—the company had accumulated investment capital of some $90 million—and, seeking diversification, invested it in General Motors and Chevrolet Motors Company (soon thereafter merged into General Motors). This investment gave Du Pont a 23.83 percent interest in GM and, thus, a powerful voice in the corporation. Durant had solicited the money during another one of his heroic and ceaseless stock market manipulations.

In exchange for the capital investment, the Du Pont board of directors had secured Durant's promise that they would control GM's financial decision making. That agreement was carefully spelled out by Du Pont chairman of the board, Pierre du Pont, and Du Pont treasurer, John Raskob. The desire for such control, and the need for a formal agreement conceding it, came in response to Billy Durant's established record of unilateral decision making and informal administration.

Pierre du Pont, guided by his long-time, trusted advisor Raskob, had faith in Durant's business genius. He was far less sure of Durant's ability to balance his zest for risk and General Motor's need for stable management. Pierre du Pont was also painfully aware that Durant was loathe to listen to others who sought to advise him. Durant felt perfectly competent to act as he wished.

Only a year earlier, in 1916, after Pierre du Pont had invested several million dollars of his personal fortune in General Motors, he wrote plaintively to Durant, "Am I wrong in waiting for advice from you relative to GM matters? It is my understanding that you wish to talk to me on the subject. As I have not heard from you I fear that through misunderstanding I have failed to communicate with you as to a convenient date of meeting."[1] A misunderstanding had occurred but not the one for which du Pont courteously allowed.

Despite what Durant might have said during the financial courtship stage, he had no interest in consulting with Pierre du Pont as to the future of General Motors. Billy Durant enjoyed building his empire and sought no limits on his activities. Thus, in 1917 the Du Pont board of directors, being quite concerned about Durant's financial enthusiasms and free-wheeling management style, had insisted on contractual oversight. They wanted to see GM become a more fully integrated, stable organization. Placing United Motors within the GM corporate structure was just one small step toward greater corporate rationality.

As a result of the enfolding of United Motors, Alfred Sloan became for the first time both a shareholder and executive in General Motors. His title was vice president. His primary responsibility remained the same: running the accessory companies he had been managing for some two years. In addition, he was made a director of General Motors and a member of the GM executive committee. Sloan's GM days had formally begun.

As vice president, Sloan moved into the General Motors offices in New York on Fifty-seventh Street. His office was right next door to Durant's. The sort of business practices he saw being conducted in Durant's office appalled him. For the next two years, Sloan endured a slow burn as he tried to devise a logical response to Durant's administrative slovenliness.

Sloan was not unaware of Durant's gifts. Billy was a magnetic presence. Even those who suffered most from his approach to business respected, if not always admired, his ability to take immense financial risks and to carry off plans of grand imagination. From his first forays into the automobile business in 1904, Durant had reached the highest highs and the lowest lows, amassing tens of millions of dollars, a fortune that he would alternately lose and then regain. He played the stock market like few others ever had, divining madcap speculations that often worked, driving prices high, trading shares of one corporation for another, each of which had been manipulated by Durant and the stockholding syndicates he had sweet-talked into existence for the sole purpose of making a killing. He never seemed to stop. The money, diverted here and there, appeared to be only a marker in a game he alone played for reasons few others could fathom. Even for the psychoanalytically disinclined, it is hard not to put his absent, alcoholic, bust-of-a-father on Billy Durant's shoulder, like a cartoon figure, whispering words of uncanny power into his left ear while Durant sits at his desk with a phone at his right ear, talking to stock market players in every corner of the nation, "charming the birds right out of the trees," as his onetime subordinate, Walter Chrysler, once said. Durant's great public charm, not unlike that of Ronald Reagan, another remarkable son of an alcoholic father, came at a price; he had almost no real friends or close relationships. Not even his loving daughter felt she knew him.[2]

Durant was always on the phone. Most of the time he was buying and selling stocks. That was one of the many things he did that tied Sloan and all the other efficiency-minded executives into emotional knots. Durant, in those telecommunication-challenged days of the 1910s, had phone after phone installed in his office. Sloan, in a rare moment of exaggeration indicative of his disgust, claimed that twenty phones crowded Durant's private office; Walter Chrysler remembered a mere "eight or ten lined up on his desk." Regardless of the exact number, the phones were always ringing and Durant was always lifting one or another to his ear.[3] He took and initiated call after call while his top executives waited. Walter Chrysler, who ran Buick for Durant at a salary of over six hundred thousand dollars a year, and who was not a patient man, remembered taking the train from Detroit to New York "in obedience to a call from him. . . . For several days in succession I waited at his office, but he was so busy he could not take the time to talk with me. It seemed to me he was trying to keep in communication with half the continent. . . . To this day I do not know why Billy had required my presence in New York."[4] Sloan never doubted Durant's love of GM or of his desire to make it a great corporation, but he did not at all care for his way of doing business.

Above all else, Sloan could not stand how Durant made corporate decisions. Even when Sloan was able to avert a Durant blunder, he hated the procedure, or more accurately, the lack of procedure, that necessitated his intervention. Once, he was invited into Durant's office in the middle of a meeting—a conversation, really—about putting up GM's massive new office building in Detroit. It was a multimillion dollar decision. Sloan quickly understood that Durant was about to buy a site based on the most casual of analysis. "Almost hesitantly," he recalled, "because it was not my responsibility, I volunteered an opinion." Durant, with little further debate or fact gathering, changed his mind, took Sloan's advice, put him in charge of the process, traveled with him to Detroit, picked an exact location out of the air, and told Sloan to spend "whatever you need to pay" to buy the site (which became a $20 million building). Sloan was appalled: "[N]ot withstanding a successful outcome, I contend that in a corporate organization of our size there should have been, somewhere, as a carefully chosen part of the corporation's manifold intellect, some specialist giving all his thinking to problems in that category. I did the best I could, but it might not have been the best that was possible."[5]

Sloan tried to admire Durant's talent for big thinking and creative financing but his administrative approach, Sloan concluded, might well lead to disaster. Too many decisions were made too casually. Too much of Durant's time was spent playing the stock market. Too often the many division heads of General Motors did as they wished. And when the division heads needed additional capital, they competed with one another for the funds not on some rigorous objective basis but by virtue of the personal relationship they had developed with Durant. In sum, Sloan concluded, Durant's approach to running General Motors could only be called "management by crony."[6] Over time, as Sloan saw it, the result could only be disaster. By 1919, Sloan feared for his financial future; almost all of his capital was tied up in shares of General Motors stock.

Sloan was far from the only man frustrated by Durant's administrative laxness. With tens of millions of dollars at stake, Pierre du Pont, chairman of the Du Pont board of directors, and others of that company's executives constantly pushed at Durant to formalize his procedures and shore up his capital investment strategy. Having only recently gone through their own period of rapid growth and subsequent corporate reorganization, the Du Pont executives were quite forceful in their demands for reform.

Under Du Pont pressure changes were made. In 1918, Du Pont interests pushed through a series of administrative moves aimed at centralizing authority and tightening up GM's financial decision-making process. The plans stemmed from the corporate structure the Du Pont company had itself initiated only a few years earlier. An executive committee, made up of the heads of all the major divisions, was formed to create general policies and to establish some kind of performance standard in an attempt to rationalize how GM's various and varied divisions competed for in-house capital. A finance committee, comprised mainly of du Pont family members and company executives, would work out the amount of stock dividends and set securities policy, thus reigning in Durant's more erratic manipulations of the stock market. Finally, the du Ponts sent two trusted non–family members over to GM to work with Durant as senior officers in the New York general office: J. Armory Haskell, who had done much to modernize the Du Pont company's own administrative procedures and operations, and John Raskob, the treasurer of the Du Pont company who had been the first to direct corporate attention to the possibilities of the motor industry in general and of GM in particular. The

Du Pont board of directors pushed hard to expand the staff of the New York General Motors office so that Durant could have able people aiding him in making rational general corporate policies.

The financial stake in General Motors on the parts of du Pont the immensely wealthy family and Du Pont the chemical and explosives company blur during this period. Both entities had major investments adding up to some $50 million. Where the personal financial interest of, say, Pierre ended and the corporate interest of the eponymous company began is a question of some subtlety. This intertwining of du Ponts, Du Pont, and General Motors proved to be a matter in which the federal government—after World War II—would investigate and litigate, causing an older and more powerful Alfred Sloan much annoyance.

Most of the changes spelled out by Du Pont representatives had little impact on Durant's way of doing business. John Pratt, a smart, hard-nosed executive sent over in early 1919 by Du Pont to appraise the efficacy of the reform effort on GM's operations (to spy, Durant loyalists would have said) bluntly reported: "No one knew just how the money had been appropriated, and there was no control of how much money was being spent." Durant was a visionary, a business genius, Pratt reported, but he was careless and scattershot in his methods. Pratt went on to echo Alfred Sloan's own conclusions: "When one of them [division heads] had a project, why he would get the vote of his fellow members; if they would vote for his project, he would vote for theirs. It was sort of a horse trading. In addition to that, if they didn't get enough money, Mr. Durant, when visiting the plant, would tell them to go on and spend what money they needed without any record of it being made."[7] Though neither Pratt nor Sloan thought in such terms in 1919, GM, ironically, was being run in accord with the oldest of legislative political traditions—"logrolling"—in which votes are traded without concern for the common good in order to secure "pork" for each representative's district. It was, Sloan believed, no way to run a business.

In 1920, Durant's auto empire began to collapse. Sloan saw it coming. So did Walter Chrysler, who would soon be Sloan's dearest friend and the best of the GM car production and operations men. Chrysler, like Sloan, had invested more than time in GM; he, too, had invested his money, which he now saw to be stupidly and unnecessarily at risk. Throughout 1919, Chrysler, to Sloan's pleasure, had publicly challenged Durant about his investment strategy, denouncing various physical expansion schemes (e.g., a new frame assembly plant, tractor manufacturing, employee housing) as overblown, ill conceived, and poorly timed.

He demanded that Durant clarify corporate policy and stop his casual, inopportune meddling in operational matters about which he knew little. Durant, more often than not, answered with a charming laugh. During a board meeting in early 1920, however, Chrysler openly and rancorously attacked Durant's planned expansions. Nobody was laughing anymore. In March 1920 Chrysler reached the end of his rope. He went to Durant and announced he was quitting: "Now, Billy, I'm done." He walked away from his $600,000 a year salary (that would be over $5.78 million in 2000 dollars) with nothing specific in mind as to what he would do next.[8] Sloan, who had great respect for Chrysler's abilities, tried to talk him into reconsidering but to no avail.[9]

Chrysler had correctly foreseen General Motor's situation. Right after World War I, during 1919 and into early 1920, the car business had boomed. Wartime government spending and overseas orders for food and goods of all kinds had stimulated the entire American economy. In 1919, General Motors had a record year, selling almost 20 percent of all passengers cars in the United States (Ford sold 50 percent of the market). But in mid-1920, even as Durant, supported (some say pushed) by the Du Pont-appointed treasurer of GM, John Raskob, spent some $79 million on plant and property expansion, the car market broke. As farm prices begin to plummet in the face of diminished European demand and industrial production contracted in the postwar conversion, new car sales petered out. General Motors, stretched financially thin, needed huge revenues to cover its bottom line. Suddenly, the money stopped coming in.

Ford, ever aggressive on the sales front, slashed prices on the Model T 20–30 percent, forcing his dealers to eat most of the discount out of their own revenues. General Motors tried to compete with undiscounted prices. By November of 1920, sales had dropped 75 percent from June's figures. Unsold inventory overwhelmed the company. John Pratt, the Du Pont man brought over to GM earlier to instill some discipline in the company's affairs, counted up some $210 million in unsold vehicles and parts. It was a disaster.

Sloan was distressed but not surprised. Throughout 1919, on his own initiative and in addition to his long list of operational and managerial duties as head of the accessory division, he had devised administrative plans to rationalize how General Motors was run. Sloan's major concern was that the company's many operating divisions—especially Buick Motors, Cadillac Motor Car, Chevrolet, General Motors Truck, Oakland Motor Car, Olds Motor Work, Samson Tractor, and Fisher Body—lacked financial discipline. The executives in charge of each division spent what money they wanted and no one paid attention to the results in any systemic way. Sloan was in complete agreement with those Du Pont men who sought to provide a rational method to General Motors capital expenditures. His attempt to change financial procedures at General Motors, not surprisingly, was unsuccessful.

Durant responded cordially to Sloan's time-intensive, carefully considered rethinking of General Motors administrative, organizational, and financial procedures. When Sloan submitted his third and final report, "[Durant] appeared to accept it favorably," Sloan remembered some forty years later, but "he did nothing about it."[10] The time Sloan had spent, the facts he had so carefully compiled, the logical arguments he had built—all of it was a waste.

In the face of Durant's failure to act, even before it became clear that General Motors was to endure a devastating downturn, Sloan began to consider other professional opportunities. Like Walter Chrysler, he was at the end of his patience with Durant's manner of running General Motors.

Early in the summer of 1920, Sloan began speaking with the investment banker James Sorrow about joining his Boston banking firm as a partner specializing in industrial analysis. Sloan had become well acquainted with Sorrow during the Hyatt days. Back in September 1910, Durant had calamitously overextended General Motors. Sorrow had led the investment banking group that refinanced General Motors and, in so doing, wrested control away from Durant. Sorrow himself had taken over the financial affairs of General Motors from 1910 to 1915, a period during which GM became Hyatt's second most important purchaser of bearings, and Sloan and Sorrow developed a mutual respect. After Durant regained control of General Motors, Sorrow had kept his hand in the auto business by becoming the principal financial backer of Nash Motors, a major car manufacturer run by the former General Motors president, Charles Nash. In 1916, Sloan demonstrated his faith in Sorrow's financial judgment (and Nash's ability) by buying stock in the brand new Nash Motors Company of Kenosha, Wisconsin, using some of the gain from selling Hyatt Roller Bearing to Durant. The investment paid off very handsomely.[11]

In 1920, Sorrow's investment house, oriented as it was toward the auto industry, represented a natural opportunity for Sloan's talents. That Sloan, at this moment of possible professional redirection, would turn not toward either an entrepreneurial endeavor or a position in production but instead would consider becoming an investment banker specializing in industrial analysis reveals the kind of cerebral "white collar" adventure that had become most attractive to our corporate protagonist. The manufacture of correct assessments, not physical products, is what most gratified Alfred Sloan.

Before making such a personally momentous decision, Sloan needed the time to carefully consider his situation. Casually, and not in complete honesty, he announced to Durant that he wished some time off to recuperate from the intensity of his recent work for the corporation. Durant, his mind clearly focused on the darkening financial clouds, wished Sloan bon voyage.

Mr. and Mrs. Sloan left by ship for England in late July. It was not their first trip abroad. The previous year, Sloan had been involved in a working vacation with several top GM men and their respective spouses. It was during that sea voyage, aboard the luxurious *S.S. France,* that the Sloans became acquainted with Walter and Della Chrysler (Chrysler would quit GM right after the trip). Until his death in 1940, Walter Chrysler was Alfred Sloan's closest friend. Between business obligations, which included a tour of the Citroën car works in France (GM was considering its purchase),[12] the Chryslers and the Sloans had a grand time sightseeing and exchanging points of view.

Walter Chrysler was a warm-hearted, expansive, profane man; a bootstrapping "Alger-boy" who relished tough talk, hard work, and good times. In his memoirs, proudly titled *Life of an American Workman,* Chrysler detailed his boyhood days growing up in the frontier community of Ellis, Kansas: "Out where I grew up, if you were soft, all the other kids would beat the daylights out of you."[13] (Consider Sloan's boyhood days, in which text books, not fistfights, provided the greatest stimulation.) Chrysler was proud to be a hard case, but for all to read he also wrote this about Della Forker, the woman who would become his wife: "Her olive-tinted young throat was soft in a wrapping of velvet; just at the level of my mouth was her dark hair that waved back from her forehead into a Psyche knot."[14]

The passionate relationship between Walter and Della Chrysler could not have been more different from that of the decorous Sloans. Then, too, the obvious love the Chryslers shared was complicated by Walter's sometimes blatant affairs with younger women.[15] Yet, their differences seemed to draw the two couples together rather than push them apart. Irene Sloan seemed to have enjoyed watching others enjoy themselves and perhaps, too, suffer through tempestuous times, even as she maintained a more careful set of proprieties. Sloan himself, already having some problems with his hearing, had no trouble following Walter

Chrysler's noisy stream of sharp-edged observations. Sloan, whose foulest words were "horse chestnuts" and "chicken feed," seemingly relished the earthy expressions of enthusiasm offered up at volume and in quantity by a man who had won his permanent respect by performing so ably in the hard-nosed world of auto production. In his choice of closest friend, Alfred Sloan showed a desire for levity and unpredictability that was carefully veiled by the professional image of cool, even mechanical calculation he so carefully fostered in his work and in the public representations he offered the world over the course of his life.[16]

During that 1919 voyage when the Sloans and Chryslers had begun their friendship, Sloan, undoubtedly out of earshot from the ladies, had attempted to convince Chrysler to stay with General Motors. The two men held regular shipboard meetings with the other junketing GM executives including Charles Mott, who nearly two decades earlier as an independent axle manufacturer had helped to make Hyatt Roller Bearing's foray into the auto parts business a success, and Charles Kettering, GM's resident genius inventor (the self-starter, most famously). With Sloan in the lead, they discussed overhauling General Motors administrative procedures (shades of a boyish Sloan's lunchtime talks about mismanagement at Hyatt Roller Bearings with Pete Steenstrup, nearly a quarter of a century earlier). The shipboard meetings had produced the seeds of several intelligent plans that Sloan then formally developed and later presented to Billy Durant. None of those plans, to the men's displeasure, had germinated under Durant's hand.[17]

Now just a year later, far less confident that solutions were even possible, and with no one urging him to stay the course, Sloan debated the direction of his professional life. Irene, who loved the sea and sea voyages, must have been hard pressed not to ask what machinations at General Motors had left her husband so moody during their cruise across the Atlantic. Mr. and Mrs. Sloan did not discuss business.[18]

Shortly after their arrival in England, news of some kind must have reached Sloan though no record of Sloan's correspondence regarding GM's 1920 crisis has turned up. Suddenly, Sloan informed his wife that they must return to New York immediately. Their plan had been to purchase a custom Rolls Royce and, just the two of them (the chauffeur would not count), make a grand auto excursion. Sloan canceled the Rolls and, with some haste, he and Irene set sail for home. Romance would have to wait. General Motors was in play and opportunity beckoned.

Throughout 1920, Durant navigated in a heavy sea of financial dangers. Based on the strong car sales of 1919, he had, as already noted, committed to major corporate expansion.[19] To raise money, he had taken the advice of John Raskob, Pierre du Pont's man, who had taken over as GM treasurer; GM would sell some $85 million in corporate bonds. Alas, in the uncertain financial markets of 1920, the bonds sold at a disappointing rate. By May, buyers had taken possession of only $12 million of the bond issue. During this period of slack bond sales and an increasingly dubious auto market, General Motors stock price began to fall. The resignation of Walter Chrysler and subsequent sale of his entire block of General Motors stock contributed to the downward turn. Durant, ever optimistic, saw the stock slide as an opportunity.

King of the stock market bulls, Billy Durant hated to see his stock fall in value and he also believed that it was in his power to punish those naysayers who were selling General Motors stock short (which further contributed to the downward pressure on GM's stock price). Short sellers operate by contracting to sell a stock at a specific future time at a given price that is less than the current market price. They make money if the share price has fallen below the price at which they have contracted to sell; they lose money if the value of the stock rises above the contracted price. Durant began a massive effort to turn the tide and manipulate General Motors stock upward by organizing a stock-buying syndicate. Never a man of smallish plans, Durant meant to corner the market in General Motors stock; he meant to own outright or own options on all available GM stock, or receive guarantees from other GM stockholders that they would not sell their shares until the syndicate had so decided. If Durant could pull off the corner, short sellers of GM stock would be forced eventually to pay very high prices for the stock shares they were legally obligated to sell at a specified date but which they had not yet actually purchased. While such stock manipulations would be illegal today (since the establishment in 1934 of the Securities and Exchange Commission), they were not illegal at the time. They were, however, extremely risky.

As only Durant could, he began working the phones, putting together his syndicate. At this point in time, it is worth noting, ownership of General Motors stock was still closely held. As late as the beginning of 1918, all General Motors stock was owned by just 894 individuals or institutions. And while this number rose during the 1919–1920 period, GM shares were still held closely enough to make a corner feasible.[20] As Durant and his allies bought, GM shares soared. In just a couple weeks' time in March the stock rose by sixty points. The stock market bears who had bet against Durant and GM were being crushed as they were forced to pay exorbitant rates for stocks they were obligated to sell at much lower rates. In

April, in a complicated deal that leading members of the New York Stock Exchange brokered in order to stave off the financial collapse of certain speculators and the brokerage houses that had supported their gamble, Durant willingly ended his corner in seeming triumph.

Durant's victory was, however, partially an illusion. While Durant, on paper, had seen his fortune increase as GM's stock price soared, he had a major problem. Overwhelmingly, he and his syndicate had raised the purchase price of GM stock by buying on margin, paying as little as 10 percent, up front, of the actual cost. He had only a certain amount of time before he had to pay off the rest of the purchase price; his only means of doing so was to sell GM stock. As soon as he and the other speculators began selling, GM's manipulated high share price would fall, possibly very hard and very fast. Durant might end up owing more money than he could realize through the sale of his shares. Durant was, personally, in a weakened financial situation.

Durant's timing could not have been worse. GM, throughout the spring and summer of 1920, continued to have great difficulties raising the capital it needed to pay for its various expansions. The company issued more stock, which, despite a major investment by the English explosives company Explosives Trades Ltd. (like Du Pont, awash in war profits), struggled to find buyers. Money men looked with growing distrust at Durant and, thus, GM's stocks and bonds, as the news spread of his grand adventure manipulating GM's share price. They saw his financial sleight of hand as a clear indicator of Durant's inability to maintain a necessary focus on his corporation's industrial capacities.

Durant's downfall began. Already by April, he was beginning to feel pressure from the bankers at J. P. Morgan. In response to GM's severe need for capital, Raskob had brokered a deal giving the Morgan interests six seats on GM's board of directors and the right to buy a huge block of GM stock at a discounted price, far under market value. In return, the House of Morgan would underwrite a GM stock offering of some $28 million. In addition, Morgan senior partner Edward Stettinius would operate a $10 million pool aimed at stabilizing the price of GM stock. (Sloan, angrily watching the declining value of his own investment in General Motors, supplied five hundred thousand dollars of this pooled capital.) Durant promised to keep out of the market while Stettinius managed the stabilization campaign.

Throughout the late summer, GM tottered. As car sales plummeted and GM's finances became more precarious, its share price dropped. Durant and Stettinius covertly began to operate in what each considered his respective organization's own self-interest. Stettinius, acting on behalf of the House of Morgan, surreptitiously began dumping GM stock ahead of what he saw as a sure and precipitous decline in value. Durant, also surreptitiously, began buying up shares in an attempt to manipulate GM's stock price upward. Throughout the fall of 1920, the House of Morgan and Durant dueled. The price of GM stock kept dropping.

As conditions worsened, Sloan came home. Financially, he decided that aside from participating in the Morgan administered capital pool, he could do nothing but watch and wait. Selling his GM shares into a major bear market would do great damage to his accumulated wealth. Selling off his shares at such a time, Sloan also believed, would be dishonorable, a blow both to the company and to Durant, who was struggling to maintain the company's share price and financial future. Sloan worked through the decision on his own. The major players at this time were not men in whom he could confide or from whom who could expect guidance. Nor did he necessarily trust any of them. Durant was operating in a near frenzy, calling on the multitude of stock market players with whom he had become acquainted over the years, trying to keep their faith in GM alive, even going so far as to guarantee them that he would cover their losses if the stock did not rise as he promised them it would. The House of Morgan was home to men unknown to Sloan. Not yet had Sloan developed a relationship with the du Ponts. While he did have both a social and business relationship with John Raskob, who as GM treasurer was the du Ponts' man most focused on the corporation's travails, it is unlikely that Sloan trusted the ever optimistic, Durant-supporting, and speculatively oriented Raskob to provide level-headed advice.[21] Sloan could do little more than endure the crisis and try to situate himself for its inevitable shake out.

His one major affirmative action during this suspenseful time was a strategic one. Shortly after returning from England, Sloan went around the stock-obsessed Durant and communicated directly with chairman of the board Pierre du Pont. In a letter, Sloan forthrightly explained that he had, the previous year, worked out a plan for reorganizing the administration of General Motors; many senior executives approved of the plan. Du Pont expressed interest. Sloan immediately followed up with the written document: "Organization Study."

For anyone familiar with the history of corporate management in the United States, indeed, in the world, bells and whistles, shouts and hosannas, should now sound. Alfred P. Sloan announced his creative genius with this work.

"Organization Study" is that rarest of business documents: it has a canonic quality. Among students and practitioners of management, for whom history and the historical is not generally held in high esteem, its status as a touchstone for management theory and practice endures. "Organization Study," in numbered points, details how to organize and how to administer a corporation without destroying the spur of self-interest or the spark of creativity that make a market economy perform. Sloan understood the predicament large corporations faced: key executives had to be made responsible for the operations they oversaw and rewarded for the success they produced. If no such responsibility and reward were granted to these individuals, they had no freedom or incentive to innovate and to make their corporate operations as profitable as possible. At the same time, these key operations executives had to abide by the greater strategic purposes and organizational efficiencies that made overall corporate profitability more likely. Sloan intended to use the principles expressed in "Organization Study" to balance these potentially competing aims by creating a rational decentralized corporate structure. In this decentralized structure, divisional managers would have clearly demarcated responsibilities and freedoms; the better they performed their duties, the greater would be their financial rewards and the larger the scope of their autonomy. Harold Livesay, the eminent historian of American enterprise, best describes Sloan's achievement: "Whatever one thinks of the consequences, Sloan . . . bureaucratized the entrepreneurial function without destroying it."[22] Nothing quite like "Organization Study" had previously existed in the world of capitalism.

Sloan began: "The object of this study is to suggest an organization for the General Motors Corporation which will definitely place the line of authority throughout its extensive operations as well as to co-ordinate each branch of its service, at the same time destroying none of the effectiveness with which its work has heretofore been conducted."[23] The Durant era of "seat of the pants" management at General Motors was almost over. Alfred Sloan was about to invent modern corporate management of the large-scale, decentralized business corporation. Pierre du Pont, who understood what he had been given, would provide him with his opportunity.

First, however, the final chapter of Durant's reign must be played out in all its tragedy. For while the details of Durant's downfall are not essential to the story of Sloan, they do provide a useful context (and are, for those who find corporate finance stimulating, quite dramatic). Furthermore, Sloan's precision about how to represent his company and his concern about the integrity of information pertaining to it, while deep-seated and formed through multiple influences, was almost surely affected by his reflections on the unpleasantness caused by his one-time boss's flair for invention before and during the debacle of 1920.

Between September and November, Durant struggled to keep General Motors' share prices from collapsing. He relieved anxious friends and supporters of their shares, or promised to support their risk if they held onto their stock rather than have them dumped into the bear market. He continued to buy shares on margin, cantilevering himself financially farther and farther out over the chasm of personal collapse. In a desperately creative but unsuccessful bid to raise share price by increasing the number of buyers, Durant invented a new marketing scheme to sell GM stock to small investors on the installment plan. He borrowed over a million shares of GM stock from Pierre du Pont in an attempt to stave off margin calls on his own shares in a complex game of asset switching.

Throughout the crisis, Durant tried his legendary charm on Edward Stettinius of the Morgan Bank. He wanted—he needed—Stettinius to expend the capital pool that had been specifically set up by the major shareholders to shore up the stock price of GM. Stettinius, in the clearest sign the end was near, refused to do so. Inoculated against Durant's charm, perhaps, by his commodious reservoir of arrogance, he coolly noted that given the fundamentals of the auto market, GM's share price could not be rescued artificially.

By November, Durant was doomed. His great gamble to rescue GM's share price had failed. His creation, and much of his fortune, would be taken from him.

On November 10, Durant, Pierre du Pont, John Raskob, and an array of Morgan bankers met at the House of Morgan at 23 Wall Street to determine the future of General Motors. Less than two months earlier, on September 16, in the midst of the so-called Red Scare (precipitated by the Bolshevik revolution), a cart bomb—a horse-drawn wagon filled with dynamite and some five hundred pounds of cast-iron slugs—exploded just outside the Morgan offices. The bomb had gone off just after the noon hour so as to kill and maim the greatest number of people. Thirty-three men and women died from the blast and some two hundred more had been seriously injured. Though the explosion had been intended to strike at the heart of capitalism, almost all the dead and wounded were clerks, stenographers, and runners. J. P. Morgan was away in England and other Morgan bankers of note, as luck would have it, were safely ensconced in a conference room far from the blast. The bomb had been set—though no one knew this at the time—by Mario Buda, an anarchist, to avenge the arrest of his colleagues and friends, Nicola Sacco and Bartolomeo Vanzetti, for murder and armed robbery. Despite a reward of one hundred thousand dollars and a nationwide search for the unknown bomber(s), no one would ever be charged with the terrorist deed. (Mr. Buda made his way back to Italy, where he continued to agitate for an anarchist revolution until he was arrested by Mussolini's fascist regime.)[24]

Into the still shattered and edgy environs of the Morgan bank stepped William Crapo Durant. Dwight W. Morrow, senior partner of J. P. Morgan and Company (and later U.S. ambassador to Mexico and father-in-law of Charles Lindbergh), ran the meeting. Morrow had been trained as a tax and utilities lawyer before becoming a Morgan banker and he had little patience for the flamboyant financial maneuvering of Billy Durant. Pierre du Pont, a man of stiff and formal manner in almost any setting (simple shyness was at the root of his cool demeanor), led off by stating that du Pont holdings of General Motors stock were being held "unpledged, and that we are not buyers or sellers of stock in an any amount." He further stated in his precise way that "none of the individuals in the du Pont group were borrowers on the General Motor's stock or operating in any way." Morrow made the same basic claim, which seems to have been true at that point—the pooled capital raised to shore up the price of GM stock was not in use, and Morgan sales of GM stock had ceased some weeks before. Morrow then asked Durant to explain his position in the market.

Durant, no neophyte when it came to discerning others' motives, was undoubtedly aware that the entire reason the meeting had been called was to ask him this question. Morrow had been privately questioning Pierre du Pont and Raskob for some time about Durant's financial maneuvers. While both men had their own thoughts about the matter, and were aware that at least through October Durant had been operating in the stock market, they had told Morrow "that we know nothing of his personal affairs and that he had never confided in us." Du Pont, always the gentleman, told Morrow that if he wanted to know Durant's situation then Morrow best ask Durant directly.

So Morrow asked. Durant, in a manner of strategic equivocation, answered in such a way as to leave unpleasant facts veiled. He told Morrow that he knew of no "weak" accounts regarding General Motors shares in the stock market. He left the impression with Morrow and du Pont that he was not "a borrower on the [GM] stock or operating in the market in any way." Pierre du Pont wrote his brother fifteen days later: "Knowing

Mr. Durant and the peculiarities of his makeup, I do not think that he intended to deceive us in any way; but Mr. Morrow, who was not inclined to be as generous, I think censures Mr. Durant severely for his failure to be frank with us."[25]

Morrow was sure that Durant was lying. He conferred with his partners—not with representatives of Du Pont—and then sent word to Durant that the Morgan Bank believed that it would be in the best interest of General Motors if he stepped down. The next day Durant called Pierre du Pont and asked if they might have lunch. He broke the news of the Morgan demand to a surprised du Pont and Raskob and said that he was willing to resign to save General Motors from any hostile actions by the bankers (such as calling in GM loans, an action du Pont insisted was extremely unlikely). He then allowed that he might be in some personal financial difficulties.

The degree of Durant's personal difficulties emerged slowly, in part, because Durant himself did not have clear accounts of his own financial dealings—or perhaps he did not care to come clean about them; the record remains murky. He would only admit to a startled Raskob, shortly after the lunch meeting, that he was not sure if his stock market debts were $6 million or $26 million. By the November 17, after a frenzy of bookkeeping and consultation with myriad stockbrokers, Durant stated that he believed his debt to total some $38 million (or $366 million in 2000 dollars). He needed piles of money immediately to pay off margin calls at various brokers. If he dumped his stock onto the market to pay off those margin calls, the share price of GM stock would be devastated and General Motors financial position, its creditworthiness in particular, might well be destroyed, resulting in the destruction of the corporation and even a financial panic of national proportions. Durant had stopped smiling.

On November 20, 1920, Durant stepped down from the presidency of General Motors. He was never to return. The details of Billy Durant's later life lie outside this account. Still, a brief summary shows how differently he and Alfred Sloan came to perceive the role of the American business leader and the development of corporate capitalism. Durant owed tens of millions of dollars, and though he was offered a remarkable settlement (what today would be called a "golden parachute"), in large part engineered by a generous Pierre du Pont, he claimed that by the time his stock market accounts were settled he was ruined financially. Nonetheless, he immediately plunged back into action. Within weeks of his ruination he began Durant Motors and, by January 1923, his start-up automobile company had more individual stockholders—remember, his plan to market GM shares to the "little people"?—than any American corporation save the immensely larger American Telephone and Telegraph. His car company, however, was just a sideline for Durant's main business: stock market adventuring. Durant was the king of the stock market bulls of the 1920s. By 1928, the press reckoned that Durant had $1.2 billion personally invested in the stock market and controlled a shareholder syndicate worth some $4 billion (about $11.5 billion and $38.4 billion, respectively, in 2000 dollars). In April 1929, Durant became concerned that the Federal Reserve Bank might increase credit costs which, he believed, would produce a stock market sell-off. He met secretly with President Herbert Hoover and asked the president to do what he could to use monetary policy to shore up the fragile market. Hoover declined and Durant, throughout May and June of that year, began to dump shares into the market. Other major players followed Durant's lead. The rest, of course, is history—the market collapsed on October 29, 1929. Durant, ever the optimist, then made his fatal mistake. He trusted that the mighty downturn was just another situation to be manipulated. He came back into the market with every dollar he had and more. A few months later, as the market dropped ever lower, Durant lost—again—his fortune. The Great Depression was too much even for Billy. Durant Motors was liquidated in 1933 and bankruptcy took the last of Durant's assets in 1936. Broken by a stroke in 1942, he lived on until 1947, aided financially by Sloan and some of the other GM men who remembered what he had created through the magnificence of his nerve and vision.[26]

* * *

With Durant gone, all eyes turned to Pierre du Pont. The bankers wished him to step forward as General Motors president. So did the members of the finance committee of the Du Pont Company, who feared for their immense investment in GM. Alfred Sloan, still only a corporate figure of the second rank, had a view honed by careful observation. He saw only two men of sufficient status and influence for the GM presidency: Pierre du Pont and John Raskob. He saw only one man who also had sufficient ability and the appropriate temperament to save General Motors: "Mr. Raskob was brilliant and imaginative where Mr. du Pont was steady and conservative. Mr. du Pont was tall, well built, and reticent. He would not put himself forward. Mr. Raskob was short and not reticent . . . a man of big ideas. I remember his often coming into my office with an idea and wanting to get it into action by waving a magic wand. . . . Both Mr. Raskob and Mr. du Pont had their strong points, but on balance it seemed to all of us who were concerned that Mr. du Pont was the man we needed." (Sloan seemed to have some general distrust of short men, like Durant and Raskob; he worried that they might have an irrational need to compensate for their size by engaging in ill-conceived, flashy, exuberant behavior.)[27]

From this summary of his analysis, presented many years later by Sloan, the reader would never know an intriguing aspect of Sloan's thinking on the matter, one that is indicative of his decision-making processes. Sloan barely knew du Pont; their relationship was entirely professional and had only developed as a result of Sloan's decision to directly submit to him the plans for administrative reform. His relations with Raskob, never referenced in any of his own accounts of those early years with GM, were quite different. They were close friends. Two years earlier, the Sloans and the fun-loving (and short) Raskobs had taken the train together down to Palm Beach and spent a pleasant few days in the sun. Later, they had advanced their friendship by sharing a table at a merry New Year's Eve celebration at the Ritz-Carlton in New York City. They had developed a warm, even intimate social relation.[28] Such intimacies, however, were easily bracketed by Sloan when calculating organizational imperatives. Du Pont was the better man for the position, Sloan correctly deduced, in part because he would not allow personal proclivities to interfere with reasoned corporate decision making.

Pierre du Pont took over the presidency of General Motors on December 1, 1920. Raskob, who had stood at his shoulder for twenty years, urged a reluctant du Pont onward, telling him that General Motors had in place everything necessary for corporate greatness, including extraordinarily talented executives. The company simply needed "a leader with the common sense to permit them to operate . . . with the least interference." Du Pont, Raskob admonished, was the only man who could both unleash GM's potential and convince the financial community of the corporation's profitable future.

Pierre, as Sloan undoubtedly understood, had no personal interest in the long-term direction of General Motors. By 1920, he looked wistfully toward retirement from business affairs. Though only five years older than Alfred Sloan, du Pont had long carried a heavy load of responsibilities, not the least of which had been acting as guardian for his nine brothers and sisters from his teenage years onward, after his father was killed in a tragic explosion of nitroglycerin in 1884. Pierre du Pont had then managed the incredible growth and profitability of the Du Pont Company. His leadership had been brilliant and the company's success had made him and many members of his family fabulously wealthy. Decisions he had made in regard to the corporate direction and management of Du Pont, necessary though they were, had also torn apart the closely knit but greatly extended (and unevenly talented) family and so placed an unwelcome emotional burden on the sensitive, family-oriented Pierre. Though only fifty, du Pont wanted to step away from active management, increase his public stewardship of his native Delaware, and throw himself into the development of Longwood, the two-hundred-acre estate outside Wilmington he had purchased in 1906; its gardens, greenhouses, and elaborate fountains gave the shy, uneasy industrialist a rare pleasure. He liked nothing better than to plan and oversee the endless perfecting of his grounds.

Still, duty called. Pierre du Pont, though engineer-trained like Sloan at MIT (class of 1890), and thus quite forward-looking in his approach to industry and corporate administration, was most Victorian in his devotion to duty. Immediately, he threw himself completely into resuscitating General Motors. From the beginning of the du Pont presidency, Alfred Sloan was central to the cause.

Sloan's corporate ascent was almost complete. On December 7, 1920, Sloan and other key GM executives accompanied du Pont on a train ride from New York to Dayton, Ohio, where the relatively new General Motors Research Corporation (GMRC) was located. GMRC was developed by Charles Kettering, who had established the research facilities as an independent company some years earlier, later bought by Durant at roughly the same time as he acquired Hyatt Roller Bearing. At the research center, du Pont wanted to examine an apparent technological breakthrough: an air-cooled engine that used copper fins attached to its engine walls and a simple fan to reduce the high temperatures produced during combustion. Kettering had developed the engine and heralded his invention as a revolutionary and profitable replacement for the traditional water-cooled engine which required a pump, radiator, and an assortment of ungainly plumbing devices. Du Pont was nearly as enthusiastic about the technology as Kettering. Sloan, firmly anchored against the rising tide of optimism on the parts of his fellow executives (might he have been contemplating the fate of the Hygienic Refrigeration Company?), was not impressed. "It is a long way from principle to reality in engine design," he unemotionally hurumphed.[29]

While Kettering's air-cooled engine was the focus of much of the on-board conversation, it was not the issue most relevant to Sloan's rise to corporate preeminence. On the train ride, amid other critical conversations, du Pont and Sloan discussed administrative reorganization. After years of administrative neglect, General Motors was a mess. No one had paid enough attention to which parts of the corporation made money and which did not. Corporate policies governing corporate capital flow, intracorporate purchasing and technical cooperation, marketing and dealerships, financial planning, and production forecasts were nonexistent, poorly articulated, or barely implemented. Du Pont believed that establishing formal lines of authority and rational intracorporate relationships was an immediate necessity. Sloan's reports, derived in part from the executive bull sessions aboard the *S.S. France* back in 1919, became the basis for the reforms. While the corporation fought for financial stability, greatly aided by Wall Street's sanguine view of du Pont's acceptance of the presidency, Sloan began to oversee administrative reorganization.

"Organization Study" was at the heart of the plan. While Sloan was no prose master, the study has the elegance associated with lucidity. To understand Sloan—and to understand how General Motors gained corporate rationality—the key elements of "Organization Study" should be read with some care. Two great, overarching principles introduce the plan. The first is the need to maintain the entrepreneurial independence of the men who ran the decentralized operations that had allowed General Motors to successfully manufacture multiple lines of vehicles, parts, and accessories, and to assimilate numerous other corporate enterprises (such as its research facilities and its loan operation, the General Motors Acceptance Corporation). The second principle is the need to create efficient, centralized oversight of those numerous decentralized operations and divisions.

> 1. The responsibility attached to the chief executive of each operation shall in no way be limited. Each such organization headed by its chief executive shall be complete in every necessary function and enable to exercise its full initiative and logical development.
>
> 2. Certain central organization functions are absolutely essential to the logical development and proper control of the Corporation's activities.

Sloan had, of course, produced a paradox: he states that each operational chief executive "shall in no way be limited" and then in the next breath that "certain central organization functions are absolutely essential." At the time, neither Sloan nor other executives pointed out the linguistic knot. But years later, in *My Years at General Motors,* his ode to management, in the book's single recognition of the pleasures of the administrative mind, Sloan writes: "I am amused to see that the language is contradictory, and that its very contradiction is the crux of the matter."[30]

Just so. Sloan's study was not an exercise in administrative logic. Like many a well-trained engineer, his statement of principles existed in relationship to the problem at hand and workable solutions.[31] He had heard plenty from his boon companion, the operations genius Walter Chrysler, about the unproductive, time-wasting phone calls and New York meetings Durant had forced on him. Sloan himself, as head of the parts and accessory division, had learned a great deal about the live wire that ran between central office and manufacturing plants, between men focused on producing profitably for a mercurial marketplace and men charged with keeping corporate order through administration and finance. Sloan, in the years since he had sold Hyatt, had been on both sides of the organizational divide. He understood the paradox; divisional managers needed autonomy to innovate and to manage their diverse operations effectively and divisional managers needed oversight to stay within corporate financial and strategic guidelines.

It was a matter of checks and balances. Sloan, who had received the barely passing grade of 67 in American history some twenty-seven years earlier, perhaps the last time he had given even a small piece of himself over to history lessons, was not much concerned with the grand political theory and debate that might have dressed up his attempt to create a kind of constitutional order to General Motors' internal governance. More important, he understood the problem, he could describe it, and he had a very good idea of how to go about implementing a solution.

Sloan had somehow found the time—between running his division, taking on numerous corporate duties, and cleaning up after Billy Durant—to examine each aspect and each operational unit of the General Motors labyrinth both in itself and in relation to all other parts. His study transcended the paradox of controlled autonomy by describing the nature of the unified, decentralized corporation General Motors could become. It was "a big chew," in Sloan's words. Five "objects," Sloan wrote, followed from his two "principles":

> 1. To definitely determine the functioning of the various divisions constituting the Corporation's activities, not only in relation to one another, but in relation to the central organization.
>
> 2. To determine the status of the central organization and to coordinate

the operation of that central organization with the Corporation as a whole to the end that it will perform its necessary and logical place.

3. To centralize the control of all executive functions of the Corporation in the President as the chief executive officer.

4. To limit as far as practical the number of executives reporting directly to the President, the object being to enable the President to better guide the broad policies of the Corporation without coming in contact with problems that may safely be entrusted to executives of less importance.

5. To provide means within each branch whereby all other executive branches are represented in an advisory way to the end that the development of each branch will be along lines constructive to the Corporation as a whole.[32]

In Sloan's enumeration of the "objects" lies a new kind of corporate music, a symphony of controlled, decentralized production, operation, and administration in which there is reward for the virtuoso performer and regard for the conductor. Recognition of its beauty, of course, takes a trained ear. Pierre du Pont was transfixed.

"Organization Study" goes on into the details promised and necessitated by the two "Principles" and the five "Objects." Most dazzling of the materials that followed was the organizational chart that brought shape and hierarchy to the tangled web of affairs that General Motors had become under Durant's exuberant, often high-handed, and occasionally ill-considered leadership. Sloan drew eighty-nine boxes on his chart. Each division and each General Motors company had its place in the order. Chevrolet, on the chart's far right corner, oversaw a mini-empire of linked affairs: Chevrolet Motor and Axle Division, Chevrolet Motor Company of St. Louis, Chevrolet Motor Company of New York, and so on down to the last box in the line, the Toledo Chevrolet Company. Parts Division had its own corporate tree as did the Accessory Division (Sloan's old group). Cadillac, Buick, Olds, and Oakland were each a box unto themselves, admirably fixed on their own affairs. Like every other box on the chart, however, an upward angling line pulled them, sometimes through intermediaries, sometimes directly, to the one box that controlled them all: the corporate president.

On December 29, 1920, with the enthusiastic support of Pierre du Pont, the board of directors of General Motors accepted a slightly modified "Organization Study." Implementing the plan would take much of the next three years of Sloan's life.

SLOAN NAVIGATES A NEW COURSE

An individual ruler, if he has been educated by the law, may be expected to give good decisions, but he has only one pair of eyes and ears, one pair of feet and hands, and cannot possibly be expected to judge and to act better than many men with many pairs.

—Aristotle, *The Politics*

"You might say," Alfred Sloan reminisced half a century after he began his work in the automobile industry, "that beginning with January 1, 1921 we commenced to make an organization out of General Motors, and you might go so far as to say that it is continuing right up to today and still continues . . . and probably always will continue."[1] Billy Durant had built General Motors through inspiration, creative risk, and an element of genial cronyism. He left it at the brink of destruction. Sloan, at first under the gentlemanly but firm hand of Pierre du Pont, and then as chief executive, would use harder instruments to take General Motors from near extinction and lead it upward, past the Ford Motor Company—which rejected, for a dangerously long time, much of what Sloan engineered—and onward to national triumph. Sloan, in partnership with men like himself, made General Motors one of the world's most productive and profitable business corporations and a symbol of American free market genius.

To be the right person in the right place at the right time is a gift of synchronicity given to few individuals. Sloan, at forty-five years of age, had been given this gift. In the 1920s, he and a few other men would lead some of America's great corporations into a new era of consumer capitalism. Sloan, as well as anyone in the country, saw the challenge. He was ready to throw himself into the enterprise.

The first year of the post-Durant era was exhausting. GM president Pierre du Pont had made Sloan his principal assistant immediately. Within six months, he was executive vice president in charge of operations. Though he had never run an auto plant, Alfred Sloan oversaw all that General Motors produced.

Never a man to brag, Sloan came close to doing so while looking back to that first year when he and du Pont and the other men of the New York office began to recreate General Motors. Organizationally, they worked through the executive committee, devising the tools and command structure to rein in GM's auto barons and rationalize the corporation's finances. "The Executive Committee," Sloan remembered fondly, "worked without respite throughout 1921. We met during that year exactly 101 times in formal session. Between sessions, individually and together we were absorbed in the innumerable problems of the emergency and of the future, and were constantly on the go visiting the divisions and their plants in Detroit, Flint, Dayton, and elsewhere."[2] For Sloan such endless work, rationally devised, and proven in its results, was the stuff of dreams. He was fully occupied.

In New York, Sloan worked all day and then after his dinner hour worked some more. He rarely took a lunch break; he usually ate at his desk or wherever his duties took him (he often carried a sandwich to work, wrapped in wax paper—this became a lifelong habit). He worked on the biweekly train rides to Detroit and back. In Detroit—surprise—he did little but work. To improve his use of time while there, Sloan had a small bedroom suite installed in the new General Motors building. Most every night he retired at a relatively early hour so that he would again be sharp for the work day that followed. "Without hard work," he patiently explained to his fellow executives at General Motors, "nothing can be accomplished, no matter what the principles may be. . . . There is no short cut."[3]

To manage in the Sloan manner took a great deal of time. To manage in some other manner never made sense to Sloan. Those who refused to put in the hours to manage in the way that Sloan believed necessary were viewed by him as deficient not only in accomplishment but also in character. (Sloan reserved his special disregard for those who seemed not to know or to honor the necessity of hard work. Professors, he believed, precisely fit this contemptible category. "They may rust out but they never will wear out," he observed.)[4]

Sloan worked hard—putting in long hours of diligent concentration—because he believed above all else that decisions had to be based on all the available, pertinent facts and then accepted by all executives affected. As an old man, in his nearly unadorned office at 30 Rockefeller Place, he had a plaque engraved with the words of his longtime associate at General Motors, research director Charles Kettering: "One cannot make the best decision if the technological facts are not known."[5] Hour after hour, Sloan gathered facts. When in New York, he read reports all day long. When he was not reading or writing reports, he was in meetings listening to others present information based on the reports they themselves had read and written. Sloan spent many hours in 1921, working alone and with others, figuring out how to get the right kind of reports, filled with the right kind of facts, that would permit him and other executives to make the right kind of decisions. Instinct, gut reaction, feelings—these had no place in the corporate decision-making process. ("Horse chestnuts," Sloan would surely have muttered, had he been alive to hear the credo of the *Star Wars* films: "Trust your feelings, Luke.")

"I think it would surprise business, in general, if they appreciated how we see facts before we make an executive decision," Sloan ruminated. "No amount of trouble, no amount of time is spared in the getting the facts to put constructively and dramatically before the executive or group that has to make the decision."[6] With the pertinent facts before them, Sloan believed, rational men could and would come to agreement on the best available course of action and therefore devote themselves as a team to its implementation. The goal of the team, it should be underlined, was presupposed: corporate profitability.

Sloan understood that his job consisted of mastering the information that enabled him to manage men, money, machines, and markets. He was not the first to think of management in this way but he was among the first to act on this principle with rigor and devotion. And it is worth noting that Sloan's fierce belief in the necessity of fact-based decision making and rationally devised organizational structures was not his alone or even unique to the culture of large business corporations. In big law firms, urban hospitals, research universities, and even government agencies (with Herbert Hoover in the lead!), such organizational and managerial reform was sweeping the nation. Sloan was at the forefront of a national movement that was creating large-scale efficient organizations in more and more spheres of American life. (In 1929, the new Social Science Research building at the University of Chicago was inscribed with this quote from Lord Kelvin: "When you cannot measure it, when you cannot represent it in numbers, your knowledge is of a meagre and unsatisfactory kind.")

Sloan did not want to use his hard-earned information to manage the individual operations of General Motors. Each operation—Chevrolet, Buick, Cadillac, AC Sparkplug, and all the others—would be responsive to its own needs and run by its own executives. The information served not so much the imperatives of operation but the rationalization across all aspects of the corporation of administration, finance, and strategy. This rationalization would serve both to channel the development of each operating unit of the great corporation and also to measure—on a regular, case-by-case basis—the efforts of each of those semi-autonomous operating units. Those units that could not meet the criteria of the overall strategy or the test of such regular measurement would see change of management or, if remediation proved profitless, full unit annihilation.

Sloan was far from alone in reorganizing the structure and rethinking the strategy of General Motors. In the New York corporate office he was surrounded by men who saw the world as he did. Working within a set of established premises and united by similar professional training, they formed a kind of hermeneutic circle. Together, they solved GM's management problems.

Pierre du Pont, an MIT graduate himself, had placed well-trained men from the Du Pont company in key administrative and financial positions. With the partial exception of John Raskob, Sloan found these men admirable partners in his pursuit of corporate reason. In particular, Sloan judged John Lee Pratt to be an exemplary member of the new corporate office. Pratt had come to GM in 1919 to rationalize Durant's casual approach to capital investment within the corporation. Through sheer tenacity and Durant's general blessing, by 1920 Pratt had set up the General Motors Inventory Committee, which aimed to regulate corporate purchasing decisions and, thus, capital flow concerns. Under Durant, the committee was a site of limited sovereignty. Restructured, it become central to the du Pont–Sloan system of coordinated effort. Du Pont and Sloan charged Pratt with analyzing the flow of corporate dollars and his work became an essential aspect of the central administrating committees—the finance committee and the executive committee—Sloan devised for General Motors.

Sloan deemed Pratt "the best businessman I have ever known."[7] Like Sloan, Pratt was a university-trained engineer when such were relatively rare in the senior levels of industrial management. He had been born in Fredricksburg, Virginia, in 1879, making him just four years younger than Sloan. Pratt earned his degree in civil engineering at the University of Virginia in 1905 and immediately went to work for the Du Pont Company.

During this early period of professional business management men such as Sloan and Pratt—as they became mature, senior executives—saw themselves as proven problem solvers rather than experts per se, in automobile manufacturing, chemical production, or cost accounting. Few rival elites, especially those involved in politics, they felt, shared their disciplined, rigorous, and proven approach to solving problems. Not without reason, they trusted the wide applicability of their analytic tools, even across quite varied areas of human activity.[8]

Pratt and Sloan spoke the same language. They also shared a relentless approach to their corporate responsibilities. Like Sloan, Pratt was married but childless. His wife, Lillian, to whom Pratt seemed deeply devoted, was even more removed from General Motors than Irene Sloan. For many years, John Pratt lived comfortably but not luxuriously in midtown Manhattan at the Hotel McAlpin, a modern, efficiently managed, full-service hotel built by Coleman du Pont.[9] His wife resided at Chatham, an impressive eighteenth-century estate in Fredricksburg, Virginia. Pratt worked such long hours during the week and did so little socializing that the arrangement seemed sensible to husband and wife.

Like many of the top GM executives, including Sloan, Pratt got away—in his case, far away—on most weekends. Friday night he took the train "home" to Chatham; the Pratts summered there as well, usually staying all of August. When Lilian was, as she put it, "bored" with the amusements of Fredricksburg, she visited her husband at the Hotel McAlpin and submerged herself in "opera and theatre." Nothing in either Pratts's correspondence reveals any discontent with the episodic nature of their marriage or the rigidly separated spheres of their life together.[10] Away from work, Pratt could be lighthearted and displayed a sentimental side to those he cared about. Something, however, troubled John Pratt—maybe the work load, maybe the divided life, maybe the strain of endlessly butting heads with the operations men. Eventually, doctors determined that a hole had been burned in Pratt's stomach lining; the ulcer would plague him for the rest of his life. He rarely mentioned his discomfort and it is likely that Sloan knew nothing of it. A tall, broad-shouldered man with deep-set dark eyes, Pratt had a commanding presence. His tough-guy demeanor worked well with the up-from-the-mechanics-shop auto operations men who were suspicious of the college-educated, by-the-numbers executives who staffed the New York offices.

The other significant du Pont import was Donaldson Brown, another southerner and, in fact, a close friend of John Pratt's. Brown came to GM early in 1921 to work under John Raskob. Raskob, the original du Pont man, would remain head of the finance committee and keep his title as GM treasurer until 1928 (when, as shall be discussed, national politics complicated life within General Motors' executive suite). On his arrival at GM, Brown was named vice president in charge of the financial staff and it was he who would initiate General Motors' corporate financial reforms. He and his staff (including the rising star, Albert Bradley, perhaps the first holder of a Ph.D. employed by GM) would create or institute key elements of the financial instruments General Motors would use to measure profitability and to steer operational units' performance. Put simply, Brown institutionalized data flows and corporate performance forecasts. By funneling all the facts bearing on the production, marketing, and sales of General Motors products into the finance staff offices, Brown's team made it possible to evaluate the past performance of each unit and to set the future needs and goals both for individual units and for the entire corporation. In the new corporate order, which took several years to conceptualize and implement, statistical information flowed in every ten days from each General Motors' dealership and every month from each GM division. The corporate office used these reports to orchestrate production, inventories, employment, and other cost factors—though not with as much precision as a good conductor would have wished—to meet predicted sales. Sloan wanted a system in which a few corporate officers could oversee semi-autonomous operations and still produce the highest possible profits with the lowest possible risks. Brown and his financial team created the means by which Sloan's goal could be met.

Donaldson Brown was a memorable character. Fellow Du Pont alum John Pratt's gift for straight talking earned him respect from the most educationally deficient of General Motors operations men. His friend Brown confounded even the best-educated GM men. The management writer, Peter Drucker, who knew Brown during the World War II years, remembers that "most General Motors managers tried to have as little to do with him as possible. They simply could not understand a word Brown was saying. He completely depended on Sloan to translate him. . . . He would recite, like the very worst of Germanic professors, all the footnotes, qualifications, and exceptions in a language that was half mathematical equations and half social science jargon, without any indication where he was headed."[11] That Brown would indulge in such opaque language indicates a critical aspect of his character: he cared little for what others—

with Sloan and a very few others excepted—understood or felt or knew. He was an elitist, sure of his genius and right to lead.

If Alfred Sloan came of age almost bereft of political consciousness, Brown was imbued from his childhood days with the ideals of genteel southern conservatism tempered by the realities of capitalist imperatives. His paternal grandfather was a banker, the patriarch of an old, distinguished and wealthy Virginia family. Young Donaldson, born in 1885, spent his summers on the family's four-thousand-acre estate—the summer home—outside Richmond playing with little "negro boys," who, he explained, "regarded us as superiors."[12]

Most of the year, Brown had lived in Baltimore, where his father was also a banker. Wonderfully adept at mathematics, he went off at the age of thirteen to Virginia Polytechnic Institute and graduated at seventeen with a degree in electrical engineering. Shortly after he graduated, his father's bank went bust during the Panic of 1903. It seems his father had unwisely invested much of the bank's assets in Mexican bonds, which failed. Father, Brown reports, had never been the prudent banker that Grandfather had been, having flirted with disaster several times previously. Fortuitously, Brown's older sister had married into an extremely wealthy family. She ensured that all the Browns weathered the unpleasantness. (Of course, what Brown does not say is that bank depositors in those preregulatory days would not have done nearly so well, a facet of the story Brown lets go unrecorded in his stilted memoir.)[13]

Young Donaldson had no intention of going into the banking business, anyway. He saw his opportunity in the burgeoning world of industrial corporations. He first worked for General Electric. Then as Sloan had done a decade earlier, Brown attempted to organize his own manufacturing concern. But while Sloan's father had been able to give his son financial backing, Brown's father was bankrupt and unable to provide start-up capital. Brown would never experience his entrepreneurial moment nor develop the business range Sloan had fostered running the Hyatt Bearing Company.

At twenty-four, Donaldson Brown joined Du Pont (his path paved by a cousin who served as a Du Pont executive). Pierre du Pont recognized Brown's mathematical ability and nine years later Brown became the corporate treasurer as well as a board member. Three years after that, du Pont concluded that Brown's talents were desperately needed at General Motors. Brown would stay with the company until his retirement in 1946 (not coincidently the year Sloan stepped down).

Brown used his numbers to keep a hawk's eye on each operating department's rate of return on capital. While internal financial oversight was Brown's *raison d'être,* more than almost any other GM grandee, Brown watched and weighed and wished to emphasize the force external affairs—political perturbations, macroeconomic developments, and international shifts—had on General Motors' well-being. An odd man of limited social graces, Brown regularly contemplated American socioeconomic developments, anxiously matched them against his political ideals, and sought ways of institutionalizing such concerns within General Motors' administrative circles. Rarely if ever did this brilliant corporate executive consider how his social reality might appear to people who worked for wages.

From early 1921 until May 10, 1923, Sloan, Pratt, and Brown worked under Pierre du Pont's leadership to restore General Motors' financial stability by developing statistical measures that enabled GM's executives to control their far-flung operations. While such administrative and financial reforms were necessary to establish General Motors' corporate empire on a more businesslike footing, they were not sufficient to ensure General Motors' success. General Motors had to build, market, and sell cars that people wanted to buy. Above all, they needed to take market share from the industry leader, Ford. Henry Ford did his best to help in this regard. Famously, Ford and General Motors chose different market directions throughout the 1920s and 1930s.[14]

For nearly twenty years Henry Ford mass-manufactured one car. From 1908 through 1927, he made the Model T (and, as all auto hobbyists know, he eventually began to make a few thousand high-end Lincolns annually). In 1908, the Motel T runabout cost $825 and the touring car was $850. In 1927, when Ford begrudgingly retired the Model T, the coupe cost $290. Ford sold over 15 million ever-more inexpensive Model T's, creating what Sloan later labeled a "mass market" for the automobile. It was the perfect *first car* for millions of Americans: mechanically sound, remarkably economical, and charming in its novelty. In 1921, when Sloan became head of operations at GM, the Model T accounted for just over half of all cars sold in the United States.[15]

That same year, General Motors produced ten cars manufactured by several different divisions: Chevrolet, Buick, Cadillac, Oldsmobile, Sheridan, Scripp-Booth, and Oakland. To some extent, Durant, in buying these various car lines, had simply gone after what companies he could, sometimes aiming high (Cadillac and Buick), sometimes targeting wisely (Chevrolet), but also just shooting wildly to see what he might hit by accident (Sheridan and Scripp-Booth). Though Durant had not rigorously thought through the organizational rationality or even compatibility of those divisions, he did have a general plan in mind when he made his acquisitions. Durant meant to follow the model he had created when he had run his carriage business. The Durant-Dort Carriage Company had manufactured and marketed not one but many models of horse-drawn vehicles aimed up and down the consumer marketplace: costly and elaborate carriages; simple, economic wagons; and many models in between. While Durant had not successfully carried that idea over in a hardheaded way to his auto business—here, as elsewhere, Durant failed to follow up on his pathbreaking insights into the marketplace—he had deliberately laid the general foundation for a product policy quite different from that of Henry Ford. (Alfred Sloan, in his own writings, never gave Durant any credit for this product policy foundation.)[16]

Whatever Durant's intent, the car lines Sloan and the other key GM executives inherited from Durant's acquisitions policy had one obvious problem: none of the ten could compete in price with Ford's Model T. Whatever strengths Durant had seen in GM's car lines, the bottom line was that in 1921, GM sold just 12.73 percent of the entire auto market. Sloan believed, with reason, that General Motor's car lines were not organized to compete with Ford for buyers seeking an inexpensive new car nor were they effectively structured to take a greater share of the rest of the auto buying market—especially the growing number of individuals ready to replace an old, low-priced Model T or a mechanically unsound or simply unappealing auto with a more expensive, improved automobile. While the nation's economic troubles in 1920–21 were the root cause for GM's sales slump during this period, Sloan believed the corporation could never take a more significant share of the market until it stopped competing with itself across divisional lines and established a more rationally devised and intelligently marketed line of autos. He was not alone in his point of view. The central office was in general agreement that something had to be done about the GM auto offerings.

So on April 6, 1921, even as Sloan was working to restructure both GM's internal governance and financial measures, he was asked—and though the record is unclear, he almost surely asked to be asked— to oversee a special committee to address "product policy." The new GM corporate elite—no Durant loyalists were invited to participate—went to work. In setting the committee's corporate mission, Sloan underlined what he called "the ABC's of business." GM existed, "not . . . to make motor cars," but "to make money."[17] Sometimes, Sloan believed, even good corporate men forgot that most basic fact of all.

On June 9, 1921, Sloan presented his report on product policy to Pierre du Pont and the other men of the executive committee (Sloan, of course, was also a member of the committee). Working closely with him on the report were several men for whom Sloan had great respect and on whom the burden of recreating GM would disproportionately fall. One of them, Charles Mott, head of the car, truck, and parts division, and a hale fellow known as neither a "Durant man" nor an "anti-Durant man," took a leading role in formulating the product policy report.[18]

Sloan had known Mott since the turn of the century when the two young men—born ten days apart in 1875—had both staked their businesses on the fortunes of the fragile auto market. Mott, born into a well-to-do family, had taken over the Weston-Mott Company while in his mid twenties, following his father's untimely death. The wheel-building company had been bought at the height of the Gay '90s bicycle craze. Unfortunately for Mott, that fad had faded by 1899 and Mott had to find new markets. He tried pushcart wheels, wheelchair wheels, carriage wheels, rickshaw wheels, and wheels for automobiles. Paralleling Sloan's adventures with Hyatt Roller, Mott took to the road looking for customers and along the way met the men who were creating the automobile industry. Told by them that they needed axles, Mott labored thirteen hours a day for months on end working out the design and manufacture of automobile axles. He used Sloan's roller bearings for his axles and the two men grew rich together.

Mott's entry into General Motors, like Sloan's, came in stages. The most important of these came in 1906, when Mott moved his factory from Utica, New York, to Flint, Michigan. He had done so at the invitation of Billy Durant, then running the Flint-based Buick Company, which had become, by far, Mott's biggest customer. (In 1908, General Motors bought 49 percent of the stock of Weston-Mott and then in 1913 Mott traded his remaining 51 percent of his company for GM shares, becoming a director of GM, as well as a very rich—and eventually, very, very rich—man.)

Sloan and Mott greatly respected each another's reliance on facts and hard work, but they were not close friends. Though of similar mind in regard to business affairs, they were men of quite different personalities. Mott, for example, in simple pursuit of adventure, had dropped out of the engineering program at Stevens Institute of Technology to go to sea for several months with the New York State Naval Militia. He followed up that un-Sloan-like experience by crossing the Atlantic and bicycling his way across Great Britain and the Netherlands. And then on April 26, 1898, the day after the United States went to war with Spain, Mott again took leave from the straight and narrow to volunteer for the Navy. He served on the USS *Yankee* as a gunner's mate first class and was pleased to see quite a bit of action along the Cuban coast, shelling Spanish positions and being shot at. Needless to say, Alfred Sloan felt no similar desire to serve during America's "splendid little war" (as Secretary of State John Hay called it). Later on, Mott embarked on an even more eccentric adventure, at least from Sloan's vantage point. He became a community leader.

Mott had moved to Flint in the midst of its automobile-spurred boom times; the city population grew from 13,193 in 1900 to 38,550 by 1910. Most of the men who had moved there did so to take jobs as factory workers in auto-related industries. In 1911, the relatively well-paid proletariat disappointed their bosses by electing a socialist mayor. In response, Mott ran for mayor in 1912 on the Independent Citizen's Party ticket. Despite a poor public speaking style and a decided lack of charisma, Mott won (and was reelected in 1913) by promising "good schools, good and properly cared for streets, public parks, and free public baths."[19] His support came from across the class spectrum, though no one doubted he represented the interests of the more community-minded business elite. An editorial in the *Flint Journal* concluded that the voters had "declared for a business administration of the city government with a capable businessman at the head."[20] Mott represented the conservative end of the progressive movement: nonpartisanship with a tight focus on municipal efficiency, economy, and planning, all of which contributed to strengthening property values, stimulating commercial activity, and, in the long run, lowering tax rates. He was also, like many other conservative progressives, a strong supporter of women's suffrage: "It is absurd to argue that if women gave proper attention to their homes and families they would take no time for voting. . . . I have never heard any logical argument against woman suffrage."[21] For the rest of Mott's long life, he would continue to spend great sums of money and much time trying to solve Flint's social and political ills. Mott exemplified an early-twentieth-century conservative domestic political viewpoint. He acted on his belief that local elites, most especially business leaders, best understood how to engineer safe, orderly, and healthy communities and had the duty to do so. Agree or disagree with the principle, Mott did his best to live by it.

Sloan would have almost surely agreed with all of Mott's public positions, if he had known of them. The difference between the two men was simply that Sloan did not care about any of those public issues sufficiently to divert his attention from his business concerns. The Spanish–American War, women's suffrage, "municipal housekeeping," and the like registered, if at all, most lightly on Sloan's mind. (And what of Mrs. Sloan? What did she do, while all alone, childless, and left by Alfred for days on end? Did she listen from a distance to suffragettes as they spoke of women's need to gain the vote? Had she turned the pages of the *Ladies Home Journal* and read Jane Addams's plea for well-to-do women to enter the urban fray? Did she stare from the well-appointed rear seat of her chauffeured Cadillac at the human parade as she made her visits to mid-Manhattan's finest stores? Would Alfred listen to her, before he closed his eyes, as she recounted her day in the city? It seems that no record exists of Mrs. Sloan's participation in women's clubs, charitable organizations, or civic societies.)

Despite Charles Mott's interest in the community in which he resided, Sloan, so closely identified with the new GM circle in New York, and Mott, a man well known and liked by the Flint–Detroit men, made a good team. The report on GM's product policy they and their associates came up with was thoroughly of one mind. On June 9, 1921, in GM's New York offices, Sloan presented their findings to the executive committee and its chair, GM president Pierre du Pont. Sloan, as was his fashion, reported what he believed to be true, not what he knew key members, including his boss, wanted to hear. Still, Sloan did not directly confound expectations. He attempted to work with du Pont's ideas, even as he subtly turned them in a somewhat different direction, following the facts as he saw them. Sloan had a gift for using dry reports to inspire his corporate peers to bold strategic reorientation.

Du Pont believed that GM should beat Ford at his own game. Using a technological breakthrough, GM might be able to build a low-cost car that could outperform the Model T. Du Pont had been sold on this idea by Charles Kettering, GM's resident car genius. As described in chapter 2, "Boss" Kettering (about whom more is written later) had been working on a "copper-cooled" engine since 1918. By using copper fins attached to the walls of the auto engine, air blown across the engine could draw heat away from the motor without the use of a radiator and its attendant paraphernalia. Kettering believed that the new engine could be made to perform better than the traditional, water-cooled auto engine. He had convinced du Pont that the copper-cooled engine would deliver a devastating market blow to the Model T.

Sloan was not convinced. Most assuredly, he was not convinced by Kettering's testimony. The engine's tested performance did not satisfy Sloan, and he envisioned endless problems with the breakthrough technology that would compromise any claims for its reliability. He was even more dubious about how it would coordinate with the rest of the auto's mechanical operations. Sloan stated his strong reservations to fellow members of the executive committee as early as December 1920, but he was outvoted. Sloan accepted the corporate decision, but his concerns were not lessened. He feared that technological innovations mandated from above would not meet with enthusiasm from the men who ran the car divisions. The rule of coordinated effort was being threatened before it had a chance to be properly implemented.

The product policy report provided Sloan with a way around du Pont's commitment to the copper-cooled engine. Sloan did not directly confront the executive committee's prior decision to use the new engine in both the four- and six-cylinder Chevrolets, which were already GM's least expensive autos, and in the Oakland, as well. He simply took the Chevrolet division, and the Oakland, as he found them, technologically enhanced or not, and enfolded them within a larger conceptual scheme. Sloan focused his powers of rational persuasion on what he considered the most important strategic reorientation: using GM's productive muscle in an interdivisional spirit of cooperation and coordination to create a coherent, comprehensive line of cars. Sloan explained:

> [T]he corporation should produce a line of cars in each price area, from the lowest price up to one for a strictly high-grade quantity production car. . . . [T]he price steps should not be such as to leave wide gaps in the line, and yet should be great enough to keep their number within reason, so that the greatest advantage of quantity production could be secured; and . . . there should be no duplication by the corporation in the price fields of steps.[22]

Sloan aimed to make a virtue out of a necessity. Ford, he believed, could not be overtaken at what he did best: producing a functional auto at the lowest possible price (Sloan did believe that Chevrolet could eventually take a sizable chunk out of the upper part of the low end of the market but would not base his entire product strategy on such direct competition). Sloan, however, believed that auto manufacturers could not develop the consumer auto market most profitably by focusing on the low end. Rather, the manufacturer who could sell across all income levels—what GM would call "the car for every purse and purpose"—would come to dominate the marketplace. Sloan would not beat Ford at his own game, but rather planned for a new auto marketplace. He later wrote:

> [T]here was the period before 1908, which with its expensive cars was entirely that of a *class* market; then the period from 1908 to the mid-twenties, which was dominantly that of the *mass* market, ruled by Ford and

> his concept of basic transportation at a low dollar price; and, after that, the period of the mass market served by better and better cars, or what might be thought of as the *mass-class* market, with increasing diversity. This last I think I may correctly identify as the General Motors concept.[23]

Consumers, Sloan firmly believed, would find the stratified choices offered by GM more compelling than the single car Ford had chosen for them.

To make the plan a reality, Sloan first wanted to realign the car divisions. Chevrolet was supposed to restrict itself to producing the company's low-end vehicles. Oakland was to manufacture a slightly higher-priced car. Buick would make the next two autos in the price ladder. Then came Oldsmobile and, finally, at the luxury end of the mass market, Cadillac. Sloan insisted that Scripps-Booth and Sheridan had no role to play in a more rational production system. By 1922 both were gone; the first simply dissolved and the second sold away. The price location of each car within the product line would be partially reshuffled over the next few years; and the price point separating each car make was not rigidly observed. The idea, however, of producing different cars with different qualities along a coherently formulated price spectrum would become essential to the success of General Motors. More marketing breakthroughs would follow but this rational price spectrum was the paradigmatic first from which the others would spring.

The executive committee accepted Sloan's product policy report, but not with great enthusiasm. Du Pont expected that Kettering's technological breakthrough, not Sloan's marketing scheme, would allow GM to surpass, or at least effectively to compete with Ford. Sloan would have to await the effects of the copper-cooled engine on the corporation's competitive position.

As all auto buffs know, the copper-cooled engine failed. Sloan knew best. As far as the record shows, he took no pleasure in being right. Certainly, he took no pleasure in sorting the emotional and financial difficulties the copper-cooled engine produced within GM. Some forty years later, when he wrote his account of managing General Motors, Sloan took an entire chapter to detail the saga of Kettering's copper-cooled engine. Nowhere else in his long volume—not when speaking about the great sit-down strikes, the coming of war, or even his greatest triumphs—does Sloan reveal so much about the emotional tides that ebbed through the highest reaches of GM.

Quoting letter after letter, almost as if to remove himself from the narration, Sloan tells us what went wrong and what he had to do to make men and machines conform to market needs. Du Pont to Kettering, fall 1921: "Now that we are at the point of planning production of the new cars I am beginning to feel like a small boy when the long expected circus posters begin to appear on the fences."[24] Then in November, from the Oakland division, where the copper-cooled engine was being tested, to du Pont: "[I]t is going to be impossible to get into production in the time specified, in fact, to get this car to the point where all tests are complete and we are ready to put our O.K. on same, it will take at least six months."[25] Mr. du Pont's circus was not coming to town, at least not soon. The executive committee had no choice but to scrap the production schedule that called for mass production of an air-cooled Oakland in early 1922.

Kettering was shattered. The executive committee felt compelled to write him a letter of mixed encouragement. First came the du Pont position: "We are absolutely confident in your ability to whip all problems in connection with the development of our proposed air cooled cars." Immediately following this upbeat sentiment came a rather different message, almost surely crafted by Sloan: "We will continue to have this degree of confidence and faith in you and your ability to accomplish this task until such time as we come to you and frankly state that we have doubts as to the possibility or feasibility of turning the trick and you will be the first one to whom we will come."[26] Sloan always had a gift for reminding others that a sword hung above all their heads. The saying had not yet been coined but Sloan surely felt it: Sorry, it's nothing personal, just business.

The Kettering engine saga was far from over. Besides the purely technical problems—no small matter—the executives running the specific car divisions were far from pleased with the whole reengineering procedure to which they felt themselves captive. As several of the operations men saw it, they were being made responsible for a risky piece of technology for which they had never asked. Their decided lack of enthusiasm, as well as a clear means for coordinating their production processes with Kettering's innovative engine, led neither to technological progress or a manufactured car in good working order. Tensions between Kettering in research, the car division executives, and the executive committee were becoming unpleasant and counterproductive to efficient operations. As Sloan later explained, throughout 1922 and into 1923 "the air-cooled car continued to distract the corporation and to keep its leading officers in a state of tension over the question of what the future product of the corporation was to be."[27]

The turmoil over the air-cooled engine, as Kettering called it (du Pont thought that "copper-cooled" better explained the wonder of the new design), annoyed Sloan greatly. From his perspective it was an unnecessary, even ill-conceived, debate. Even if the engine succeeded, Sloan believed, it would do relatively little to enhance GM's competitive situation or market growth. If it failed to pan out, it would prove to be a waste of time and money, at the least. Worse, if consumers bought GM cars with the new engines and the engines performed poorly, the fiasco could undermine public belief that GM cars were reliable. Sloan had not yet placed his full energies into navigating the consumer marketplace or finding the right tools to measure the mind of the consumer. But he knew that poor performance could be a marketplace catastrophe.

Sloan tried to convince his fellow executives, most especially Pierre du Pont, that GM did not need to lead the industry in automotive technological improvements. Instead, he argued; GM's competitive advantage would come through its coordinated efforts. That managerial imperative—coordinating GM's operations—is what Sloan believed that the other executives should focus on. Efficient internal governance of GM's massive corporate capacities, he insisted, would lead to superior performance in all areas, thus allowing every GM product to be economically produced and effectively marketed. Scale and scope, if properly coordinated, were GM's competitive advantage. Betting on cutting edge technology was a foolish gamble for a major market player to make, reasoned Sloan.

So even as the copper-cooled engine crisis played itself out, Alfred Sloan worked to make General Motors run more efficiently and profitably. He struggled to put GM's finances and financial structures in order. He traveled from coast to coast in a specially outfitted Pullman car to see GM's independent automobile dealers and learn the facts of their commercial situation. He moved across the nation from production unit to production unit, learning the business of each operation.[28]

Sloan's travels rarely revealed—at least, in a conventional sense—the man beneath the suit. When he met with the far-flung employees of GM, mainly he listened to them talk. Sloan went into the dealerships, parts companies, production facilities, and engineers' offices and he asked pointed questions and heard out concerns. He was no Durant. He offered few pleasantries, made no motivational speeches, and wasted little time. In large cities, he saw as many as ten car dealers in a single day. Sloan asked the dealers and production men questions meant to reveal their challenges, as well as their successes. He never lectured them or puffed himself or the central office. While he would not, perhaps could not, show an interest in the individual men with whom he met, he did demonstrate that he valued what they could tell him about the workings of their businesses. Politely, even urgently, he asked them to instruct him on how the corporation worked from their positions within it. So little did he talk about himself or his concerns that sometime in the early 1920s, the others, half jokingly and never to his face, began to call him "Silent Sloan." In person, he was always addressed as Mr. Sloan. He, in turn, replied to each man formally, addressing him by his last name.[29]

Sloan, as must be clear by this time, did not look or act like most of the men with whom he met. He was not the typical "man's man" that most auto dealers, at least, might have expected from an auto industry executive. Sloan weighed no more than 130 pounds. In his mid-forties, he was bony and narrow-shouldered, a whippet of a man.

Whether visiting a car dealership in Texas or an accessories factory in the Midwest, Sloan dressed just as he did in New York City. He wore custom suits, beautifully tailored, usually double-breasted and made of the finest wools, and starched, hand-tailored white dress shirts with high stiff white collars. His broad, silk ties were carefully tacked down with an inconspicuous pearl stick pin. A silk scarf, folded just so with three peaks, usually graced his coat pocket. He wore hand-cobbled spats that accentuated the narrowness of his feet. Fastidious about his appearance, Sloan was a dapper man. Surprisingly, given the gray public image he would later work to create, Sloan had an eye for style and he exercised it. He dressed quite deliberately in the grand manner of the New York business elite. Sloan's sartorial elegance also reflected his simple precision in all matters. Finally, it might be said, that his impeccable, expensive, buttoned-down clothing worked, deliberately or not, to armor Sloan during his endless meetings from the misapplied intimacies of the often gregarious, less than well-polished men of GM.[30]

Not that Sloan was cold or rigidly composed during meetings. He was not a passive listener. As others spoke, his knees jiggled, his feet tapped, he squirmed in his chair. On occasion, he pulled his knees up and leaned far forward. He stared intensely at each man who spoke, fixing him with his total concentration.[31] (An image of the iconic capitalist character from the *Simpsons,* Mr. Burns, sitting vulpine behind his desk, springs to mind.) In the early 1920s, at least in part, the intensity of Sloan's expression, his fixed gaze on the man or men with whom he was meeting, and the relative paucity of his replies were the result of his partial deafness. Not until he was much older, and his hearing was much worse, would

Sloan refer to his difficulties. With mechanical aid, his hearing was adequate to his needs and he seemed to worry little, if at all, about it.[32] It was a technical problem.

Sloan's transcontinental journeys during the early 1920s served a purpose more subtle than the simple transmission of information upward through the ranks. Sloan visited the dealers, the production men, and myriad other GM executives in their operational homes to evoke, demonstrate, and cement a corporate relation. While Sloan's rationalization of information was a critical aspect of his managerial genius, his organizational vision contained a human aspect, as well. The men of GM must learn to pull as one, even as the decentralized structure of the corporation lent itself to loyalties of a more localized nature.

Transforming GM's corporate culture—a phrase unknown in 1920s corporate America—from the Durant era of a loose confederacy to a more centralized, if still federalist regime, took more than simply instituting financial controls and executive committee strategic decision making. Sloan knew he must manage men as well as numbers. He made sure that the corporate central office had a face—a sober, intense, profit-minded face.

Yet Sloan knew that such old-fashioned, one-on-one visits were not enough to manage the centripetal forces at work in General Motors. He and Pierre du Pont were in accord on this matter. Something more needed to be done to unify the company and break down any estrangement between center and periphery, production men and financial overseers, dealers and manufacturers. For Billy Durant, remember, GM had been above all the initials issuing forth from a stock ticker. Each member company—an already existing business before it had been bought by Durant—had been its own, self-contained universe of promise and possibility. Buick was real. AC Sparkplug was real. GM was not; it was a holding company. As one of Sloan's allies said in the early 1920s, for most people inside and outside the corporation, GM meant "the name of a security."[33]

In late 1922, Sloan began to gather information about how GM was perceived by the diverse publics with which he thought the corporation should connect. Sloan saw several purposes behind this imaginative project. In part, he hoped to survey the public and gather data useful for his new product policy: How could GM link their segmented line of cars in the mind of the auto buyer? Second, and at least as important, Sloan had begun to consider how he could at least soften, in the minds of GM's myriad lords and their various vassals, the hard instruments of centralized financial control and strategic planning. Could General

Motors apply the balm of corporate brotherhood onto the injured pride of GM's divisional knights errant?

Sloan devised several solutions. While he did not order up an Arthurian Round Table, he did craft a variety of interdivisional committees. One of the most important of these was the general purchasing committee, composed of divisional purchasing agents and Sloan and his central office associates. Together they forged cooperative, cost-saving approaches across the corporation.[34] More broadly, Sloan looked to the emergent fields of advertising and corporate public relations to simulate and, therefore, possibly stimulate GM corporate unity both internally and in the minds of the American people.

In his understanding of the central role that image making could play in business, Sloan was far ahead of his time. Not that he was the first to consider how a profit-making operation could be transposed onto a gentler plane of human endeavor. Other captains had first charted the waters of the corporate imaginary. But being first had never much interested Sloan. Being right was what mattered. Better to learn from others' ventures into the unknown and then improve on their accomplishments. The right thing to do for General Motors in the early 1920s, Sloan observed, was to create a useful image that would give General Motors—not its individual divisions—a primary place in the minds of its employees and its consumers.

In September, Sloan began to orchestrate his image make-over of General Motors. Step by logical step, he moved forward while carefully maintaining consensus among the men who ran the divisions. He began cautiously with some circumlocutory management by memo: Did the divisional managers, perhaps, perceive any need for some greater attention to the public presence of the General Motors corporation? Receiving no negative responses to his subtle but not misleading memo, he stepped further along the path he wished to take. He then wrote all divisional managers that, in accord with a general sense throughout the corporation, a campaign of institutional advertising would be undertaken as a supplementary form "properly coordinated with what I term the product advertising of the Divisions."[35] Sloan had laid the groundwork for the first attempt to situate each product line of the corporation within a General Motors brand—an externally oriented marketing move. At the same time, he was publicizing for all employees, dealers, contractors, and shareholders their stake in the "parent" corporation—an internally directed corporate culture move. Sloan was turning Durant's speculative holding company, in which each operational piece had run on its own, into a functional, integrated corporate entity.[36]

Next, Sloan went to the finance committee. It, and it alone, could provide the necessary funds for an institutional ad campaign. As GM president Pierre du Pont was already on board, and since Sloan carried great weight with the committee—he had been instrumental in its creation and had been a member of it since April 25, 1922—the deed was done.

To create the General Motors institutional ad campaign, Sloan contracted with a relatively new ad agency, Barton, Durstine, and Osborne (founded in 1919). It was Barton—Bruce Barton—who had attracted Sloan to BDO. Barton, just thirty-six years old in 1922, was the ad man extraordinaire of the 1920s. He made a great deal of money out of what literature professors call the "pathetic fallacy." Barton, like the great romantic poets, knew how to imbue bloodless entities with great human emotion and spirituality. This knack seemed to sell product. Nowadays, most global citizens consider it normal to attribute sexiness to a car or good cheer to a coffee brand, but in the 1920s this anthropomorphism was ground-breaking stuff. Barton was the king of such conceits and as is true of most breakthrough artists, he tended to go over the top.

Bruce Barton must have seemed a piece of work to Alfred Sloan. The Barton Sloan knew was a bundle of enthusiasms, can-do certainty, and effervescent creativity. He radiated, all who knew him said, supercharged "sincerity." Barton's major professional breakthrough had come in 1914 when he had penned a rather fantastic biography of Jesus. In *A Young Man's Jesus,* Barton pictured a Jesus "glowing with physical strength and the joy of living." His Jesus had "perfect teeth" and "hot desires." A minister's son, Bruce Barton's trademark creative move was strapping the language and imagery of a virile but spiritual Christianity onto the manly business of business. In 1925, this vision reached its apogee with Barton's publication of *The Man Nobody Knows,* a breakaway best-selling book that once again told the story of Jesus but this time as "the founder of modern business." That Barton's brio hid a more melancholic, anxious self—Barton spent part of 1928 in a sanatorium—was not something Sloan knew or would have cared to know.[37]

The direct line that led Sloan to choose Barton almost surely originated during World War I when Barton began his adventures in advertising. Then a New York City magazine writer, Barton volunteered to write copy for the Victory Loan campaigns. To sell New Yorkers on the Liberty Bonds, he imagined New York City as a person ("For I am New York, the dwelling place of honor. 'A city that hath foundations'—whose corner stone is FAITH.") Somehow the "I am New York and This is My Creed" advertisements were meant to ennoble New Yorkers by leading them to appreciate what a high-minded city they lived in, which in turn would prompt their buying war bonds. Whether this campaign was effective is unclear. What is certain is that it put Barton on the commercial map and set him on his ad-man way.[38]

Barton's specific pitch to GM particularly charmed Pierre du Pont. Barton wrote: "I like to think of advertising as something big, something splendid, something which goes deep down into an institution and gets hold of the soul of it. . . . Institutions have souls, just as men and nations have souls." Du Pont found these word so apt, so moving, that he had them sent out to all shareholders of General Motors.[39] The shy tycoon, orphaned early and thrust into family and corporate leadership while hardly more than a youth, took pleasure in the sincere certainties of one of the greatest business boosters of the 1920s. Barton told Du Pont something quite dear; his creations, his businesses, transcended the material grit of the bottom line. They were somehow, in some way, beings vested with the glory of God's own most sanctified gift. At the turn of the century, as noted earlier, some businessmen liked to think that they were God's stewards on earth. What did it mean, that by the 1920s, businessmen of sober mien were willing to think that the corporations to which they had given life had also been endowed (by whom?) with souls?

Barton offered General Motors more than a soul. Specifically, he wished to picture for one and all the great car company as a family, a "famous family." Chevrolet, Oakland, Buick, Cadillac, GMC Trucks, and Olds would all be enfolded—even as each retained the special individuality due any blessed child—within the paternal embrace of General Motors.

That spring of 1923, as Bruce Barton spun his family romance, the corporate paterfamilias—or stepfather, in the minds of the Durant loyalists—made a decision that Sloan at least had not anticipated. Pierre du Pont was done. He was satisfied that he had accomplished what was most necessary in protecting the family investment in General Motors. GM was on sound footing. Its finances had been stabilized. Sales had grown. Corporate governance had been rationalized. And the heir apparent had been groomed.

Du Pont knew the corporation's future was far from certain. Troubles still loomed, not least a final reckoning over the fate of "Boss" Kettering's copper-cooled engine (and at least one historian has argued that du Pont stepped down when the failure of the engine—Pierre's "circus" attraction—had become painfully clear). Still, Pierre could now retreat to his gardens knowing that he had done what was necessary and that he had achieved a great deal.

On May 8, 1923, du Pont met privately with Sloan. He told Sloan that he would, in short order, resign. He also said that he would call for a special meeting of the board of directors, where he intended to nominate Sloan for the presidency of the corporation. Sloan was . . . pleased. He had known the job would become his eventually. That much had been apparent since Sloan had spoken to du Pont in 1920, urging him to assume the position of corporate president. Du Pont had accepted the responsibility back then, in the corporation's darkest days, but had lightened it from the start by telling the board that the operating burdens of the corporation had to be placed on someone else's shoulders: Sloan's. And Sloan had performed. As an associate would later say, he performed just like the roller bearing that had made his first fortune: "self lubricating, smooth, eliminates friction and carries the load."[40]

On May 10, 1923, Alfred P. Sloan Jr. was named president of General Motors by the GM board of directors. No letter or speech or scrawled remark has been found that reveals Sloan's emotions on the occasion. Mrs. Sloan's feelings remain similarly lost to history.

(Did Sloan tell his wife the news on that first night of May 8? Did he call her on the phone? Or, as his own father had done almost exactly seven years earlier, did he hide the news from his family, waiting until it had become official, and unavoidably public, on the May 10? A guess: he came home at his regular hour on the May 8 and explained to Irene his upward assignment. To guess at more than that—about an embrace or exclamations or a quiet talk about what his new role would mean for her and for him in the long halls and large rooms of their splendid home—would be to make assumptions about aspects of his personal life that Sloan was careful never to reveal.)

Everything known suggests that Sloan was moved by his ascent. And everything known would indicate that he let those feelings show where no one could see them.

He did write some seventeen or so years later (or more likely approved the ghostwritten passages that read):

> I believe it is reasonable to say that no greater opportunity for accomplishment ever was given to any individual in industry than was given to me when I became president of General Motors. I fully realized that, and I fully appreciated it. And I always have been grateful for the confidence that made it possible. I determined right then and there that everything

> I had was to be given to the cause. No sacrifice of time, effort, or my own convenience was to be too great. There were to be no reservations and no alibis.[41]

Some twenty years later still, he tried again to find the words to communicate what he wished to share with a general public:

> As to myself, I recognized that my election to the presidency of the corporation was a big responsibility and a business opportunity that comes to few, I resolved in my own mind that I would make any personal sacrifice for the cause and that I would put forth all the energy, experience, and knowledge I had to make the corporation an outstanding success. General Motors has been for me a dedicated activity ever since, perhaps to a fault.[42]

Perhaps to a fault?

SLOAN IN CONTROL

He stops upon this threshold,
As if the design of all his words takes form
And frame from thinking and is realized.

—Wallace Stevens, "To an Old Philosopher in Rome"

The middle line of a corporate haiku: "work flowed on without a break."[1] So reads Sloan on becoming president of General Motors, awash in work but not at sea.

Much had been accomplished by May 10, 1923. More still needed to be done. Sloan had put his stamp on the corporation, even as he had worked in subordination to Pierre du Pont. Now, as GM's president as well as chairman of the executive committee, he would (always in coordination with the other men of GM) lead the company forward, past the Ford Motor Company.

During the 1920s, Sloan would make style a critical aspect of the General Motors automobile line. Though he had no personal interest in the ballyhoo of the Jazz Age, he understood that the emergent culture of celebrity, publicity, and spectacle would be good for the auto business. The American people, at all social levels, were embracing the notion that the "good life" included consumer products and mass entertainments. Sloan meant to make General Motors a critical piece of that new consumer culture.

In such a culture, Sloan saw the need to make a public place for himself. He would become a minor national celebrity as he invented a new role in American society: corporate man. The president of GM, Alfred P. Sloan Jr., would not be just another flamboyant celebrity, however, making the newspapers with witty statements or entertaining exploits. He would instead present himself as a quiet productive engine of the good life, humming along, bringing to the American people—in the most cost-efficient manner possible—the good things that made their good lives possible. Even with the attendant difficulties, these years were for Alfred Sloan the best of times.

Before Sloan could move the corporation in the directions he saw as most useful, he first needed to solve permanently the major problem he had inherited from Pierre du Pont: the copper-cooled engine. The problem entailed more than a technical decision. Charles Kettering, head of the research corporation, had to be managed as well. Kettering refused to believe that his breakthrough technology was to be discarded. If the engine was to be cast away he would leave with it.

Kettering had never fit easily within General Motors' corporate structures. He did not really want to fit in. Self-consciously and proudly, he was a man between two worlds. "I'm always a screwdriver and pliers type," he declared toward the end of his extraordinary life, "but then someone threw a monkey wrench in there."[2] Kettering, with his first-rate technical mind, tended to talk in cracker-barrel aphorisms. Sloan found such utterances, and Kettering's sense that no meeting was complete without a few of his observations on his favorite subjects, trying at times. Still, the man produced and Sloan could usually ignore irrelevant habits of personality on the parts of his men so long as they didn't interfere with their production.

Kettering was born in 1876, making him a year younger than Sloan. He came from central Ohio, where he had grown up on a small farm. No one in his family had expected him (nor helped him in any way) to push on and make his way through Ohio State University with a degree in electrical engineering. Kettering was twenty-seven when he graduated. Unlike Sloan, who rushed into the twentieth century, Kettering kept something of the nineteenth century within him. Long of limb, with clodhopper-clad feet, his head cocked forward in a peculiar fashion, he was something of a Natty Bumpo in a brown suit, roaming his laboratory with tools at the ready, his cantankerous common sense always on call. Even after he became immensely rich, he sometimes acted—and it was an act since he could turn it on and off—the part of the rube (though he would have been the smartest rube on earth). His life story, he believed, not unlike Henry Ford, was the genuine American article. His "kind," by which he meant men of uncommon good sense, technological know-how, and get-up-and-go who were not afraid to tackle conventional wisdom, had built America. Back home, after earning wealth and renown, he told the people of Londonville, Ohio:

> Now I didn't know at that time that I was an underprivileged person because I had to drive the cows through the frosty grass and stand in a nice warm spot where a cow had lain to warm my feet. . . . I thought that was wonderful. I walked three miles to the high school and I thought that was wonderful, too. I thought of all that as an opportunity, and I thought the only thing involved in opportunity was whether I knew how to think with my head and how to do with my hands.[3]

Kettering had proven to the business community by 1923, when Alfred Sloan became his boss, that he could make very lucrative products with his head and with his hands. "The business of engineering was business" was how the American Institute of Electrical Engineers saw it, and no one engineered for business better than Charles Kettering.[4] Despite his country-boy manner, Kettering ran one of the first modern industrial research laboratories, a linear descendant of Thomas Edison's "invention factory" and close kin to the corporate labs at General Electric, Du Pont, and Bell Telephone.[5]

In his first serious job, with the National Cash Register Company, he invented marvelous machines for registering sales. He invented not by whimsy but to meet the market on its own terms. By 1908, Kettering had recognized the market for automotive technology and he rushed in and used his genius to invent new parts systems for cars, most famously the electric self-starter. Kettering twinkled when he told appreciative audiences: "I didn't hang around much with other inventors or the executive fellows. I lived with the sales gang. They had some real notions of what people wanted."[6] Kettering loved to talk and out of his mouth streamed the business common sense of the 1920s, a language he played no small role in creating: a rough idiom of country-boy plain speech and big-city hustle. Kettering listened less well.

In the spring of 1923, Sloan needed to make Kettering listen. But Sloan needed to be careful in his remonstrances because he wanted to keep Kettering's genius for General Motors. Kettering had begun his relationship with General Motors in 1916, just as Sloan had. Billy Durant bought Kettering's Dayton Engineering Laboratories Company—DELCO— at roughly the same time as he had bought Hyatt Roller Bearing. He folded both into the United Motors Corporation, which was soon after brought directly into the General Motors family. Sloan had been put in charge of the new combine and was, thus, nominally Kettering's superior. Kettering was not much one for bosses and Sloan had, for much of the next seven years, gently tried to bring Kettering's creativity and practical know-how within the administrative structures Sloan was working so diligently to craft. Throughout the late 1910s and early 1920s, this corporate relationship had been tense as GM's new cost-conscious managers tried to calculate the utility of a cost-producing research laboratory.

Kettering, from 1920 onward, was president of the General Motors Research Corporation, a breakthrough division charged with innovating for the entire corporation. GM was one of only a handful of corporations willing to spend its money on a research lab. At Kettering's insistence, the research facility and Kettering himself had stayed put in Ohio. Kettering was happily married and proud owner of a mansion on a hill a few miles outside Dayton. His wife, Olive, had become the philanthropic benefactress of Dayton. Kettering, by 1923, was a leading member of the Society of Automotive Engineers (president of the organization in 1918) and a national spokesman for American ingenuity and mechanical innovativeness. He was well known among the industrial set. He was also, through the deal that brought him into GM, a major stockholder in the corporation (and possessor of a growing portfolio of stocks and bonds). He was rich and he had a life apart from General Motors and he knew he had opportunities for further wealth, status, and technological innovation apart from the corporation. He did not, by May 1923, trust anyone at General Motors. All of them, he was sure, meant to thwart his engine due to jealously, bull-headedness, and short-sightedness.

Sloan was neither bull-headed nor short-sighted, and he was not jealous of Kettering's technical skills. Sloan believed in Kettering. He saw him as a man of the first order, "a man of . . . marvelous ability."[7] But he believed that Kettering had fallen prey to an enthusiasm that was not substantiated by proven facts. He had pushed his air-cooled engine on the production men before its reliability had been proven to them and before the divisional engineers had time to make the new engine work in the cars already under production. In sum, regardless of the specifics of the new engine's performance, Kettering—and Du Pont—had created an administrative mess and an impediment to good corporate order. And at a practical level the copper-cooled engine was beside the point.

In the economic good times of 1923, the water-cooled Chevrolet was selling in record numbers. No need existed for a breakthrough engine. Advertising copy for the copper-cooled engine painfully indicated the indifference, even antagonism, of the Chevrolet division to the product:

> Chevrolet Motor Company announces an important development in economical transportation, consisting of a motor embodying new application of established principles governing the efficient control of motor temperatures under all weather conditions. . . . Chevrolet cars, equipped with these new motors, are now being marketed in limited quantities . . . along with its present successful line of New Superior Models.[8]

Of course, worst of all, the engine did not work, at least not in the cars for which it was designed. It was supposed to be put into parallel production in the 1923 Chevrolet, along with the "successful line" of traditional engines, but production problems arose. Those cars that were produced with the new engines did not work well at all. William Knudsen (about whom more is written later), who had inherited the copper-cooled engine when he had been put in charge of operations at the Chevrolet division in March 1922, fumed over the technological imposition. He told off Kettering: "This car isn't any good. . . . You and the people you have working on it down in Dayton, and principally the people working on it in Dayton aren't automobile people." Later, he bluntly informed Sloan that the copper-cooled engine was a disaster: "This copper-cooled car isn't any good. . . . It won't stand the gaff. We've got seven or eight million dollars tied up in it, but it is my decision to abandon this car altogether, and I am putting that decision down on paper and sending it to you."[9]

Sloan recorded the production of 759 copper-cooled Chevrolets. Of these, 239 worked so poorly that they never made it beyond the factory gates. Of the remainder, only a hundred were sold to car buyers; most of the rest stayed within the organization, driven by salesmen or factory representatives or tinkered with at the dealerships. Complaints about the new car's performance flooded in. Kettering, not without reason, blamed the divisions for the mishaps, accusing them of misengineering the Chevrolet in the process of accommodating the new engines. Sloan believed the new engine itself was the main problem.

At the first meeting of the executive committee run by President Sloan it was decided to test Kettering's engine before any attempt was made to introduce it into the Oldsmobile—as had been planned under the presidency of Pierre du Pont—so as to preclude any possibility of "serious embarrassment to the Olds Motor Works organization at the factory and throughout the world."[10] Now that he was corporate president, Sloan began to push harder at one of his growing concerns: that as a maturing corporation General Motors must do nothing to damage its reputation in the minds of its growing number of customers. Technical innovation must take a backseat to product reliability. GM autos needed to perform as well as—not necessarily better than—the corporation's competitors. This relative reliability, Sloan believed, had to be considered the base line on which all other decisions would be judged.

The facts, as recorded by the test engineers, bore out Sloan's beliefs. On May 28, 1923, just eighteen days after Sloan took charge, three of GM's leading engineers reported their findings to the executive committee. The copper-cooled engine did not work properly: "[M]ajor difficulties plus several minor ones which can be reported in detail, if you so desire, lead us to the conclusion that the job is not in shape for immediate production. We recommend that we set it aside for further development."[11] The executive committee stopped the planned introduction of the copper-cooled Oldsmobile. William Knudsen, at Chevrolet, recalled every copper-cooled car that had been built.

Kettering was devastated. It was his first major failure and it was caused, he felt, not by his own mistakes but by the divisions' incompetence. Kettering believed that he had not sabotaged Sloan's principle of coordinated effort. The operating divisions were at fault for refusing to take advantage of the corporation's research laboratory. Desperate, he tried to get Sloan to give him the money to develop his own independent production capacity. Days later, when he came to understand that GM was not going to go forward as he wished with his engine, he wrote a letter of resignation to Sloan: "I have definitely made up my mind to leave the corporation unless some method can be arranged to prevent the fundamental work done here from being thrown out and discredited through no fault of the apparatus."[12]

Sloan understood Kettering's emotional state but rather than appease him he worked to educate him into understanding the principles of management as Sloan saw them. In a long, carefully detailed, calmly worded letter, he reminded Kettering of the facts; the copper-cooled cars were not working properly and Knudsen and the other production men did not believe in the technology. The whys and wherefores were important but did not and could not trump the facts: the cars did not function properly; the production men had no faith in the technology. He then explained how he worked, how the corporation under his presidency worked, and what Kettering must do as a result: "What we have got to do is to make our people see the thing as you see it and with that accomplished then there will be nothing more to the problem. I do not think that forcing the issue is going to get us anywhere. We have tried that and we have failed. We have got to go it in a different manner if we are going to succeed."[13]

Four days after sending the letter, Sloan himself arrived in Detroit. He had arranged for Kettering to join him, along with the well-respected, problem-solving Charles Stewart Mott and the equally powerful and respected GM giant, Fred Fisher. As equals they talked through the problem. Sloan wanted Kettering to come on his own to the right conclusion as to why the project had failed. Kettering also had to learn how to manage future work at the research laboratory so as to avoid such unpleasant—and financially adverse—outcomes. The operations men, most importantly Knudsen, who could outproduce anyone in the world in an industrial setting (and who had only a couple of years earlier quit the Ford Motor Company over Henry Ford's autocratic and overbearing manner), were pleased with Sloan. Sloan, himself, had hoped that the matter was moving along in an appropriate fashion.

Kettering did not yet, however, share in the bonhomie. The very next day after the Detroit meeting, Kettering fired off an angry letter to Sloan: "Since this thing with the Copper-Cooled Car has come up . . . the Laboratory has been practically isolated from the Corporation's activities. This I resent, as I also resent the criticism upon the work of the Laboratories."[14] Kettering demanded that Sloan support him. If Kettering came up with an engine that proved out and the men in the division still refused to cooperate, Kettering said, then Sloan should fire them. When not giving public talks to large audiences or interviews to friendly reporters, Kettering used few country-boy colloquialisms.

Sloan tried again. He wrote Kettering:

> The Executive Committee can remove anybody in the organization; it can make any changes in personnel it wants to; it can adopt any policies that in its judgment are desirable for the benefit of the Corporation, but there are certain things it cannot do and that is, it cannot order a co-operative spirit to be developed in the organization—it has got to be done in an entirely different way.[15]

Kettering had to be made to understand that General Motors could not make progress while hampered by internal acrimony. The men in charge of the car divisions, so long as they operated profitably, could not simply be ordered into compliance. They had to be convinced. Thus, Sloan told Kettering, he would not give such orders or make such demands.

Sloan walked a fine line with Kettering. Just barely, they stayed in balance. Sloan, of course, did not leave it at that. Management had to be more than *ad hoc* responses to personnel crises.

In September of 1923, Sloan sent around a letter to Kettering and the key car men. He asked them if it would not be useful to create a new committee devoted to general technical matters. The chief divisional engineers, Kettering and his own hand-picked men, and some of the key men from New York, including Sloan, should meet regularly, he suggested, and consider how to move forward together in technological harmony. All agreed that such a regular meeting could prove useful and so it came to pass. Together, over time, they would develop their common ground and work out how to test new technologies, creating the GM Proving Grounds in the process. Sloan hoped that scheduling a few more hours of meetings would prevent another copper-cooled engine fiasco.

The committee did not solve everything; divisional ties and competing concerns did not just fall away. The committee did, however, greatly increase the chance that different branches of the corporate family could sound one another out, at an early stage, about possible constraints and creative opportunities. Maximizing cooperation within the corporation did not guarantee success, Sloan believed, but it offered a clear competitive advantage over GM's less well organized or less well developed rivals. The price paid for such executive comity was a degree of corporate inertia—the many committees through which any one idea must pass did not make for speedy changes. This price Sloan was willing to pay, however. He believed that efficient production at reasoned costs guided by strategic marketing and precise accounting techniques would produce steady growth and sure profits for the giant enterprise.[16] (Sloan did not leave the matter of technological integration solely in the hands of the technical committee. In November 1924, to break down the geographical barrier separating Kettering's lab boys and the operation men, Sloan managed to get Kettering to move his research outfit from Dayton to Detroit. In his new Detroit office, Kettering installed a plaque reading: "Any problem, thoroughly understood, is fairly simple.")[17]

Kettering's bitterness evaporated within months, in large part due to the fruition of another of his long-term research laboratory projects. Kettering's lab would produce a patented fuel additive that would change engine performance. Once again, a Kettering breakthrough would cause Sloan much anxious maneuvering. This time the corporation's problem would be very much in the public eye. And this time Sloan would decide that the possible profits were worth the problems.

For several years, beginning even before DELCO had become a GM division, Kettering had overseen research into the problem of engine knock—that sharp pinging noise that comes from within the engine's chambers.[18] Kettering, demonstrating the keenness of mind that made him such a valuable member of the GM family, perceived that engine knock was a fuel, not an engine, problem. In 1917, having decided that a chemist had too many ingrained notions about fuels to look at the problem creatively, Kettering counterintuitively assigned a mechanical engineer named Thomas Midgley Jr. to the engine knock project. After years of work, Midgley was able to prove Kettering right; knocking was caused by a "premature combustion of the fuel–air mixture."[19] This "premature combustion" wasted fuel and also reduced engine performance. It also damaged the engine. In December 1921, Midgley solved the problem, after much trial and error, by adding tetraethyl lead—TEL—to gasoline. Kettering called the new additive-enriched fuel "ethyl." By curing engine knock, ethyl not only reduced engine damage and provided better gas efficiency, it also allowed for more powerful high-compression engines, which allowed cars to go faster and to accelerate more quickly. By May 1923, ethyl-fueled race cars took first, second, and third at the most prestigious auto race in the United States, the Indianapolis 500.[20] General Motors owned the patent for TEL, and if an economical system for producing the substance could be devised, GM had a major money-maker under its control.

Just weeks after the copper-cooled engine had come to its unsatisfactory end, Kettering and General Motors made a deal with Du Pont to begin manufacturing TEL. Kettering also set up a pilot manufacturing program under his own control in Dayton. Sloan, in part to demonstrate his faith in (and to) Kettering, created a new division, the General Motors Chemical Company. He made Kettering its boss (even as he continued to run the research division) with full responsibility for producing and marketing his lab boys' products.

Almost immediately, disaster struck. At the Du Pont manufacturing plant in Deepwater, New Jersey, in the first month of operations, a worker died of lead poisoning. Then another died while more were stricken. In April 1924, two factory operatives died at the Dayton pilot plant and by June some sixty other men were suffering serious health problems.

Kettering and Midgley knew of TEL's toxicity. Midgley had already suffered a severe bout of lead poisoning in his own experimental work. Kettering insisted that safety precautions simply had to be observed. Sloan, we only know, was "gravely concerned about the poison hazard."[21] He and Kettering put together a committee composed of outside experts to investigate. The report revealed the grave risks of working with TEL. Du Pont chairman Irénée du Pont, whose people had the major commitment to the actual production of the fuel additive, dismissed the warnings. He told Sloan, "I have read the doctors' report and am not disturbed by the severity of the findings."[22] He reminded Sloan that Du Pont manufactured numerous dangerous products, including nitroglycerin, and that his people could be counted on to come up with a perfectly safe process for the manufacturing of TEL.

But the terrors of TEL production were far from over. Standard Oil of New Jersey had won from Kettering a contract to produce TEL, too. Seemingly, Standard had come up with a more efficient process of production, which was quite timely, as demand for the gas additive was far in excess of supply. Sloan sounded a warning about the Standard contract. He preferred that GM get completely out of the business of manufacturing TEL. Let Du Pont produce it; as Irénée du Pont had emphasized, Du Pont knew how to work with dangerous substances. As was his rule, Sloan did not insist, as the decision was operational in nature and thus under the purview of Kettering and the General Motors Chemical Company.[23]

On October 26, 1924, a worker at Standard's TEL plant in Elizabeth, New Jersey died after a short burst of tortured raving. Over the next month, four more men died after suffering the same symptoms of insane outbursts and violent behavior. Dozens of other plant workers suffered neurological damage caused by lead poisoning.

Standard Oil of New Jersey issued a statement noting that the company's production of TEL was "still more or less in a stage of development. This has occasioned unforeseen accidents." Standard Oil executives then informed reporters that they believed all workers at the plant understood the dangers of the operation: "[D]aily physical examinations, constant admonitions as to wearing rubber gloves and using gas masks and not wearing away from the plant clothing worn during work hours should have been sufficient indication to every man in the plant that he was engaged 'in a man's undertaking.' "[24] Standard's reminder that its employees were engaged in "a man's undertaking" was not just a bullyboy aside; it was phrase redolent with legal implications. In 1905, the Supreme Court had ruled in *Lochner v. New York* that working men—women under the law were treated differently—had "intelligence and capacity . . . to assert their rights and care for themselves without the protecting arm of the State."[25]

Standard of New Jersey, the largest industrial concern in the United States, was no rogue company. It had been a leader in employee relations since the violent Bayonne plant strike of 1915–16.[26] With the TEL disaster, Standard executives felt compelled, however, to revert to an earlier, less progressive policy governing industrial relations.

Standard Oil was counting on the industrialist-friendly trinity of legal principles concerning occupational safety in the early twentieth century: contributory negligence, assumption of risk, and the fellow-servant rule.[27] In other words, industrial workers knew they were doing dangerous work; it was their own responsibility to be careful; and they had a duty to be attentive to unsafe conditions created by other workers. If they got hurt it was their own problem, fault, and/or responsibility. In the nineteenth century, court decisions upholding these interpretations of the legal principles had allowed industrialists to escape almost all responsibility for harm suffered by their workers while on the job.

By 1924 industrial life in the United States, thanks to Progressive Era reforms and large corporations' belief that worker protection would reduce the likelihood of labor union agitation, was operating under somewhat different legal ground rules. New Jersey had a workers' compensation statute; the workers' compensation program was administered by an efficient industrial commission; and some state insurance money was awarded to those harmed workers and to the families of the dead. As far as Standard Oil of New Jersey saw it, that was the end of the unfortunate affair.[28] A grand jury agreed with Standard executives. They found the company (patent holder General Motors was not investigated) not responsible for the deaths or injuries. On a moral note, the grand jury did recommend that "before it resumes operations the company try to perfect some machinery by which ethyl gas can be manufactured without endangering life."[29]

New Jersey government officials, amid the general panic caused by the deaths, took a harder line, banning Standard Oil of New Jersey from further production. The proximity of the plant to New York City—it was directly across the Hudson River—ensured that the entire matter received abundant press (unlike the deaths in Dayton and Deepwater). Amid the bad press—"loony gas" was one of the labels attached to ethyl—Kettering and his counterparts at Du Pont and Standard put ethyl out of production and came up with a plan to reengineer the public's feelings about leaded gasoline.

Kettering and leading men from Du Pont and Standard met on the quiet, Christmas Eve 1924, with U.S. Surgeon General Hugh Cummings in Washington, D.C. They asked him to lead a Public Health Service investigation into the safety of ethyl gasoline. In May 1925, at a very public meeting convened by the surgeon general, the ethyl interests announced that they would keep the product off the market until a new expert opinion ordered by the surgeon general regarding the safety of leaded gasoline was delivered.

Sloan's inner feelings and actions regarding the safety and suitability of the manufacturing of TEL are unknown. That he worried about TEL seems certain. That he kept those concerns within the corporation is equally certain. Sloan appeared to take the reported dangers and the men who died working on a General Motors product far more seriously than the other leading executives, but how seriously and exactly what he said remains, again, unknown. No word on the horrors is recorded in any of Sloan's published writings. As far as the record shows, the dead and damaged men, working far from GM's core business, haunted him not at all. Industrial accidents happened, and in the early years of the twentieth century, with little state regulation and none at all from the federal government, they still happened with regularity. As the TEL tragedy unfolded in New Jersey, a single cave-in killed fifty-three miners in North Carolina.[30]

Sloan did decide that despite Kettering's energetic public and political response to the difficulties, he was not the man to manage General Motors' stake in the ethyl business. Quietly, he relieved Kettering of his management responsibilities. Kettering does not seem to have minded the change in status. Kettering did remain completely committed to his lab's product and began a campaign of public speeches in praise of TEL as a marvelous marker of technical progress. Such progress, he allowed, did on occasion bear some costs. Kettering proved to be a remarkably effective speaker. His down-home manner and avoidance of technical language coupled with his lucid presentation of complicated scientific issues did wonders with the general public. His point of view was completely shared in by all leading members of the federal government, most especially both President Calvin Coolidge—it was he who said that "the business of America is business"— and Secretary of the Treasury Andrew Mellon, administrative overseer of the Public Health Service. That Mellon's family controlled Gulf Oil, which had just signed a lucrative contract to distribute ethyl gasoline, was not a fact known to the public at the time.[31]

On January 19, 1926, the surgeon general's appointed committee, whose membership was quite sympathetic to the needs of industrial progress, reported the happy news that gasoline treated with TEL created no safety problems. (That they were wrong was a fact suspected but unproven by a diverse group of engineers and scientists that included the president of the Society of Automotive Engineers and key members of the American Chemical Society. By the 1960s, as the problem of air pollution became more widely understood, the fumes produced by leaded gasoline were shown by scientists to be a major health problem. The federal government ordered the phasing out of leaded gasoline beginning in 1974. GM management was completely in agreement. Its patent on TEL had expired in 1947 and the Ethyl Corporation division had been sold off in 1962). The committee left unexamined the difficulties of producing TEL, which had caused so many men to die and suffer. Standard and General Motors had by this time already agreed to join together to market the leaded gasoline through the jointly owned Ethyl Gasoline Corporation. Du Pont, which did know how to manufacture dangerous chemicals safely, became the producers of TEL.[32] With the surgeon general's clean bill of health, the Ethyl Corporation began an advertising onslaught that ignored the safety issue while highlighting ethyl's contributions to engine power.

Sloan had little to do with the marketing of ethyl. General Motors owned the patent and needed to do little but collect its rent, which would amount to some $43.3 million between 1924 and 1947. Its share of the profits on sales made by the Ethyl Corporation amounted to another $82.6 million.[33] It was a highly profitable piece of the General Motors empire by the mid-1920s and helped bring home the capital necessary to take on Ford and improve both General Motors' share price and stock dividends. Ethyl made Sloan look good even as it concerned him almost not at all.

In both the flap over the copper-cooled engine and the messy business of getting ethyl into the marketplace, Sloan kept himself out of the public eye. Unlike Henry Ford, Sloan did not thrust himself forward at every chance. He thrust himself forward, in fact, not at all. He was always willing to have public credit go to others—and blame, as well. His only business, as he understood it, was to manage the corporation. Still, Sloan knew he could not avoid the limelight. He understood that his corporate position demanded a certain kind of public visibility. As president of the corporation, he saw that he could and that he must contribute to the public image of General Motors.

In the 1920s, shaping the public images of leading businessmen, as well as politicians, movie stars, sports heroes, and myriad other celebrities, was becoming a regular aspect of a new, more nationally integrated American culture. Such celebrity mongering was a part of the emergent consumer culture in which mass circulation magazines, newspapers, billboards, movies, and the radio trumpeted the latest, newest and most exciting products and personalities. National products like the Model T and the Chevrolet were sold coast-to-coast and national celebrities were touted around the country. Hollywood was coming into its own in the 1920s, selling stars like Rudolph Valentino, Mary Pickford, and Douglas Fairbanks. Sports heroes such as Red Grange and Babe Ruth, aided by the advent of the radio and national broadcasting systems, were being mass produced as never before. In an alchemical stew of mass media, mass production, national marketing, and unprecedented economic prosperity, the "ballyhoo" years had arrived (seemingly, never to depart).[34]

Sloan appreciated the changing world of publicity, even as he struggled to understand its meaning for General Motors and the business corporation. The public—at least its designated representatives in the business-oriented sector of the mass media—wanted to know more about him. He understood that duty and opportunity directed him to answer their call. So Sloan began to become a national public figure.

Before May 10, 1923 the public presence of Alfred Sloan had been almost entirely nonexistent. He had appeared not at all in the general press and, despite his considerable wealth, had not even been listed in the national compendium of success, *Who's Who in America.* When he first became GM president, newspaper editors from around the country besieged General Motors with requests for information on a man about whom they said they knew nothing.[35] That the press was so intrigued by the new leader of General Motors indicates, too, how seriously some, at least, saw the role of General Motors in the nation. In the Age of Normalcy, as President Harding had called it, Big Business was Big News.

Sloan personally did not enjoy the process of publicity. He had, however, recognized the need to advertise GM's consumer products, as well as GM itself. And he knew full well that consumers did not want gray facts and figures when they were making their product choices. They seemed to far prefer ads that sold goods through drama and personality. The consuming public was not driven by reason alone, as far as Sloan could tell. How then to fit himself, apostle of corporate reason and fact-based decision making, into this irrational realm?

Sloan never fully accommodated himself to a contrived public role. He was hard pressed, at times, to cooperate with the effort. As his appointment secretary once told a *Wall Street Journal* reporter seeking to do a profile, "[H]e has been too busy to even get a haircut, and besides, he hates publicity. But I will ask him."[36] Still, while he found the process annoying,

Sloan clearly understood he could not shirk his duty to the corporation and throughout the 1920s worked at creating an appropriate public role for himself. He chose to be, only even more so, what he genuinely was: a professional corporate manager. Sloan was the first American of his stature to present himself to the American people in this role.

Sloan crafted his persona in such a way as to distance both himself and GM from the public images of two figures familiar to many. The first was that of GM founder Billy Durant who, while long gone from GM, was still a major public figure in the United States. Durant was once again a leading auto manufacturer, energetically promoting Durant Motors to middle-income Americans. He was also well publicized as one of the most vocal "bulls" of the booming 1920s stock market. Durant was a booster, a cheery if not completely trustworthy type well known to Americans. In the nineteenth century, men like him had sold newly platted lands to families eager to settle the frontier and railroad stock to those looking for a shortcut to wealth. In the patter of the booster, every deal and every opportunity, as one 1890s pitchman assured, "was pregnant with certainty."[37] Sloan meant to sever, with a vengeance, any lingering connections between Durant boosterism and General Motor's public image. Americans, especially shareholders and prospective shareholders, would know that GM was no stock market gamble but a rock solid corporation run on the most unerringly modern management principles possible.

The second image Sloan meant to distinguish himself from was that of Henry Ford. Ford's public image was more important than Durant's legacy by the time of Sloan's ascent to the corporate presidency. It was even more pressing an issue by the mid-1920s as GM began to challenge the Ford Motor Company for the auto industry leadership. Henry Ford was one of the most famous men in the world. The simplicity of his Model T was neatly reversed by the extravagance of his own public role.

Ford had come a long way since Sloan had first met him at the dawning of the auto age. A man of many opinions, he was a public character beloved by millions of Americans across the nation as much for his folksy wisdom as for the Model T. Ford volubly offered his advice to the American people on everything from their diet—he championed the carrot and the soybean—to the values that made the nation great, quoting on regular occasion from his favorite writer, Ralph Waldo Emerson, and emphasizing the role of hard work, discipline, and individual genius.

Ford was no Jeffersonian democrat. He held little faith in the average man, about whom he mused that "above all he wants a job in which he does not have to think."[38] Despite his public skepticism about most Americans' abilities ("the unevenness in human mental equipment"), many nevertheless took his public declarations as a defense of the common man—at least the common man's right to decent wages—and praise for what a later generation would call "traditional values."[39]

Not content merely to offer his views on matters domestic, Ford also took an interest in world affairs. He had gained his first non-auto-related fame in 1915 for his game if painfully naive effort to stop World War I by sending a "Peace Ship" over to Europe to sort out the international difficulties. Like his "Peace Ship," Ford's fame crossed the oceans. In the new Soviet Union he was lionized for bringing mass production techniques to industry and both the political left and right in Weimar Germany proclaimed the genius of *Fordismus.*[40]

Ford expended great energies promoting his vision of a better America. Beginning in May of 1920, Ford decided to educate Americans about the forces conspiring against a productive, hard-working, and just society by publishing the *Dearborn Independent,* which he distributed nationally through Ford auto dealerships. The attractively designed magazine featured stories on the treachery of the "International Jew." Borrowing heavily from standard European anti-Semitic diatribes, Ford's magazine explained that "the Jew" sought to tear down America through a cunning amalgam of money lending, jazz music, short skirts, rolled stockings, and Bolshevism. Ford had the collected anti-Semitic canards of the *Independent* published in a popular volume entitled *The International Jew.* Both the magazine and the book were welcomed throughout rural and small-town America (and most of Europe, as well, where Adolph Hitler read them and became an enthusiastic Ford booster).

"Jew hating" was popular and respectable in the 1920s. Anti-Semitism provided many Americans with a ready explanation for both economic transformations (e.g., chain retail stores, Wall Street, and Big Business) and cultural changes (e.g., jazz music, "flappers," and "petting parties") that disturbed them. The Ku Klux Klan, among the most successful of national fraternal organizations in the mid-1920s with a membership in excess of 2 million men, a majority of them residing outside the south, fed the American people a regular diet of anti-Semitism, calling Jews "vermin," "scum," and "a national danger."[41] Ford's championing of anti-Semitism brought him much appreciation from a segment of the American people. In 1923, Henry Ford, banking on his widespread public support, expressed interest in the presidency. He backed away from a campaign only after the flinty champion of small-town virtues (but not anti-Semitic) Vice President Calvin Coolidge took over the presidency following the untimely demise of the card-playing, whiskey-drinking, womanizing President Harding.[42]

Sloan could not and would not compete as that kind of industrial celebrity. Carrot diets and anti-Semitism did not interest him (as far as the record shows, Sloan never made anti-Semitic remarks either publicly or privately). Sloan would not be a booster or a Babbitt. Instead, he would portray himself as a man of singular talent and singular dedication. Sloan offered the public the image of a new kind of American hero: the corporate genius.

In his first major public profile, which appeared in the leading business magazine *Forbes,* Sloan demonstrated his iron discipline by carefully staying on point throughout the interview. He combined two themes: the GM family and the science of corporate management. After a paragraph noting the immense size of "the General Motors family" (135,000 employees), and several more on Sloan's approach to management ("I never give orders. . . . It is better to appeal to the intelligence of a man than to the military authority invested in you."), Sloan outlined the advantageous nature of the new business corporation if it was properly managed:

> General Motors is a group organization. . . . All of us have some weaknesses, but most human beings do not like to admit to themselves that they have human weaknesses and limitations. Therefore it is often extremely difficult to get a man in the frame of mind where he will gladly seek to gather from other people in the organization what would offset, what would remedy his own weakness. Yet, this must be done in a large organization to bring about a maximum of efficiency and effectiveness.[43]

In this interview, Sloan offered readers a new sort of American exemplar. He was no nineteenth-century frontier hero of "colossal proportions and Herculean strength."[44] He never tried to pass himself off as another Andrew Carnegie, rising from a humble background to industrial statesman. And he was certainly no Jazz Age personality of the sort written about by F. Scott Fitzgerald. Sloan sought out no celebrity, eschewed the brighter hues, and offered little at all in the way of personality. As the *Forbes* writer explained: "He has not a hard, domineering mien. He radiates earnestness, but not severity. He talks in a moderate tone and is totally without swashbucklerism."[45] Deliberately, Sloan distanced himself from the pioneering auto men, "the hard-muscled and strong willed."[46] He was a new men representing a new kind of corporate organization.

The Harvard economist Joseph Schumpeter in his 1942 modern classic *Capitalism, Socialism, and Democracy* described Sloan's new corporate man and the economic order he inhabited. Characterizing what he called "the civilization of capitalism," he argued that it was both "rationalistic and 'anti-heroic' ":

> The two go together of course. Success in industry and commerce requires a lot of stamina, yet industrial and commercial activity is essentially unheroic in the knight's sense—no flourishing of swords about it, not much physical prowess, no chance to gallop the armored horse into the enemy, preferably a heretic or heathen—and the ideology that glorifies the idea of fighting for fighting's sake and of victory for victory's sake understandably withers in the office among all the columns of figures.[47]

While Schumpeter was no cheerleader for the "civilization of capitalism," Sloan would have found this aspect of his analysis quite acceptable.

In the 1980s, the Big Men of the American economic reorganization, the bond traders and the mergers and acquisitions heavyweights, would fight the image Sloan bequeathed the business and financial elite of the corporate age. Many of them had grown up in the 1950s and 1960s when the Sloanesque figure of the dutiful, unemotional corporate professional—the white collar man—had come under withering national scrutiny. The second post-Sloan generation would insist that they *were* warriors, eager for battle and macho combat. Sloan would have found such representations absurd posturing that hid, for reasons best not discussed, the real work of gathering the facts and working through solutions to profitable ends.

Still, even in his own time, the business-happy 1920s, Sloan's carefully crafted and disciplined self-representation was not without its public detractors. One can only wonder if any of Sloan's novel-reading friends ever showed him *Dodsworth* (1929), by Sinclair Lewis, the best-selling author and scourge of the small-minded businessman. *Dodsworth* tells the story of an honorable auto manufacturer whose business was bought out by a company, the "Unit Automobile Company," that looked very much like General Motors: "the imperial U.A.C., with its seven makes of motors, its body-building works, its billions of dollars of capital." The president of the GM-like company, Mr. Alex Kynance, was pictured as a hyped-up booster whose vulgarity was only matched by his buffoonlike pattern of speech: "I haven't been hinting around. Hinting ain't my way. When Alec Kynance has something to say, by God he shouts!"[48] Sloan's total disinterest in literature probably saved him from encountering this distorted fictional representation of himself.

Sloan painted a simple portrait of himself to reporters. He was a facilitator of correct judgments, reached through consensus, achieved after exhaustive consultation with all relevant members of his corporate enterprise. He took pains to counter any possible apprehension on the part of the public that General Motors was a too-powerful, too-big, autocratic industrial giant that churned out cars at the cost of crushing human creativity or individuality. Always, he emphasized the numerous men who each contributed in a valued way to collective decision making. He warned a *Wall Street Journal* reporter against attempting to portray General Motors as Sloan's creation:

> Remember, General Motors is not a one man organization. We have many operations, each headed by the best man we can find for the job, and he is charged with the full responsibility for the success of his organization. We are all partners in the management of General Motors working together with executives who do not rule as much as they cooperate.[49]

Sloan would have expected businessmen and stock investors who read such passages to understand his implicit criticism of Henry Ford's tyrannical and egocentric management of the Ford Motor Company. (And by 1928 that image of Ford was gaining a toehold; on January 8, 1928, the cosmopolitan *New York Times* characterized Mr. Ford as "an industrial fascist—the Mussolini of Detroit.")[50]

In a perhaps deliberately ironic, even paradoxical twist, Sloan suggested in his interviews that he, the most powerful man at General Motors, was useful because he had the ability to listen to others, to collate their insights and to parcel them together for appraisal and validation by the organization itself. He was newsworthy, he insisted, only insofar as reporters understood that he embodied the form of corporate management that successfully allowed General Motors to bring automobiles and other worthy products to the consumer (a word Sloan was among the earliest in the business community to use regularly).

Sloan made it appear as if he had little to no life outside the corporation—or much use for such a life. Never in his magazine and newspaper interviews and profiles did he present himself as an individual with his own agenda: personal wealth, political power, or self-aggrandizement. Sloan managed. He was a manager among mangers. He existed to assist in the effective running of General Motors, and GM existed to manufacture and to distribute automobiles, refrigerators, and other industrial goods that pleased the American people. Success in this mission allowed the corporation to employ, directly and indirectly, hundreds of thousands of American citizens and to pay them good wages, thus ensuring the economic prosperity of the nation.

Sloan always avoided discussions of profit and remuneration, preferring instead to discuss sales and industrial capacity. His only concession to the pecuniary was to note that "liberal profit-sharing with those who carry out the actual management of the business [ensures] we are in a position to hold and, whenever necessary, to reach out for the brainiest men in the whole industry."[51] Sloan never spoke of his own compensation nor did the press ever mention it.

At the end of 1927, in what turned out to be nearly the last article of its kind (an unabashed puff piece), the widely circulated *New York Journal* ran a feature story under the title "Cylinder Battlers Square Off! FORD VS. SLOAN." The article was a pared-down version of an extended profile that had run in the mass-circulation magazine *Hearst's International Cosmopolitan.* Above the story were cameo photos of Sloan and Ford. Ford offers a twinkling smile. Sloan stares blankly at the camera. Under each photo was a stark description of each man culled from several years of their public-image making. Ford's profile reads, in part: "Plays much. Eats carefully. Has many hobbies. Likes books. Plays with many friends. . . . Has 'good line.' No 'education.' A business despot." Sloan's reads: "Works every hour. Eats anything. Has no hobbies. Never reads. Too busy for friends. Never drinks. Doesn't smoke. Never tells stories. College Man. Never gives an order." In the body of the article Sloan is further described: "Sloan works twelve hours and then works some more. His recreation is work. His whole life and heart are bound up with work and the supremacy of General Motors."[52]

Sloan's public image as depicted in the *New York Journal* had a fundamental truth about it. He did work very hard and had few interests outside GM. The portrait, however, one that Sloan himself helped create, is much exaggerated. In this piece and others he offered an image of what today we might think of as a kind of corporate cyborg: a man whose heart beat inside the corporate body of GM.

In real life, Sloan had friends; he and his wife were close with Walter and Della Chrysler. In the 1920s, the Sloans enjoyed New York City nightlife with them, GM treasurer John Raskob and his wife, as well as others. Sloan was a regular at dinner parties among the New York City financial and business elite. And throughout the 1920s, he and Irene vacationed lavishly for several weeks a year; going to Europe in the summer (where, it is true, he spent much time visiting GM investments and rival auto manufacturers) and to Florida in the winter (though perhaps only Sloan would privately defend his vacationing to Charles Kettering thus: "We can discharge our responsibilities better by getting a change of thought and scene, especially when the responsibilities are as great as ours"). By 1925, Sloan was well ensconced in his richly decorated Fifth Avenue apartment. Around the time he was appointed president of GM he purchased a summer and weekend getaway—Snug Harbor, a large, tasteful estate on Long Island, not far from the Chryslers' opulent mansion.[53]

Sloan quite deliberately hid his private life and the less work-obsessed aspects of his personality from the public. Not surprisingly, he also did his best to keep private his great and growing wealth. He told one inquiring reporter, not with complete honesty, "Making money ceased to interest me years ago. It's the job that counts."[54] Sloan presented himself to the public as a corporate servant; a selfless contributor to the go-go, economic good times of the 1920s. What was a cooperative press in those days helped ensure that this image prevailed.

Sloan's ascetic, self-sacrificing image dovetailed with the nearly sacred aura President Calvin Coolidge commonly attached to America's industrial leaders. Among the president's pronouncements: "The man who builds a factory builds a temple. The man who works there worships there."[55] The public legitimacy of Big Business in the 1920s, both Coolidge and Sloan seemed to indicate, was built on its clear success in providing spiritually satisfying economic sustenance and consumer riches to an appreciative people. For tens of millions, a new era of mass production and potential mass consumption had dawned, and it was good. One Emile Coué, a Frenchman with a mission, taught Americans to start every day by repeating: "Day by day, in every way, I am getting better and better."[56]

Economic life, for many Americans at any rate, was getting better and better. From 1922 through 1928, per capita disposable income in the United States rose an immodest 50 percent. Industrial productivity in the twenties nearly doubled. The average wage of working Americans—with auto workers doing considerably better than the mean—was the highest in the world and, as best as these things can be measured, the highest that had been recorded in human history.[57] Average life expectancy in the 1920s, as compared to the previous decade, jumped an astounding seven years (from 51.8 years to 58.7 years).[58] President Calvin Coolidge opened his first elected term by announcing that the United States had achieved "a state of contentment seldom before seen."[59]

President Coolidge will always be remembered for his proclamation, made during the third longest sustained period of economic growth in the twentieth century, that "the chief business of the American people is business."[60] More interesting than this oft-quoted remark is how Coolidge justified his sense of Americans' extraordinary business-mindedness. It is worth quoting at length for it offers a noble gloss on a vital aspect of Alfred Sloan's America (and our own):

> They are profoundly concerned with producing, buying, selling, investing, and prospering in the world. I am strongly of the opinion that the great majority of people will always find these are moving impulses of our life. . . . Wealth is the product of industry, ambition, character and untiring effort. In all experience, the accumulation of wealth means the multiplication of schools, the increase of knowledge, the dissemination of intelligence, the encouragement of science, the broadening of outlook, the expansion of liberties, the widening of culture. Of course, the accumulation of wealth cannot be justified as the chief end of existence. But we are compelled to recognize it as a means to well-nigh every desirable achievement. So long as wealth is made the means and not the end, we need not greatly fear it.[61]

The industrialist in the mid-1920s carried with him the imprimatur of government and press. His needs were carefully protected by the Republican administrations in power throughout the decade. His individual fortune was safeguarded by Treasury Secretary Andrew Mellon, himself one of the nation's richest men, who worked assiduously and with unmitigated success to reduce the federal income tax burden on the wealthiest citizens. Prosperity—and, moreover, the belief that even more prosperity was on its way—gave the business community widespread, enthusiastic support. In this cheery atmosphere, Alfred P. Sloan saw great opportunity for General Motors.

Sloan himself had no use for movie stars, professional sports teams, or jazz music. He did see in the public's love of these things a kind of desire General Motors could tap. But finding some way to tap into the public's enthusiasm, Sloan understood, was necessitated in large part by the new shape of the auto market. First-time car buyers were becoming far less plentiful. A great many people with money already had an auto. And by the mid-1920s, an abundance of used automobiles was flooding the marketplace and complicating the sales of new cars to first-time buyers, as well as to the more frugally minded car shoppers. Sloan believed he must accelerate his strategic reshaping of the auto market. The plan he had first formulated in 1921—to take market share from Ford by offering a well-ordered, attractive line of autos, differentiated by price and thus appealing to different class elements within consumer society—was about to be more fully and imaginatively implemented.

Chevrolet figured prominently in those plans. Sloan needed Chevrolet to sell hundreds of thousands of cars to lower-income Americans who would otherwise buy a Model T. By 1925 the Chevrolet division was coming along nicely under the expert guidance of William S. Knudsen, who performed as well as any car man before or since. Knudsen had come to the United States from Denmark in February 1900 when he was twenty years old. He was one of about 15 million immigrants who ventured to the United States between 1896 and 1915. Like most of the others, Knudsen came because American industry needed workers and, to get them, employers offered the highest wage scale in the world. Like most immigrants, he arrived uncertain of how long he would stay (during the early years of the twentieth century about one person returned home for every three new arrivals).

Knudsen came to the United States with only a little English and no connections. He stood six feet three inches tall and, once he filled out, weighed well over two hundred pounds. He could work harder and longer—and given any kind of chance, smarter—than anyone around him. Knudsen hauled garbage, worked at the shipyards in the Bronx, got a job repairing railroad locomotive boilers, and then went to work at a bicycle factory. He liked America. The American was different, he wrote his mother: "Whatever the object is, he is trying to stand out from the crowd and represent something."[62] Knudsen could imagine himself as an American. He saw opportunity in America. He never left.

Knudsen could make anything out of metal. Better, he could organize other workers to produce. His talents were recognized. The man who ran the bicycle company he worked for in 1904—like C. S. Mott—faced a downturn in bicycle sales; he started making parts for automobiles. Knudsen figured out how to make the parts and how to produce them as cheaply as possible. Henry Ford, for whom most of the parts were made, took an interest in Knudsen and by 1913 Knudsen was laying out new assembly plants for Ford. In 1918 he was Ford's production manager. In 1921, he was making better than fifty thousand dollars a year (more than four hundred thousand in 2000 dollars). He was also through with Henry Ford. The money was not worth the aggravation (not unlike how Walter Chrysler, another bootstrapper or "Alger-boy," felt about working for Billy Durant). Ford, himself, explained the problem: "Mr. Knudsen was too strong for me to handle. You see this is my business. I built it and, as long as I live, I propose to run it. Mr. Knudsen wanted to run it his way."[63] Knudsen could not accept Ford's interventions into his operations.

Alfred Sloan's decentralized operations fit Knudsen's need to exercise control perfectly. Once the copper-cooled engine difficulties had been resolved, Sloan did his best to get himself out of Knudsen's way. Sloan understood that Knudsen could produce and he meant to give him every opportunity to make Chevrolet perform. If General Motors was to become what Sloan believed possible, the industrial leader, Chevrolet would have to succeed.

Just as Sloan recognized Knudsen's talent, from the beginning of their relationship Knudsen understood Sloan's evolving marketing plan. Knudsen had mastered auto production at Ford but he did not intend to build Chevrolets like Henry Ford built his Model T. First, he began to manufacture an inexpensive car that did not look cheap: "[We] modernized its appearance so as to remove the inevitable stigma which rests on low priced articles that show it." Second, Knudsen built flexibility into his assembly process. He rejected Ford's reliance on "single-purpose" machine tools. Instead, he installed "new heavy type standard machines" that permitted "flexible mass production." Knudsen was creating a manufacturing process to regularize consumer-appealing changes—by the mid-1930s annual model changes—in the Chevrolet's appearance and its mechanical components.[64] Knudsen's manufacturing breakthroughs were critical to the success of Sloan's still germinating idea that consumers did not just want a car that worked and that they could afford, they wanted an automobile that pleased them because of how it worked and how it looked and how it made them feel.

Knudsen was a car genius. Part of his genius was that he understood his own limits. In his blunt fashion, he told Sloan that he needed help: he did not know how to create a sales organization within Chevrolet that could align what he and his men manufactured with what consumers wanted and with what Chevrolet dealers around the country sold. Knudsen understood that cars did not sell themselves.

Sloan was pleased when Knudsen asked him for assistance. It meant that he grasped what Sloan was trying to accomplish with his organizational strategy: the GM president and the executive committee would not tell Knudsen how to run his division, but they could help him run it better. Sloan went to work, conferring and studying the matter, spending the necessary hours to determine which executive among the hundreds of possibilities working within the many divisions of the corporation would serve the needs of the situation at Chevrolet. He believed that this work, finding the appropriate person for high-level positions within the corporation, was among the most important tasks he personally performed. As Sloan described it to the business writer Peter Drucker:

> There are only people who make people decisions right, and that means slowly, and people who make people decisions wrong and then repent at leisure. We do make fewer mistakes, not because we're good judges of people but because we're conscientious. . . . The decision . . . about people is the only truly crucial one. You think and everybody thinks that a company can have "better" people; that's horse apples. All it can do is place people right—and then it'll have performance.[65]

Sloan found Knudsen exactly the right man, Dick Grant. That Grant had never sold an auto before coming to Chevrolet was irrelevant to Sloan. Grant was a proven sales manager. He had done an extraordinary job running sales for DELCO, and when Sloan had placed Frigidaire—GM's foray into the fledgling refrigerator business—under DELCO's organizational control, Grant had figured out how to sell tens of thousands of the new product. The Harvard-educated Grant, almost a foot shorter than Knudsen, would work as hard as Knudsen at making Chevrolet a success.[66] Grant began to systematically gather information on consumer preferences and sales estimates based on economic data. He worked closely with Chevrolet dealers, listening to their concerns and ideas while melding them into an enthusiastic sales force. Further, Grant led the production worker and the salesman to recognize that their efforts were both critically joined in creating a strong team.

Finding the correct man (like Grant) to manage a particular task and then stepping back and letting him perform, when done correctly, was an act of precision. Sloan allowed himself to take a measure of pride in this aspect of his work.[67]

In 1925, Knudsen's efforts paid off. A newly designed Chevrolet, the K model, was a resounding success. Knudsen had corrected most of the Chevrolet's technical problems, applied the newly developed, appearance-enhancing Duco paint to its body, and chose to make it a closed car (a majority of Model T's were sold as "open" cars). The Chevrolet, in the parlance of a later generation of Americans, was "new and improved."

The previous year, his first as president (though he had been running operations at Chevrolet since early 1922), Knudsen was asked by Dick Grant to tell an assembly of some two thousand Chevrolet dealers at the Palmer House in Chicago his goal for the Chevrolet division. In a speech of startling brevity, punctuated by his pronounced Danish accent,

Knudsen raised his huge hands in the air, put up the index finger of each and shouted: "I want vun for vun!"[68] After a few moments of uncertainty, the dealers understood: Knudsen meant for Chevrolet to sell one car for every Model T Ford sold. It would take Knudsen, all told, some six years to make good on what had once seemed the unthinkable goal of catching Ford. The sales of the 1925 Chevrolet demonstrated that it could happen.

Sloan saw the improvements at Chevrolet as but one aspect of his strategy. He worked across the divisions, cajoling, counseling, suggesting, meeting, presenting possibilities, and listening to his men as they looked for ways that would allow them to capture more sales of more vehicles. Sloan saw a gap in his price spread and worked with Chevrolet engineers and Oakland's factories and then sales network to produce and market a new car, the Pontiac. Sloan's management through cooperative effort worked. Introduced on time for the 1926 model year, the Pontiac priced out perfectly at $825, almost midpoint between the Chevrolet and the Oldsmobile coach models.[69]

As Knudsen's efforts on behalf of the Chevrolet division demonstrate, by the mid-1920s Sloan had come to believe that selling across the price spectrum was not enough. From his earliest days in the automobile business, Sloan had perceived that carmakers saw their products in too narrow a light. In their hearts, they were tinkerers: men who worked at lathes and handled tools, burning the midnight oil to make their machines run better. That was all good and well, but Sloan, who never saw himself as the tinkering sort, had long believed that the auto needed to be more than a set of engineering problems. Even in the early years when he ran Hyatt Bearings and visited auto manufacturers seeking their business, he had, in his own words, "visualized an organized effort [by the auto manufacturer] to promote the maximum in eye appeal." The auto, Sloan believed even then, should have "a styling approach separate from the usual engineering approach."[70]

Henry Ford in those early days would have certainly found Sloan's visualization more than a little suspect, probably an indicator of insufficient manliness. Ford famously mocked all auto ornamentation as girlish "knickknacks."[71] And, in accord with Ford's predilections, contemporaries, not without humor, praised the tough, so-called masculinity of the Model T. The *Los Angeles Times* reported in 1920: "In a Denver divorce case . . . the suffering wife testified that her brutal husband forced her to ride in a Ford car. In the face of this fiendish disclosure the sympathetic judge promptly granted a decree."[72]

Alfred Sloan was not concerned that his corporation's products might somehow reflect poorly on his own manliness. His mind simply did not turn in those directions. While other men felt the need to hit some kind of ball or to shoot things or to tell ribald locker-room stories, Sloan took his personal satisfaction in managing his corporate responsibilities. Manliness was not a factor. Nor was Sloan interested in realizing some idealized image of the auto. He wanted to manufacture products that would sell in great quantities at the highest possible profit. But in an age of ballyhoo, Sloan also believed the time had definitively come to sell people cars that did not simply run but that captured their imaginations as well.[73] Demonstrating again his unusual ability to find the perfect man to perform a difficult task, Sloan turned in an unexpected direction: westward. A product of Hollywood, Harley Earl, would become central to Sloan's plan to increase General Motors' sales through "eye appeal."

Harley Earl was not first discovered by Sloan; Lawrence P. Fisher found him. Fisher had been asked by Sloan in 1925 to take over the struggling Cadillac division. He was at that time only thirty-six years old but had been a major figure in the auto business for nearly half of those years. His background was in auto bodies. Lawrence Fisher and his brothers had been building bodies for autos since 1908. Billy Durant, in one of his best investments, had brought the Fisher Body Corporation—and the Fisher brothers—into General Motors in 1918 (Durant had bought 60 percent of the company; in 1926, Sloan engineered the purchase of the rest of the company and formally made it a GM division). Lawrence Fisher was known as one of the more forward-thinking and dynamic men in the corporation (and also was a well-known bon vivant, which explains in part the trip to Hollywood). He had Sloan's complete trust.

In early 1926, Fisher was out in Los Angeles doing the rounds of Cadillac dealers. One of those dealers, Don Lee, ran a side operation in custom cars, aimed at the Hollywood set. Lee's custom operation, which featured a Cadillac chassis, was Fisher's main purpose in making the trip. The director of the custom car operation was thirty-three-year-old Harley Earl, whose father had started a coach building business and then, in the 1910s, had helped to create the custom car body business in southern California. Fisher loved what Earl was doing: turning boxy, square production cars into long, sleek, low-riding roadsters. He played out his custom designs in modeling clay, working every part of the car's body, including the hood, fenders, and running boards, into a newly imagined whole. Hollywood moguls and high-priced screen stars like Mary Pickford, Fatty Arbuckle, Tom Mix, and Cecil B. DeMille drove Earl's custom autos.

Fisher brought Earl to Detroit in the early spring of 1926 to design a fresh look for the La Salle, a new, lower-priced luxury car Cadillac wanted to bring out in 1927. Earl worked fast. When he finished, he had a car that was rounder, lower to the ground, and more aesthetically coherent than any other mass production car on the market. For Sloan and the other decision makers, Earl had produced four different designs. Each one of them was a full-size model finished off with a superb japan (a varnish that produces a brilliant, hard coating) and then a light coat of Duco. The models were polished acts of showmanship. And at nearly six and a half feet, dressed as impeccably but with a good deal more flair than Sloan (or any of the other executives), Earl was, himself, a master showman.

Sloan saw a high potential for increased sales in Earl's work. His basis for this judgment was strategic: eye appeal would transform the car market. Consumers would purchase cars not just for utilitarian transportation but for personal pleasure and self-expression. General Motors had the production capacity and organizational know-how to take best advantage of car styling. While Sloan based his judgment on his analysis of the maturing consumer marketplace, he admitted to a rare personal insight. Harley Earl argued aesthetically that "oblongs are more attractive than squares." Sloan felt that way, too. Back in the last days of the Durant years, Sloan had bought his first Cadillac (remember, he was about to buy a Rolls-Royce in England when he hurried home to participate in the GM shake-out). He respected the car's performance but he found its ungainly height and its resulting squarish appearance singularly unappealing. To change the Cadillac's silhouette, he brought it closer to the ground by installing custom, small wire wheels (correct: Sloan is an unsung godfather to the East LA low rider). As his impeccable dress indicated, Sloan, gray-man image aside, had an eye for style. And he believed in Earl.[74]

Earl's stylish La Salle was produced. A few months later, on June 23, 1927, Sloan asked the executive committee to consider establishing a special department "to study the question of art and color combinations in General Motors products." Supported by Fisher, the committee agreed to establish it. Sloan personally invited Earl, who had returned to Los Angeles, to direct the department.

Earl agreed. He was told to set up shop in Detroit in the General Motors Building Annex. As a sign of changes to come he placed mauve curtains in his office. The executive committee provided the department with fifty people. None of them were engineers and Earl would make a point in the years ahead of doing his best to ignore all engineering influences in his creative work. Earl, the very large (and heterosexual) man with mauve drapes and unorthodox suits, also broke the mold in another way: he brought some of the first well-paid professional women into General Motors as designers. Their contributions were premised on the notion that they would "express the woman's point of view."[75]

Sloan understood the probable difficulties of getting his production men and the divisions' engineering staffs to accept the design ideas generated by Earl's shop (soon enough nicknamed by GM men with the tauntingly feminine sobriquet "the "beauty shop"). So Sloan intervened. As Earl remembers it, Sloan told him: "Harley, I think you had better work just for me for awhile till I see how they take you."[76] Sloan then began one of his many management-by-memo strategies. He wrote the more conservative William Fisher, president of the Fisher Body Corporation: "To sum up, I think that the future of General Motors will be measured by the attractiveness that we put in the bodies from the standpoint of luxury of appointment, the degree to which they please the eye, both in contour and in color scheme, also the degree to which we are able to make them different from competition."[77] Fisher had to be brought around since it was his operation that would have to turn much of what was envisioned by the art and color department into car bodies capable of being mass produced.

Sloan also worked to convince the sales sections to welcome more visually stimulating vehicles and not to fear any sort of dicta coming from a corporate-imposed, fashion czar (the imposing Earl). In December 1927, he wrote the head of the corporate sales section (who was, in turn, to assuage the fears of the divisional sales managers):

> The exact working out of the new set up is not yet completed, but if I have my way and I shall influence a program so far as I can that provides an organization having artistic ability and while it may be dominated from the operating standpoint by one individual, it will have in its organization a sufficient number of individuals to develop a diversity of ideas.[78]

In the increasingly prolix, elliptical, and even confusing writing style Sloan was unfortunately developing, perhaps as a deliberate way of tempering his growing power and authority, Sloan was again trying to demonstrate his respect for operational autonomy—within acceptable limits. During these critical years, he was seeking a balance between his perceived need for centralized processes of innovation (like Kettering's shop) with his belief in the operational divisions' needs for stability, independence, and their own innovations. Keeping all parties in a cooperative spirit and yet open to change was among his primary goals. Managing that process was as satisfying as anything he did.

Sloan made sure that the changes he oversaw in the style and performance of the car divisions' models reached consumers. Though product advertising, too, was a decentralized process in which divisional heads made their own budgeting decisions, Sloan urged the divisions to spend their money on it. Massive advertising budgets, by the 1920s, were nothing new. Between 1880 and 1910 national corporations and major urban retailers had pushed advertising costs from about $30 million to $600 million. In 1917, department store magnate John Wanamaker expressed the new business common sense when he remarked: "The time to advertise is all the time."[79] Automakers, with the exception of Henry Ford, agreed.

Under Sloan's leadership, by 1924 GM was spending an average of about ten dollars per car in advertising and was the single largest buyer of magazine advertising space in the nation.[80] Ford was so incensed over GM's massive spending—and the American people's acceptance of advertising messages, with their emphasis on style—that in 1926 he openly rebelled. He cut his own advertising costs to the bone and delivered a manifesto that appeared in newspapers and magazines around the country. It read in part:

> The stability of the substantial bulk of the American people is most definitely evidenced by the continued leadership of Ford. Despite confusion, in the minds of many, of extravagance with progress, a vast majority cling to the old-fashioned idea of living within their incomes. From these come and are coming the millions of Ford owners. . . . They possess or are buying efficient, satisfactory transportation.[81]

Ford was not alone then—or ever after—in seeing style-based advertising as a malicious trick aimed at exciting consumers' passions and fooling people into buying what they did not need for reasons that could not stand up to moral scrutiny.[82]

Sloan saw things differently. He was undoubtedly in closer touch with how most Americans felt, as well. Writing about the 1920s-era debates over the propriety of style-based advertising, the historian Roland Marchand concluded: "[C]onsumers were voting in the marketplace every day for style, beauty, 'extravagance,' and the installment plan. They were voting against automobiles defined simply as 'satisfactory transportation.' "[83] Sloan was not interested in challenging business common sense about the utility or morality of advertising. He was interested in results and under his steady hand, it was all working: profits, sales, share price, market share, dividends.

General Motors by decade's end had triumphed. Many men, Sloan would insist, had produced the corporation's success. Pierre du Pont's leadership during the immediate post-Durant era had made success possible. John Raskob, the original Du Pont export, had created the General Motors Acceptance Corporation (GMAC), which changed the motor business by providing car buyers with ready credit (and GM with steady profits). And Raskob, Pierre du Pont, and Donaldson Brown, with Sloan's enthusiastic support, had also contributed in a more subtle fashion by devising a stock bonus structure for GM's leading executives that enabled them to share generously in the corporation's success (and which also gave them financial incentive to stay with the corporation). Kettering had improved GM cars and through the invention of "ethyl" had brought in a steady source of profits. Donaldson Brown had revolutionized corporate finances by creating breakthrough financial controls that made profitable operations predictable. Knudsen, Pratt, Mott, the Fishers, and other key men had performed at an extraordinary level.

The results were astounding. At the beginning of the 1920s, when Durant had left the corporation, bankruptcy had seemed possible. At the end of the 1920s annual net profits after taxes hit $265,824,911. In 1921, General Motors sold 193,00 vehicles, just 12.7 percent of the auto market. Ford owned 55.7 percent of that market. In 1927 General Motors passed Ford, selling over 1.8 million motor vehicles.

General Motors had become an American corporate giant, a mainstay of the nation's economy, and a leader of the great Bull Market of the 1920s. As late as 1917, only 894 people owned all of the outstanding shares of General Motors stock. In 1929, GM shareholders numbered an astounding 176,693. General Motors was among the most popular stocks in America, with roughly half its shareholders owning ten or fewer shares.[84]

Sloanism had defeated Fordism. Ford had tried everything he could within the system he had devised. He cut prices. He speed up the assembly line. He pushed his dealers mercilessly so that in 1926 seven of ten lost money. And still, GM, led by Chevrolet, cut away his market share. In 1926, Ford cut production of the Model T to 1.3 million cars. Without his massive volume he was lost. Shocking even Sloan, Ford conceded defeat—temporarily. On May 27, 1927, Ford officially stopped production of the Model T and closed down his assembly plants. Some six months later, he rolled out the first Model A, a much improved vehicle.

Still, Ford clung to the belief that the public just wanted one type of reliable transportation.[85]

The great auto historian James Flink concluded: "The Model T was intended as a farmer's car for a nation of farmers."[86] As America became more urban, and the Model T did not, the results were inevitable. Sloan, years later, put the matter bluntly: "The old master had failed to master change."[87] Sloan knew better. He understood what Americans wanted.

SLOAN ENTERS SOCIETY

[M]any ultimate ends or values toward which experience shows that human action may be oriented, often cannot be understood completely, though sometimes we are able to grasp them intellectually. The more radically they differ from our own ultimate values, however, the more difficult it is for us to understand them empathically. . . . [S]ometimes we must simply accept them as given data.

—**Max Weber, *Economy and Society***

In the spring of 1925, high above Times Square, atop the General Motors building at Fifty-seventh Street, Sloan had installed the largest electric sign Americans had ever seen. One hundred feet long and containing five thousand individual lamps, the sign promised "A car for every purse and purpose." Indicating the changing corporate order, the lamps continuously spelled out "General Motors"; blinking on and off, in sequence, flashed Chevrolet, Oldsmobile, Buick, Oakland, Cadillac, GM trucks, and "body by Fisher."[1]

Every other week during the 1920s, Sloan boarded the New York Central's *Detroiter,* traveling between GM's corporate offices at Fifty-seventh Street and Broadway in New York to GM's massive building at Grand Boulevard in Detroit, and back again. He also made the corporate rounds: Trenton, Baltimore, Atlanta, Indianapolis, St. Louis, Oakland, and here, and there, and most everywhere in the United States, personally linking factories, dealerships, plants, and offices into a decentralized empire. As GM's domestic affairs become more settled, he steamed across the Atlantic in the fall of 1926, 1927, and 1928 to explore the possibilities of expansion and oversee the growth of General Motors across Europe. By 1929 GM had built nineteen foreign assembly plants not only in Europe but also in Asia, Latin America, Australia, and Africa.[2] Data, personnel files, and committee reports flowed upward through the organization from all directions into his office. He institutionalized operational autonomy, responsibility, and culpability. He built centralized controls. By decade's end his authority within the corporation was secured. General Motors was triumphant.

Within the intertwined worlds of Wall Street, Big Industry, and the business press, he was a figure of the highest regard. Although most comfortable within the fluid boundaries of his corporation, Sloan did begin to venture beyond its confines into American society, into a landscape populated by men and women he knew best as consumers. Pressed by events usually not of his own making, Sloan became increasingly caught up in the workings of his nation. He had to consider what public roles he and the other top men at GM could and should play in American society. He had to decide which activities pursued by corporate men brought prestige or honor to GM and which public acts risked alienating consumers from GM. Sloan would have to act when GM men crossed the ill-defined line between their roles as American citizens and as corporate representatives of General Motors.

* * *

By the late 1920s, Sloan was a very wealthy man. His holdings in General Motors stock, the share price of which soared in the great bull market, were the basis of his wealth. In 1923, a generous bonus plan, the Managers Securities Company, had been created to reward GM's key men, most especially Sloan. His GM shareholdings, as a result, increased with every passing year. Stock dividends, his salary, and outside investments—Sloan had large holdings in the stock market—created an abundant cash flow. Great wealth and high position provided him opportunities to participate in new endeavors and to join a wider circle of acquaintances.

John Raskob, GM treasurer and member of the board of directors, offered Sloan his guidance in this realm. Raskob, too, had grown immensely rich, in large part due to the spectacular rise in General Motors stock. Unlike Sloan, who was so circumspect in all matters, Raskob was a prince of "Roaring Twenties" New York City. He was a boulevardier who knew all kinds of people: those with new money, those with old money, those with political connections, and those who controlled the great financial institutions that underwrote the era's booming stock market and economic expansion.

In New York, Raskob was best known as a high-rolling stock market operator. Alongside his old friend Billy Durant, he was an oft-quoted king of the stock market bulls. A *Ladies Home Journal* article, titled "Everybody Ought to Be Rich," made him a national celebrity. In the article, he urged every American to invest whatever they could in the roaring bull market (alas, the piece was published just two months before the market crash).[3]

Raskob knew the biggest of the money men. In large part, his relationship with them built on his role in both the affairs of du Pont and General Motors, and, specifically, Raskob's financial dealings with Morgan bankers, who played a pivotal role in the 1920 GM financial debacle and who, thereafter, sat on the General Motors board of directors. Raskob mixed business and pleasure with such men and sought to connect Sloan with them. In 1926, Raskob proposed Sloan for membership in the New York Yacht Club, a bastion of Morgan bankers and other members of the New York financial elite.[4] Back in 1901, J. Pierpont Morgan, proud commodore of the Yacht Club, had provided the land on Forty-fourth Street on which the club's spectacular beaux-arts-style clubhouse was built. In the 1920s the Yacht Club was among the most elite of gentlemen's clubs for New York's most avid and most wealthy yachtsmen. J. P. Morgan had grandly pronounced: "If you have to ask how much it costs [yachting], you can't afford it."[5]

Raskob arranged for Junius S. Morgan Jr., and Thomas Lamont, Morgan bankers (the first by reason of blood, alone; the other through extraordinary talent), as well as GM board members, to support Sloan's application. Raskob also asked George F. Baker Jr. of the First National Bank, and a GM board member, as well, to add his good name to the cause. Baker had recently taken over the chairmanship of the bank from his more illustrious father. Baker Sr., famously private, had broken a long-standing public silence in 1923 when he told an inquiring newspaperman: "Businessmen of America should reduce their talk two-thirds. Everybody should reduce his talk. There is rarely ever a reason for anybody to talk."[6] Sloan, having already embraced the emerging field of public relations, perhaps had found the senior Baker's comment quaint. The son was a more modern sort, and a GM board member besides; Sloan would certainly have appreciated his support.

Raskob undoubtedly saw business utility in having Sloan mix with the men of the New York Yacht Club. He also probably hoped to lure Sloan into a bit of yachting fun. Raskob definitely liked his own fun and often seemed interested in coaxing his friend into having a bit more. Since the 1880s, yachting, by which was meant ownership of spectacularly large, ocean-going vessels such as J. P. Morgan's various *Corsairs,* which took some seventy men to run, had been a leading hobby of the very wealthy.[7] It is also possible that Raskob, who knew of Irene Sloan's love of the sea, was seeking to bring some additional pleasure into Mrs. Sloan's life. If so, that mission failed, at least in the near term.

In the end, Sloan did become a member but he did not yet find the time to buy a yacht or, seemingly, go yachting. How often he went to the Forty-fourth Street clubhouse is not clear but, on occasion, he almost certainly did. Sloan was becoming more involved in the elite world of New York City. He joined the Bankers Club and then other exclusive establishments. Careful to keep such activities out of the public eye, by the mid-1920s Alfred Sloan Jr. spent a good deal of the little leisure time he had with the nation's most powerful bankers and industrialists.

Sloan's heightened position among New York's financial elite brought with it certain rewards. In all likelihood assisted by Raskob, by 1927 Sloan was added to the very short list of wealthy individuals given extraordinary stock market opportunities by the Morgan bank. In those days the securities markets were subject to practically no public oversight. Also during those days—and after a long era of tough regulation, not so unlike our own—the largest banks could and did take on many roles, including making loans, accepting deposits, and issuing stocks and bonds. Moreover, the largest banks and the largest corporations almost always worked together on exclusive terms. To put the best face on it, bankers and corporate leaders placed a long-standing strategic commercial relationship well ahead of any sort of rigorous scrutiny or open competition for the best possible financial terms (not unlike how the Japanese corporate financial system worked throughout most of the twentieth century). The Morgan bank stood at the top of this system.

One result of both the system and Morgan's great power within it was the bank's ability to sell a portion of a public stock offering it was issuing for a corporate client to private individuals at a discount price prior to the stock's open sale on the New York Stock Exchange. From a certain perspective this practice looks like a scam in which wealthy individuals were almost certainly guaranteed a large profit in return for what appeared to be a sympathetic outlook on the Morgan bank. That the list of favored individuals included several key corporate decision makers and powerful government officials, "men of affairs and position" in the Morgan bank's own terms, made the purpose of the practice, at the least, suspect.[8]

Sloan certainly did not see the matter in this light. No one could bribe him to accept less favorable terms for his corporation in exchange for a personal favor. He would have supported the explanation for the practice J. P. Morgan and Company later gave (before an unfriendly New Deal congressional committee): "We wished, therefore, to sell part of [the stock offering] as a business man's investment to those having knowledge of business and general conditions."[9] Sloan was pleased to accept the Morgan "business man's investment." On July 1, 1927, he bought one thousand shares of the Manville Corporation at $57.50; at its subsequent public offering it went for $79 (Morgan partners did even better selling themselves shares at $47.50). Extant records next show Sloan buying thirty-five hundred shares of United Corporation at $75; it sold openly at $93; then ten thousand shares of Allegheny at $20, which then sold openly between $31 and $35 a share; and finally seventy-five hundred shares of Standard brands for $32, which then sold openly for $36.50–$37.[10] Sloan, unlike his friend Raskob and his ex-boss Billy Durant, was not a major speculator in the stock market frenzy of the late 1920s. With the help of his Morgan associates he did not have to gamble to do well in the bull market. It was a good time to be wealthy, a state of affairs Sloan took as appropriate because earned through performance.

Raskob was not the sole instigator of Sloan's movement out into the world. Sloan himself was exploring. In 1925, he had reached his fiftieth birthday. The occasion seemingly evoked no self-examination but in the mid-1920s, with his success assured and his opportunities for extracorporate involvement greatly expanded, Sloan did begin to turn his mind in new directions. Some thirty years after his graduation from MIT, he had begun again to think about higher education. He acted in two related directions.

Within the bounds of the corporation, Sloan championed a GM takeover of the Flint Institute of Technology. The local school had been established in 1919, inspired in large part by Charles Kettering and fostered by Walter Chrysler, then working for Durant and head of the Flint YMCA Industrial Committee. In 1916, at Chrysler's request, Kettering had come up from Dayton to give a YMCA talk on education. A supporter of the relatively new "cooperative education" program at the University of Cincinnati, Kettering had promoted a new kind of higher education in which "theory and practice" were intertwined—that is, students should be able to combine book and classroom learning with hands-on, real-world work experience. He concluded, "[T]he cooperative job is the student's laboratory in which he learns the details of his profession."[11] Out of Kettering's speech, the Flint Institute of Technology took fledgling form. At first, it served primarily to train highly skilled workers for Flint automakers, such as machinists and tool and die makers. Later it developed engineering programs. Similar "cooperative" programs in which industrial work and engineering courses were combined so as to best prepare young people for corporate management jobs spread around the nation (they are still popular today).

In 1926, Sloan decided that the Flint school could be usefully reengineered and offered economic stability through a direct attachment to GM. Sloan, in cooperation with other GM executives, had General Motors take over the Flint school and rename it the General Motors Institute of Technology. In opening the new four-year school, Sloan himself explained that GMI would create corporate-ready engineers for both GM and other employers "through practical training in the theory and practice of engineering and its application to modern industry, particularly the automobile industry." Students would alternate between four weeks of instruction in the classroom and school labs and four weeks working in factories. Sloan described GMI as "a cooperative management engineering course."[12] The fluff—liberal arts and such—Sloan had endured in his years at MIT would be kept to a minimum, replaced by a narrowly tailored education that properly prepared young people for corporate industry.

Sloan was always careful not to injure the feelings of his colleagues—such as William Knudsen—who had moved up the corporate ladder without benefit of higher education. But he fully believed in the professional training of engineers and he wanted General Motors to hire such men. GMI was a commitment in that direction at a time when few Americans had the means or opportunity to attend a four-year college and when many of the operations men at GM lacked such academic credentials. Sloan took a personal interest in making sure that the school offered ambitious and capable young hourly-workers within GM's plants a possible avenue upward into management. In addition, GM executives created a variety of educational programs for foremen and other lower-ranked GM employees. GMI was a useful tool for extending corporate opportunities to more GM employees. The institute was not an aspect of GM's affairs that Sloan had to manage; he took an avid interest in it because he wanted to. Sloan was beginning to think more seriously about how to link GM to other social institutions that offered the technical outlook and business approach in which he believed.

Sloan's interest in GMI percolated through the corporation's top ranks. In the summer of 1928, N. F. Dougherty, one of GM's top men and director of industrial relations, asked his fellow executives, "enriched" by the corporation's unparalleled success, to create an endowment for GMI equal to that of other top colleges and universities. He then asked his colleagues to consider with him what more they could do to reform education in the United States. The basic problem, Dougherty argued,

> was that the entire creative and directive genius of the country . . . is less than 1% . . . [while] 95% of the population . . . occupy positions in which all that is required is the knowledge of one or more tasks that will be performed under the direction of others. . . . It is my opinion that our educational institutions are attempting to develop people for the 1% class instead of for the 99% class.

To solve this problem, Dougherty suggested that GM might fund schools from kindergarten through the tenth grade (at which point students would go to work) "devoted largely to scientific and manual activities" which "would best fit [the] natural aptitudes" of the 95 percent of Americans who really needed no "book knowledge." Dougherty was clearly no devotee of philosopher John Dewey's pedagogy, laid out during the same period, which argued that democratic citizenship demanded a rich, broad-based education for all Americans. Sloan's thoughts on his colleague's scheme are not known, but GM during this period did not attempt to charter new elementary or vocational schools.[13]

Sloan's own educational efforts did extend outside the company. Around this same time, he began to become more involved with his alma mater, MIT. He was an enthusiastic member of the advisory committee that oversaw "Course XV, Engineering Administration," one of MIT's major innovations (though Carnegie Tech had actually been the first to develop such a course). As the course's historian, David Noble, recounts: "Instruction in Course XV covered all aspects of works management, economic, finance, accounting, business law, and marketing."[14] Sloan fully believed in the course's goal, which was to prepare the elite engineering students enrolled at MIT for industrial leadership. Sloan exemplified the possibilities and he was not alone. Serving alongside him as an advisor to the course was his electrical engineering classmate ('95), and then General Electric president, Gerard Swope. Pierre du Pont had also served on the committee, as had numerous other leading industrialists who had gone through MIT's engineering programs. Sloan was delighted with the institute administrators' efforts to make higher education and corporate enterprise a working partnership. Just as Sloan had helped to develop a rational structure for decision making at General Motors he was pleased to see higher education moving toward a rational integration with the corporate system to which he had devoted his life. In the 1920s, Sloan saw a corporate society, driven by the free market, emerging in the United States; and while he carefully limited the time he gave over to extracorporate affairs, he happily lent a hand and supportive words to the endeavor.[15]

Sloan enjoyed his expanding involvements and interests. Always, however, he was careful to do nothing that could in any way cast a shadow on the reputation of General Motors. Alas, from his perspective, not everyone in a position of great responsibility within the corporation showed a similar equal concern. Once again, Raskob figured centrally in Sloan's movement into the uncertain realm outside of the closed GM corporate circle.

Sometime in the late 1920s, probably in 1927 or early 1928, Sloan got into a terrific argument with John Raskob. It occurred at such volume as to allow Sloan's executive secretary to overhear choice passages—and pass them along. As the story was told within the corporation, a tabloid had published a photo of the bland-appearing Mr. Raskob, treasurer and board member of General Motors, on the Atlantic City boardwalk in the company of an attractive young woman who was not his wife. The newspaper photo found its way to the desk of Alfred Sloan, who was mortified. He insisted that Raskob immediately come to his office and talk over the matter with him.

"John," Sloan loudly admonished (according to our source), "we can't have that kind of publicity, that's very bad. Indeed, I wish you could be more careful."

Raskob yelled back, "Listen, what I do when I'm not on duty here is nobody's damned business."[16]

Raskob then stormed out of Sloan's office, watched with interest by Sloan's staff, who had heard their boss yell before but never over such a scandalous affair.

Sloan was probably not shocked by the particulars of his Catholic friend's situation. Sloan's closest friend, Walter Chrysler, was an unabashed womanizer known for mixing his five o'clock cocktails with visits from New York showgirls. Around the time Raskob was caught having an Atlantic City fling, Chrysler was beginning a long-term, quasi-public affair with the notorious and, evidently, extraordinarily beautiful Peggy Hopkins Joyce. The term "gold digger" was coined by the Hearst newspapers to describe the often-married and divorced, onetime Ziegfield Follies sensation.[17] It was not Sloan's moral sensibility that was being strained by Raskob's behavior.

He knew Raskob and he knew what kind of man he was. The two men were good friends. They socialized together. Raskob was practically the only person Sloan knew who kidded him. In a letter from Raskob to Sloan, as the two men and their wives made plans to see the "passion play with Lang" in Lucerne, Switzerland the summer of 1922 (Sloan's attendance produced, almost surely, by some combination of Raskob's charm and his wife's request), Raskob wrote in his jolly way: "Hope you are behaving yourself while in Paris from under my watchful eye and with best regards to Mrs. Sloan."[18] Only Raskob, the bon vivant, would write to the sober and monogamous Sloan in such a fashion.

Raskob was, like Walter Chrysler, a man who embraced life on his own terms—as something that had to be, in general, accepted and enjoyed. Sloan had more difficulty analyzing how Raskob's well publicized extra-corporate affairs and General Motors' public image could be kept in harmony. Increasingly, Raskob was becoming involved in matters further and further from his duties with General Motors.

Some of Raskob's activities seemed relatively reasonable extensions of his corporate responsibilities. He was, for example, a member of the board of directors of the U.S. Chamber of Commerce (begun only in 1912). He mainly used the position to lobby Congress on several issues dear to his heart and pocketbook, most importantly income tax reduction. This sort of low-key, business-related activity, conducted mainly behind closed doors, probably caused Sloan little concern.

Raskob had also become a major public benefactor of the Roman Catholic Church. By the late 1920s, he had donated substantial sums of money, well over a million dollars, to various Catholic causes. In honor of his support, Pope Pius XI had made Raskob a Knight of the Order of St. Gregory the Great.[19] This public honor came at a time when Roman Catholics in the United States were regarded with suspicion by the much more numerous car-buying Protestants; in the 1920s, anti-Catholicism competed with anti-Semitism in many Americans' hearts. Sloan's feelings about Raskob's enthusiastic Catholicism remains unknown. Sloan likely chalked up this sort of religious business, despite the potential corporate complications, as an unavoidable matter of personal spiritual obligation.

More vexing, Raskob was also a major financial backer of organized anti-Prohibition efforts. Raskob was a "wet," in part for personal reasons: he enjoyed his cocktails. But he opposed national Prohibition mainly for ideological reasons and reasons of economic self-interest. Like several other wealthy conservatives in the 1920s, Raskob feared that Prohibition was but "the opening wedge of tyranny" by the federal government. It was, he warned, a frontal assault on individual rights and, potentially, the first salvo in a governmental barrage against constitutional principals of limited government that protected the rights of property against democratic hysteria. Translated into simpler terms, Raskob feared that the federal government, spurned on by the hoi polloi, would seek to increase income taxes to replace lost federal excise taxes on alcoholic beverages—which before World War I had been a major source of federal revenues (some $223 million in 1913, when no federal income tax had existed).[20] Raskob hoped to end Prohibition and instigate a not insubstantial "beer tax." If working men would then drink the amount of beer consulting economists estimated they would, some $1.3 billion would flow out of their pockets and into the federal coffers, allowing for a 50 percent reduction in both corporate and individual income taxes (almost all of which came from America's wealthiest citizens in those days).[21] In these fears and hopes, he was joined by his long-time friend and business mentor, Pierre du Pont, the prior president of GM and still GM chairman of the board. Du Pont, by early 1928, was perhaps the single largest financial supporter of anti-Prohibition efforts,[22] and he earnestly sought to involve the reluctant Sloan in the cause. At one point, du Pont tried to light a fire under Sloan by writing him that if Prohibition was not soon ended, "our form of government shall be destroyed."[23]

Raskob, too, gently prodded Sloan on the issue. A letter Raskob wrote to Walter Chrysler indicates the amusement Raskob found in both of his friends' hypocritical neutrality on the subject of prohibition:

> I am having a lot of fun taking a crack at you and Alfred every now and then about denying the workingman his glass of beer, with your lockers filled with vintage champagnes, rare old wines and selected brands of old whiskey, liqueurs, etc. However, I am not mentioning any names, because sometime I might want to borrow some money from you, and you might remember too much. Anyway, I love you and nothing else much matters, so God bless you and good luck.[24]

Prohibition was an immensely controversial subject. Americans were divided over it. Automobile and refrigerator buyers were divided over it. As Sloan saw it, General Motors—and men clearly identified with General Motors—should not take a public position on such a controversial matter. Business corporations, Sloan believed, could not afford to be identified with either side of any public controversy. Neither could their corporate leaders. Sales could be lost. But Raskob and du Pont disagreed with Sloan. They believed they had a right to their positions.

Raskob did not see himself as a simple extension of his corporate duties. He had his own interests, both personal and financial. One of his interests, clearly defined by 1926, was politics. He found it fun. And it gave him a chance to do big things.

Raskob probably first met New York governor Al Smith in 1925 when they were introduced at the Tiger Room, located high atop an office building on Fourth Avenue and Twenty-third Street. William F. Kenny owned the building. He had set up the Tiger Room, replete with tiger-theme interior design—tiger rug, tiger statuary, stuffed tigers—as his own sort of private club (no Morgan bankers would be in attendance). The tiger, it need be said, was the symbol of Tammany Hall, the Democratic Party Irishman's club that played an incomparable role in New York City politics from the mid-nineteenth century right into the 1920s. Photos of Tammany leaders such as William Tweed, who brought the Bengal tiger symbol to Tammany and whose "Tweed Ring" stole some $50 million out of the public trough, lined the walls. About a year before Raskob's first visit to the Tiger Room, the well-known Tammany ward boss, George Washington Plunkitt, had died. Plunkitt, in a remarkable political primer published in the earlier years of the century, had defended "honest" graft in public life by providing the men of Tammany Hall with a credo: "I seen my opportunities, and I took 'em."[25]

William F. Kenny had grown up with Al Smith on the mean streets of the Lower East Side. A man of great charm, fierce ambition, and excellent political connections, Kenny had become a construction magnate worth many millions of dollars. The Tiger Room was a private hideaway where Kenny and his cronies, including Governor Smith, could have a few drinks, play cards, and talk politics.

Raskob, through his varied connections, made his way to the Tiger Room, where he met Governor Smith. The two self-made Irish Catholics (Raskob was actually half Irish and half Alsatian), both of whom had bootstrapped themselves up from poverty without benefit of much formal education, immediately hit it off. Raskob become a Tiger Room regular. He found that he enjoyed the exuberant game of politics and the men who played it. By 1926 he was one of several wealthy men—almost all of them self-made—who became a part of Governor Smith's so-called Golfing Cabinet, offering him advice on a range of public affairs.[26] Raskob was probably the richest of the crew and through his long-standing relations with the du Ponts and other leading industrialists and financiers, the best connected.

By spring 1928, Governor Smith was well on his way to securing the

Democratic Party nomination for presidential candidate. Raskob was his chief fundraiser. Over the course of the campaign, in one form or another, Raskob would personally contribute some $540,000 to Smith and would sign promissory notes for $150,000 more.[27] Raskob made it his job to line up support from among his well-to-do friends and associates. In newspaper interviews, as well as in private clubs, Raskob championed Smith. Raskob and Smith were becoming a well-publicized duo.

Shortly before Smith's nomination a well-known political writer, Frank Kent, published a pointed essay, "Fat Cats and Free Rides," about the prominence of wealthy men in national politics. It appeared in the *American Mercury,* the nation's "smart" magazine run by the country's sharpest social critic, H. L. Mencken. While Alfred Sloan probably did not read the article, he would have found it a useful guide to the new enthusiasm of his friend and business colleague, Raskob, who was in 1928 just one year short of the half century mark. Kent wrote:

> A Fat Cat is a man of large means and no political experience who having reached middle age, and success in business, and finding no further thrill . . . of satisfaction in the mere piling up of more millions, develops a yearning for some sort of public honor and is willing to pay for it. The machine has what it seeks, public honor, and he has the money the machine needs.[28]

Unbeknownst to Sloan, Raskob had decided to make formal his support for Democratic Party stalwart Al Smith. He asked Smith to appoint him head of his presidential campaign. On July 11, 1928, Smith announced that John Raskob, chairman of the General Motors finance committee and member of the GM executive committee, was to run his presidential campaign, and had his support to be chairman of the National Democratic Committee. General Motors chairman of the board, Pierre du Pont, joined Raskob, his old friend, in publicly supporting Al Smith, the ardently "wet" and seemingly pro-limited-government candidate.

Raskob all along had kept du Pont abreast of his deepening political involvements and had specifically talked with him about his role in the Smith campaign. Raskob had told Sloan nothing. Perhaps he meant to break the news to him prior to its public release; but tragedy intervened. A few days before the news was made public, one of Raskob's twelve children was killed in a car accident. As a result, Raskob was both preoccupied and out of touch with his GM colleagues. He never got hold of Sloan. Regardless of the circumstances, Sloan was not happy that he learned about Raskob's new position from the newspapers.[29] Though no secretary passed along Sloan's immediate response, shouts of "horse apples" and other of Sloan's choicest epithets were probably heard echoing off the wood-paneled interior of his austere office.

Political insiders, including Franklin Roosevelt, who was to run for New York governor in Smith's stead, were sure the Catholic Smith had made a colossal blunder by appointing the Catholic Raskob to head his campaign. Many of Smith's supporters worried that their candidate's Catholicism was political problem enough. Adding Raskob, Knight of the Order of St. Gregory the Great, was salt in the wound. They predicted that the white Protestant south, home of the Democratic Party's most faithful supporters (since the days of Lincoln and then the post-Reconstruction disenfranchisement of the southern African-American population), would rebel.

Such electoral particulars interested Sloan not at all. He simply could not accept what Raskob had done. One of the most public of General Motors' men had leapt into partisan politics in the most public manner imaginable. Such publicity could not be good for the corporation.

Sloan's fears were immediately inflamed by two events that occurred almost immediately. The day of Raskob's announcement General Motors' share price declined. Second, the day Raskob's Democratic Party chairmanship was announced, a GM shareholder fired off a letter "c/o General Motors" that made its way to Sloan's desk within twenty-four hours of its mailing: "I am afraid that your [Raskob's] action will have a bad influence on the sale of General Motors products, because you know men will take sides and become very bitter in a political campaign."[30] Sloan answered the letter personally: "A man's standing on political questions is a personal matter in which he cannot involve his corporation. . . . As you well know, the law does not permit a corporation to subscribe to a political campaign, directly or indirectly. General Motors, of course, observes the law." While Sloan's letter attempted to calm his shareholder's concerns, Sloan himself was furious. He sent both sides of the correspondence to GM chairman Pierre du Pont as a sign of troubles ahead.[31]

Sloan began to make it clear to GM's leadership that he wanted Raskob gone. Some years later, in a tone far more temperate than he probably displayed as the actual events were playing out, he summarized his concerns:

> You will remember it was a time of considerable speculation and Mr. Raskob was issuing statements to the financial press and so forth, so they came to look at him as the spokesman for General Motors. The management of General Motors, particularly myself, felt that it would be very unsound

for an individual who was managing a political campaign to continue as spokesman of General Motors. We felt that it put General Motors in politics, and we had worked very hard to get General Motors where it was. We were selling to the ultimate consumer, and the campaign was quite an important one, so far as the psychology of it was concerned, and we felt that it was unfair to the management for Mr. Raskob to take that position. . . . It was particularly important to us because the consumer can discriminate very easily against General Motors products.[32]

Between July 11 and July 17, Sloan talked to the board of General Motors. He wanted Raskob to resign his position on the finance committee. Raskob thought it would be fine if he just took a leave of absence, a position strongly supported by Chairman Pierre du Pont. But by the summer of 1928, the outcome of a contest between du Pont and Sloan was not close. A majority of the board sided with Sloan. One of Sloan's firmest supporters was Walter Carpenter, the vice president for finance at Du Pont, a GM board member, and, like Sloan, a professional manager of the first order. In full agreement with Sloan's concerns, he later wrote a tough-minded letter to his boss at Du Pont and fellow GM board member, Irénée du Pont, arguing that Raskob's public political activities were "more serious than we have appreciated. I can think of no way in which the duP-GM interests could have dissipated the good will and respect of the country in so short a time as has been done."[33]

With little choice, Raskob submitted a letter of resignation on July 17, 1928. Privately, he vented his anger. Sloan, he felt, was overreacting. Like Carpenter, he also wrote du Pont president and GM board member Irénée du Pont. Looking for moral support, if nothing else, he argued that his support for Smith was in the interests of GM and the Du Pont corporation:

Governor Smith's ideas of protecting big business are quite in accord with yours and mine. . . . . Furthermore, I happen to know that the Governor believes that there is too much interference of the Government in business. . . . Personally, I can see no big difference between the two parties except the wet and dry question, and, of course, some people say the religious question, which I think both of us can agree should form no part of politics.[34]

Raskob was right on the issues. Franklin Roosevelt, at least on business policy, agreed. He headed the Democratic Party Division of Commerce, Industry, and Professional Activities and sent businessmen fundraising letters that noted: "Some of Mr. Hoover's regulatory attempts are undoubtedly for the good of our economic system. . . . But I think the policy of Governor Smith to let businessmen look after business matters is far safer for our country."[35]

But the issue, in Sloan's mind, was not a matter of public policy. It was public relations. And in a letter to Sloan, Raskob calmly conceded the problem of appearances. He understood, he said, Sloan's concern: "[T]he corporation must not be put in the light of taking sides for or against political parties, personages, or questions."[36] Sloan took no pleasure in the process; he had only done what was necessary. Of course, his friendship with Raskob could not affect his thinking. Sloan was helping to invent a new role for the American businessman: corporate manager. Blatant public partisan political maneuvering was not appropriate behavior in a corporate officer.

On July 24, Sloan issued a press statement announcing that Raskob had chosen to resign from his position as General Motors corporate executive (quietly, he kept his GM board membership) in order to devote himself to the 1928 presidential campaign. A flurry of newspaper stories and editorials covered the announcement, seeing it as a milestone in the relationship between the political process and business interests.

Sloan was particularly impressed with the editorial disseminated by the Boston News Bureau, which represented, Sloan believed, "the *Wall St. Journal* interests." He sent this editorial, and others as well, to Pierre du Pont, Irénée du Pont, and in all likelihood a number of other men involved with overseeing General Motors. The editorial intoned:

> Chairman Raskob [Democratic Party chairman] could not remain Chairman Raskob [GM finance committee chairman] when those two titles were not at all synonyms, and threatened a confusion of identity and performance. An old truth gets now a new personal expression—and a prominent one. That truth is the necessary cleavage between politics and business. They are indeed as oil and water, and will not fuse. . . . Stewards of business must emulate Caesar's wife in avoidance of suspicion. . . . The truth persists that there is no true serving of two masters.[37]

Sloan could not quickly put the matter behind him. Pierre du Pont was displeased with Sloan. Du Pont believed that leading businessmen had to be public stewards and as public stewards in a democracy they had to be politically active. He wrote his cousin Coleman du Pont, "The only way that we can improve political service is to get better men. We cannot get the best from corporations if we impose the penalty of resignation from corporate work at the same time."[38] Sloan was wrong to force Raskob's resignation, just as he was wrong to shirk active involvement in the political life of the nation. As a matter of principle, du Pont decided to write his own letter of resignation.

Sloan did not want du Pont to resign, even though he was playing an increasingly public role in the anti-Prohibition movement and was an avid supporter of Al Smith's presidential candidacy. On the other side of the issue, the Fisher brothers, who also sat on the GM board, did think Du Pont should resign, just as they had strongly supported Sloan's push for Raskob's resignation from the chairmanship of the finance committee. Arguably, they were not acting on the high-minded principles that drove Sloan's thinking, for out of the public eye the Fishers were strong supporters of Republican presidential candidate Herbert Hoover. Partisanship played a role in their anger with both Raskob and Pierre du Pont. The Republican Party, they and most of their friends in the auto business believed, was the proper party of Big Business. In their defense, they did take some pains to keep their strong support for Hoover and the Republican Party discreet. Discretion, they believed, was the only proper condition under which well-known corporate officers could involve themselves in electoral affairs.

Sloan, in general, agreed with the Fisher brothers. He wanted Pierre du Pont to understand that the very public mixing of politics and business was too dangerous for the corporation. Du Pont surely could understand that public actions by well-known GM officers affected GM's public image. Sloan explained his position—the proper corporate position—to Irénée du Pont, Du Pont company president and Pierre's cousin: "[T]he Corporation's interest is the only interest I have, as of course, you know. . . . I personally feel—perhaps I am right and perhaps I am wrong—that much injury has been done the Corporation [by mixing business with politics]. Naturally, much of it can be overcome, but I cannot help but feel that there will be a certain permanent loss of prestige for what has gone by."[39]

Sloan respected Pierre du Pont for his role in the recovery of GM in the 1920–21 financial crisis and for his wise choice of successor—respected him too much, in fact, to allow him to resign as chairman of the board without attempting to prevent it. He also felt—perhaps not with the total objectivity for which he prided himself—that du Pont was not immediately recognized by the public as a representative of General Motors. So, at a General Motors board meeting on August 9, "at the longest meeting that body has held in several years," Sloan engineered a compromise—one that was not made available to Raskob.[40] Du Pont was "granted leave of absence" as GM chairman so that he might fully pursue "his activities in connection with the association against the prohibition amendment."[41] Sloan's heavy-handed statement to the press explained that du Pont thought it best to leave, otherwise, "[he] might cause confusion in the public mind and give the impression that General Motors was involved in that movement. . . . Mr. du Pont's activities in connection with the association's work are entirely those of an individual and did not concern the corporation. The resignation was, therefore, not accepted and Mr. du Pont was accorded a leave of absence instead."[42]

Sloan did not leave it there in his attempts to manage the public's understanding of the affair. He also released his earlier statement to Raskob, explaining GM's position on politics and the corporation:

> [T]he corporation takes no part in political affairs. . . . On our part, as a corporation, we recognize the necessity of always keeping clear of politics, which is of no concern of ours, at the same time fully recognizing to the full the right of all our officers, employees, dealers, and stockholders to take their individual stand on political questions as they think best.[43]

Then, while in Flint on company business, Sloan made one of his relatively rare public speeches in which he attempted to make the whole matter crystal clear. He told a respectful audience: "GM is not in politics."[44] Sloan had the address printed and distributed to all GM shareholders and made widely available to GM dealers and employees.

Sloan was trying to craft a delicate position. For several years, he had announced himself as a Republican in his *Who's Who in America* annual entry.[45] Only days earlier, in the midst of the controversy, Sloan had quietly sent a check for $250 to Republican congressman Jas. C. McLaughlin who represented a nearby Michigan congressional district. He had sent the check after Roy Chapin, president of both Hudson Motors and the National Automobile Chamber of Commerce, the auto industry's lobbying group in Washington, D.C., requested the contribution to thank the congressman for his successful fight in the House of Representatives against an automobile excise tax. Sloan was one of twenty-six auto industry leaders Chapin contacted, almost all of whom sent in contributions ranging from fifty to two hundred dollars.[46] It is true that the money was Sloan's, not GM's. And Sloan was certainly no leader in the effort to raise money for this particular fellow. But he sent it for one reason alone—the congressman had supported GM and the auto industry. Still, Sloan could claim that his statement that "GM is not in politics" was faithful to the truth. GM was not attempting to influence voters. Sloan was only trying to reward a politician who supported his corporation's policy needs. And since no one other than Chapin and the congressman knew about the donation—contributions were not publicly disclosed back then—GM had kept itself out of politics. In other words, as long as the involvement of GM or of General Motors executives in national politics was private, it was permissible. Sloan, himself, would have a hard time adhering to this subtle rule soon enough, when America's politics, as they affected business, became more contentious.

Delaware's U.S. senator Coleman du Pont, one of Pierre's first cousins—offered a pointed private rejoinder to Sloan's view of the circumspect relationship between public duty and corporate responsibility. The Republican senator wrote Pierre:

> I think when you and John [Raskob] went in to help your country, the directors of the General Motors Corporation should have said, "For you gentleman to take on additional patriotic work and responsibility we have nothing but praise. Your salaries are doubled until after the election." I think someone should give you both medals for patriotism. If more of our able, successful, and unselfish men were to follow your example, we would have a much better Government.[47]

Neither Coleman nor Pierre seems to have thought it useful to pass along such sentiments to Sloan.

Sloan was not amused by the public attention the Raskob–du Pont affair had attracted. Raskob, never the shrinking violet type, had pointedly thumbed his nose at Sloan by renting office space for the Democratic National Committee in the General Motors Building on Fifty-seventh Street and Broadway in New York City. The move bothered Sloan. Not surprisingly, it also rankled many Democratic Party regulars. Frances Perkins, a Smith insider (and later, secretary of labor under President Franklin Roosevelt) noted: "Raskob thought he'd bought the Democratic Party, and he was going to run it on his own way, like a branch of General Motors."[48]

After stewing over the matter and Raskob's actions for several weeks, Sloan decided he had to make a more affirmative response to the difficulties in which Raskob had placed the corporation. He issued a lengthy statement to the press in which he declared his support for Herbert Hoover. His decision to announce his support was driven, he said, by the public's awareness that key figures identified with General Motors were avidly supporting the Democratic presidential candidate Al Smith. Sloan's statement began:

> I have received a considerable number of inquiries from associates in business, members of various organizations with which I am connected, and from other sources. It seems necessary that I should state my personal viewpoint on the political situation. I am in favor of the election of Mr. Hoover for president. In making that statement I want to emphasize that it is my position as an individual and has nothing to do with any business enterprise in which I may be connected.[49]

Raskob kept a clipping of the newspaper story in which Sloan's statements appeared, but no correspondence on the matter seems to have passed between the two men, who were moving apart.

Sloan was not happy to have publicly entered the political stage. He felt himself to have been forced into a public performance by his associates' poor judgment. His public statement on behalf of Hoover, while reflecting his genuine support, was meant only to neutralize car buyers' perception that GM as a corporate entity supported the Democratic Party. Sloan hoped his declaration would ensure that the public understand "we had a divided house on the political question."[50] Both Democrats and Republicans could buy General Motors with a clear conscience.

Publicly, Sloan was done with the 1928 election. Privately, he sent a check for twenty-five thousand dollars to Hoover's campaign. The five Fisher brothers sent Hoover five times that amount. Circumventing the federal law against corporate donations to federal political campaigns and Sloan's stated position as well, the Fishers also arranged for another one hundred thousand dollars from the Fisher Body subsidiary of GM to make its way into Hoover's campaign coffers. All of these donations were made with no publicity.[51]

Sloan had, of course, backed the right man. Hoover easily won the election with 21.5 million votes to Smith's 15 million. The dependably Democratic southern states of Florida, Texas, North Carolina, Virginia, Tennessee, Kentucky, and Oklahoma all went for the non-Catholic, Republican Hoover. Anti-Catholicism contributed to Smith's defeat, but "Republican prosperity" ensured Hoover of victory. In words that would come to haunt him, Hoover had told cheering Republicans at the convention that had nominated him: "We in America today are nearer to the final triumph over poverty than ever before in the history of any land. . . . We shall soon, with the help of God, be in sight of the day when poverty will be banished from the land."[52] In November 1928, obvious economic problems existed; most visibly, farmers were not doing well. But America was rich and people expected Hoover to help make the nation even richer.

Photographs

218

Sloan, Alfred Pritchard Jr. son of Alfred P. Sloan 240 Garfield Pl Brooklyn

Born: May 23, 1875

Date	Subject	Grade	Date	Subject	Grade
Oct '92	Algebra.	satisf ✓	Oct '92	Chemistry.	satisf
	Chemistry.		May '93	Drawing: Mechanical.	L
Jan '93	Drawing: Mechanical.	P.		Drawing: Freehand.	P
	Drawing: Freehand.	F		French.	March '95 (alleg)
Oct '92	English.	satisf ✓	Oct '92	Military Drill.	exc
	French.		May '93	Political History.	P
	Geometry.	satisf ✓	Oct '92	Trigonometry.	satisf ✓
	Military Drill.				

Date	Subject	Grade	Date	Subject	Grade
Jan. '93	Acoustics	60 P	May '93	Acoustics	80 C
	American History	67 P		Carpentry	60 P.
	Analyt. Geom.	85 C		Diff Calculus	90 H
	Carpentry	61 P		[illegible]. Literature	L
	Descript. Geom.	Sept '93 P	May '94	[illegible] ~~and Mach. Tools~~	50 L
	English Lit.	L		[illegible]	
	German		May '94	[illegible] Drawing	F May '95 L
Jan '94	Mechanism	70 P ✓	May '93	Physics	75 C
Jan '93	Metal Turning	70 P.		Phys. Lab.	P
	Physics	75 C		Phys. Meas.	65 P
	French, Elem.	62 P		Wood Turning	50 P
				French, Elem.	55 L
			May '94	Machine Tools	50 L ✓
				Mechanism	80 C ✓

Date	Subject	Grade	Date	Subject	Grade
Sept '93	Int. Calculus	100 H	May '94	App. Mechanics	44 L ✓
Jan '94	App. Mechanics	57 P ✓		Boilers	63 P ✓
	Business Law			Business Law	60 P ✓
	Electricity	60 P ✓		Elect. Meas. Insts.	C ✓
	German			Engin. Lab.	C ✓
	~~[illegible]~~			German	April '95 [illegible]
	M. E. Drawing	P ✓		M. E. Drawing	P ✓
	Phys. of Heat	75 C ✓		Phys. Lab.	C
	Phys. Lab.	P ✓		Pol. Econ. & Ind. Hist.	58 L ✓
	Pol. Economy	C ✓		Thermodynamics	70 P ✓
	Telegraphy	P ✓		Theoret Elect.	75 C ✓
	Thermodynamics	98 H ✓			
	Valve Gears	70 P ✓			

Date	Subject	Grade	Date	Subject	Grade
Jan '94	Least Squares	C ✓	May '94	Diff. Equations	65 C ✓
Jan. '95	Altern. Currents	P.		Diff. Equations	
	[illegible]	50 P ✓		Elect. Math. (3)	
	[illegible] Mach.	68 P ✓	May '95	Elect. Engineering	P
	[illegible]	90 C ✓		Engin. Lab.	P
	[illegible]	P ✓		Phys. Lab. (2)	
	[illegible]	P ✓		Precision of Meas'ts	90 C
	[illegible]	89 C ✓		Quaternions (1)	
				Telephone Eng.	L
	[illegible]	P ✓			
	Phys. Lab. (Lab. / Ex.)	C ✓ / 70 P ✓			
	R. R. Signals	72 C ✓			
	Steam Eng.	68 P ✓			

Entered September 1892

Dec 12. Admitted on certif. from Brooklyn Polytechnic Institute.

English
Algebra
Geog.
History

Arith.
Geometry
French
German

Sept. 92: Satisfactory for admission to American History (4) and Acoustics.

Oct-7-92 Special VI (Second Year)
Omits: Desc. Geom., and Mechanism. Substitutes French for German
Takes also: F. H. Draw. (1) and Mech. Draw. (1).

Feb-17-93 Special VI. (Second Year)
Omits: Mechanism & M. E. Draw.
Takes also: F. H. Draw. (1) Mech. Draw. (1) and Pol. Hist. (1)

Mch. 15 Attention called to his low standing in first year subjects.

Apr. 11 Removed from care of Committee on Provisional Students.

Oct. 8-93 Regular VI (Third Year)
Omits: German and Int. Cal.
Takes also: Mech. (2) and Least Sq. (4)

Sept. 27-93 Granted special examinations in Des. Geom. (2) and Integral Calculus (3)

Feb. 5-94 Regular VI (Third Year)
Omits: German
Takes also: M. E. Draw. (2) and Mechanism (2) and Diff. Equations (4)

March 7-94 Granted extra time in the Phys. Lab. (3)

Oct. 4-94 Special VI (Fourth Year)
Takes full course except Least Squares
Takes also: French (3) and German (3).

Dec. 5-94 Petitions to be granted special examinations in French (1) and German (3) referred to Prof. van Daell with favor (granted)

Feb. 18-95 Special VI Fourth Year
Omits: Diff. Equations
Others: "Physical Lab."

May 31-95 Recommended for the degree.
Thesis: A Study of the Methods of Testing the Efficiency of Transformers.

Alfred Sloan meant to put his youth behind him as quickly as possible. In order to graduate from MIT in just three years, Sloan took a crushing course load, as can be seen above in the transcript from 1895. As a partial result, his grades were a mixed bag. Still, he succeeded in his overarching goal; he was the youngest member of the class of '95. Courtesy Office of the Registrar, Massachusetts Institute of Technology.

Cylinder Battlers Square Off!

FORD VS. SLOAN

Auto Kings Throw Two Billion Dollars into Ring.

ALFRED P. SLOAN, JR.

HENRY FORD.

ALFRED P. SLOAN, JR., who will wage the big fight against Henry Ford for supremacy in the automobile manufacturing business, is vastly different from the daugh'erless father of millions of "Lizzies."

Sloan, the president and the real spark plug of General Motors Corporation, is sharply contrasted with his rival in the economic battle of the century in an article by Allan L. Benson for the January issue of Hearst's International-Cosmopolitan.

Business all over the world is watching this gigantic contest between two supermen. It has stimulated the imagination of every reader on earth.

Ford's past performance was well known, and when General Motors invaded the low-priced automobile field the dopesters laughed, so much confidence did they have in the Detroiter.

SLOAN

Age 53.
Six feet tall.
130 pounds.
Works every hour.
Eats anything.
Has no hobbies.
Never reads.
Too busy for friends.
Never drinks.
Doesn't smoke.
Never tells stories.
College man.
Never gives an order.

FORD

Age 65.
Five feet nine inches.
147 pounds.
Plays much.
Eats carefully.
Has many hobbies.
Likes books.
Plays with many friends.
Never drinks.
Doesn't smoke.
Has good "line."
No "education."
A business "despot."

Up, Up, Went "G. M."!

Then something happened. Eyes began to focus on a man named

By 1927, Sloan was a celebrated business leader and General Motors was triumphant. The *New York Journal* could not resist a head-to-head comparison of the twinkling Henry Ford and the sober-minded Mr. Sloan. From the *New York Journal*, December 1927, courtesy Hagley Museum and Library.

Left: John Raskob, who served as Pierre du Pont's right-hand man and as the top Du Pont import to GM, was an early supporter of Sloan; the two men were good friends by 1920. But in 1928, Raskob's extracorporate activities became too much for Sloan, who engineered Raskob's departure from GM's executive ranks. Photograph courtesy Hagley Museum and Library.

Right: Donaldson Brown came to GM from Du Pont in early 1921. A mathematical prodigy, he introduced numerous effective financial and statistical systems that greatly contributed to the stability and profitability of General Motors and helped to end the wild gyrations of the Durant years. While Brown and Sloan never became friends—Brown was a bit of an odd duck—Sloan greatly respected Brown's genius. Photograph courtesy Hagley Museum and Library.

This photograph of most of the GM leadership was taken in the mid-1920s. The supposedly "gray men" of GM display a marvelous assortment of sartorial ensembles. *Top row, left to right:* Charles Kettering, Donaldson Brown, Henry F. Crane, John L. Pratt, Charles S. Mott, E. F. Johnson. *Bottom row, left to right*: George Whitney, Junius Morgan Jr., Alfred P. Sloan Jr., C. E. Wilson, William S. Knudsen, Walter S. Carpenter Jr., R. Samuel McLaughlin. Photograph courtesy Hagley Museum and Library.

Irene Sloan loved the sea. Here she is with her husband, beaming with pleasure on the deck of the Sloans' just launched but not yet outfitted "Rene," September 19, 1929. Alfred rarely found the time to go yachting, or to do much else, with his wife of fifty-eight years. Photograph courtesy Hagley Museum and Library.

Sloan and his old boss, Pierre du Pont, pose in front of the White House before meeting with Herbert Hoover to discuss the stock market crash and economic downturn, November 21, 1929. Throughout the Great Depression, Sloan did his best to display in public a calming equanimity, whatever the current crisis. In the 1930s, Pierre and several members of his family became the leading supporters of the vehemently anti–New Deal organization, the Liberty League.

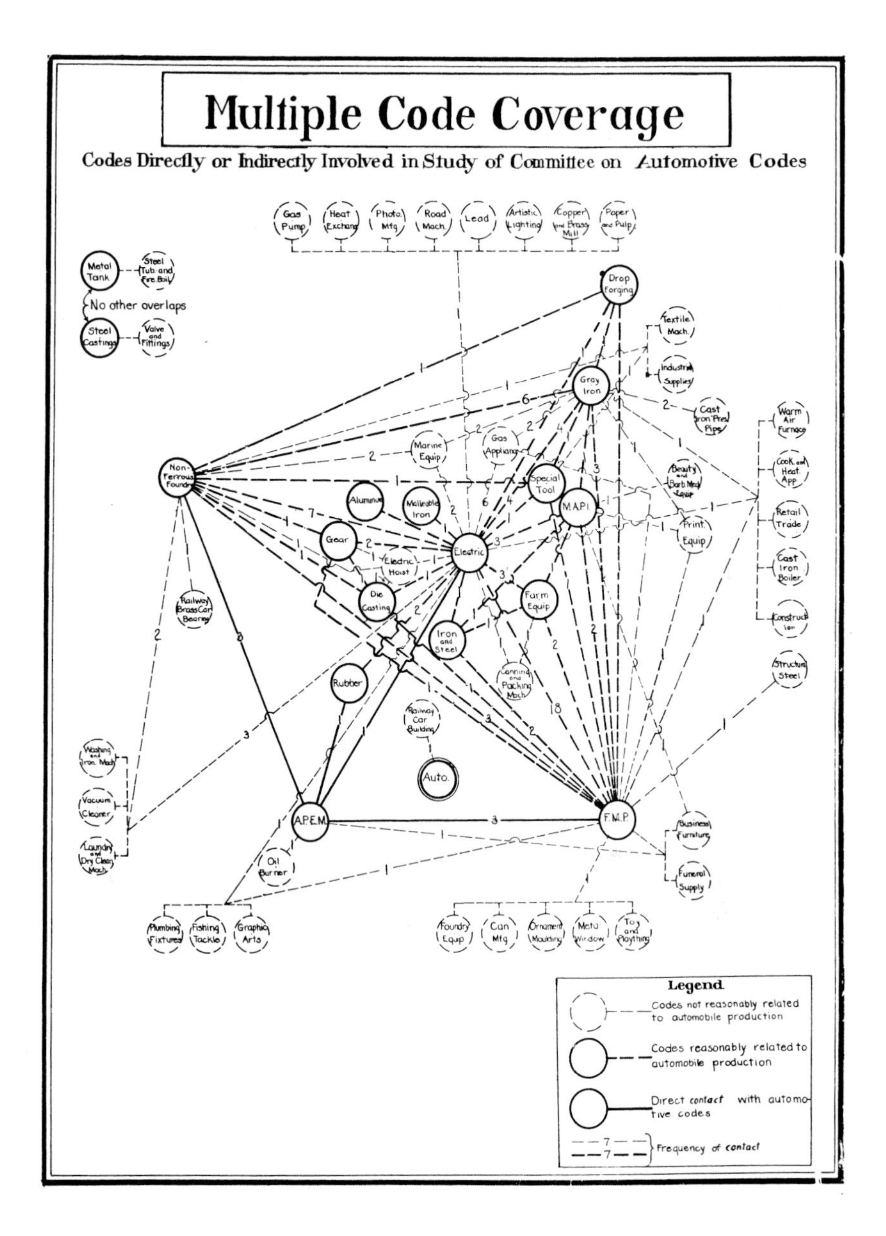

The New Deal's National Recovery Administration attempted to codify industry standards and practices in order to stabilize the economy and end downward spiraling wages and prices. In 1933, Sloan supported the effort. By early 1934, Sloan rebelled, believing that coercive government intervention and bureaucratic red tape were handcuffing his management of General Motors. This bewildering diagram, prepared by NRA officials, explains in part why Sloan came to regret his early support of the NRA.

The first woman to hold a cabinet position in the United States, Secretary of Labor Frances Perkins emerged as Sloan's nemesis during the Flint sit-down strike of 1936–37. As historian Arthur Schlesinger wryly observed, Perkins was "intent on beating sense into the heads of foolish people who resisted progress." To Perkins's way of thinking, Sloan was one of those foolish people.

Walter Carpenter, one of twentieth-century America's greatest corporate managers, became the first non–family member to become president of the Du Pont Corporation. He was, as well, a board member of General Motors. The warm but sometimes sharp correspondence between Sloan and Carpenter contains many gems, including Carpenter's savvy attempts to convince Sloan that cooperating with the government during World War II was the only acceptable course of action, at the very least from a public relations point of view. Photograph courtesy Hagley Museum and Library.

FEDERAL BUREAU OF INVESTIGATION

Form No. 1
THIS CASE ORIGINATED AT DETROIT, MICHIGAN NY FILE NO. 100-355 OG

REPORT MADE AT	DATE WHEN MADE	PERIOD FOR WHICH MADE	REPORT MADE BY
NEW YORK CITY	8/2/41	7/16,25,31/41	L. A. LANGILLE

TITLE	CHARACTER OF CASE
ALFRED PRITCHARD SLOAN, JR.; GRAEME KEITH HOWARD, with aliases Graeme K. Howard, Graham K. Howard; JAMES DAVID MOONEY	INTERNAL SECURITY (G)

SYNOPSIS OF FACTS:

Confidential Informants of the New York Field Division confirm loyalty and allegiance to U.S. of subject MOONEY. Some indication that he is admirer of industrial efficiency of Nazis but disagrees with Nazi idealogy. His apparent attitude, explained by informants, is due to the large interests of General Motors in Germany which would require him to appear in favor of Nazi regime as a matter of business policy. Another confidential informant who had known MOONEY in Europe explained MOONEY's activities by stating that he had originally miscalculated in estimating that there would be 20 years peace in Europe as a result of which he authorized investing huge sums of money by General Motors in Germany and that in order to protect his position before the stockholders of the company, he had to maintain the appearance of holding certain sentiments which in fact he did not actually believe in.

- R U C -

REFERENCE: Report of Special Agent L. L. Tyler dated at Washington, D.C. 7/23/41.
Report of Special Agent L. A. Langille dated at New York City, 7/15/41.

COPIES DESTROYED

APPROVED AND FORWARDED: O. J. Donegan SPECIAL AGENT IN CHARGE

DO NOT WRITE IN THESE SPACES

100 - 25806 - 27 RECORDED INDEXED

COPIES OF THIS REPORT
5 - Bureau
2 - Detroit
3 - New York

AUG 1941

U.S. GOVERNMENT PRINTING OFFICE : 1941—O-291858

One of many documents generated by the World War II–era FBI investigation of GM executives Alfred Sloan, Graeme Howard, and James Mooney. The investigation focused on Mooney, who had received the Merit Cross of the German Eagle First-Class from Adolf Hitler on August 10, 1938. The FBI cleared all three men of any wrongdoing.

The new president was a Stanford-trained engineer. To the American people, to many around the world, Hoover was the "Great Engineer."[53] As was noted several chapters ago, during and then after World War I, while Sloan moved from riches to greater riches, the self-made multimillionaire mining engineer retired from the hunt for private gain and devoted his extraordinary administrative talents to saving Europe from starvation. Serving both Harding and Coolidge as secretary of commerce, Hoover became the most dynamic cabinet officer the nation had ever seen. He had won substantial popular support in 1927 when he had personally, and successfully, coordinated the giant relief effort that followed catastrophic Mississippi River floods (over 16 million acres of land flooded, some 160,000 houses lost, as many as 500 killed).[54]

Hoover was no politician. Before winning the presidency, he had run for only one prior office, that of treasurer of the Stanford student body. Shy by nature, gruff in manner, and a poor public speaker, he had no common touch. In the days prior to mass media exposure, such limitations in one seeking to lead a democratic nation were not fatal. Hoover's leadership was built on his extraordinary competence and his proven skills.

In general outlook, Hoover's views were not dissimilar to Sloan's. He, too, was a modern manager. He looked back not to the days of laissez faire and unfettered individualism. Instead, he sought to bring to government and to society new administrative methods built on notions of cooperation. Unlike his presidential predecessor, Calvin Coolidge, Hoover saw a useful role for government in the economy. Government, he believed, could help businessmen to work together, voluntarily, to coordinate America's dynamic economy and so reduce needless competition and wasteful practices. As secretary of commerce, he had coordinated efforts by various industries to standardize parts and to share useful information. The auto industry had been a forerunner in this movement. In 1921 the Society of Automotive Engineers (SAE), to which Sloan belonged, had overseen an industrywide effort to standardize voluntarily some 241 auto parts.[55] Such cooperation along voluntary lines made for certain efficiencies that produced economies benefiting all those who had the good fortune, proper skills, and accepted group identity to be included in America's world-leading free market system.

Volunteerism was key for Hoover. He in no way approved of government coercion of business. While running for president, Hoover had declared: "I have witnessed not only at home but abroad the many failures of government in business. I have seen its tyrannies, it injustices, its undermining of the very instincts which carry people forward to progress."[56]

Like Sloan, Hoover believed without reservation in a well-managed private enterprise system. Although he did not personally know Hoover, Sloan understood and approved of his principles.

In one socioeconomic regard, however, Hoover and Sloan did differ. Hoover had some sympathies for labor unions. In 1909, when he was still running his mining business, he wrote that labor unions are "normal and proper antidotes for unlimited capitalistic organization."[57] Hoover, to put it bluntly, was a progressive conservative. While Sloan would not so identify himself—he had not yet thought through his political beliefs sufficiently to attach any kind of label to himself—he would have been comfortable with Hoover's general approach to government. Sloan approved of the more progressive direction Hoover was taking the Republican Party, the party with which Sloan was quite comfortable if not yet actively committed. Neither Sloan nor Hoover could have imagined that Republican prosperity was soon to end.

MR. SLOAN GOES TO WASHINGTON

Like human, everyday wings
That he has not ever used,
Releasing his hair from his brain,
A kingfisher's crest, confused.

—James Dickey, "Drowning with Others"

Herbert Hoover had been careful when he promised Americans that "poverty will be banished from this nation." In this endeavor, he said, he would need "the help of God."[1] That help did not arrive in time for Hoover. Talented, intelligent, and disciplined, he was nonetheless to have a very bad presidency. Alfred Sloan's presidency of General Motors, during the first years of crash, panic, and contraction, would be better. He would feel compelled to operate in strange realms but he would emerge from the depths of the Great Depressions confident both in his beliefs and in the future of GM. The nation would, in his opinion, make poor choices during the first years of the Great Depression. He would not.

Herbert Hoover, the poor orphan who had become a millionaire mining engineer and then dedicated himself to public service, took over the presidency on March 4, 1929. During the first few months of his administration, economic confidence was sky-high—at least among those whose opinions were heard in newspapers, in boardrooms, and on Wall Street. Hoover and almost every other member of the economic and political elite expected the American economy to continue to expand. Unemployment was estimated at just 3 percent of the labor force (though no one really knew—the federal government, its bureaucrats still few in number, had not yet begun to calculate a reasonably accurate, official statistic). In the first quarter of 1929, the construction industry was strong, factory orders were high, and general domestic economic investment was running ahead of the previous quarter. The stock market continued to soar. John Raskob had picked the wrong presidential candidate but when his article promoting the stock market, "Everybody Ought to Be Rich," appeared in the early summer of 1929, he seemed on the money.

On September 3, the stock market reached yet another stunning high mark. Investors celebrated, unaware this would be the market's high point for many years to come. General Electric, a high-technology, new-economy stock, had gone from $128\frac{3}{4}$ on March 3, 1928 to $396\frac{1}{4}$ in just six months. RCA, known as Radio, top stock play for the exploding new media–new technology sector, was personally championed by GM's departed founder Billy Durant, who directly and indirectly had billions tied up in the market. Radio sold on September 3, 1929 for $505 a share, up 420 points from its original offering price in 1928 (when adjusted for stock splits). General Motors stock was not one of the highest flyers. Still, during the last eighteen months of the bull market it moved from $139\frac{3}{4}$ to $181\frac{7}{8}$ (adjusted for a $2\frac{1}{2}$ to 1 stock split)—a respectable 30 percent increase in value.[2]

A few insiders had the prescience to fear the extraordinary stock market speculation. Russell Leffingwell, perhaps the most farsighted of the Morgan bankers, wanted to cut off, or at least cut down on, broker loans. Such loans allowed speculators to buy on highly leveraged terms. In 1929, stock speculators could front as little as 10 percent of the total purchase price of a stock; the rest of the purchase price was arranged through borrowed money, easily paid back so long as share prices continued their upward march. It was called buying on margin.

A small chorus of Wall Street bankers joined their voices to Leffingwell's. Too many New York banks, they concluded, had loaned out too much money for highly speculative stock purchases. If the market corrected, numerous speculators would have to liquidate their stock holdings to pay off accounts that had fallen below the margin of their own investment (often, as said, as little as 10 percent of the purchase price). Such forced sales would put greater downward pressure on stock prices, which could cause more liquidation and, quite possibly, a situation in which people could not pay off their loans because hard-falling stock prices had destroyed their financial position. As a result, those bankers who had loaned the money to brokerage houses and to individual stock purchasers would face massive defaults, which would put their banks at risk and, in turn, could create a crisis in the American financial system.

Leffingwell and the others hoped that high interest rates would squeeze out some of the most speculative stock market operations. They may well have been wrong. In 1929 stock market returns had been so high that a couple of points extra interest might not have stopped speculators' borrowing. On the other hand, higher rates would certainly have reduced the numbers of those borrowing for less speculative but lower-return investment activities, thus contracting the overall economy. Leffingwell understood the problem. Still, he privately urged members of the Federal Reserve Bank to raise the federal discount rate substantially. He wanted to make broker loans more expensive for the speculators—and thus less tempting. The Fed bankers, concerned about the overall economy, chose not to follow Leffingwell's advice, tightening the discount rate only by a point during the summer of 1929. Leffingwell noted to his Morgan colleague, Thomas Lamont, "I expect we shall all have to reap the whirlwind."[3]

Billy Durant, while many hundreds of millions of dollars ahead, had not forgotten the unpleasantness of 1920–21. He feared that tight credit could panic the stock market. In April, he arranged a visit to the White House and told President Hoover that the market was fragile and that the president must keep the Fed from tightening money policy. Hoover was not sympathetic to Durant's fears. One of his first actions as president was to urge Richard Whitney, vice president of the New York Stock Exchange, to curb speculation. He agreed with Leffingwell and others that interest rates were too low and banks had too much money available for highly speculative loans. As a consequence, as noted earlier, Durant and several other major stock market bulls quietly began selling off large parts of their holdings.

For those on the lookout, signs of a more general economic trouble began to appear, or became more visible, throughout 1929. Over the summer, construction slowed down. Consumer spending declined. In just a few weeks time, business inventories shot upward. Wholesale prices began to drop. The faltering farm economy, more or less a drag on national economic growth since shortly after the end of World War I, began to weigh more heavily as other economic sectors lost forward momentum. Though largely out of the headlines during the Roaring Twenties, rural people still made up 40 percent of the American population. From 1926 onward, in the United States and around the world, crop prices, especially wheat and cotton, began to fall from global overproduction. Farm families bought even fewer consumer goods, like automobiles, that fueled the economic expansion of the 1920s.

At first, as other investment opportunities, such as business expansion or real estate development, lost their luster, money flowed into the markets. Plenty of the new money was used to secure broker loans, making for more margin buying. Brokerage houses continued to push margin buying as a way to increase stock purchases, which, in turn, increased stock broker commissions. About $7 billion in broker loans were outstanding by late 1929. For many small investors, as well as major players, the lure of margin buying, in the face of explosive stock market gains, was hard to resist. Speculators were leveraging relatively small amounts of money into spectacular returns, creating a number of well-publicized fortunes.

Share prices kept rising in the fall of 1929, even as a variety of economic indicators showed that corporate profits and consumer spending were not rising with them. This disconnect was not a good thing from a rational point of view. Some big investors had noted the economic slowdown earlier and had gotten out of the market. It was only a matter of time before many others decided that a certain irrational exuberance had taken over the stock market.

On October 23, 1929, for no particular reason (some say economic bad news from London gave a few cautious investors the jitters), the market broke. Shareholders, large and small, began to sell and then sell more as prices began to drop across the board. As a few of the most speculative issues took a particular drubbing, margin accounts began to be closed out putting a great deal of downward pressure on the market.

The next day, October 24, was much worse. It was "Black Thursday." Overnight, all kinds of investors across the country had lost their nerve. Most had held on through the sell-off the previous day. But as the market ticked downward again, hundreds and then thousands and then tens of thousands of investors demanded that their brokers sell out their positions. The panic was on. And again, as the market plummeted, many margin investors who might have stayed the course were forced out of the market to cover their loans. At the height of the sell-off, Thursday morning, for some of the most highly speculative stocks, buyers could not be found. Two hours after the market had opened, $10 billion in stock value had disappeared.

At noon, with panic spreading on the stock market floor and at brokerage houses around the country, several of Wall Street's grandest figures met. They were led by Thomas Lamont of the Morgan Bank. Morgan Bank historian Ron Chernow puts it perfectly: "For the last time, they enjoyed the heroic stature that the Jazz Age had conferred upon them."[4] The leading men of Wall Street worked up a pool of some $240 million aimed at stabilizing the market.

The next day, Friday, their cool heads seemed to have prevailed. The market stabilized. That day and over the weekend, while the market was closed, the nation's leaders tried to put a cheerful face on events. President Hoover did his part, reporting in his bland fashion: "The fundamental business of the country, that is production and distribution of commodities, is on a sound and prosperous basis."[5] Across the land, brokers and bankers and leaders of Big Business gamely assured the American people that all was well. Sloan joined in. With unusual directness, he stated, "Business is sound."[6] Exactly what Sloan meant by this phrase is not certain. He did, of course, believe in the essential soundness of the private enterprise system. He also knew, based on GM's own data, that the American economy in the fall of 1929 was fragile and, in all likelihood, was contracting. Whatever his exact meanings or motives, the leading newspapers reported what at least sounded like his encouraging words.

GM's record of the last few years, Sloan knew, had made him an industrial leader. In the past, John Raskob, who enjoyed such things, had usually served as corporate spokesperson on matters relating to the stock market, the economy, and finance. His departure in 1928 had left some uncertainty about how to convey GM's perspectives on economic matters. Sloan, his duties evolving once again, was pondering how to sustain GM's public persona on economic and financial matters, even as he himself began to feel the absence Raskob's departure had created.

Alas, the comments of Sloan and the many other business and political optimists were not enough. Monday, the market fell. Brokers, fearing loan default, pressured investor sales and forced the liquidation of margin accounts. General Motors, whose stock had not been as hard hit as the most speculative issues, took a tremendous beating. GM shareholders sold in an attempt to recoup what money they could from the market before it was too late.

Tuesday was much worse. Panic hit again, but even harder. Some 16 million shares were sold, a record that would not be toppled until the end of the 1960s. At the end of the day, overall stock prices were down 25 percent from just a couple of days earlier. Two weeks later, the market had lost 40 percent of its value. By November 13, 1929, GM's stock price had fallen almost exactly 50 percent from the market's high point just over two months earlier. Some thought the market had bottomed out and shopped for what they trusted were bargains. In the short term, they were right. The stock prices of U.S. Steel, GE, GM, AT&T, and many other leading industrial corporations came back at the end of 1929 and gained ground through the early spring of 1930. Then, it all went bad. And the longer the seemingly prudent investor hung on, the worse he or she was hit. Inexorably, from June 1930 through the summer of 1932, the market fell. On July 8, 1932, to get a bit ahead of the story, General Motors stock sold for $8 a share (as did U.S. Steel, which had sold for $262 a share in September 1929).[7]

The conventional wisdom is that the stock market crash of October 1929 was more a catalyst than a cause of the years of economic depression that followed it. And surely, the length and depth of America's hard times, and the nearly worldwide depression, is not directly related to the stock market debacle. But the failure of the market and the revelations of unethical and unsavory practices by brokerage houses and Wall Street banks that followed the crash had a great deal to do with the politics of the 1930s. The crash changed the image Americans had of the big men of the capitalist system. Stock market boosters and Wall Street bankers, always a suspect group in the eyes of Main Street and rural Americans, lost the "heroic stature" jazz-age apostles as diverse as President Calvin Coolidge and Bruce Barton had bestowed on them. Businessmen were out. Within a few years time, politicians, social reformers, labor leaders, and populist demagogues had replaced business leaders as the people's champions.

This reduced public stature did not mean that corporate chiefs and Wall Street operators lost all influence or credibility within elite political and policy-making circles. Far from it. But the exercise of their power at a time of economic despair, heightened political threats, and increased fragmentation within business circles did demand a certain amount of retooling. Corporate leaders would find that staving off political threats while hunting for hard-to-find profits demanded strategic reorientation. Alfred Sloan would turn his talents in these directions. Remember his adage: "Everyone of us has a certain talent in a certain direction and in other directions we may be completely devoid of talent."[8] Sloan was too smart to be entirely clueless about anything to which he turned his mind. But like the history courses he had been forced to take at MIT so long before, which he found both useless and ridiculous, politics during the Great Depression would not be a subject in which he would do well.

Alfred Sloan, like most of his friends and business associates, did not see the market collapse coming. He seems not to have sold off any stock before the fall, nor did he sell any during or after. It is unlikely that he found any irony in the collapse of his holdings in the special stock offerings with which the Morgan Bank had supplied him. Allegheny, a mismanaged holding company, would fall particularly hard and Sloan was annoyed by the mess of its affairs. How he felt as he watched his shares in

General Motors plummet in value is unrecorded. Well acquainted with many leading Wall Street bankers through his clubs and corporate board memberships, he probably did not agree with treasury secretary Andrew Mellon's acid comment to President Hoover that the group "deserved" their comeuppance.[9]

More significantly, Sloan better understood the general state of the economy than many of those who shared their thoughts with Hoover. Commerce secretary Robert P. Lamont deduced that "recent fluctuations" (the stock market crash) would only "curtail the buying power, especially of luxuries, of those who suffered losses in the market crash. There are present today none of the underlying factors which have been associated with or have preceded the declines in business in the past."[10] On the face of it, Lamont seemed to have the facts on his side. Only about 1.5 million out of 150 million Americans owned stock in October 1929. But that number was deceiving, and masked other, more critical facts regarding the American economy at the end of 1929.

The American people as a whole had enjoyed tremendous economic expansion in the 1920s. The aggregate increase in national income, however, hid the tremendous disparity in the distribution of that income. Most Americans in the 1920s had seen only modest improvements in their incomes. In 1929, one of the first American public-policy think tanks, the Brookings Institution, issued a report that had shocked the few intellectuals and policy makers who read it: the nation's richest 27,500 families had a total income equal to the poorest 11,450,000 families. Despite massive improvement's in the nation's productive capacities, only about 30 percent of all Americans had family incomes over $2,500 ($24,323 in 2000 dollars). And about 80 percent of American families had no savings whatsoever in 1929.

The mass consumer society made possible by assembly-line manufacturing, mass marketing, consumer credit, advertising, and high-wage employment was balanced precariously on a minority of American families. It was estimated that fewer than 8 million families had enough disposable income to keep buying the flood of new goods American manufacturers were capable of bringing to the marketplace. By late 1929 the American economy was already slowing down, in part due to the relatively thin ranks of Americans prosperous enough to keep consumer spending growing. The stock market crash, while only directly affecting a million and a half individuals, was nevertheless a very hard blow to those American families whose disposable income had given the Roaring Twenties its economic oomph. As they bought less, fewer good were produced, less production was needed, which caused layoffs, which lowered aggregate national income (remember, no national unemployment compensation system existed), which further reduced consumption, all of which accelerated a downward-coursing economic spiral.[11]

General Motors had a great year in 1928. Profits reached $276,468,000. No corporation had ever made that much money. The new year started even better, and not just for GM but for the auto industry in general. Car factories churned out vehicles. Everyone expected 1929 to run even ahead of glorious 1928. By May, however, auto and truck sales were proving somewhat disappointing, less so, actually, for GM and Ford than for most of the other manufacturers. "Bad weather," was the industry consensus. June and July brought no sales relief. The weather (it had been an unusually cool spring in large parts of the country) was still blamed by the more sanguine.

Sloan doubted that the weather had anything to do with the sales figures. He pored over his statistical reports as did GM men throughout the divisions. The reports had been created for just such a tricky market. While most other auto concerns kept manufacturing vehicles well ahead of sales, GM tried to match production to sales. Sloan would not allow GM to become an overstocked monstrosity. He had been there, after all, in the recessionary era of 1920–21, when Durant's overproduction and overcommitment of funds had brought GM to the brink of disaster.

By midyear, GM production was slowed down. Still, even as the stock market collapse began in October, GM's business remained relatively strong. And when Ford chose to cut prices in November to punch up faltering consumer demand, GM saw no need to follow. Still, Sloan saw difficulties ahead. On October 4, 1929, almost three weeks ahead of the crash, he wrote a general policy statement widely distributed throughout the corporation. He warned that the rapid expansion of the last few years was not likely to continue: "What I am trying to convey is the thought that in the future it should be the prime consideration of every division and subsidiary to put the energy previously directed toward expansion and development into the hardest kind of a drive in the direction of economy."[12] Sloan foresaw a slowdown, though as he later admitted, "I was, of course, not pessimistic enough."[13]

GM, despite the warning signs, still turned out too many cars in late 1929 and early 1930. Back in 1927, in one of Sloan's frequent attempts to maintain amiable relations with car dealers—the most difficult members of the GM family—he had stated that it "is absolutely against the policy of General Motors to require dealers to take cars in excess of what they should properly take." But as one GM historian, Anthony Patrick

O'Brien, has written, "the number of cars that dealers 'should properly take' turned out to be quite an elastic concept in late 1929 and early 1930."[14] Despite Sloan's policy, and maybe even because he had articulated it so clearly to them, a number of dealers felt betrayed in early 1930 when GM's sales divisions forced them to fill their lots with what they knew were more cars than they could sell.

Even as GM dealers scrambled to sell cars in the early days of the downturn, many of their competitors faced far worse. Sloan watched with interest as a trend begun earlier in the 1920s began to take on greater force. As the overall auto demand slid, the smaller manufacturers showed a decided inability to compete against GM's organizational might and Ford's powerful market position. Already by 1929, dozens of auto manufacturers had been driven out of the industry. Only fifteen remained, and several of them were on shaky ground. The Chrysler Corporation, begun only in 1925 by Sloan's dearest friend, Walter Chrysler, bucked the trend by turning out an abbreviated GM-like range of vehicles. By the end of 1929, the so-called Big Three—GM, Ford, and Chrysler—sold over 75 percent of the market.[15] The down market was killing off many of the vulnerable, smaller companies.

Sloan was not surprised by the slowdown in car sales in late 1929. He had been worrying about a stagnant American market for new cars for several years, even as GM sales had increased. His trips to Europe in the late 1920s had been focused on that problem and on the opportunity international development afforded General Motors for growth and increased profits. In the early spring of 1929 Sloan had traveled to Europe to visit GM plants and to expand GM investment in the growing European market. While in France, he ran headlong into a problem that would plague his international strategy, both in the United States and abroad—economic nationalism. French newspapers, fueled by French auto interests, attacked "American domination" of the European market.

Sloan met the attacks head on: "I was in Europe ninety days ago. . . . I am back again because of the great importance these markets now have for us. The American car is coming into its own in Europe. The people over here are realizing more and more that automobiles are not a luxury but a necessity and an economic benefit. As this realization develops, so will the sale of our product."[16] At the beginning of the decade, Sloan had been one of several GM executives who had visited the Citroën works in France. They had concluded that Citroën was too poorly run to acquire. As a result, GM had begun its own assembly operations in France, an effort necessitated in part by that country's exorbitant tariffs on imported cars (a minimum of 45 percent by 1924). Sloan, in responding to the public attacks on GM's supposed "American domination," was not telling the French to buy GM cars made in America. He was far more politic, urging France's middle class to buy the more affordable American-brand cars that were being assembled in France. Profits from GM's overseas operations flowed back to the United States, a fact Sloan saw no need to mention.

During the same trip, Sloan launched a much more aggressive plan of expansion in Germany. In April 1929 he oversaw the purchase of a controlling interest in Germany's biggest auto producer, Opel. The cost was only $26 million, a relatively small piece of the huge capital reserves garnered from the previous year's profits. This investment was along Sloan's preferred lines: the takeover of an up-and-running, successful operation that could be integrated into GM's decentralized administrative model.

Sloan returned to Germany in October 1929, shortly before the stock market crash, to explain GM's overseas operations to a meeting of Opel car dealers. He told them that Opel would remain, essentially, a German company. German executives would run operations just as German workers would continue to build Opels. German dealers, he assured, would continue to sell to the German people. He explained to them that American executives would be involved in Opel only at the policy level. And he bluntly stated that American-made GM cars would continue to compete for market share in Germany. Sloan concluded with the closest he could come to a pep talk:

> We have at all times advocated . . . the highest standard of living for our employees, have advanced the interest of our dealers, have maintained the highest standards of product quality, all for the purpose of supplying customers with the best possible motor car. . . . The motor car contributes more to the wealth of the United States than agriculture. The automobile industry is a wealth-creating industry.[17]

Mainly, Sloan believed what he told the German dealers. Opel was an excellent investment in 1929. Sloan had no way to see what a headache it would shortly become.

Back in the United States, Sloan publicly promoted the idea of pursuing further exports of American-built GM cars to foreign markets (almost no imported autos or auto parts competed successfully in the American high-volume marketplace). Given the reality of the now immense used-car market and the lack of buying power available to tens of millions of Americans, Sloan believed in the necessity of developing the international vehicle market.[18]

GM's foreign investments did not go unnoticed by politicians in the postcrash hunt for villains. For the first time, General Motors came under political attack. For the first time, Alfred Sloan was personally lambasted by a politician, and a leading Republican one at that. Indiana senator James ("Sunny Jim") Watson, majority leader of the Senate Republicans, famous for his old-fashioned political oratory (frequently punctuated by the homey phrase, "but by the eternals!") accused Sloan of selling out his countrymen.[19] First, Senator Watson said, Sloan made a fortune for himself and for General Motors in the United States. Then, "to produce where wages were only two-fifths those paid in the United States," Sloan moved his corporation's capital, and with it American jobs, to foreign lands. "In other words," said the conservative, isolationist, anti-free-trade senator:

> These great masters of production, after having enriched themselves and their corporations in this country, are using the wealth they thus obtained to set up competitive industry in foreign countries and to produce their products by men who receive from a quarter to a half the wages paid in those factories in the United States. General Motors wants free trade in those articles so that the corporation can compete in our market with the product of their own mills in this country where they pay 50 per cent more wages than in the competing production in foreign countries. General Motors wants to destroy the very conditions which made possible the accumulation of that wealth by transferring that production to foreign countries.[20]

Watson insisted that high tariffs, embodied in the proposed Smoot–Hawley legislation, would stop the flight of American investment capital abroad and the unfair competition it unleashed on homegrown American producers. "If this bill is passed," orated the longtime champion of high tariffs, "this nation will be on the upgrade, financially, economically, and commercially within thirty days, and within a year from this date we shall have regained the peak of prosperity."[21] Small-town America's Main Street, represented by conservative, insular men like Senator Jim Watson of Rushville, Indiana, no longer looked with so much awe and respect at Wall Street financiers and Big Business leaders like Alfred P. Sloan Jr.

Sloan must have been incensed. Almost nothing GM produced abroad, except profits, came back to the United States. GM did produce overseas for foreign consumption, but it also sold American-made GM products around the world. Watson's remarks were completely off base. Publicly, at least, Sloan made no direct comments to defend GM business policy. He was, however, willing to fight the general impression created by Watson's remarks.

Sloan believed in free trade. GM's position in the world economy alone made such a belief a necessity. He tried to make the case publicly, even as he saw which way the political winds were blowing. "All nations," Sloan argued, "should encourage the greatest possible volume of world trade by means of facilitating the exchange of goods and services."[22] Higher tariffs, Sloan believed could only hurt competitive American industries, reduce world trade, and exacerbate the contemporary economic situation.

Sloan's criticisms of the tariff legislation were met by Senator Watson with more personal attacks: "Mr. Sloan issued statements denouncing this pending Bill. . . . The motives of these international financiers and industrialists are obvious and portend only unemployment or cheapened labor in this country."[23] Politicians, Sloan was discovering, played by different rules than the ones that governed his corporation. Despite his protests, and the independent opinion of nearly a thousand liberal economists rounded up via petition by University of Chicago professor Paul Douglas, the politicians were fast moving toward protectionist legislation—the infamous Smoot–Hawley tariff—that would, as Sloan knew, further damage both the American and the international economy.

The downturn in the economy did not go unnoticed by President Hoover. To restore fast-fading public confidence, the president called a series of White House meetings of business, farm, and even labor leaders. On November 21, Sloan dutifully attended a meeting of the leading men of industry. John Kenneth Galbraith, author of the classic *The Great Crash,* acerbically described this meeting as "one of the oldest, most important—and, unhappily, one of the least understood—rites in American life. This is the rite of the meeting which is called not to do business but to do no business." The "no-business meeting," Galbraith explained, served

> to create the impression that business is being done . . . . Even though nothing of importance is said or done, men of importance cannot meet without the occasion seeming important. Even the commonplace observation of the head of a large corporation is still the statement of the head of a large corporation. What it lacks in content it gains in power from the assets back of it. . . . The no-business meetings at the White House were a practical expression of laissez-faire. No positive action resulted.[24]

Galbraith, the wittiest economist of the last half of the twentieth century, wrote not in total sympathy with Hoover's program.

Sloan was impressed by Hoover's exercise in public psychology. Consumer confidence and investors' confidence, he believed, must be manipulated to restore economic progress. With each passing month, as troubles multiplied, he would ponder the means by which he could play a role in restoring economic spirits. Without that restoration, he knew, investors would not invest, consumers would hold back on purchases, and GM would not prosper. Simulating economic confidence in a free market society, Sloan understood, could stimulate economic growth. Sloan, the rational corporate manager who believed all problems could be solved by collecting the right data, pondered how he could convince the American people to ignore the economic facts staring them in the face and to act on faith. If they could be convinced to spend their money—even as unemployment or its specter haunted so many of them—they could reverse the downward economic spiral.

Sloan hoped he could rationalize, somehow, consumer capitalism. He understood that the least rational and controllable aspect of the private enterprise system was the consumer, so often driven by irrational desires and fears. He was encountering a kind of paradox: though seeking a rational economic order, to effectively manage the national economic problem of aggregate consumer demand it was necessary to use irrationality; to develop techniques that would manipulate consumers' emotions. The lessons he had learned from selling cars in the 1920s—for example, that style sold better than economic efficiency or mechanical quality—he would begin to apply to a larger public sphere.

By 1930, Sloan knew he had to expand his activities to fight both the economic contraction and the dangerous political fallout it was producing for General Motors. These activities, he believed, must always be tied to the primary goal of ensuring the profitability of General Motors. On occasion, personal emotions would enter into Sloan's decision-making process. But such feelings were almost always unwelcome. The facts were enough: the auto industry, in all its myriad manifestations, had become the largest single engine of economic progress in the nation. If it faltered, so would the nation's economy. Likewise, if the nation's economy faltered, so would its leading sector.

As the car and truck business slackened, Sloan sought new opportunities. General Motors had never been just a car and truck company. Profits had flowed in from many revenue streams. While GM had not avoided some overproduction in early 1930, the record profits of the previous two years meant that the corporation was financially fit. Sloan began to seek out new businesses. He moved GM into radio production. The company invested in aviation. Based on Kettering's groundbreaking research in diesel engines, GM acquired diesel-engine manufacturing capacities (soon to be a highly profitable enterprise). Sloan refused to be passive in the face of a downturn in the vehicle market. The corporation was dedicated to making money for its shareholders and Sloan would do everything possible to find profits even in an economic depression.

Managing the "men" of General Motors, by which Sloan always meant his fellow executives, also demanded greater creativity in the midst of widespread pessimism and growing gloom. In an odd twist on this theme, Sloan announced that for $2 million he had purchased a state-of-the-art, clipper-bow-type yacht in early 1930 to help corporate morale. The yacht—named *Rene,* after his wife—would serve, he stated, as a "floating conference room." He wanted the key men of General Motors to join him on regular occasions on board, away from their offices and everyday business routines, so that they might breathe in the invigorating sea air and "think" more freely and expansively about new directions for the corporation. In fact, Sloan had ordered the custom-built yacht from the Pusey and Jones Corporation of Wilmington, Delaware, long before the depression had begun, undoubtedly at the urging of his wife, whose love of the sea has already been commented on, and by his friends (including Fred Fisher, who had ordered a matching vessel at the same time). At an impressive 236 feet, the yacht was hardly going to remain a secret; seemingly, Sloan chose to make public his extraordinary purchase in order to control publicity about it, while demonstrating his commitment to fighting the economic slowdown through continued consumer spending.

Sloan paid for the yacht in a rather complex fashion. As a tax measure (personal income taxes were small by contemporary standards—though the New Deal would soon change that—but more than sufficiently annoying to Sloan at the time), Sloan had set up a private holding company. He named it the "Rene Corporation" after his wife, who was the cotrustee of the company. The Rene Corporation actually bought the yacht, which it chartered to Sloan. It was all perfectly legal and several of Sloan's friends had set up similar holding companies to purchase their homes, cars, yachts, and other expensive items so as to minimize their income taxes.[25]

While no record of the ocean-loving Irene Sloan's unaccompanied use of the yacht has been found, it is possible that between GM junkets she cruised the seas with her friends. Perhaps, once in a great while, she and Alfred stood at the rail and watched the Long Island coastline move by at fifteen knots an hour, under the moonlight, while sipping dry martinis (Sloan did enjoy the occasional martini cocktail, newspaper reports of his temperance to the contrary). A charming photo taken around 1932 shows the Sloans yachting aboard the *Rene,* accompanied by Walter and Della Chrysler and another couple. At least on that occasion, the *Rene* was not simply a "floating conference room," as Sloan described his yacht for public consumption. The formally posed photo shows a remarkably informal Sloan. He has traded his usual tailored suit for a light-colored cardigan touched up with a jaunty tie. (Not surprisingly, Sloan did not go in for a more nautical yachting outfit.) Walter Chrysler stands to his left. In keeping with his personality, Chrysler is laughing and his hands are gently wrapped around his wife's shoulders. Sloan stares at the camera; his nervous hands are perched on the back of his wife's chair back, almost but not quite touching her.[26]

While the yacht purchase, whatever had been said publicly, was not strictly for business purposes, Sloan was absolutely determined to create new forums for his top people at GM to meet together in congenial settings and get to know one another better. Over the summer of 1930, as the economy contracted, Sloan decided to hold a lavish conference for GM's leading men at the Greenbriar, a tony resort located at White Sulphur Springs, in West Virginia. Sloan wrote to John Raskob, alienated from Sloan but still a director of the GM board, defending the conference expense at a time of declining sales volume:

> The question may arise in your mind as to whether the expense of such a gathering is justified under prevailing circumstances. We naturally gave consideration to this point and it seemed to us that the benefits to be derived and the opportunity presented of placing our problems before the organization, together with the good-will that will be developed by a better understanding that such a meeting should create, both as to our objectives and of each other individually, warranted us in going ahead with the program, irrespective of present conditions.[27]

In his wordy letter to Raskob, Sloan outlined a commitment that would guide him throughout the downturn: GM's executives would not turn on one another during hard times. They would pull together as one. No senior executives would lose their jobs over GM's declining revenues.

In August 1930, Sloan shared with Kettering his blossoming feelings on the need for corporate solidarity in a time of difficulties. With the copper-cooled engine difficulties receding into the distant past, he and the productive Kettering were becoming increasingly friendly. Sloan was finding his quirky research director ever more valuable for advancing both GM's public image and profitable opportunities. In unusually flowery language he told Kett: "I feel that every opportunity should be developed of cultivating a more intimate acquaintanceship and a closer bond of sympathy and understanding among all of those who are carrying the important executive responsibility of the corporation."[28] Though the phrase would not appeal to Sloan, he had decided to use corporate resources in the midst of economic uncertainties to build up the "class cohesion" of his top executives and GM board members.

In holding the conference, Sloan would spend the money to instill the lesson that corporate cooperation and corporate coordination would get them through periods of contractions just as successfully as through expansions. Over three days of golf, formal presentations, informal conversations, and many heavy meals, the 241 leading GM men refined their corporate connections.[29] GM was not just a symbol on a stock ticker. Nor was it the unified "family" of assembly-line workers, foreman, white-collar men, dealers, customers, and shareholders. When it came down to it, GM was a corporate enterprise run by the key executives and members of the board—every one a white man—whom Sloan had invited to his executive conference. Throughout the Great Depression, Sloan personally oversaw an annual luxury retreat for the key executives and board members of GM.

Is it by now unnecessary to say that at these conferences Sloan played no golf and wore no short pants? In 1930, Sloan was fifty-five. His silvery-gray hair was receding. He was no longer thin as a rail, though he was by no means portly. His light woolen suits fit perfectly, more boxy as was the fashion and cut full at the shoulder. A hearing aid was now a necessity but Sloan still carried himself with the same taut, nervous energy. He never complained about any ailment. He gave no indication that his age slowed him down. In sum, Sloan cut a dashing figure at the retreats. He was doing what he thought necessary to buck up his men in the face of unfavorable economic conditions. He, himself, was ready to do whatever was necessary to keep GM profitable.

As the economy continued to contract, Sloan considered numerous plans, including international investments, to improve GM's financial situation. As the Smoot–Hartley imbroglio indicated, Sloan's zeal for opening new markets went well beyond the conventional wisdom of many Americans. In early 1932, he became involved in a plan involving the sale of a huge fleet of used American cars to the Soviet Union. Sloan hoped to convince Hoover's new secretary of commerce (his old friend Roy Chapin), to champion the idea.

Chapin, before his cabinet appointment, had run the Hudson Motor Company. He had also been the president of the National Automobile Chamber of Commerce (NACC). He and Sloan had long been on friendly terms. They had first met in 1917 when Sloan, though working for Durant at GM, still put a good deal of his energies into selling Hyatt bearings to the industrial market at large. Sloan had taken Chapin and a number of other vehicle manufacturers on a carefree trip by rail to Fremont, Nebraska. Sloan took no particular pleasure in such junkets but they were a part of the salesmanship game and he did what was required. Once in Fremont, they attended the annual national tractor exhibition, watching state-of-the-art motorized tractors perform in Nebraska farm fields. Traveling from Chicago in a private, custom Pullman, attached to their own "club car," complete with barber, comfortable bathing facilities, and undoubtedly liquid refreshments, they had themselves a good deal of fun. Chapin, in particular, had found Sloan a charming host. Over the years the two maintained a friendly, if not intimate, relationship.[30]

Sloan outlined for Secretary Chapin a plan to use money supplied by the recently created Reconstruction Finance Corporation (RFC) to help the Soviet Union buy American used cars. Sloan understood that the RFC had not been created by the Hoover administration to loan money to foreign governments (mainly, it existed to loan emergency funds to American banks to prevent their insolvency—some twenty-three hundred had closed their doors in 1931). Sloan was also aware that the U.S. government did not recognize the communistic, atheistic Soviet government, making a nation-to-nation loan more than a little awkward. This particular diplomatic problem Sloan found entirely unfortunate. He wrote Chapin:

> In studying the proposal [to use the RFC to finance the car sales to the USSR] it seemed to me that in view of the attitude of mind that existed in Washington with respect to the whole Russian situation—which to tell you frankly, I am entirely out of accord—any plan, irrespective of how sound it might be otherwise, would just be impossible. In view of the fact, however, that I have a very close friend, Colonel Hugh L. Cooper, who I believe is closer to the "powers that be" in Russian than any other individual and who recently left for four months' stay in Russia, I took the liberty of asking if he would discuss the matter with Mr. Stalin, whom he stays several days with

each time he visits Russia, just to see if there was any possibility of it—all other things being possible.[31]

Sloan believed that American political pressure to restrain American trade opportunities in the Soviet Union was ridiculous. The Soviet Union was unaffected by the capitalist world's economic contraction. It needed to import a variety of manufactured goods. Here was opportunity for commerce.

Sloan's business interest in the Soviet Union actually had begun to develop almost two years earlier. In the fall of 1930, James D. Mooney, president of General Motors Overseas Corporation since 1922, toured the Soviet Union. He liked what he saw and by phone and letter told Sloan that GM should "capitaliz[e] upon the opportunities that exist there." Mooney laid out his general international investment policy for Sloan:

> I confined my official observations very definitely . . . to the economic considerations in which, as a business man, I am exclusively interested. The questions which I asked myself in this connection involved only one which touched upon the political aspect of things in any way, and that was the question that we have to ask ourselves in any market—including the United States—where we contemplate doing business; the question, simply as to whether or not the Government is stable.

Mooney believed that the Soviet Union, under the control of Josef Stalin, was "as stable as any Government in the world."

Mooney made it clear that he was not passing judgment, one way or the other, on Stalin or the Bolshevik government he ran: "I think that as business men we cease to be interested in whether that government is autocratic or democratic or bolshevik, or whatever it happens to be in the hands of Methodists or Catholics or Mohammadans or Atheists." Mooney concluded with a note of humor:

> If my trip to Russia convinced me of anything, it convinced me that we cannot give credence to half the detrimental things we hear about Russia, any more than we could believed the things we heard about Germany in 1917, or the things we hear on every side today here in Europe about that most imperialistic and despicable of all nations—the United States. There is so much sheer bunk going around on every side to-day that if we really swallowed a tenth of it, we would never invest a penny in any undertaking.[32]

Sloan was in complete accord with Mooney. How nation's chose to govern themselves, except as it interfered with General Motors' business, was of no concern to Sloan. And the experiences of Hugh Cooper in the Soviet Union only confirmed Mooney's favorable appraisal. Cooper was no Bolshevik sympathizer. He was an engineer of extraordinary competence and accomplishments. Like Sloan's first engineering mentor, Henry Leland of Cadillac, Cooper (ten years older than Sloan) had gone directly into engineering without benefit of higher education. By the 1890s, he had become a leading engineer in hydroelectricity projects. In 1901, Cooper founded a highly successful consulting firm and traveled the world building hydroelectric dams. In 1927 he became the chief consulting engineer for the Dnieprostroy hydroelectric project in the Soviet Union, Stalin's showpiece of Soviet industry and technology. Between 1927 and 1932, Cooper had spent between one and two months every year at the construction site at the falls of the Dnieper River. He reported that he was treated with great consideration by the Soviet authorities; they even imported his favorite American food. Cooper had, as Sloan stated, enjoyed regular meetings with Stalin and was the first foreigner to receive the Soviets' Order of the Red Star.

Not a man prone to enthusiasms or overstatements, Cooper had shared his positive accounts of the Soviet Union and Stalin with Sloan. Cooper assured Sloan that Stalin would take a reasonable approach to business matters if they were in the Soviet interest. Stalin, Cooper also believed, was remarkably intelligent and "kindly minded," if a bit too "firm and confident that their economic plans are correct."[33] While perhaps not a keen student of human psychology (few people would share the view that Stalin was "kindly minded"), Cooper did have an excellent business sense and he persuasively outlined the economic advantages of working with the Soviet government.

Sloan was convinced. By 1932 he chose to ally General Motors with the American–Soviet Chamber of Commerce, presided over by Cooper. Sloan was far from alone in making this decision; General Electric, Westinghouse, Chase National Bank, American Locomotive Company, and many other financial and industrial concerns participated in the American–Soviet Chamber of Commerce. Given the current economic realities, Sloan wrote Chapin in 1932, business with the Soviets could not be overlooked. Inducing the Soviets to purchase a large number of used cars would provide a positive boost to the American car industry.

Sloan's strong support for a kind of "constructive engagement" with the arch-communist, murderous Soviet dictator Josef Stalin did not represent a break with the thinking of most major American industrialists, as the membership of the American–Soviet Chamber of Commerce demonstrated. Of course, some did oppose trade with the Soviets based on ideological and moral grounds. Back in 1927, Julian Barnes, president of the Chamber of Commerce, had given the more conventional American business approach to the Bolsheviks: "Trade relations prosper only when founded on mutual good faith and integrity and no such foundation exists today in the whole Russian record of repudiation, of conflicting and confiscatory edicts, of bad faith and misrepresentation in international relations, and in the treatment of their own people."[34] While such sentiments were certainly in line with a staunch commitment to a high standard of conduct, with decreasing trade and plummeting internal demand numerous American businessmen sought stronger trade arrangements with the Soviet Union in the early 1930s. Henry Ford had never accepted anti-Soviet trade policy and right before the stock market crash had signed major trade and investment agreements with the Soviet government. Sloan, like GM's head of overseas operations, James Mooney, found morally based approaches to trade issues and international investment, such as the fierce anticommunist attitudes espoused in the 1920s by presidents Harding, Coolidge, and Hoover, almost entirely irrelevant to sound business decision making.

Sloan failed to convince Chapin to support a giant, government-sponsored used-car loan for the Soviet Union. Colonel Cooper may well have discussed used cars with Stalin, perhaps while sipping Stalin's favorite Georgian wine, *Khvanchkara,* or over after-dinner shots of *Peretsovka.* But Sloan, having received no clear support from Chapin, did not write back to the secretary of commerce explaining the results of any such meeting.[35] As was usually the case, Sloan's plan for RFC support of a Soviet trade deal was not as improbable as it might seem; less than a year later, the RFC provided a $4 million credit to the Soviets (via the Soviet trade corporation, Amtorg) to purchase American cotton.[36]

The used-car plan had come to Sloan via one of his many correspondents, a Buffalo, New York manufacturer.[37] During the early years of the economic contraction, Sloan was constantly importuned by a stream of individuals. As he was remarkably open to possible avenues of economic stimulation and accustomed to churning rapidly through piles of paper in search of useful data, he often was willing to correspond with a great variety of economic promoters. At times this proved awkward; his eager, sometimes desperate, correspondents took his casual interest as sincere commitment to their schemes.

In the fall of 1932, for example, a reasonably reputable Cleveland stock broker named John T. Blossom took great offense at Sloan for failing to move forward on his hazy plan to launch a national "Million and One Campaign" to sell automobiles. Blossom had met with Sloan in Detroit for an hour in early 1932 and was under the impression that Sloan would fund the effort (and pay Blossom a substantial commission). By September, however, Sloan refused even to answer Blossom's numerous, increasingly agitated letters, phone calls, and wires. Blossom complained to Secretary of Commerce Chapin: "His secretary, Mr. Brandt, stated that . . . he had been so busy with the affairs of the company that he had not found the time to reply, but would do so at an early date. We have still to hear from him."[38] By 1932, Sloan was simply inundated with outside requests for his support in all matter of public and private work. These demands came even as his direct responsibilities at General Motors were all the more demanding.

Above all, Sloan's first concern throughout the early 1930s—as in all other times—was the maintenance of General Motors' profitability. He tried to parcel out his time in a rational fashion that reflected that imperative. So while schemes abounded, some of which caught his eye, he tried to put the most energy into the most pressing matters.

As the economy continued to decline, Sloan found it necessary to become more engaged in work outside of General Motors. Political forces—an amalgam of Democrats and Republicans—were increasingly impinging themselves on General Motors operations. Sloan was particularly worried about federal tax legislation and a variety of budgetary measures being considered by Congress. Sloan had no idea that over the next eight or so years he would be spending a considerable amount of his time, energy, and money fighting federal public policies and the politicians who championed them.

As a first step in countering what he considered anti-industry policy initiatives, Sloan began to spend numerous hours working in coordination with the other leading men of the auto business—with the not inconsequential exception of the uncooperative Henry Ford. Most of these cooperative efforts occurred through the works of the National Automobile Chamber of Commerce. The NACC dated back to 1914. It was a successor to a series of earlier trade associations within the auto industry that had been primarily dedicated to working out patent issues (most importantly the infamous 1895 Selden patent that gave controversial patent protection to the basic design of the gasoline-powered engine) and structuring a patent-sharing system among its members.[39] GM had long been a leader in the NACC and Sloan, by 1930, was an active participant. Sloan was adept at such cooperative endeavors in which reasoned discussions among like-minded men produced concrete actions.

Throughout 1931 and 1932, Sloan became quite caught up in an auto industry lobbying campaign against a congressional initiative to create an auto excise tax. The auto industry, Sloan was shocked to discover, was being threatened by Congress because of its very success. Congress, fearing a runaway budget deficit caused by a dramatic fall in tax revenues, sought a means to balance the budget. Since auto sales, though falling fast throughout 1931, still amounted to a substantial sum, Congress had decided to raise money by taxing auto sales. Sloan became a forceful member of the taxation committee of NACC (led by Chapin—who was not yet secretary of commerce). He threw himself into defeating the tax initiative, which he believed would be devastatingly bad for car sales. In a time of shrinking family incomes, the added price burden could only drive away additional prospective customers.

Sloan was joined in the campaign by almost all of the leading auto manufacturers. Ford alone remained aloof to the collective effort. Edsel Ford, who suffered under the heavy hand of his increasingly difficult father, gently apologized to the NACC leadership: "I think you know that our policy is of not joining associations or trade committees, and we are endeavoring to maintain this independent position whether it is right or wrong."[40]

Sloan worked closely on the antitax campaign with NACC's major lobbyist, Pyke Johnson, who by this time was an experienced hand in Washington politics. Most of his work, up until that time, had been aimed at increasing federal contributions to road-building efforts. Johnson was quite good at his work, one of the hard-core group of successful associational lobbyists, whose numbers had exploded during the business-friendly federal government of the 1920s. Sloan found him a useful guide to politics and the political process, a realm in which Sloan knew himself to be still ignorant.[41]

During the winter and spring of 1932, Sloan met in Detroit and on occasion in Washington, D.C. with fellow executives like Alvan Macauley of Packard, Chapin, and Chrysler to discuss the situation. Each man applied pressure where he could. Pyke Johnson kept up a barrage of communications with the men, pointing out key votes on the critical House Ways and Means Committee and in the Senate. Michigan's Republican senators, James Couzens and Arthur Vandenberg, assured Pyke Johnson and the NACC members that the situation was manageable. They were wrong. Sloan and his comrades lost and they lost big. Many Republicans ended up supporting the auto industry's position, but the Democrats lined up neatly against them. Not only did Congress pass the motor excise tax, they joined the states in taxing gasoline purchases. On top of state gas taxes that ranged from two to six cents a gallon, the feds added another penny a gallon.[42]

Auto lobbyist Pyke Johnson was devastated. In an emotional, somewhat rambling letter to the NACC, he wrote:

> We have fought the fight and lost—lost by virtue of trickery in high office . . . [who] jam[med] down the throats of a fear-driven Senate a nauseous dose necessary to "balance a budget." Tonight I confess to heart-sickness, not that I care about the defeat itself, but because I know how you must feel. . . . .My sole regret is that reliance upon the words of Couzens and Vandenberg should ever have led me to tell you we would win.[43]

Sloan was again forced to recognize that politicians played by rules he understood poorly.

By the time of this legislative defeat, Sloan most have felt himself under siege. In 1931, despite the general economic downturn, GM had astounding net profits of $116,739,956. But in 1932 the crash caught up to it. Only Sloan's relentless management and nonvehicle business enabled GM to eke out a tiny profit of $8,359,930; the closest GM came under Sloan's leadership to actually losing money.[44] Bad as the particulars of the economic slide were—and remember, Sloan and most of his colleagues still assumed that the contraction was a short-term predicament— the political scene seemed almost as troubling. On top of the tariff bill and the excise tax difficulties, in early 1932 the railroad interests had begun to use their influence on Congress to raise additional problems for the motor industry. Sloan was dumbfounded by the temerity of the railroad people and the credulity of Congress.

The long-suffering railroad industry was being hit hard by the economic downturn. To make any money, they needed to maintain high freight volume to counter their high fixed costs. By late 1931, the volume was just not there. Flexing what political muscle they still retained, the railroad interests managed to convince President Hoover to convene a national conference on transportation issues. Hoover, in turn, had induced Calvin Coolidge to step out of retirement and chair the conference. Rather cleverly, the organized railroad interests banded together under the unlikely name of the National Highway Protective Association. They had two major goals. First, they wanted to regulate their main competition—big-rig trucks—out of existence. Long-haul trucks, they meant to show both the public and Congress, were too dangerous to be on the nation's highways alongside the family car. Second, they wanted Congress to take a piece of the federal gasoline tax and use it for the support of the rail infrastructure. It was only fair, they argued.

Sloan would not stand idle before this threat. Congress had already shown itself willing to hammer the auto industry. Now with the railroad people on the offensive, more would need to be done. For Sloan and the other leading auto men, state gasoline taxes had long been a necessary evil: the gas tax funded highway construction that made autos and trucks more useful. Sloan had always felt it was unfair that the auto user alone was targeted for a special tax but, at least, the auto user benefited from the charge. But now, at a time when Sloan believed that states and Congress were looking to soak the auto user with even higher gasoline taxes (and most states in the early 1930s would raise gas taxes to fight revenue shortfalls), the railroads were looking to steal the money for their own noncompetitive industry's needs. Anything and everything that made auto use more expensive made people less likely to drive, which made new car purchases less frequent. The political situation was becoming increasingly frustrating.

Sloan saw the need for a strong counterattack. NACC was a necessary aspect of the process, but as the congressional setbacks demonstrated it was not sufficient. Back on February 17, Sloan had met in Washington, D.C. with Chapin, Pyke Johnson, and a number of other men to discuss the possibilities of strengthening their political countermeasures. Johnson, in all likelihood, argued for a larger coalition. He had long been active in the highway and good roads movement in the United States. And through his work in Washington on behalf of the auto makers, Johnson knew the men who represented the trucking industry, highway and road construction firms, and many other concerned parties.

At the end of May, with the loss in Congress and the railroads steaming up for their attack, the need for some new organization had become a pressing matter. Threatened with tough, even punitive regulation, it is not surprising that truck interests were particularly agitated. In the new economic situation, it seemed more and more that every industry was turning inward, looking out narrowly for its own self-interest. Something, Sloan knew, had to be done to align sympathetic sectors of the industrial economy.

In late June, Sloan again met with Pyke Johnson and a couple of other key men to lay out a plan to move forward with the aptly named National Highway Users Conference (NHUC). Sloan wanted a big group but he also wanted to make sure that auto interests, rather than those of long-haul trucking, were central to the organization's agenda. Probably to ensure the centrality of the auto interest, and to give the new organization the greatest degree of credibility, he decided to become its first chairman.

On June 28, 1932, NHUC had its first formal meeting. Pyke Johnson had signed up forty-three national organizations, including gasoline interests, chain store interests, farmer interests, truck and bus interests, the auto clubs, and other auto manufacturers. They met not in Detroit or in New York, but at the Raleigh Hotel in Washington, D.C. Increasingly, Sloan had to put a third leg into his regular travels. GM's profitability and autonomy, he unhappily perceived, increasingly depended on his ability to manage the nation's changing political climate. Alfred Sloan was becoming a regular visitor to the nation's capital.[45]

NHUC was a relatively open pressure group. Both Johnson and Sloan believed that NHUC's goals were in the public interest and welcomed and sought out public support. Johnson, perhaps still smarting from his failure in the motor excise tax fight, wrote Sloan regularly about his efforts and the public support he received. Sloan thought it useful to be straightforward about GM's role in NHUC and probably appreciated Johnson's reports, such as the one sent after a public appearance in Minnesota: "The [newspaper] clipping may interest you as evidence that there was no 'under-cover' appearance on behalf of the motor industry. Everybody there knew who I represented."[46]

While Johnson toured the nation seeking public support, the closed-doors skull sessions engaged in by the NHUC were not meant to be a matter of public record. Sloan, as chair, was blunt in setting out the issues. The privately circulated minutes of one of the first meetings reveal Sloan's ability to cut to the chase, a skill he had mastered after countless GM meetings. After very brief introductory remarks, Sloan outlined for his highway coalition partners the strategy to which they needed to commit: "We have two common enemies. 1. The railroads. 2. The legislatures, to which might be added the Congress of the United States. [We] should attempt to work together to settle difficulties and develop ways and means to protect ourselves against common enemies." With just the right amount of prodding and polite interjections, Sloan moved the meeting efficiently forward (undoubtedly winning the affections of all those who had sat through too many meetings that ran too long).[47]

Under Sloan's leadership, the unified highway users met with the railroad interests and settled most of their differences without government intervention. From GM's perspective, the key victory—and Sloan's only real concern—was a concession from the railroad interests that they would not push Congress or state legislatures to use the gasoline tax for nonhighway purposes. The "highway protectors" did still demand truck regulations, an issue of secondary concern to GM.[48]

After the meeting, a GM-approved press release stated: "It is always wiser that economic problems should be solved by conference than by legislation."[49] Such sentiments were in complete accord with the thinking of President Hoover. The Hoover-appointed National Transportation Committee rubber-stamped the general agreement, siding with the highway users' group on the gas tax issue and, indeed, condemning the railroads for their attempt to use their economic troubles to challenge the nation's successful transportation system.[50] On this issue, Sloan had beat back the main thrust of the political attack made cynically by a competing industry in the name of the general public.[51]

Within GM, Sloan did not face his new political burdens alone. At the end of 1930, aware that political pressures caused by the economic slowdown were not likely to turn around any time soon, Sloan reassigned Edward Stettinius Jr. from John Pratt's office to his own. Stettinius was given a newly created title, "Assistant to the President." In a memo circulated among top executives, Sloan explained that among Stettinius's key duties was the "development of good will . . . [which] requires more specific consideration in the future than in the past."[52] Stettinius was going to be Sloan's external affairs man. Stationed part of the time in Washington, D.C., he was to look after the political situation, mind GM's public image, and coordinate GM's position with appropriate business allies. But Pratt, Stettinius's friend and corporate protector, feared this reassignment took his former assistant off the corporate fast track. Washington, D.C. had not been where important GM men performed rewarding corporate duties. Twice removed from the traditional business of GM—working neither in Detroit at the operational level nor in New York on strategic, financial, or product policy—Stettinius was in uncharted corporate territory.

Stettinius was an unusual GM man. He did not have the engineering or finance background typical of Sloan's executive circle. However, he did have a characteristic unique in GM's top rank: he was charming. His father, Edward Stettinius Sr., had been a leading Morgan banker. Like a number of other Morgan partners, Stettinius Sr. had died at a relatively young age, but not before accumulating tens of millions of dollars (and a thirty-four-acre estate on Long Island). Stettinius Jr. was to the manor born and he looked the part. He was famously handsome and infallibly polite. Some thought his upper-class manner hid a mediocre intelligence.[53] While it is likely that he was no intellectual match for, say, "Boss" Kettering or Don Brown, he had a talent for which Sloan had use. He mixed well with others, something Sloan did not.

* * *

The last year of Hoover's presidency, as the Great Depression deepened, brought an unexpected personal misfortune into Sloan's life. Both his parents died.

Alfred P. Sloan Sr. died on August 30, 1932. He had been ill for most of the summer and at eighty-two years of age, his death, while unexpected, could not have been a complete surprise. Sloan Sr. had retired from the coffee business almost immediately after Alfred's sale of Hyatt to Durant had made them both rich. For the last sixteen years of his life, Sloan had devoted himself primarily to religious works. He had donated well over a hundred thousand dollars to the Central Methodist Episcopal Church and the Methodist Episcopal Hospital in Brooklyn, and had been happily occupied with various denominational boards and church affairs. With his full beard and old-fashioned glasses, he looked, in his last years, very much a man of the nineteenth century. Sloan Sr. had never graduated from high school and with his religious bent and parochial concerns, the common ground he shared with his intense first-born son most have been small. Still, Alfred Jr. had arranged for his father to have an office in the General Motors building at 1775 Broadway from which to run his philanthropic endeavors. Father and son must have passed some few minutes in conversation on occasion, sometime or another during the business day, even if no record of such meetings has been uncovered. Surely, they must have.

The old man's death, in homage to his son's success, received respectful attention in the *New York Times*. The son offered, however, no comment to the *Times* about his father's passing.[54]

The day before Christmas of that same year, Alfred Sloan's mother died. Sloan spoke to the *Times*' reporter about his mother. He told the *Times* that "his mother was an old fashioned wife and mother who had devoted herself entirely to the making of a home for her husband and children. She had few other interests. The death of her husband, to whom she was married nearly sixty years, was a great shock to her."[55] With those cold, few words Sloan summed up what he wished the world to know about his mother. Whether he intended his curt sentences to reveal anything about his feelings toward the small, plain woman who bore him is unknown. Christmas Day, 1932, Sloan was bereft of parents.

His period of mourning, if he found the opportunity or had the need to take any such time, was quite brief. At the end of 1932, much needed to be done in the realms in which Alfred Sloan operated best.

SLOAN AND THE NEW DEAL

Nothing more clearly reveals the truth of this self-interested questioning than the ruling fraction's obsession with the "economic information of the citizens." Inspired by their dream of a dominated class possessing just enough economic competence to recognize the economic competence of the dominant class.

—**Pierre Bourdieu, *Distinctions***

In the fall of 1932, with the depression deepening and the presidential election nearing, Sloan wanted Hoover to remain in office. He and Secretary of Commerce Roy Chapin worked together, behind the scenes, to raise substantial sums from auto industry leaders for the president's reelection campaign.[1] At least once during the campaign, Sloan and Chapin had met privately with Hoover in the White House to discuss the economic situation. The meeting led to nothing, which was no less than Sloan had expected. Sloan was neither inspired nor charmed by his access to the president. The White House—as historical site, as place of power, as architectural curiosity—held no interest. His enthusiasm for Hoover was limited.[2]

In the months prior to the election, Sloan had begun investigating alternatives to Hoover's attempts to resolve the nation's economic downturn through limited government action. Roosevelt's victory, while not Sloan's preference, did not appear to him as a threat to General Motors. Certainly, he had no fear of Franklin Roosevelt. The Democrat had indicated his preference for sound money principles and had said little during the campaign that did not meet with Sloan's approval. Walter Chrysler, a lifelong Republican, publicly supported Roosevelt; that alone would have likely assuaged any major concerns Sloan might have had.[3] In 1932, Sloan had no idea how much he would come to despise Franklin Roosevelt and his New Dealers.

For months preceding the 1932 presidential election, times were certainly not good for most Americans; neither were they good for Sloan. Demand for autos continued to be poor. Within the corporation, among the men who counted, pessimism ruled. John Pratt, the no-nonsense problem solver, was among the most negative. As far back as May 1931, far earlier than Sloan, Pratt had concluded that the economy was shot. He wrote Walter Carpenter, probably the smartest executive at Du Pont and a member of the GM board: "I am forced to the conclusion that unless we can find some new industry with a product comparable with the automotive industry . . . [we] have got to look forward to a different state of employment."[4]

Thanks only to the nonvehicle side of the business was GM able to eke out a tiny profit in 1932. But sales and revenues were down catastrophically. By late 1932, GM had laid off half its workers. Those that remained had seen two hourly wage cuts of about 10 percent each. Their weekly hours had been cut from an average of around forty-five hours in 1929 to only about thirty-one hours in 1932.[5] GM's top managers did not suffer the same economic shortfall. In fact, led by Sloan, they engineered an expensive corporate bailout of the General Motors Managers Corporation, a stock option plan that had been set up in 1930 to provide the top men with a generous bonus. Not everyone at GM would face the same consequences from the economic downturn.[6]

The Great Depression impressed upon Sloan a heightened sense of responsibility. GM was so intertwined, by this time, with the nation—and with the larger economic fortune of much of the world—that Sloan came to believe that he had to change the scope of his concerns. Everything was connected: public confidence, political leadership, policy choices, international relations, market demand, unemployment, profitability. Each piece, Sloan had come to understand, affected the other.

Sloan, however, did not yet know exactly what role he should play in the national crisis. In the business-friendly 1920s, despite his rapidly increasing status and visibility as president of General Motors, Sloan had not been among those businessmen who had promiscuously entered public life. Outside of his corporation, the auto industry, and his few memberships in New York elite clubs, he had not been active in the various business associations, policy-oriented organizations, and private enclaves in which powerful people met and considered how they might manage the large issues of the day. Not only had Sloan spent little time thinking about broad national issues, he possessed only limited social capital at the advent of the business community's greatest twentieth-century challenge.[7] That is to say, he was not a man who had built many bridges into the diverse, if often overlapping, elite circles of financiers, industrialists, politicians, and other useful people. As Sloan perceived an ever-more pressing economic and political crisis, he would try in his disciplined way to build those bridges, even though such work did not come easily to him.

Sloan had decided that General Motors, the leading industrial corporation in the United States, had to play a major role in the nation's economic crisis. As GM president, he would have to learn how to position the corporation more directly in the nation's public life. He saw a dual role for GM. Most important, the corporation needed to be perceived by the public, as well as its elected representatives, as a productive citizen of the nation—one with an active role to play in the democracy's conversations about the economic crisis and its remedies. In addition, GM could offer the nation the benefits of its practical experience in economic problem solving. The leaders of the corporation had economic and managerial expertise; they could provide models of corporate rationality to help policy makers address the nation's economic concerns. Though much of the American public had lost faith in America's business leaders and their corporations, Sloan never believed they were part of the problem. He knew they could be part of the solution. But for that to happen, both the American people and the government had to recognize their rightful role as corporate citizens.

* * *

Political work did not come easily to Sloan and, at first, he tried to delegate much it. Most of the responsibility, however, remained his. On top of his already enormous corporate tasks, the new obligations were a wearying burden. The economic situation made for more work and fewer tangible rewards.

Even in his own industry, Sloan found himself unable to control events as he would have wished. Earlier in 1932, he had attempted to convince the leading auto industry executives at the National Automobile Chamber of Commerce (NACC) that they needed to negotiate with Congress. They should trade away federal road-building monies for an end to the gasoline tax. Whatever the merits of his suggestion (and Sloan wrote many words in defense of his plan) the NACC had not pursued his approach. His time had been wasted and Congress had gone ahead with the tax plan while it spent money it did not have on roads that were not, in Sloan's opinion, necessary.[8] The facts of the situation, as Sloan saw them—that Congress was spending the government into deficit and that increasing taxes on autos would only hurt sales at a time of a contracting market—did not seem to enter into Congress's calculations. As Sloan saw it, the politicians seemed either unaware of the economics of their decision or they were allowing some sort of political pressure to interfere with rational, economic decision making.

Sloan let Roy Chapin, at that point still head of the NACC, know that he was displeased. Whether he pointed a finger at the association's lobbyist, Pyke Johnson, is not clear. Probably he did not. Sloan generally voiced his concerns to the man in charge of a given operation and expected that man to take care of the problem. Chapin did certainly let Johnson know that Sloan was angry about Johnson's failure in representing Sloan's views to Congress. Johnson wrote back to Chapin a telling analysis:

> As I see it, the essential difference between the industrialist and the politician is that the former can bridge the gap between the present and the future in his retrenchment. The man in politics cannot. He must be concerned with immediate effects. As between the man who has and the man who has not, all the weight of the vote is with the latter. . . . I wouldn't want Mr. Sloan to think that I am opposing his views on economy. I believe fully in them. But Shopenhaur [*sic*] expressed it pretty well when he spoke of the mariner who, caught in a storm, must tack in order to achieve his final objective.[9]

Sloan needed to hear this lesson. He would have appreciated it, even as it would have angered him. But Chapin never passed along Johnson's gentle lesson in democratic politics.

By mid-1932, Sloan was anxious for economic and political solutions. In May, he wrote his old superior, Pierre du Pont, and suggested that some sort of committee of twenty-five leading industrialists be formed to offer the nation economic guidance during the presidential campaign. Pierre, who had suffered through Sloan's admonitions during the 1928 election to stay away from politics and controversial issues like Prohibition, might have found Sloan's sudden interest in public policy ironic. He demurred.[10] Sloan, unsure how to proceed, stepped back.

Among the financial and industrial elite, Sloan was far from alone in his concerns. His corporate colleagues were highly agitated. Solutions, both hardheaded and less so, were floated. James Bell, head of General Mills, suggested "the dropping of a certain amount of our mechanical equipment in the country and using hand labor instead."[11] Bell was not alone in believing that the tools of mass production were at least partially responsible for unemployment figures that approached 25 percent. Everywhere, people were without work and without money. Americans waited for leadership.

Just as Sloan had wanted, corporate leaders during the summer of 1932 began seeking each other out in an attempt to provide leadership. Roy Chapin organized industrialists in Detroit. General R. E. Wood, who ran Sears, was doing similar work in Chicago. Owen Young, chairman of General Electric, the *Time* magazine man of the year in 1929, leading light in international financial reforms, and deputy chair of the New York Federal Reserve Bank, brought together a group of key men in New York. Sloan readily agreed to participate in this group. He respected Young and had high hopes that the New York committee would "do a good deal toward handling the situation there."[12]

Sloan was in regular contact with Roy Chapin and undoubtedly was pleased with Chapin's confidence that in Detroit "the leading business interests . . . are now all set up to take care of almost any eventuality."[13] Chapin left unsaid what "eventuality" he most feared, but he wrote as thousands of desperate, out-of-work World War I veterans were massing in Washington, D.C. The veterans wanted the government to pay out a service bonus they were not scheduled to receive for several more years. Congress and President Hoover had no intention of giving them the money. It was the 1893 "Coxey's Army" confrontation all over again, only far worse. The threat of violence was real. Exactly how the Detroit industrialists were "all set up to take care of almost any eventuality" remains a mystery.

By the time Roosevelt was elected in the November landslide, America's Big Business leaders were divided. Several business and financial leaders supported Roosevelt. Russell Leffingwell, at the Morgan Bank, who had known Roosevelt for many years, assured his fellow bankers that the Groton- and Harvard-educated Democrat was "a pleasant, kindly, well meaning chap with a pleasing smile" who supported sound economic principles.[14] Some, like GE's Owen Young (a Raskob-style Democrat who had been a contender for the 1932 Democratic presidential nomination), believed they had a role to play in the new administration. Whatever their specific feelings about the new president, many feared that if business and corporate leaders did not come up with sound economic recovery proposals, others would. A number of Hoover-supporting businessmen simply waited to see what would happen. Alvan Macauley, the president of Packard, and new leader of the NACC, spoke for many in the auto industry in a letter to Roy Chapin: "Since we lost the election I am glad it was a landslide with everything in the hands of the enemy and so, no reason for alibis. . . . Meanwhile I shall do what all businessmen I believe will do, viz., pitch in and do everything we can to give Roosevelt all the help possible."[15] At the dawn of the New Deal, Macauley used the word "enemy" lightly; soon enough he and others would lose their sense of humor.

Sloan probably got a similar letter from Macauley (or Chapin passed his letter along). He was not pleased with Macauley's genial passivity in the face of the political and economic unknowns that faced the auto industry. Sloan was angry: the leading men of the auto industry did not know what they were doing. "As an industry," he wrote Macauley in January 1933, "we are unhappy about our present economic position and we are worried about that position in the future. . . . We have no concrete objective for discussion. . . . What are we going to do about it?" Sloan wanted to form a small working group of four men—Don Brown of GM, B. E. Hutchinson, treasurer of Chrysler, a third from another company (by which he did not mean Ford), and "an economist of some standing." These men should figure out what policies or actions the industry should support to bring about recovery for the automobile industry specifically and the national economy in general. Sloan concluded:

> I should like to support the above idea by saying that it is a very modern and up to date way, and a very intelligent way, of dealing with controversial subjects in which there are contending forces. It seems to me as the world should have found out by this time that it does not pay to fight—it destroys both the loser and the victor. To my mind, industrial controversies should be taken out of the realm of conflict and dealt with on a basis of intelligent thought, consideration, and compromise.[16]

Sloan's hopes that industrial controversies could be "taken out of the realm of conflict" were soon enough to be dashed on the shoals of New Deal politics and labor strife.

The clash of interests between Sloan and the New Deal did not come right away. Sloan's first communiqué from president-elect Roosevelt, at the very end of 1932, seemed to promise a cooperative spirit. Roosevelt sent a telegram to Sloan and several of his colleagues congratulating them on their work in the Share the Work Movement. Sloan co-chaired the group which, as the name suggests, aimed to fight unemployment through a program of job sharing. GM had instituted the plan among its hourly workers, as had several other major corporations. Sloan read Roosevelt's cheery telegram to a large assembly of industrialists at a New York City banquet aimed at publicizing the practice.

Sloan's leadership in this particular program came out of his involvement with the group of New York corporate and financial leaders Owen Young of GE had put together earlier in the year. By time of Roosevelt's election the group was formally organized as the Industrial and Banking Committee of the Second Federal Reserve District. Roosevelt probably did not know, though it is likely he would not have cared, that the share the work program probably originated within a semi-secret organization called the Special Conference Committee, comprised of the dozen-or-so largest industrial firms in the United States. Each corporation was represented by a top executive. The committee had been meeting monthly since 1919 to share, on the quiet, labor-management strategies. In the early years of the depression they also shared general economic information, the best of which was supplied by the statistical department of AT&T. (The federal government's numbers were neither as comprehensive nor as reliable.) Since his promotion to assistant to the president, Edward Stettinius had represented GM at the meetings. He ably promoted the share the work strategy to Sloan as an antidote to greater worker frustration and agitation.[17] The interregnum between Hoover's electoral defeat and Roosevelt's inauguration was full of political intrigue and policy maneuvering. No one, including the president-elect, knew exactly what the New Deal would bring.

Sloan had Stettinius head up an *ad hoc* policy group to consider GM's immediate challenges. Stettinius's group responded with two programmatic statements. The first, which they called "The Institutional Objective," sought to ensure the corporation's freedom from outside interference. The second, "The Competitive Buying Attitude Objective," had the goal of maintaining and improving GM's competitive position. The reports were distributed among the top executive team. Sloan believed GM's core group of managers had to acknowledge the new political environment: even as they sought new means of increasing sales of General Motors products, they would have to counter political attempts by the new administration and Congress to limit the rights of GM's corporate officers to run their enterprises as they saw fit.[18]

Still, at the end of 1932, with President-elect Roosevelt still an unknown quantity, politics ran a distant second to GM's primary concern:

making money. To counter plummeting auto sales and general corporate revenues, Sloan was open to new ideas and new people. In this spirit, in December 1932 Sloan personally approved of the hiring of Edward Bernays, the leading public relations counselor of the era.[19] Bernays was a likable, if immensely self-confident man. While he was not the first to identify himself as a professional public relations man, he was among the first. Given the corporate world's general anti-Semitism, it is worth noting that Bernays was Jewish, a fact about which Sloan seemed indifferent. Bernays was not hired primarily to burnish GM's reputation. Sloan wanted him to come up with innovative, relatively inexpensive means for promoting GM products. Public relations, Sloan hoped, might be an economically efficient means of replacing costly advertising expenditures.

Sloan's enthusiasm for experiments with public relations was not shared by all of his fellow executives. Bernays, in first meeting several of the GM's top corporate executives, was not impressed with them. In turn, they did not welcome him. In notes he made for his memoir (material he would later soften when he published his autobiography), he reports that Sloan's right-hand man and GM's chief financial officer, Donaldson Brown, "as stuffy and self important man as I ever met . . . was too opinionated even to know that a public existed, a Bourbon of old." According to Bernays, John Pratt was "a professional backwoods man." John Thomas Smith, GM legal counsel, "another self-important man," was an anti-Semite. And Edward Stettinius was "very handsome and not so wise." However, Bernays did set one man apart from the rest: "There was one hope I had as I came into this room of troglodytes for the most part. That was Sloan."[20]

Despite his respect for Sloan, Bernays feared that even the GM president did not recognize the new political world within which corporate America was suddenly forced to operate. GM executives, Bernays believed, did not understand that the election of Roosevelt threatened their traditional ways of doing business. He observed: "They had no idea that a broad ideological revolution was taking place under their noses."[21] At the end of 1932, Bernays felt, Sloan and his men still did not take government action into account when formulating their corporate plans.

Bernays was wrong. Sloan had made corporate freedom from outside interference a strategic goal. He had, just prior to hiring Bernays, ordered a large-scale survey (Sloan had made GM a leader in the developing field of public opinion surveying) testing Americans' attitudes about General Motors, the nation's leading industrial corporation, in light of the economic downturn. Sloan knew, as of late 1932, that there was "no threat of hostile public attitudes requiring an 'institutional' defense. . . . [GM's] standing is so high as to require only enough effort to maintain it."[22] (To safeguard GM's reputation, Sloan authorized the production of an "independent" company history to honor the corporation's twenty-fifth anniversary in 1933.)[23]

Sloan understood the political threat mass unemployment created for the private enterprise system. But what Sloan related to Bernays was a narrower message in keeping with their professional relationship. Bernays did not know what Sloan was thinking because Sloan saw no need to tell him. Sloan had not hired Bernays as a political consultant; he had Stettinius, Pyke Johnson, and others for that work. Sloan wanted Bernays to create a cost-effective campaign to sell cars. Bernays produced such a strategy.

By late 1932 GM was moving steadily, if uncertainly, toward a program of announcing model changes on a yearly basis. The general idea for regular, publicized model changes dated back to the mid-1920s when Sloan was formalizing the policy of "a car for every purse and purpose." The program, as an annual practice, was not fully and regularly implemented until the mid-1930s.[24] Still, several of the new 1933 GM cars had been engineered with novel selling points such as no-draft ventilation and composite steel and wood bodies. Rather than simply advertise these new touches, Bernays set into motion a somewhat devious plan to *simulate* demand for these changes. Bernays meant to use an illusion of demand to produce actual demand—and increased sales.

Bernays created the Better Transportation Ventilation Committee, whose membership of dozens of prominent architects, engineers, and designers was led by the famous New York City architect Ely Jacques. (How he induced Jacques to head up this front group—if money changed hands—remains unknown.) The *New York Times* duly reported that the committee, which announced favorable findings about GM products, was created "to safeguard the health and promote the comfort of three million New Yorkers."[25] The *Times,* along with other public organs, had been duped by Bernays into providing GM with free advertising. A similar "independent" group of engineering experts, actually created by Bernays for the express purpose of promoting GM's autos, announced the superiority and desirability of cars made with composite bodies. GM again reaped free publicity for having produced such advanced autos.

Unfortunately for GM, Bernays let his success go to his head. He got sloppy. His third effort along the same lines, to create an association of supposedly public-spirited citizens to contrive a ground swell of support for an already manufactured GM product (in this case, a new form of front wheel suspension), blew up in GM's corporate face late in 1933. This time Bernays used one Doctor Franklin Goodchild, supposedly a well-known New York City doctor (actually a more humble Brooklyn general practitioner), to organize a group of health care professionals and engineers to support the development of an auto with a more comfortable ride such as that produced by "knee-action," GM's new suspension system.

This effort failed when several of the people contacted by Goodchild (actually, the letters seemed to have been generated by Bernays's office with Goodchild playing little if any role) saw through the veil of supposed medical expertise and complained about the inherent duplicity of the effort. An engineer, Thomas Estep, wrote directly to Charles Kettering: "I regret very much that General Motors found it necessary to go out and beg free advertising for an untried device under the guise of rallying the engineering profession to approve it. It reminds me very much of the contortionist begging on the city streets under the guise of being a cripple." New York City commissioner of health, Thomas Parran, wrote directly to Sloan: "shyster methods such as this will do nothing but create ill will for your products among the medical and public health professions in this country."

Sloan was not happy. He expressed his disappointment in Bernays to Paul Garrett, an ex-newspaperman who had been hired to manage GM's brand-new public relations efforts: "We have got to be rather careful in this type of propaganda."[26] Garrett, in turn, seems to have read the riot act to Bernays. Bernays argued that a few negative letters, three by his count, were meaningless given the scope of the public effort. Sloan did not accept this argument. Public exposure of what Parran called GM's "shyster methods" might have serious consequences: public outrage could result in lost car sales; GM's competitors and critics might use this information to attack the corporation. The tangible risk was not worth the unsure reward. Bernays's consulting contract was up for renewal just a few days after this flap. It was not renewed.[27] Such straightforward manipulations of the car-buying public through simulated citizens' groups seems to have disappeared, at least for the duration of the New Deal Era, with the end of Edward Bernays's contract.

Throughout 1932 and into early 1933, Sloan had greatly increased his public presence. Quite deliberately, he was taking on a new role, that of the corporate citizen. Identified forthrightly as the representative of General Motors, Sloan had decided that he must speak out on economic issues in a "nonpartisan" fashion. He had made speeches calling for an end to Prohibition, in large part as an economic stimulus. He had spoken on the need for "rigid economy in Federal, State, and Municipal expenditures as the first step toward economic recovery." He had called for reform in the intergovernmental debts left over from World War I and for lowering global tariffs. He had publicly suggested that "the chief executive officers of large corporations would well organize a quite unofficial advisory council to consider in the light of their experience and the facts, leading problems of the day."[28] Sloan closed out 1932 with a tough-minded "New Years' Statement," which the *New York Times,* and probably many other newspapers, printed. Not surprisingly, he called for cuts in federal spending to ensure a balanced budget (a "sound money" principle dearly beloved by his fellow industrialists). Less predictably, he also called for "real leadership of a militant type. If that be forthcoming—and I certainly hope it will be—the nation should rally around and support that leadership from a patriotic standpoint and in the interests of the people."[29] Sloan was undoubtedly pleased that his brief for sound money and militant leadership was complemented by the *Times*' headline story: "Roosevelt Works with House Chieftains for Federal Cuts."[30]

Under Bernays's direction Sloan had also sent out a New Year's telegram to 150 leading men in industry, research, and finance. The telegram and responses to it were to be publicized across the land by Bernay's public relations machinery. In the painfully hortatory, Latinate, and nominalized prose Sloan employed (or approved) to address the public on political matters, he offered assurance that the "inevitable progress and momentum of America go on in spite of depressions and that the large corporations which play so great a part in shaping America's civilization recognize their moral obligation to allow no lag due to adverse conditions to retard their scientific advance or detract from their achievements." The *New York Times,* whose publisher had become an occasional dinner companion to Sloan, quoted in full that inspiring sentiment in its front-page story on Sloan's initiative, which the paper titled, "Leaders Put Faith in the Machine Age to End Depression."[31]

Public response to Sloan's flurry of speeches and good tidings is difficult to measure. The popular writer Gerald Johnson, referring to business leaders in general, had observed: "It will be many a long day before Americans of the middle class will listen with anything approaching the reverence they felt in 1928 whenever a magnate of business speaks. We now know they are not magicians. When it comes to a real crisis they are as helpless as the rest of us, and as bewildered."[32] Sloan knew he faced a wary and anxious public.

Sloan also knew that the quality of his public performances was not at the level he desired. With rare exception, he was not pleased with the speeches that were written for him or with the press releases that went out under his name. He had hired Paul Garrett and created the public relations department to take on this very responsibility; but Sloan found their efforts wanting. Garrett complained to Edward Bernays (right before he fired him): "What Mr. Sloan wants is a Walter Lippman or a Thomas Woodlock."[33] (In the early 1930s, Lippman was the nation's leading newspaper columnist, pundit, and public intellectual; Thomas Woodlock, who let it be known that he read Euripides and Aristophanes in the original Greek, wrote the erudite "Thinking It Over" front-page column for the *Wall Street Journal.*)[34] Sloan never felt this problem was adequately solved. The quality of many of his speeches, in which one apt word was almost never used if two, three, or more opaque phrases could be substituted, indicates that Sloan correctly recognized the problem if not its remedy.

Speeches were far from Sloan's primary concern as FDR took over the presidency in March 1933. All over the country, banks were crashing. Detroit's leading banks, the First National Bank and the Union Guardian Trust Company, had come undone (in part through paying out huge dividends to shareholders even in the dark year of 1931). Their failures forced Michigan's governor to declare a "bank holiday," shutting all banks in the state just prior to Roosevelt's inauguration and subsequent declaration of a *national* bank holiday. The ever-public-minded Henry Ford had helped to force the bank closings by refusing to cooperate in the complex efforts the federal government had masterminded in an attempt to save the state's fumbling financial institutions: "Let the crash come. Everything will go down the chute. But I feel young. I can build again."[35]

Sloan, who had prior to 1932 shown little interest in the particularities of life in Michigan, decided to step into the breach. In the dreary days of late 1932, Sloan, in his new role as public man, had signed on as the chairman of the Detroit Civic Group. Composed primarily of the leading auto men (Henry Ford was represented by his son Edsel, who attended meetings sporadically), the group meant to offer the city some sort of guidance through the economic crisis.[36] Sloan, after several weeks of negotiation, committed GM to an extraordinary effort to save Detroit's two leading banks.

Sloan was not the indispensable man here. President Roosevelt and his New Dealers led the charge to reconstruct the American banking system. On March 12, 1933, eight days after the inauguration, Roosevelt gave his first Fireside Chat—"I want to talk for a few minutes with the people of the United States about banking. . . . It is your problem no less than mine. Together we cannot fail." Roosevelt spoke to the American people as a wise, old friend. He asked for their help, their trust, and their faith. And, as events showed in the spring of 1933, most Americans were ready to do what he asked. Sloan's call for "militant leadership" was being met.

As Sloan had promised, he was willing to follow. He sent his president a telegram: "Highest commendation of your financial program . . . we are ready to accept whatever losses may result to ourselves in the workout of your program of facing the facts . . . above all we must preserve the integrity of the American dollar."[37]

Sloan had his men work closely on the Detroit banking problem with federal officials of the Reconstruction Finance Corporation (Hoover had started the RFC but Roosevelt gave it credibility, if not a fundamental change in its mission). Without insisting on the usual expected high rate of return on capital invested, GM supplied some $12.5 million, neatly matched by the RFC, to reorganize Detroit's failing main banks. Out of the mess emerged the solid National Bank of Detroit.

In a lengthy statement, widely distributed throughout the Detroit area both in pamphlet form and via daily newspapers, Sloan personally explained General Motor's action to "the people of Detroit." After detailing the nature of GM's involvement—primarily limited to financing and administrative structuring—Sloan stated: "I am sincerely anxious that the people of Detroit appreciate that the only interest which General Motors has in this connection is to be of service to the people of Detroit." He concluded:

> In my various contacts with you the people of Detroit I feel that you understand the position which General Motors has taken and that you will lend your support to those men who will be designated to carry on for you a sound type of banking which has been made possible through the sympathetic and financial cooperation of the United States government.[38]

General Motors had a keen interest in stopping financial meltdown in Detroit; it was home to their core production facilities, suppliers, and multitudes of employees of all ranks. Financial chaos in Detroit would badly hurt the corporation. And by riding to the rescue, Sloan expected the corporation to reap a public relations bonanza.[39] Still, similar concerns had not motivated Henry Ford. Corporate Citizen Sloan showed remarkable flexibility and strategic insight in recognizing the role GM could play in remedying a bad situation not of its own making.

Sloan proved, in the Detroit banking matter, his willingness to cooperate with the Roosevelt administration. No rigid partisan, Sloan recognized (as some businessmen did not) that Roosevelt's banking policies kept the capital markets firmly under the control of capitalists. Americans less sympathetic to bankers had hoped for much more aggressive policies, that Roosevelt had meant it when he had stated during his inaugural address, "The money changers have fled from their high seats in the temple of our civilization. We may now restore that temple to the ancient truths."[40] The North Dakota populist, Congressman William Lemke, spoke for those who had expected radical solutions: "The President drove the money-changers out of the Capitol on March 4th—and they were all back on the 9th."[41] Sloan approved.

Roosevelt had promised the American people "action, and action now." Congress felt the same urgency. By the spring of 1933, the New Deal rush was on. The same legislative fervor spread to the states, as well. From his New York office, Sloan fought to ride the political whirlwind.

Pyke Johnson, in Washington, sent bulletins almost daily. A major agricultural bill was in the works. Sloan did not care. Roosevelt continued to suggest support for "sound money." That was good. Congress was bestirring itself. Generally that was bad. (During the interregnum Sloan had turned down an offer to testify before the Senate Finance Committee, probably because he was still smarting over the tax legislation the committee had moved in the previous session and but also because he did not want to march in a disorganized parade of uncertain Big Business leaders propounding diverse policies that had little chance of being enacted.) Roosevelt's sound money principles were being crowded out by congressional demands for a major public works program (Pyke Johnson wrote him, "While the President is essentially a sound money man he is also a political realist"). That was worrisome but not tragic. (Sloan sent word to both the NACC and the National Highway Users Conference that if public works legislation passed they should lobby for major road building; if it did not pass, to aid in balancing the budget, they should lobby for cuts in highway money.)[42]

Sloan's first public foray into the New Deal legislative blizzard of the first hundred days came on May 5, 1933. On behalf of the National Automobile Chamber of Commerce, he testified favorably on the Thirty-Hour Work Bill. Here, and in the months that followed, Sloan showed himself more willing to cooperate with New Deal legislation than almost any other major figure in the auto industry—including most of his fellow executives and board members at GM.

Sloan began his testimony with an unqualified support for what he called the "dividing the available work movement." This "emergency" initiative, after all, was a nationalizing of the Share the Work Movement Sloan had headed in 1932. Sloan's pre–New Deal efforts, however, had been strictly aimed at voluntary compliance by his fellow employers. The Thirty-Hour Work Bill aimed at mandatory, government-regulated compliance during the economic emergency. Sloan saw no problem and went even further. He testified that the bill would only work if the government also mandated a minimum wage policy for the emergency period to ensure that employers did not "share the work" while simultaneously impoverishing the increased number of workers. Sloan was no nineteenth-century laissez-faire capitalist.

During his lengthy testimony, Sloan argued that the good work of the congressmen would be defeated if they wrote legislation insufficiently flexible to meet the changing employment needs of different industries. His industry, for example, would need to average work hours on a yearly basis, not on a weekly basis, due to the cyclical nature of its production runs. Sloan also made sure that Congress understood that managers and other corporate professionals could not be restricted to any set of work hours. For such men, he stated, "it is frequently a case of day and night work 7 days in the week because of the limited time and the absolute necessity of meeting a definite object."[43] Sloan and his men would never be limited to a thirty-hour work week.

The House Committee on Labor saw a side of Sloan few witnessed outside his corporate circles. He answered their questions precisely, factually, and with total mastery of detail. The opaque phrasing and prolixity that affected his public speeches and much of his written work disappeared. His sobriety, however, was unchanged. Sloan rarely saw the need for charm or chatter. He did make an exception, however, late in the hearing when asked by a friendly Michigan congressman, "What is a saturation point . . . in the automotive industry?" Sloan invited a discussion: "I wish you could tell me. I would like to know." When the congressman asked Sloan to explain what he meant, he said simply that demand for automobiles was determined by "purchasing power." Incredulous, Congressman Welch from California asked, "Then you would have an automobile for every person in the United States, is that it?" Sloan, perhaps with the hint of a smile, replied, "Two for every person."[44] Congressman Welch seemed to believe that aggregate auto consumption should be ruled by some standard need for the product. Sloan knew better. If people could afford more than one car, Sloan was confident that General Motors could find ways to convince them to buy more than one car. Automobile consumption, Sloan believed, had no natural limit and no relation to some standardized need or use. He understood that in the new culture that had developed in the United States (before it was stalled by economic depression) cars were not simply transportation. Automobiles—as well, as many other products—were a means through which consumers expressed themselves. It was a small point in his testimony but it indicated how differently (and more insightfully) Sloan perceived the marketplace from many of the congressmen who were struggling to restore the American economy.

Sloan would need all of his committee-work skills to meet the first major New Deal initiative: the National Industrial Recovery Act.[45] Just a little over a month after Roosevelt took office, Pyke Johnson wrote to Sloan with the news that key administration figures were discussing "government control of labor, wages, and production."[46] Sloan was not surprised. He was expecting such a development. Gerard Swope, president of General Electric, whose chairman, Owen Young, headed the New York City business group Sloan had joined during the summer of 1932, had been advocating a similar program since 1931. Sloan had listened with respect to his fellow MIT electrical engineering alumnus. Swope was an unusual character. In a corporate industrial world that rarely hired even assimilated Jews as executives, Swope was an observant Jew who had made it to the top at GE. (His sponsor was Owen Young, who also sponsored the Jewish David Sarnoff to head the Radio Corporation of America.) As a young man, as mentioned in chapter 1, he had volunteered at Jane Addams's Hull House in Chicago, where he taught technical courses to eastern and southern European immigrants. During World War I he had stepped off the corporate ladder to serve voluntarily on the General Staff of the Army, overseeing industrial procurement. As president of GE he had overhauled administrative procedures, invested heavily in research and development, and turned GE into a consumer products giant. In Sloan's view, Swope had proven himself through demonstrated performance. He was a pragmatic visionary who looked, not always with success, both within and outside his corporation for a more workable, humane, and profitable industrial system.[47]

Swope believed that the economic emergency required a nationally coordinated, economic regulatory scheme run with government sponsorship by the major business trade associations; only such a program could stop the relentless downward pressure on wages, prices, and employment. In the summer of 1932, he had publicly urged President Hoover to craft such a plan. Hoover, showing his old-fashioned, antitrust, progressive side, had blasted Swope's plan as "the most gigantic proposal of monopoly ever made in history."[48] Despite Hoover's reaction, Swope continued to speak out in favor of a national economic plan and a number of other leading businessmen and business associations, including the National Chamber of Commerce, supported him in his efforts. Sloan was among those supporters, as his work on behalf of the Share the Work Movement demonstrated.

So, as a general principle, Sloan favored some nationally organized, trade-association-directed economic plan to bolster wages, prices, and employment through cooperative industrial planning. By late May of 1933, however, Sloan knew that businessmen would not simply control the crafting of an industrial plan, and he was worried. Plans percolated all over the executive and legislative branches of government. Roosevelt charged key "Brains Truster" Raymond Moley with devising some sort of "business self-government." Moley brought in General Hugh Johnson, generally trusted by leading businessmen for the key role he had played during World War I on the War Industries Board in overseeing military–industrial coordination, as well as Donald Richberg, a tough and savvy railroad union lawyer. At the same time, another group of New Dealers operating in the Commerce Department, including pro-government-planning "Brains Truster" Rexford Tugwell and the liberal-progressive Secretary of Labor Frances Perkins, worked on another version. In the Senate, the labor-friendly Robert Wagner of New York took the lead in drafting yet another plan. Businessmen had plenty of say in these discussions. So, at least in Senator Wagner's group, did the leaders of organized labor.[49]

By late May the labor aspect of the coming legislation had the auto men worried. Again, Pyke Johnson kept up an almost daily briefing. He had good access to the Commerce Department group and one of his sources warned him that the plan being drafted by Senator Wagner "does provide flatly that the employers must negotiate with representatives of its employees."[50] Stettinius was hearing the same things from his colleagues at the Special Conference Committee; somebody had gotten hold of a draft of the legislation being drawn up by Senator Wagner that included Section 7(A), mandating workers' "right to organize and bargain collectively through representatives of their own choosing."[51] Auto manufacturers had been fighting unionization, with great success, since the industry's origins. None of them, including Sloan, wanted collective bargaining. None of them wanted to see labor unions interceding between managers and workers. Since the late nineteenth century, thanks to men like Sloan's engineering mentor, Henry Leland of Cadillac, Detroit had become known as "the graveyard of organizers."[52]

Sloan had believed that national industrial regimentation would have little impact on the auto industry. By 1933, the industry—down to fifteen manufacturers overall, with Ford, Chrysler, and GM completely dominating the market—did not in the least suffer from cutthroat competition. Prices were relatively stable, with Ford setting the pace (Sloan had long ago opted to compete with Ford and others through style changes, organizational efficiency, and scale economies rather than through price wars). And, as Sloan had testified during the hearings on the thirty-hour work week, his corporation was already seeking to stabilize wages and employment through reasonable standards. Sloan envisioned an industrial plan as affecting other, less well-managed and rationalized sectors of the economy. He had not anticipated the labor question. He was not pleased.

In late May and early June, as the National Industrial Recovery Act took final form, Sloan and other leading auto executives met and communicated often. By early June, they were hopeful that the labor problem was solved. They expected the final legislation to include a clause, crafted by the ferociously anti-union National Association of Manufacturers, stating that "nothing in this title shall be construed to compel a change in existing satisfactory relationships between the employees and employers."[53] They were wrong.

A week later, when President Roosevelt signed the National Industrial Recovery Act, which created the National Recovery Administration, no such language was in the new law. Senator Wagner had prevailed. The famous—or from most industrialists' perspective, infamous—Section 7(A) not only stated that workers had the right to organize and bargain collectively but that employers were constrained from "interference, restraint, or coercion" in the organizing process. American Federation of Labor president William Green had been responsible for the last bit of language. The New Deal, Sloan and his friends were learning, had a room at the negotiating table for labor's champions.

Despite reservations, Sloan agreed to cooperate with the new industrial plan. He accepted an invitation to participate in the Business Advisory and Planning Council, a newly formed government advisory group. Several of the key men who had been organizing the business community before the 1932 election were behind the council. Formally, Secretary of Commerce Daniel Roper created the group. Concretely, those corporate leaders with New Deal sympathies—men such as Gerard Swope of General Electric, Walter Teagle of Standard Oil Company of New Jersey, and Louis Kirstein of Federated Department Stores—gave the council its legitimacy in Sloan's eyes. The Business Council was a straightforward attempt by the New Deal administration to co-opt corporate leaders, and an equally straightforward attempt by certain business leaders to keep the New Deal in line with their private enterprise principles. In the words of the council's astute historian, Kim McQuaid, "[it] would first marry corporate expertise to federal power, and then serve as a long range economic planning council with primary responsibility for formulating industrial recovery strategy. . . . These CEOs were serving on a quasi-public advisory agency that was *in* the government, but not *of* it."[54]

By the summer of 1933, key members of the Business Council, including Alfred Sloan, had joined the Industrial Advisory Board (IAB) of the National Recovery Administration (NRA).

Proving his new broader commitments, Sloan was an active participant in the IAB. Despite reservations about the organized labor issue, Sloan believed that the NRA's attempt to create industrial codes that would end salary reductions, establish minimum wages (which would be well below the high-wage auto industry), and put a stop to price cutting could be useful in stabilizing the economy. In this regard, Sloan differed from Henry Ford, most of his fellow executives at GM, and almost all other auto industrialists, who from the beginning looked with great suspicion and even open hostility at the NRA. Here, for example, are John Pratt's intemperate remarks to the conservative congressman Walter Pierce: "[The NRA is] moving us very fast to the ideas that Russia has been trying to establish." And Pratt was generally considered a political moderate within GM and the larger auto industry.[55]

Sloan's role on the Business Council and the IAB was the most forthright and extended government-oriented public service he would ever undertake. Simultaneously, he became the head of two key IAB projects, the Committee on General Monetary Situation and the Committee on International Trade Relations. While Sloan had firm views on both matters—he was, not surprisingly, an anti-inflationist and an advocate of international trade—he felt that he and his CEO colleagues had neither the time nor the expertise to craft sound policy recommendations. So he asked his Washington-based assistant, Edward Stettinius, to have the Brookings Institution prepare reports on both issues. He paid for the work out of his own pocket.[56]

Even as Sloan was dutifully chairing the advisory committees, he was losing faith in the NRA and losing interest in working with New Deal administrators. With each passing month, his hopes of steering the New

Dealers toward what he considered responsible policies in support of free enterprise waned. Sloan wanted to see the economy stabilized. And he believed that some form of government-sanctioned cartelization of industry, à la the NRA, was a reasonable, or at least plausible means for achieving that stabilization. He did not, however, believe that the federal government had any right to tell him or any other responsible industrialist how to manage their corporations. Nor did he believe that the government had any right to interfere in his or any other industrialists' labor policies. Sloan became increasingly convinced that what he wanted and what the New Deal was becoming were not likely to be the same thing.

On November 14, 1933 Sloan wrote Louis Kirstein, chairman of the Industrial Advisory Board. He had two major complaints. First, he believed that the NRA was fast setting up a system in which government bureaucrats would have the power to tell corporate managers how to run their businesses: "A review of the codes already approved by the National Recovery Administrator and the President, disclose quite a variety of practices in which . . . government and not industry constitute the final authority." Sloan found this loss of corporate sovereignty completely unacceptable. Second, he argued that the anticompetitive practices being created by NRA codes hurt consumers as they systemically punished the most efficient producers (such as GM). He concluded: "If we must embark upon the perilous policy of regimentation of industry . . . we should try to develop ways and means that will be the least possible destructive of the initiative and aggressiveness which have given this country the highest standard of living throughout the whole world."[57] Sloan was becoming increasingly agitated over New Deal economic policy. He believed that Roosevelt was overseeing a gigantic increase in the power of the federal government to interfere in the marketplace because of political demands, not free enterprise principles, and that was something Sloan could not condone.[58]

Sloan's concerns about what he saw as the New Deal's prolabor attitudes drove much of his growing hostility. This specific hostility, however, was linked to a rising disgust with politicians in general. As a group, Sloan believed politicians had no sense of economic principles or rational decision making. They were driven by the need to make sensation for the ill-informed masses and to cater to aroused large voting blocs. In Sloan's eyes, ignorant, undisciplined men, seeking the votes of even more economically unsound individuals, threatened to radically alter the most successful economic system ever created—simply because of a temporary setback.

Sloan let loose with such feelings, in a moment of extreme frustration, to NRA czar Hugh Johnson, whom he generally respected. Sloan, Walter Chrysler, Don Brown (Sloan had charged him with overseeing GM's role in the NRA's promulgation of codes affecting autos), and several other top auto executives at GM and the other major manufacturers (excepting the ever-uncooperative Ford) met with General Johnson in a special meeting in Detroit at the General Motors Building. The car men hoped to iron out their differences with the NRA. Johnson, who was known to enjoy, at any time of the day, a drink or three, had begun the meeting with a rambling disquisition on the need for cooperation, the unpleasant but, he argued, unimportant failure of the Ford Company to participate in the NRA, and, finally, the need to trust in the men, like himself, who were administering the NRA. Sloan, who had no patience for poorly run meetings and long-winded speakers, finally jumped in: "General, everybody has so much confidence in your fairness. . . . [But] you know the industry can't afford to put itself in the hands of the politicians. There are more damn politics. . . . I would rather be in the hands of the Labor Unions than I would be in the hands of the politicians."[59]

Sloan did his best to hide his growing frustration with politicians in his public statements, but his letters to trusted colleagues are full of such sentiments. To Pierre du Pont he wrote at the end of 1933: "I like Senator Wagner—he is a fine fellow—but, after all, he is nothing but a politician and is in no sense of the word a statesman and naturally, he has his ear to the ground from the political standpoint. I do not blame him for that . . . . He recognizes the number of votes that labor has."[60]

Sloan was not being fair to Wagner. The senator was among the most principled men operating in public life in the 1930s. His beliefs, however, were quite different from Sloan's. Wagner believed that economic justice demanded that working people have government-supported rights in the work place. Sloan believed that well-run corporations rewarded working people with decent paying jobs. Government interference in corporate labor policies—and other areas of management responsibility—would only reduce corporations' ability to effectively balance the needs of their consumers, shareholders, workers, and managers. Sloan believed that men like Wagner did not understand that businesses were not simply employers but complex economic institutions that must manage the competing desires of various stakeholders if they were to remain viable. Sloan had a saying that he undoubtedly applied to Wagner: "He has never had the job of meeting the payroll at the end of a week."[61]

Clearly, any snide remarks Sloan may have made about Wagner were not really directed at the senator's character. Sloan was frustrated about the role Wagner and public officials like him were playing in his business. The New Deal was ending business leaders' near-monopoly on what had passed for economic common sense in the corridors of governmental power.

Sloan, not unlike many of the New Dealers with whom he had to contend, could not stay focused for long on any one problem. Dozens of diverse challenges came at him from every direction. Throughout 1933 Sloan was particularly annoyed by a growing movement at the state government level to regulate auto safety. On this issue, Sloan found himself taking a minority position even within the auto industry (and he was opposed within GM itself by Knudsen and other "car" men).

Sloan did not buy the idea that safer automobiles were more desirable automobiles. His own experience told him that consumers were not willing to pay extra for safety, nor did they reward a car company that installed special safety features with increased sales. The facts had been proven to Sloan's satisfaction with the 1928 Cadillac. For the first time the Cadillac windshield had been made out of safety glass. Cadillac's rival, Packard, like all other automakers, continued to use less expensive plate glass. The result: despite advertising its advanced safety feature, Cadillac lost market share to Packard. The more expensive feature did not improve sales, it only hurt Cadillac's overall profitability. At the time, Sloan wrote Pierre du Pont that "irrespective of accidents or no accidents, my concern in this problem is a matter of profit and loss."[62]

In mid-1933, the safety issue made an unwelcome appearance on Sloan's overcrowded plate. The New York state legislature was preparing a law mandating the use of safety glass in automobiles, and several other states were following New York's lead. This cost-adding legislation came at a time when car buyers were feverishly searching out the lowest possible auto prices; any extra costs would have to be eaten by the manufacturer (or bargain hunters would turn to the used auto market). Sloan had the facts to prove this; a survey (commissioned by Sloan) that showed that fewer than 25 percent of car buyers would pay *anything* extra for safety glass. Sloan demanded that the NACC fight safety glass laws anywhere they appeared.

Pyke Johnson wrote directly to Sloan, beseeching him not to make this fight. Former New York governor Al Smith's son, he told Sloan, had suffered grievous injuries flying head first through the plate glass window of his car. In New York, prominent people were testifying in favor of the bill. It was going to pass. Sloan could not let go of the issue. The facts were on his side: "[C]ompulsory use of safety glass was very costly and meant many millions of dollars of expenses to buyers of cars." At a time of limited demand and limited consumer budgets, fewer people would buy new cars that cost more. Any other consideration, moral or otherwise, was not his concern. Safety laws were not good for General Motors.[63]

Paul Hoffman of Studebaker tried to get the NACC to take a more affirmative stance on the issue. Hoffman, by far the most socially conscious of the major auto men (he alone actually supported some form of unionization), had been worrying about automobile safety for years. But with Sloan so adamantly opposed to any compromise on costly safety additions, his efforts were completely rebuffed. Sloan won; the NACC would fight the safety movement. But the issue would not go away.[64]

It was an odd time for Alfred Sloan. By early 1934, the auto business was improving. By year's end GM car sales would again surpass a million units—double what they had been in the nightmarish 1932 and more than three hundred thousand more than in 1933 (but seven hundred thousand fewer than had been sold in 1929).[65] Still, the recovery was sluggish. Labor troubles were increasing (a major confrontation with GM production workers occurred in March; it is worth noting that Sloan played no documented role in the spring labor troubles, leaving the specific problems, seemingly, to William Knudsen).[66] Sloan believed these labor problems were caused by the NRA.[67] The rhetoric coming out of the White House and the policy demands of several prominent New Dealers were not to Sloan's liking. A stream of public works programs, aimed at creating work ("make-work") for the unemployed, were throwing the federal budget deep into the red. Sound economic principles that Sloan believed would bring about economic recovery were being crowded out by Big Government measures that would bring short-term relief but long-term trouble. Even before the obvious leftward turn of the New Deal in 1935 (the Second Hundred Days produced such progressive legislation as the Social Security Act, the Wagner Act, and various new corporate and individual tax plans), Sloan had lost all faith in Roosevelt's "militant leadership."

By the spring of 1934, Sloan worried that he was simply reacting to events rather than contributing to his preferred solutions. So he began to act. Throughout 1934 and even more so in 1935, when Sloan perceived the New Deal to be fixedly prolabor and against the interests of Big Business, he greatly expanded his efforts to engage the public on matters of economic policy and, most strikingly, partisan politics. Sloan had been moving in this direction since the economic downturn had begun in late

1929. And he had, after all, been performing in an expanding series of public roles since he had taken over the GM presidency in 1923. Still, the journey outward into society and politics was not an easy one for Sloan. He was a private man and at nearly sixty years of age his intellect did not move easily in new directions.

At a practical level, Sloan probably thought he was prepared for the task he had chosen to undertake: to move the American people away from bad economic policy. Longer than most of his contemporaries, Sloan had been thinking about how to reach the general public and motivate them in the directions he preferred them to take. He had made GM a pioneer in consumer outreach through surveys, advertising, and marketing. And Sloan had been well ahead of most in seeing the possibilities new media, especially the radio, provided in delivering desirable messages to the mass of American people (in 1928 Sloan had personally decided to put GM on the radio waves with the *General Motors Family Party;* he spoke live, Christmas Eve, on the festive show that launched NBC's twenty-four-hour-a-day national network operation).[68] The tools Sloan had used in selling products and his corporation's good name were likely to be useful in selling public policy as well. Nonetheless, Sloan recognized that democracy and the marketplace were not congruent.

In part, Sloan's frustration with politicians stemmed from his sense that they had the power to shape public discourse and, thus, the public's understanding. Too often, Sloan believed, they fed the public error-filled, even dangerous nonsense on matters of vital concern to General Motors specifically and the private enterprise system in general. As Sloan contemplated his role in countering what he saw as the politicians' pabulum, he hoped that solid economic facts and clear explanations would help the public choose wisely. Good information would counter the politicians' inferior product. But Sloan also recognized that the public did not always choose—whether it was electing politicians or buying cars—based on reason alone. Reaching the public was complicated.

Sloan, throughout the New Deal years, oscillated between a belief in the ability of people to make good political choices if they were only given good information and a more jaded sense that the public was easily manipulated. Sloan was no political theorist and he never worked out this problem in any detail. Perhaps his pithiest observation on the problem of shaping public opinion came a couple of years into his political foray. In 1936, a group of advertising executives awarded him a prize for a General Motors ad campaign. In his acceptance speech, he stated: "Just as iron, steel and copper are the raw materials out of which the motor cars are built, just so is the buyer's mind the raw material out of which sales are produced."[69] While Sloan did not give up on a rational public, that image of the public's mind as a raw material, ready to be shaped by powerful tools and a sure hand, explains much of Sloan's public work in the 1930s after he became convinced that the New Deal threatened General Motor's marketplace autonomy.

Sloan committed himself to leading a kind of public relations campaign for limited government intervention in the economy. As his colleague Charles Kettering stated, "industry has always been in the doghouse because it won't tell its story."[70] In 1934, Sloan began an intense personal effort to help industry manufacture public opinion. His quarterly stockholders' messages began to express, both in tone and content, an openly anti–New Deal outlook. He increased both the number of public speeches he gave (focused on economic issues) and the budget of the GM public relations department to ensure that those speeches had public impact.

In May 1934, he broke publicly—if cryptically, it must be said—with the New Deal. He did so with the speech he gave at the reopening of the Century of Progress Exposition in Chicago. In front of the spectacular General Motors' exhibit, the largest at the fair, he let loose in his predictably less-than-perfectly-clear fashion. Among other things, he subtly compared the Roosevelt administration to ancient Asiatic despots: "All through the ages, whenever the upward spiral of material progress has dipped a little in depression, the cry has been raised that the end of human advance is at hand. Asiatic kings had that somber fallacy carved on monuments rescued from oblivion by the far reaching archeologists of our dynamic era." Indicative of Sloan's increased concern about public outreach, he had the corporation's public relations department carefully follow the impact of his remarks. With remarkable quantitative precision, the department reported that the Chicago speech had generated 670 newspaper editorials, 557 news stories, 52 radio comments, 28 magazine articles, and 16 news pictures. Sloan and his corporation took his relatively new role as public educator seriously, as did the nation's mass media.[71]

President Roosevelt also registered Sloan's comments. He sent a telegram directly to Sloan to be posted at the GM exhibit (the public relations department had solicited comments from some three hundred world leaders for public display). The president's telegram read, in part: "As I have said before, private business can and must help. The nation will remember those who are helping. It will also remember those who believe that our progress in the world is finished and make no constructive contribution in the present emergency."[72] Lines were being drawn between GM and the New Deal. Sloan's commitment to Roosevelt's "militant leadership" was just about finished.

As Sloan intensified his personal efforts to sway the public against the New Deal's economic policies, so too did he begin to find ways to join with other business leaders in anti–New Deal propaganda. Sloan's major effort along this associational line came through the National Association of Manufacturers (NAM), which in 1935 had some seventy-five thousand member firms. To NAM, in the 1930s, Sloan gave his biggest donations, both personal and corporate, and—a more precious commodity—considerable time. He attended numerous banquets, conferences, executive meetings, and special events. He was one of the organization's featured speakers: "There must be brought home to the consciousness of all that the more Government takes the less each one has. No one can possibly escape."[73] He became the NAM's fund-raising chairman and signed his name to a stream of solicitation letters during the last half of the 1930s.

NAM was not a subtle operator in the nation's public life. The liberal columnist for the *New York Post,* Samuel Grafton, called NAM "the shock troop brigade. . . . [It] does the rough work with little attempt at diplomacy or concealment."[74] Sloan was not always pleased with NAM members' "fire and brimstone" rhetoric and he used his status to instruct them, at times, that they need remember to relate their economic interests to larger societal concerns. Despite Sloan's own sense that he played a moderating role in the organization, to any New Dealer his prominent role in what would have been perceived to be a fiercely reactionary organization marked Alfred Sloan as a declared enemy of the Roosevelt administration.[75]

Founded in 1895, NAM began as a lobbying counterweight to the great turn-of-the-century trusts that were systemically crushing small-to-medium-sized manufacturers. By 1902, NAM was dedicated to preserving the open shop and destroying the labor union movement. It was among the first national associations of businessmen to explore a new technique in its fight on behalf of employers' rights: "the molding of public opinion."[76] It was this focus on public opinion that drew Sloan to it. In 1934, Sloan decided to chair the newly created National Industrial Information Council (NIIC), a NAM front group solely dedicated to shaping public opinion along lines favorable to business. NIIC's purpose was to install "in the consciousness of our [the American] people" the proper answer to "a vital question of national policy. Is the American economy of the future to be motivated by private initiative or by some form of regimentation under the domination of an all powerful State?"[77] NIIC would teach Americans how to think like Americans again, said its founders.

Between 1934 and 1938, with Sloan at the helm, NIIC oversaw an industry of information production. Some of that information was clearly produced and disseminated under the name of NAM-NIIC. Most was not.

Sloan was particularly interested in reaching the public through the relatively new media of radio and film. With his support (though the specific inspiration came from Harry Bullis at General Mills, the company that proudly had first utilized the "singing commercial"), NIIC personnel wrote and paid for a radio show called *American Family Robinson*—"a serial dramatic radio program presenting industrial facts against a background of typical American family life." The plot of the serial was simple: Mrs. Myra Robinson, with the intellectual assistance of her husband, struggled to organize the small town of Centreville against the corrupt and sinister efforts of the "Arcadians" (New Dealers by any name) to "regiment" in every possible way American life. Throughout the latter half of the 1930s, the show aired twice or more a week, usually between the hours of two and three in the afternoon ("to reach not only housewives but other members of the family") on some 270 radio stations.[78]

By 1936, NAM's overall public outreach campaign equaled the efforts of the Republican and Democratic parties. NIIC provided multiple streams of anti–New Deal information. George Skolsky, "the noted writer and lecturer," appeared with NIIC support once a week on 246 radio stations. Film shorts produced by NIIC on "progress under the American industrial system" and "how machines create rather than destroy jobs," were shown to some 15 million movie goers and many millions more school children, university students, women's club members, and even Civilian Conservation Corps enlistees. Tens of thousands of billboards demonstrated the theme, "What's Good for Industry is Good for You" (shades of "Engine" Charley Wilson's memorable testimony before Congress in 1953 about the relationship between GM and the nation). Numerous full-page "advertorials" were placed in hundreds of newspapers; millions of booklets were distributed; there was even a special division charged with providing material in German, Hungarian, Polish, and Italian for leading foreign language newspapers in the United States.[79]

An entire news service, the Industrial Press Service (IPS), was covertly funded and directed by NIIC to provide newspapers with editorials, features, columnists, hard news, fillers, and cartoons—all in support of free enterprise. By 1941, over six thousand newspapers had requested the free service.[80] Overwhelmingly, the IPS found its clients, as planned, among the newspapers of the smaller cities and towns of America. While such newspapers seemed backwater to some, it was their readership, NIIC personnel knew, who provided state legislatures and the House of Representatives with the majority of their membership. And even more important, as NIIC reported to its financial supporters, IPS readers' "representatives dominate the major committees of both houses of Congress."[81]

Sloan never seemed to have come to terms with the relative efficacy of NIIC's efforts. During his years of most active involvement, from 1934 until 1937, he helped lead fundraising efforts that saw the annual public relations budget of the National Association of Manufacturers increase from $36,000 to $793,000.[82] As to whether or not NIIC's well-funded flooding of the nation's media with free enterprise propaganda actually accomplished anything, neither the group's staff nor its corporate sponsors could clearly say. Sloan, at any rate, maintained his connection to the organization until its demise in the midst of World War II.

By the mid-1930s, Sloan was becoming much more comfortable with and interested in politics. And his commitments in that realm were multiplying. As always, however, his own industry's problems took precedence. In 1935, the auto safety issue, again, erupted onto the national scene. Sloan was needed to put out the fire.

In October of that year, *Reader's Digest* published an article on auto safety—or more accurately, the need for auto safety—by Joseph C. Furnas, a clever, young, Harvard-educated writer who styled himself as a latter-day muckraker. Furnas carefully documented "the horrors of highway accidents." His "blood curdling" depictions of human bodies slashed by shattered glass and torn apart by hard-edged steel touched off a national fervor. The article was reprinted in some two thousand newspapers and magazines and 3.5 million copies were ordered from *Reader's Digest* by police departments, businesses, and traffic courts.[83] Even the auto industry's favorite newspaper, the *Detroit News*, jumped on the bandwagon with a front-page editorial: "Stop the Automobile Slaughter . . . THE AUTOMOBILE INDUSTRY MUST NOT LET THE AUTOMOBILE COME TO BE KNOWN AS A KILLER!" The editorialist laid out the blueprint the auto industry did its best to follow: "Let the industry which has given us the cars—so necessary in American life today—establish the rules by which those same useful cars will cease to be weapons of death and injury."

Sloan helped spearhead a sophisticated response to the auto safety hoopla. Building on his experiences with the National Highway Users Conference and other intra- and interindustry associations, he participated in creating the Automobile Safety Foundation (ASF). The ASF was launched with a good deal of publicity. General Motors and the Studebaker Corporation, headed by the longtime safety advocate Paul Hoffman, provided four hundred thousand dollars (about 4.75 million in current dollars), almost the entire start-up costs of the foundation. Soon after its inception, Sloan helped persuade gasoline companies, tire companies, and other auto-related industries to contribute to the ASF.[84]

Sloan had long argued (recall the disputes over auto safety glass) that consumers were willing to pay for improvements in auto performance, which made autos more dangerous, but they balked at paying for safety features they believed they would not need. In light of this conviction, rather than examine the safety of the auto itself (which might have resulted in auto manufacturers laying out large sums, unrecoverable from consumers) to improve their vehicles, the ASF focused its attentions exclusively on "encouraging safe and efficient use of streets and highways." On the occasion of a personal gift to the ASF of twenty-five thousand dollars (nearly three hundred thousand in current dollars), Sloan declared that "traffic problems will yield to the broad application of proven techniques."[85] For the next quarter of a century, until Ralph Nader came along, the foundation successfully promoted an auto-safety agenda based on improving the safety performance of drivers and the improved safety engineering of streets and highways. These efforts saved the lives of many Americans. (In 1937, with only 42 million licensed drivers, recorded traffic deaths totaled 39,643; in 1962, with nearly 89.5 million licensed drivers in the United States, recorded traffic deaths actually dropped to 39,600.) ASF programs and projects also deflected attention away from the dangerous characteristics of cars and trucks manufactured by the auto industry. That the ASF grants leveraged improved roads, highways, street signage, and school-based drivers' education paid for almost entirely by *public* funds was no accident.[86] From Sloan's perspective, the potentially costly problem of automobile safety had been intelligently managed.

* * *

By the mid-1930s, Sloan had become more comfortable in voicing his political opinions. In his quarterly message to GM stockholders in April 1936 (which was featured in a front-page *New York Times* story), after bluntly attacking New Deal economic policies, he explained his new perspective:

> Added responsibilities must be assumed by industry. . . . Industry must assume the role of enlightened industrial statesmanship. It can no longer confine its responsibilities to the mere physical production and distribution of goods and services. It most aggressively move forward and attune its thinking and its policies toward advancing the interest of the community at large, from which it receives a most valuable franchise.[87]

Still, Sloan believed himself to be carefully walking a line in his political work. He distinguished between organizations to which General Motors belonged and organizations to which he, as a private citizen, belonged. When GM belonged to a trade association such as NACC or industrial organizations like NAM and ASF, Sloan openly worked in full public view to promote the group's viewpoints. However, when Sloan the private citizen joined an organization or supported a political candidate, he operated in a behind-the-scenes fashion. Thus while newspaper stories made it clear to the public that Sloan was a spokesperson for NAM, few Americans probably knew that he played a significant role in the rabidly anti–New Deal citizen's group, largely funded by du Pont family money, the American Liberty League.

Sloan was involved in the Liberty League from its beginnings. In July 1934, shortly after his public break with Roosevelt, he had attended a meeting with some of his closest business compatriots including Irénée du Pont, Lammot du Pont, Walter Carpenter, Don Brown, and John Pratt. Helping to guide the meeting was Jouett Shouse, a New York lawyer and former chairman of the Democratic Party executive committee during Al Smith's run for the presidency. Their goal was to organize a coalition made up of Democrats and Republicans capable of defeating Roosevelt in the 1936 election. At the meeting they brainstormed, trying to conceive of an organization that, in Irénée du Pont's words, could "include all property owners—stocks, bonds, homes or farms . . . [as well as] the American Legion and even the Ku Klux Klan."[88]

Out of this meeting, a month later, came the Liberty League. Sloan was on the organization's national advisory board. However, as Sloan told du Pont shortly after the group took form in June 1935, he would not appear publicly on behalf of the organization. He explained: [It] is absolutely essential that I confine myself to the corporation's work, and only depart in things of this character where the Corporation is rather directly involved."[89] As a result, few Americans identified Sloan with the Liberty League. While Sloan's approach probably did help to insulate General Motors from consumers' potential politically inspired anger (Sloan's primary concern), it did little to hide Sloan's position from the more politically astute (probably an acceptable risk, in Sloan's mind). From Roosevelt's perspective, and that of his political allies, Sloan's role in the Liberty League was an open declaration of war.

The Liberty League, from its origins in August 1934 to its death throes following the election of 1936, existed to tear down the New Deal. In 1935, it raised and spent almost the same amount of money as the national Democratic Party. Of that money, at least $10,000 (about $122,000 in current dollars) came from Alfred Sloan.[90]

Sloan's role in the Liberty League, because it was not a public one and likely because he did not want people to know then or later about the part he played, is difficult to trace.[91] Only some twists and turns of the money trail remain visible. Sloan helped to fund the Liberty League, even as the league's alliances and rhetoric became ever more frantic and fanatical. For example, it helped fund the fascistic, anti-Semitic Sentinels of the Republic ("Every citizen a Sentinel! Every home a sentry box!"). The Sentinels believed the New Deal was a "Jew Deal" and that Roosevelt and his minions were a part of a worldwide Jewish conspiracy. Sloan sent at least one check for one thousand dollars directly to the Sentinels.[92]

Another Liberty League beneficiary was the Southern Committee to Uphold the Constitution, a principal backer of the 1936 campaign to elect to the presidency Georgia governor Eugene Talmadge (a business-respecting replacement for the assassinated Kingfish, Huey Long). This committee and its candidate mixed anti–New Deal populist diatribes with fervent racism. Infamously, they circulated what they called "nigger pictures": photos of Eleanor Roosevelt with black Americans. Soon after the photos appeared and were nationally publicized, Alfred Sloan sent the committee one thousand dollars.

What could Sloan have been thinking? Perhaps, following the logic of the Liberty League staff professionals, Sloan thought Talmadge could split off Roosevelt's southern Democratic support to give the 1936 Republican presidential candidate a surprise victory. A case could be made that Sloan was flirting with the kind of behavior some of his corporate peers in Germany had engaged in with more deadly effect—that is, funding a demagogue who put out the fires of national crisis by pouring on the gasoline. Then, too, Sloan was probably not put off by racist, anti-Semitic sentiments, even if he himself, seemingly, never expressed them. In his business circles, such comments were commonplace.[93]

Sloan's rather casual experimentation with extremist organizations, as a means of weakening Roosevelt and the New Deal, proved to be costly.

By the fall of 1936, Roosevelt campaign was directed in part against the Liberty League and the rich men who supported it. The president had a come a long way from the jaunty fellow of 1932 who had carefully courted business leaders. Now he attacked the "economic royalists" who opposed the New Deal. At the last stop of the 1936 campaign trail at Madison Square Garden, FDR lashed out in controlled anger:

> We now know that Government by organized money is just as dangerous as Government by organized mob. Never before in all our history have these forces been so united against one candidate as they stand today. They are unanimous in their hate for me—and I welcome their hatred. I should like to have it said of my first Administration that in it the forces of selfishness and of lust for power met their match. I should like to have it said of my second Administration that in it these forces met their master.[94]

By the end of 1936, Alfred Sloan and many of his corporate peers had thrown down the political gauntlet; Franklin Roosevelt had picked it right up. Alfred Sloan soon found out, to his amazement, that he had made an enemy of a man and a political administration he actually needed.

SLOAN AT WAR

All that is akin to me in nature and history speaks to me, praises me, urges me forward and comforts me: other things are unheard by me, or immediately forgotten. We are only in our own society always.

–Friedrich Nietzsche,
Joyful Wisdom

Just before the 1936 presidential election, Alfred Sloan made a last-ditch appeal in a five-minute radio broadcast during the *General Motors Sunday Radio Hour* on NBC. He had already written a similar, direct appeal to GM shareholders. Plaintively, Sloan told his listeners:

> They have suggested that we throw away the plan that has made America unique among the nations of the world—that we cease trying to produce an abundance so that everyone can have more—that we devote our efforts instead toward dividing up what we already have. . . . Help us perpetuate the American way of life—its free enterprise—its alertness for the new and better—its rewards for the deserving. . . . Hold fast on through future years to the American system of industry that has *brought us these benefits* and that is still the envy of the entire world.[1]

Sloan referred several times to "they" but, tenuously maintaining his public nonpartisan stance, he never named them or any specific "he." He retained faith enough in the public to assume that the broadcast audience could figure out to whom he referred and what they should do on Election Day.

President Roosevelt heard Sloan's words clearly enough. He knew where Sloan stood. The president kept in his personal papers a clipping file full of speeches made during the election campaign by Alfred P. Sloan and his allies in the Liberty League and the National Association of Manufacturers (NAM).[2]

Sloan hoped right up to the bitter end that Governor Alf Landon, the bland Kansas Republican, could defeat Roosevelt. He was not alone. Henry Ford openly championed Landon. Al Smith, the onetime "friend" of the working man, had broken with Roosevelt and campaigned for Landon. Sloan did have some evidence of Landon's widespread support. A confidential memo he received from the Liberty League reported that "between 80 percent and 85 percent of the newspaper circulation of the country is now estimated to be opposed to the chief features of the New Deal. . . . No candidate for the office of President has ever been elected with so strong a newspaper opposition." Fifteen additional facts gathered by the Liberty League's staff revealed the president's nearly complete lack of support ("70% of the clergy are opposed . . . the Catholic Church is almost unanimously opposed . . . the majority of city dwellers are opposed . . . the unemployed will be opposed . . . the women of the United States in strong majority are now opposed"). Finally, the League cited the *Literary Digest* poll, which had correctly called the 1932 election. Landon, the *Literary Digest* showed, was well ahead of Roosevelt, and was predicted to win thirty-two states with 370 electoral votes. (The magazine's opinion polling techniques obviously were flawed.)[3]

Perhaps Sloan found such information heartening. But by 1936 he understood that the material presented to him by the Liberty League staff, men whose livelihoods depended on maintaining an anti–New Deal opposition, did not offer proof of victory. First, he knew that politics and politicians did not operate according to the corporate rules with which he was most familiar. And second, when it came to politics, his men and the men of his allies did not seem able or willing to provide him with the kinds of facts on which sound judgments could be predictably made. Somehow, he knew, he needed either to change the rules by which politicians played or get the facts he needed to understand and operate within their realm.

* * *

For nearly four years, Sloan had spent part of his time and energies developing an understanding of the nation's politics. By November 1936, he did not need help in seeing that Roosevelt was a formidable politician and that Landon had his limitations. The Kansas governor campaigned poorly; he had no idea how to communicate over the radio. Though sincere and generally likable, he was an easy target for his opponents.

John L. Lewis, head of the United Mine Workers of America and chairman of the Committee for Industrial Organization, which had been created in November 1935 to unionize mass production workers—especially including auto workers—was among the most outspoken of FDR's supporters in 1936. From organized labor's coffers, he would provide the Roosevelt campaign with some six hundred thousand dollars. Lewis, a master of invective, scored political points almost effortlessly against the well-meaning, if relatively unsophisticated, Kansas governor. Landon, said Lewis in a memorable attack, was "this little man out in Topeka, Kansas, who has no more conception nor idea of what ails America or what to do about it than a goat herder in the hills of Bulgaria."[4]

Between Roosevelt and his barbed-tongued supporters, Landon was overmatched. But he was not a quitter. In the last days of the campaign Landon gave hope to many of his supporters with a burst of heated rhetoric. Traveling across the country, Landon lambasted the New Deal: "No nation can continue half regimented and half free." "[The New Deal is] obsessed with the idea that it had a mandate to direct and control American business, American agriculture, and American life." "Our homes, our communities, our jobs and our business are to be directed from Washington. The profit motive is to be eliminated. Business as we know it is to disappear."[5] He sounded like a spokesman for NAM. Sloan, though not directly (and certainly not publicly) involved in Landon's campaign, sent Landon at least $89,100 in campaign contributions. In current dollars that would be a donation of about $1.1 million.[6]

Sloan had invested his social, cultural, and personal capital poorly. Roosevelt crushed Landon. Except for Maine and Vermont ("As Maine went, so went Vermont"), Roosevelt took every state in the union. He won a popular vote of 27,476,673 to Landon's 16,679,583. The congressional elections, from Sloan's perspective, were no better. After the 1936 election, seventy-six Democrats sat in the Senate, so many that twelve freshmen had to sit "across the aisle" on the Republican side of the Senate chamber. In the House, the Democrat's total soared to 331 representatives as against 89 Republicans. Working-class Americans, buoyed by FDR's support of unions, Social Security, public works, and other social welfare legislation, had voted in record numbers and overwhelmingly for Democrats. So had those African Americans of all income levels who were able to cast their ballots (black southerners, by and large, were barred from voting). The New Deal voting bloc, a force for decades to come, had taken clear form. Roosevelt's progressive legislative record and anti–"economic royalist" rhetoric had proven to be a resounding electoral success.[7]

So far as the historical record shows, Alfred P. Sloan feared no specific repercussions from the victory-flush Roosevelt administration. After the New Deal landslide a frustrated Sloan hoped to put politics on the back burner and concentrate more fully on his business. Ironically enough, given Sloan's views of New Deal tax plans, prolabor legislation, and federal deficits, at the end of Roosevelt's first term the overall economy had recovered substantially. General Motors had enjoyed a remarkably successful year in 1936. For the first time ever, GM vehicle sales worldwide topped the 2 million mark (1932 world sales were 562,970). North American sales were just short of the 1929 high point. Overall, corporate profits had been quite satisfactory and stock dividend payments had been high. Whatever damage Sloan believed Roosevelt had inflicted on the economy and the prerogatives of management, GM seemed to be back on track.[8]

In the immediate aftermath of the election, publicly Sloan kept quiet. GM's top managers could not come to a consensus as to the effect Roosevelt's reelection would have on the economy in general or on GM's business in particular. Just before the election, in early November, a number of GM's top men—it is not clear if Sloan was among them—had met privately with W. H. Swartz, an investment banker at Lehman Brothers. Swartz, in a confidential memo, reported back to his colleagues at Lehman: "Certain General Motors people also felt further capital expenditures could not be expected now, in view of Roosevelt's possible reelection. . . . [This means] a break in general business next year . . . midsummer is the logical time to expect it." Whether GM's managers meant that rational businessmen could only respond to the likelihood of New Deal "antibusiness" legislation (and the resulting "economic instability") by delaying capital spending, or if they meant that angry businessmen would retaliate politically against four more years of Roosevelt by deliberately causing an economic contraction, is not clear in Swartz's memo. Swartz did conclude: "I would suggest that the rather intense political emotions of certain of these men may have colored their thinking more than they themselves may have realized."[9]

Swartz was probably right that emotions had been running high among GM's upper people in early November. A month after the election, Swartz had returned to GM's New York offices to reassess GM's corporate outlook. He then reported more sanguine news to his Lehman colleagues. Swartz wrote that Sloan had told him that "the skies have cleared materially." Sloan predicted that 1937 would be as profitable as 1929, GM's best year.[10] But in early December of 1936, Alfred Sloan had no idea of the troubles that lay just ahead.

* * *

Sloan had never taken much interest in the men and women who worked in General Motors factories. No working men or women, not even a token representative, attended the annual Greenbriar retreats or belonged to the many management committees Sloan had created. Sloan did not appear on the factory floor, like William Knudsen, to shake hands and trade jibes with the hourly workers. He did not oversee the specifics of their employment or seek out information on the nature of their concerns. Other men— those charged primarily with production—were responsible for seeing that the hourly workers did their jobs and stayed in line. Workers had no box in Sloan's organization charts.

While Sloan had little interest in the lives of GM workers or in the particularities of plant-level labor relations, Sloan was firm in his resolve that GM workers remain unorganized individuals employed by the corporation and controlled by management directive. Unions had no place in Alfred Sloan's approach to management. Unions could provide some stability in corporate cost accounting by providing long-term contractual terms and some security against "wildcat" strikes through negotiated agreements, but those possible advantages were overridden by the threat of union interference in management's control of workplace rules and job terms. Sloan believed management to be a hard practice based on factual analysis. This process could only be corrupted by union leaders.

Union organizers did not see the corporation as he did: as a profit-maximizing institution run by professional managers. They seemed to feel that the modern business corporation should have as its priority maximizing employee wages and security. Sloan believed (and not completely without reason) that his focus on profits rather than on humane, rewarding jobs for working people produced better long-term outcomes for GM's employees. Workers might have pointed out that GM's managers enjoyed far greater job security than did hourly workers; that dividends had been paid out to shareholders throughout the Great Depression, even as hundreds of thousands of GM workers had lost their jobs; and that those workers who had kept their jobs had been forced to increase their productivity without any commensurate increase in their wages. Sloan could have replied that at the end of 1936 GM's already high hourly wage rates had been increased by a nickel, that overtime rates of time and a half were paid to workers who put in more than forty hours a week (not forty-eight as before), and that a bonus had been paid out to workers in a profit-sharing plan. GM also contributed to a major health insurance plan as well as to a savings plan, and provided an array of other benefits for its workers. These were facts. Few, if any, major corporation in the United States, Sloan believed with cause, could be said to have done better by its workers.[11]

Sloan's angry resistance to the New Deal, like that of many other industrialists, was due in large part to the protections government provided to organized labor in Section 7(A) of the National Industrial Relations Act (NIRA) (1933) and in the Wagner Act (1935). One can only imagine his response to the impassioned soliloquy the usually stoical Senator Wagner had made on the Senate floor on behalf of the working man and federal protection of union organizing:

> Who is this worker we are talking about? Is he some enemy of this country? Is there any reason why he, unlike other people, should be shackled in some way? He is a man of flesh and blood like you and me with hopes and aspirations, who wants to preserve America for himself and for his children. . . . That is the man for whom I am pleading.[12]

Senator Wagner represented New York, the home of GM's corporate offices, a fact Sloan believed that Wagner had forgotten.

In early 1934, General Motors' top divisional managers and corporate executives had begun to pay closer attention to their workers' discontent over wages, security, and job conditions. Senator Wagner's work, and the increasingly militant actions of men and women on the shop floor, had forced their hand. As a partial remedy to labor legislation and the union activity it protected, they began a concerted effort to stop labor union organizers from reaching the hourly employees. Sloan stood foursquare behind this effort. The specific role he played in the anti-union activities of 1934–36 unfortunately remains a mystery. In subsequent, extended congressional investigations into industrialists' anti-union activities, Robert La Follette, the progressive senator from Wisconsin, angrily concluded that there was at General Motors "a sort of mystic mist . . . about who actually does determine labor policy."[13]

In 1934, for the first time, the corporate office in New York had placed an executive in charge of "industrial relations." Sloan surely played a hand in this organizational development. Still, throughout 1934 and 1935, the corporate office's interest in labor—organized and unorganized—remained underdeveloped and loosely structured. Workplace operations remained primarily a divisional and plant-level responsibility. As a result, centralized oversight of the work force was unsophisticated compared to other central office duties, like financial control, even as labor concerns began to press against management decision making.[14]

Despite this relative lack of centralized oversight or openly declared corporate policy, a corporatewide approach to federally protected labor organizing did take shape in early 1934. Between January 1934 and July 1936, executives throughout the General Motors corporation expended the impressive sum of $994,855.68 to detective agencies to stop labor union activities. The Pinkertons, veterans of labor wars dating back to the railroad strife of the nineteenth century, were the main recipients of these funds. GM's hired men planted spies—many, many spies—and other informants among the workers to identify and track union activists. Their mission was simple: to foil union organizing efforts.

New Deal labor legislation—Section 7(A) of the NIRA and then after the Supreme Court found that law unconstitutional, the Wagner Act—was supposed to protect union activists from retaliation by their employers. Despite such legal protection, between 1933 and 1936 GM plant managers routinely fired organizers and their supporters. In 1934, for example, GM fired sixty-four shopfloor leaders at Fisher Body 1 and 2, and nearly twice that number at the Chevrolet plant in Flint. In May 1936, despite the Wagner Act, Arnold Lenz, general manager of Chevrolet in Flint, gave this order to his subordinates: "We expect you to discharge anyone who is found circulating a [union] petition or soliciting names for a petition inside our plant." While legal protections sometimes enabled fired unionists to regain their jobs, company officials waged a relentless campaign of intimidation and harassment against them. GM executives, Sloan included, just didn't accept the right of the federal government to protect labor union activities (they hoped the Supreme Court would find the Wagner Act unconstitutional just as the Court had ruled against the NIRA), and they refused to accede to the legal measures that had been passed by Congress and signed by President Roosevelt.[15]

GM's employment of intracorporate spies was a critical aspect of this campaign, and was not kept entirely secret. Most managers wanted the men to understand that they were being watched and that their ranks had been filled with turncoats. (Employing spies and detectives remained a

GM practice for years to come; in 1966 GM president James Roche had to apologize to Ralph Nader before a U.S. Senate committee for hiring men to pry into his private life.)[16]

GM was far from alone, among its peers, in refusing to accept New Deal legislation that protected union organizing. And compared to many other companies, especially Ford, General Motors used less vicious and less violent tactics. Irving Bernstein, in his dramatic account of labor in the 1930s, *Turbulent Years,* writes:

> Unlike Ford and Republic Steel, GM, with some exceptions, did not opt for violence as a general policy. This was, perhaps, not caused by moral restraint; rather it appears to have stemmed from the desire to maintain what nowadays would be called "the corporate image." . . . This was certainly good business judgement as Ford later learned when many people refused to buy his cars because Harry Bennett's goons beat up and murdered union workers.[17]

Here, as elsewhere, though no specific document reveals it, Sloan would have been well aware of the risks involved in balancing GM's need for good public relations with his desire for a strict, management-directed internal corporate order.

General Motors mainly financed its anti-union activity at the divisional and individual factory level. Every GM plant manager across the nation laid out funds for the effort. In response, someone with sufficient authority at the New York corporate office, probably GM's new corporate industrial relations man, chose to hire detectives to spy on the spies hired by division and plant managers. Here was an unlikely iteration of Mr. Sloan's corporate oversight committee structure. While Sloan had little directly to do with this effort, almost surely he knew about the anti-union activities in a general way, and approved of them. Strange times, Sloan believed, demanded unusual measures.[18]

GM's labor spies and anti-union tactics failed. On December 30, 1936, militant unionists in Flint began sit-down strikes against General Motors. They demanded that GM recognize their right to collective bargaining. The action caught most GM executives by complete surprise. Flint was GM's town, or so its managers believed. Sidney Fine, the author of the classic account of the strikes, *Sit-Down,* reports: "Flint was to the nation's leading automobile producer what Pittsburgh was to steel, Akron to rubber, and Minneapolis to milling."[19] A combination of management intimidation (with the help of the Flint police department), union organizers' mistakes, legions of spies, workers' fears of losing their jobs at a time of massive unemployment, and GM's relatively excellent wages and benefits seemed to have been working in Flint to keep labor troubles at bay; in the summer of 1936 only about fifteen hundred out of forty-two thousand GM workers in Flint belonged to the United Auto Workers (UAW). Management expected trouble, if it came at all, to show up elsewhere, not in their most carefully guarded citadel.

Union organizers active in the auto industry, unlike Sloan, expected Roosevelt's landslide victory to turn the tide in their favor. John L. Lewis said that the president "would hold the light" while union activists organized. UAW organizers, whose successes before the election had been relatively few—the UAW had only been chartered by the American Federation of Labor (AFL) the previous year—believed that the election of both Roosevelt and a new, liberal governor in Michigan, Frank Murphy, meant that "the government is obviously with us." Targeting Sloan himself, the UAW pitched membership to GM workers by arguing: "You voted New Deal at the polls, and defeated the Auto Barons—Now get a New Deal in the shop." In the immediate aftermath of the election, the Committee for Industrial Organizations, a newly formed umbrella organization led by Lewis that comprised the UAW and other labor unions, met in Pittsburgh and specifically decided to target the auto industry for a major organizing campaign. Forces beyond Alfred Sloan's control were lining up against him and he did not know it.[20]

Labor agitation broke out in mid-November and it did not stop. No one in the union hierarchy was behind it (though they quickly supported the actions). Militants at the Atlanta Fisher Body plant started things off on their own with a wildcat sit-down strike. Then, about four weeks later, another wildcat sit-down occurred at the Kansas City Fisher Body plant. On December 28, the Cleveland Fisher Body plant was hit. All hell finally broke lose on December 30, when the two main Fisher Body plants in Flint were taken over by sit-down strikers. Flint was GM's production bottleneck—key auto divisions could not manufacture cars in quantity without bodies from Flint.

These strikes were not directly fueled by the frustrations on the parts of the masses of GM workers—a fact the corporation desperately publicized—nor were they orchestrated by the UAW leadership. The UAW, as GM knew, had yet to make hardly any headway in organizing at GM's Flint plants. Rather, it was a small minority of workers led by militants, many of whom were communists, who had put down their tools and taken possession of the factories in which they worked.[21]

While few in number, the sit-down militants did, however, represent the frustration and anger of a great many GM workers. And at least some GM executives, public protests to the contrary, knew it. In 1934, investigators working for the National Recovery Administration had examined the auto industry and reported: "Everywhere workers indicated that they were being forced to work harder and harder, to put out more and more products in the same amount of time with less workers doing the job. . . . [T]hey are vigorous in denouncing management as slave drivers, and worse. If there is any one cause for conflagration in the Auto Industry, it is this one."[22] In Flint alone, GM had cut over nine thousand blue-collar jobs between 1930 and 1936 without reducing productive capacity, forcing remaining workers to increase their work load prodigiously when production increased in 1936.[23]

The production speedup was not new to the auto industry in the 1930s. It was intrinsic to the mass production system Henry Ford had brought to the manufacture of the automobile. But the Great Depression had greatly intensified manufacturers' ability and desire to push workers as hard as possible to get the most production out of them at the least cost. Early on in the economic downturn, at the St. Louis Fisher Body plant, when workers' complained about being shortchanged on their pay despite a Herculean bout of production, a manager bluntly told them: "Whenever you don't like the pay you are getting, go out to the gate and get your check. There are four hundred men out there every morning willing to work for less than what you men are working for."[24] Massive unemployment had made many workers afraid to speak out or to act on their grievances; despite New Deal promises, they knew they could still be easily replaced. As individuals they knew they had no way to challenge the corporation. So while only a few union militants took the dangerous step of confronting GM in Flint at the very end of 1936, a far larger group of auto workers watched and waited; their sympathies and their hopes were with the men inside.

Sloan was aware of the events as they unfolded. But William Knudsen, by this time a corporate executive vice president, had responsibility for plant operations. He took charge of GM's response to the agitation. Throughout the ordeal, Knudsen would be GM's public face. He would also handle the day-to-day negotiations with the UAW.

Knudsen was not taken by complete surprise. Even before the Flint troubles, he had begun discussing workers' grievances with the UAW's quixotic president Homer Martin, a former minister whose rise to power within the fledgling union was built on his inspirational, biblically inflected oratory, not on his disciplined mind or strategic vision. Unlike

Sloan, Knudsen (who had himself worked on the factory floor) believed unions and some form of collective bargaining at GM were an inevitability. But Knudsen by no means accepted Martin's demand that the UAW had the right to be the sole representative of all GM workers. And as a starting point, he wanted Martin to understand that labor issues with GM were not a corporate affair but a plant-level responsibility. Martin, whatever his failings as a union leader, had no intention of organizing and negotiating separate contracts at every plant—just as GM, in fact, did not leave basic wage and benefit policy at plant-level decision making. No one at GM had thought through how collective bargaining, if it came, would be managed at the corporate level.

Knudsen responded to the strike by stating that GM would not bargain with the UAW while the strikers were in "illegal possession" of the Fisher plants. Immediately, GM's legal team secured an injunction from the local county court ordering the strikers out of the plants. After the writ was issued, the UAW revealed that the county court judge who had issued the order owned a sizable bloc of GM stock. The strikers rejected the court's legitimacy and refused to leave. Martin insisted that the corporation recognize the UAW as the GM workers' sole bargaining agency and that negotiations over "a code of rules for collective bargaining" between GM and the UAW begin immediately.

Sloan tried to keep his distance physically, as well as publicly, from the strike. He stayed in New York. But the union's intransigence and the workers' refusal to leave the plants was simply too much for him. On January 5, he issued an open letter to GM employees that was posted on the bulletin boards of all General Motors domestic manufacturing operations. In five double-columned pages Sloan laid out General Motors labor policy. He wanted the workers to have the facts:

> On every count General Motors workers are earning more than they ever have in the entire history of General Motors, and as much, if not more than the workers of any other business. No one can honestly say otherwise. Yet under these conditions you are being forced out of your jobs by sit-down strikes, by widespread intimidation, and by the shortage of materials produced by similar tactics in many allied industries.
>
> General Motors grew up on the principle that a worker's job and his promotion depend on his own ability—not on the say-so of any labor union dictator. And on that principle General Motors stands and will continue to stand. . . .
>
> The real issue is perfectly clear, and here it is: Will a labor organization

> run the plants of General Motors Corporation or will the management continue to do so?

Workers' freedom and their livelihoods were at stake, Sloan explained. The UAW would force every GM worker "to pay tribute" to it. Union power would force the company to make irrational, uneconomic decisions. Sloan concluded by asking the workers to weigh the facts and to trust "the management of General Motors Corporation to make the business a good business, not only for the workers and for the stockholders, but . . . [for] the prosperity of the country, and after all, that means much to all of us."[25]

The facts could not be clearer to Alfred Sloan. Trespassers were occupying a critical corporate facility. They had no legal right to occupy the property of the General Motors Corporation. Public authorities had the legal obligation to remove them from GM property. And yet, as far as Sloan could tell, no public authority was willing to honor his sworn duty to protect the laws of the land. The new governor of Michigan, a liberal Democrat by the name of Frank Murphy, simply refused to do what Sloan believed was his legal duty. Murphy, like most every politician, was a mystery to Sloan.

Frank Murphy had been sworn in to the Michigan governorship on January 1, 1937. He was an inordinately ambitious, immensely capable, public-service-oriented man. He came to be governor after some three years as governor-general of the Philippine Islands. Before that he had been mayor of Detroit where his support of Roosevelt in the 1932 election had earned him his plum appointment in the Philippines where he had lived like a potentate. Murphy, some said, hoped to become the first Roman Catholic president.

The strike in Flint was Murphy's first order of business. He had run for governor with the support of organized labor and Franklin Roosevelt. Still, no one knew what he would do. Few, even on management's side, knew exactly what they wanted him to do. It was one thing to argue that GM's property rights were being illegally trampled by a mob and that the strikers be commanded to leave. It was another thing to order an attack on the striking workers by police or the national guard. What if the workers resisted? Should they be shot down and killed, if that is what it took?

Governor Murphy was, ironically enough, close friends with Lawrence Fisher (and though none of the principals knew it at the time, Murphy also owned a large bloc of GM stock that he discretely sold in the midst of the strike). According to the governor's executive secretary, even Fisher did not want Murphy to order a violent attack on the strikers. Fisher had told the governor, "Frank, for God's sake if the Fisher . . . brothers never make another nickel, don't have bloodshed in that plant. We don't want to have blood on our hands. . . . Just keep things going . . . it'll work out.[26]

Knudsen felt the same way about bloodshed, as did other executives. Sometimes, Sloan felt that way, too. He did not want to see people killed on GM property. But he was impatient that the government, somehow, make the strikers leave. According to Secretary of Labor Frances Perkins, Sloan early on in the strike told her, "[I]f this crazy government we've got here will just send in some troops and put them out of the shops, it'll be alright."[27] Perkins, instead, counseled patient negotiation. Yet while the government delayed, Sloan watched the sit-down strike spread to other GM plants around the country. The chaos was, in Sloan's mind, the predictable development of New Deal labor policy. As he saw it, that policy had led to a breakdown in good economic order beyond even his most pessimistic fears.

Inside the GM plants that Alfred Sloan had helped to make profitable, the workers singled him out for mockery. To keep up their good cheer they sang:

> Oh! Mr. Sloan! Oh Mr. Sloan!
> We have known for a long time you would atone,
> For the wrongs that you have done
> We all know, yes, everyone. . . .
> Oh! Mr. Sloan! Oh! Mr. Sloan!
> Everyone knows your heart was made of stone,
> But the union is so strong
> That we'll always carry on.[28]

Several centuries earlier, Niccolò Machiavelli had warned: "[M]en have less hesitation to offend one who makes himself loved than one who makes himself feared."[29] It seemed that GM's workers, at least some of them, neither loved nor feared Alfred Sloan. He had believed that he could run General Motors without fear or love; that reason alone would suffice.

In the 1920s, following Pierre du Pont's lead, Sloan had allowed Bruce Barton to publicize the corporation as a "family." But he had in fact no paternal feelings for the hundreds of thousands of hourly workers GM employed, and they knew it. Sloan had never even allowed his own marriage to get in the way of company business. The corporation, he believed, was too immense for anything personal to interfere in its governance and its good order. Far down the line, the men who worked the machines that made the cars seemed to understand just how little they meant to Sloan, and they did not appreciate it. The men on strike seemed to think that Alfred P. Sloan was nothing more than a cold-hearted slave driver.

John L. Lewis, head of the CIO, sought to cash in his campaign chips. He boldly interjected himself into the conflict. Through Secretary of Labor Frances Perkins he called on the president to settle the strike in favor of the UAW. Roosevelt, politically cautious as ever, wanted to avoid public involvement in the matter until a reasonable settlement could be worked out. While he did not approve of the sit-down tactic, agreeing with Sloan that it was an illegal act, he nonetheless refused to make any public condemnation of it. Instead, behind the scenes he made it clear that, in principle, he sided with labor.[30]

On January 11, the edgy stalemate between the strikers and GM came to a head. About thirty Flint policemen (later reinforced with fifteen additional officers), under the impression that several private plant security guards had been captured, attacked the strikers holding down the Fisher plant. They fired gas canisters into the plant. The men inside, vomiting and red-eyed from the gas, with labor leader Victor Reuther shouting orders from a union sound car, fought back. They turned fire hoses on the officers, hurled stones and bottles, and pitched with impressive accuracy two-pound steel door hinges at the police. Shocked by the barrage, and coming under additional fusillades by a large crowd of picketing strike sympathizers, the police ran away—giving the confrontation its name: "The Battle of the Running Bulls."

Afraid and enraged, the police regrouped and opened fire on the plant and the picketers with pistols and riot guns. Thirteen people were hit by the gunfire; amazingly, none was killed. Nine policemen had been wounded (one of them by a fellow officer's errant shot). From the sound car, Reuther roared that if the police did not back off the Fisher plant would be destroyed. The police lined up about one hundred feet from the plant. For the next several hours, all through the night, the police fired tear gas at the strikers, who responded by hurling whatever they could get their hands on at the police. Finally, the police used up all available gas. They were, by this time, armed with machine guns as well as additional riot guns. Facing them were the eight hundred or so men in the barricaded Fisher plant, seemingly prepared for an armed assault by the heavily armed police. By some accounts, the men were prepared to blow up the plant and martyr themselves to their cause. The attack never came.[31]

The next morning, the "riot"—as it was often called—was front-page news across the nation. Governor Murphy had called out the Michigan national guard to intercede and the *status quo ante bellum* was restored. The UAW accused GM of being behind the police attack. Knudsen denied the charge. Murphy asked Knudsen to keep the heat on in the plants and to allow the strikers to receive food and water. Knudsen agreed.

In the immediate aftermath of the crisis, John Lewis decided to stir the pot. He held a press conference. With the utmost seriousness, he charged GM with a variety of crimes, past and ongoing. GM, he told the press, should be investigated as an illegal holding company that had cheated the public by "inflating values and watering stock." GM's managers, he reported, were guilty of the "mulcting of shareholders" by paying "excessive salaries and bonuses to executives." GM's very patriotism, its loyalty to the nation and its people, was in doubt, Lewis soberly opined. The public might consider, he stated, "to what extent the policies of General Motors are dictated by British, French, and other holders of securities, in order to ascertain 'if foreign financial leaders control conditions under which our citizens work, and the speed of the General Motors assembly lines.' " Lewis added that he and other labor leaders would ask Senator Robert La Follette's committee on civil liberties to investigate "the arsenals in GM's plants" and the corporation's policy of "industrial warfare, as against collective bargaining which is recognized by law and by thoughtful citizens." He wrapped up his remarks by noting that leaders of American industry, through the Liberty League, "tried for six months to drive the President out of the White House. They are now trying to drive organized labor out of their plants."[32] All this and more was printed in newspapers throughout the nation.

Sloan and GM fought back. In Flint a group of supposedly disinterested citizens, the Flint Alliance, agitated for an end to the illegal trespass. Thousands of loyal GM workers were rounded up by the corporation to proclaim their desire to keep unions out of their lives and to get back to work. GM's public relations department kept up a steady stream of publicity releases. Newspapers reported the cascading unemployment and economic ramifications of the sit-down strike, with thousands and then tens of thousands of workers out of work as the strikes spread and as GM closed down plant after plant because of parts shortages.

The *New York Times,* the *Wall Street Journal,* and several other papers openly sympathized with General Motors in both their coverage and their editorials. According to Secretary Perkins, Sloan "had complete access" to *New York Times* publisher Arthur Sulzberger throughout the strike, and complained continually of his poor treatment by the Roosevelt administration.[33] Whatever Sloan's influence, the *Times* was particularly tough on CIO head John L. Lewis. A few days after the Battle of the Running Bulls, a *Times* editorial warned: "After what Mr. Lewis and his associates have been showing us, it may confidently be said that the system which they would contrive and set to work would look much more like a tyranny than a democracy."[34] Paul Garrett's public relations operation within GM sent copies of this editorial and others like it to newspapers and opinion leaders around the country.

One of the few papers to take the other side, and with a vengeance, was the "central organ" of the Communist Party in the United States, the *Daily Worker.* While by no means an objective commentator on events, its regular columnist Harrison George did get off a snappy reply to the *Times* attack on the "tyrannical" Mr. Lewis, noting that "what the *Times* implies is needed, is a nice democratic institution like that headed by Messrs. Sloan and Knudsen."[35]

The venerable progressive weekly, the *Nation,* also leapt to the defense of the strikers. Thanks to a 1934 New Deal measure mandating corporate reports of executive remuneration, the *Nation* was able to publicize the monies paid to GM's leading figures. In 1935, it reported, workers received a 5 percent pay raise over 1934. During the same period, "the 350 officers, directors, and managers of General Motors received an aggregate reward of $10,000,000 . . . 50 to 100 percent over 1934." It then listed the remuneration of the corporation's twenty-seven highest paid men. John Pratt and Donaldson Brown were tied at third with $249,862. Second was William Knudsen at $325,869. Topping the list, of course, was Alfred P. Sloan, who had earned $374,505 (in 2000 dollars that would be about $4,655,000).[36] (The 1936 figures had yet to be released: Sloan's GM remuneration would be $561,311, or $6,807,386 in 2000 dollars). Some individuals might have enjoyed the publicity associated with being the highest paid corporate industrial executive in the United States. Sloan did not. The New Deal government, in demagogic fashion he believed, had made him an object of public scrutiny and, by so doing, had brought unwanted attention to corporate policies best managed by corporate officials.

In the week that followed the Battle of the Running Bulls, Governor Murphy, William Knudsen, Homer Murphy of the UAW, and others negotiated at the Michigan state capital in Lansing. The National Guard kept order in Flint. Governor Murphy proved to be a heroic negotiator and by mid-January an agreement had almost been worked out. GM, however, refused to give up its right to "collective-bargaining pluralism" (Knudsen, with Sloan's approval, had stated that he would talk to the pro-GM Flint Alliance about a possible role in labor negotiations). The UAW insisted on being recognized as the sole collective bargaining agent for GM workers. Over this not insignificant issue, the talks broke down.[37]

After this disappointment, with talks seeming at a stalemate, Secretary of Labor Frances Perkins (with Roosevelt's vague support) decided to take control of the situation. Perkins was the nation's first woman cabinet officer. As a recent graduate of Mount Holyoke, just after the turn of the century, she'd found her life's calling—she was a devout Christian—working at Hull House and the Commons settlement house in Chicago. Eventually, she had moved to New York. Under the political tutelage of people as diverse as social welfare rights leader Florence Kelley and Tammany pol Big Tim Sullivan, she became a key player in social welfare policy under governors Al Smith and Franklin Roosevelt. When Roosevelt won the presidency, he took her to Washington with him.[38]

Perkins was smart, sure of herself, and she liked to talk. She had not gone to Washington with the support of organized labor. Arthur Schlesinger noted, in his Roosevelt trilogy, "her background as a social worker inclined her, on the whole, to be more interested in doing things for labor than enabling labor to do things for itself."[39] Despite her lukewarm support of organized labor—a feeling, in general, shared by her boss—her sympathies, clear as day, lay with working people. Alfred Sloan knew enough about Frances Perkins to know that she was not going to be his ally.

Perkins had a plan. She wanted to meet in Washington, as she told the president, with "the real principals," Alfred P. Sloan and John L. Lewis. She felt that if she could get the two men to talk, face to face, under her tutelage they could and would work out a settlement.[40] Sloan refused to meet directly with Lewis. He was willing, however, to travel to Washington and talk with Perkins, as well as with Governor Murphy, if she would promise him that their meeting would be held in secret. She so promised. She had been warned by Walter Chrysler that Sloan much preferred deliberating in secret. Such private negotiations, Sloan probably believed, ensured that no one need feel obligated to make statements aimed at the public rather than at solving the problem at hand.[41]

On January 20, 1937, inauspiciously from Sloan's perspective the day of Roosevelt's second inauguration, Sloan traveled with Knudsen, Brown, and GM legal counsel John Smith by private train car down to Washington. Somehow, reporters spotted them. What was to be a secret meeting became a news event. Sloan was angry. Soon, he would be much angrier.

Sloan came prepared to bargain. Even on the issue of collective bargaining, which he found so infuriating, he was willing, he believed, to be flexible in the name of rational problem solving. As a starting point, he insisted that the sit-down strikes be ended before negotiations with Lewis began. With plants reopened, workers could be paid and cars could be made. He pledged that he would negotiate in good faith with the UAW and that once an agreement was reached, retroactive benefits would be given to the workers. Lewis found Sloan's proposal insulting. He did not believe that evacuating the plants and returning to work would leave the UAW much leverage on the corporation.

Lewis, never one to avoid the limelight, chose to respond to Sloan's offer publicly. On January 21, Lewis held a press conference to inform the American people about the secret negotiations. In full voice, he announced:

> The strike is going to be fought to a successful conclusion. No half-baked compromise is going to allow General Motors to doublecross us again. We have advised the administration that [it was] the economic royalists of General Motors—the du Ponts and Sloans and others—who contributed their money and used their energy to drive the President of the United States out of the White House. The administration asked labor to help it repel this attack. Labor gave its help. The same economic royalists now have their fangs in labor, and the workers expect the administration in every reasonable and legal way to support the auto workers in their fight with the same rapacious enemy.[42]

Sloan was disgusted by Lewis's public insults. He and his men took their private train car back to New York. On hearing that Sloan had left the capital, Lewis told reporters, "Perhaps . . . he feels his intellectual inferiority to me."[43] While dead serious about the standoffs in the plants, Lewis seemed to take special pleasure in zinging Sloan. (Late at night, in his hotel room, Lewis did wicked imitations of Sloan and Knudsen for reporters.)[44] At a press conference the next day, Franklin Roosevelt gently chided Lewis for his sharp tongue with a relatively rare on-the-record statement: "Of course, I think that, in the interests of peace, there come moments when statements, conversations, and headlines are not in order."[45] The press laughed in appreciation and the remark was printed in the newspapers. Lewis did not appreciate the president's rebuke, but he was not chastened. For his part, Sloan was growing increasingly furious at the public nature of the entire enterprise.

Perkins tried again. She asked Sloan and Lewis to please meet with her in Washington. Lewis quickly agreed. Sloan would not come, he stated, until "our plants are evacuated and not before."[46] President Roosevelt was annoyed at Sloan's blunt refusal to accept the invitation of "a representative of the President" and the next day, at yet another press conference (four days after his last one and the 339th in less than four years as president!), he rebuked Sloan: "I was not only disappointed in the refusal of Mr. Sloan to come down here, but I regarded it as a very unfortunate decision on his part." When a reporter followed up by asking, "Unfortunate for whom, Mr. Sloan?" the president and the rest of the press corps simply laughed.[47] Again, the president agreed to have his remark placed on the record, and Sloan was able to read it in the next day's papers. In tone and manner, Sloan might well have felt like he was dealing with a new, far more powerful version of his former, not beloved boss: the amiable, impossible-to-pin-down Billy Durant. Such men always smiled when they told you what you did not want to hear.

Perkins piled on. She told the press that she could understand why the UAW did not "trust the word" of GM's managers. Sloan and his men "had made the mistake of their lives in failing to see the moral issues here and proceeding on them, rather than basing their position on a legal technicality and sulking in their tents." Indicating her high emotions, Perkins then read to the reporters from a letter she had written but then not sent to Sloan: "[D]o unto others as you would have done unto you; agree with thine adversary quickly; forgive us our trespasses." The religiously inspired secretary of labor was quoting the Bible to Alfred Sloan. And he could read the entire mess in the *New York Times*, the *Detroit News*, the *Flint Journal*, and probably any number of other papers from which his public relations people clipped articles.[48]

Sloan fought back. He distributed a statement to all GM employees stating that GM would find legal means to prove "that these trespassers who have seized our plants and who have taken from you the privilege of working, have not the right to do so." Then Secretary Perkins announced that she would ask Congress for the power to subpoena and, thus, force recalcitrant parties in a strike situation to negotiate.

With tempers long since frayed, Perkins somehow convinced Sloan to hold a private, face-to-face talk with her in Washington. In secret, they met for two hours. Perkins believed the meeting to be a resounding success. She understood Sloan to have backed down and had agreed to meet in Michigan with Governor Murphy and representatives of the UAW. Sloan, willfully or not, had left her with this clear understanding.

Alfred Sloan boarded the train back to New York and went home. Judging by subsequent events, perhaps he had a drink. It was the dinner hour. Then from his apartment, Sloan rang up Mrs. Perkins at her home. She was having dinner with her daughter. The secretary was famously private (in part, because her husband was institutionalized with a mental disorder) and she hated to be disturbed at home when she was with her family. Perhaps Sloan did not know this about her; perhaps he did not care. He had never before in his life, before the current difficulties, discussed a serious business matter with a woman. Perkins took his call but not happily. He had clearly stated as he left her office in Washington that he would call her in the morning about the details of their agreement.

Sloan was direct. He had decided, he told her, that he would not meet with any representative of labor in Michigan or anywhere else. His legal team had already begun legal action against the strikers. He intended to have the men removed. Frances Perkins believed herself to have been betrayed. She later described her feelings: "I was really so angry that something that wasn't me was bulging up inside of me." She really did not like Alfred Sloan.

"You are a scoundrel and a skunk, Mr. Sloan," she yelled into the phone. "You don't deserve to be counted among decent men. . . . You'll go to hell when you die if you do things like that. . . . Are you a grown man, Mr. Sloan? Or are you a neurotic adolescent? Which are you? If you're a grown man, stand up, and be a man for once."

Sloan was astonished by her outburst: "You can't talk like that to me! You can't talk like that to me! I'm worth 70 million dollars and I made it all myself! You can't talk like that to me! I'm Alfred Sloan." (Seventy million dollars would be equivalent to $848,940,000 in the year 2000).

According to Perkins, he repeated his admonishments about the 70 million dollars and not talking to him like that and his name some twenty times. Once he stopped to catch his breath, she came back at him: "Haven't you ever read what happens to the rich man! It's like the camel trying to go through the eye of the needle. If you've got 70 million dollars it's going to drown you, Mr. Sloan. It's going to sink you. For God's sake don't say those words to me again. It makes you a worse rotter than I thought you were."

Sloan slammed down the phone.[49]

Perkins believed Sloan had lied to her. She believed that Sloan lacked something fundamental in his understanding of the world around him.

After pondering the matter for some time, many years after the dust had settled, she told an interviewer: ". . . What was the matter in those days with Alfred Sloan's mind was that he had never used his mind for the purposes of thinking out a moral problem, a philosophical problem, any problem whatever, except a problem having to do with the making of money and the selling of goods. . . . He doesn't have the kind of a mind that can think in terms of what's right and wrong, what's good and bad, what's democratic and undemocratic."[50]

Alfred Sloan would not have agreed, in whole, with Frances Perkins; he did think, at least, about right and wrong, good and bad. He just thought about such things in terms quite foreign to her. Very soon after the Flint mess he would demonstrate such concern.

Perkins and Sloan reacted differently to their unpleasant phone call. Sloan seems to have called Myron Taylor, chairman of U.S. Steel. Taylor was in the midst of his own—far less antagonistic—labor talks with John Lewis, which were being held in secret. Quite possibly, Sloan knew about the talks. He was still upset when he spoke to Taylor and repeated his angry words about being worth $70 million and having no need to put up with so much aggravation. Taylor proved himself to be no friend of Sloan's. He called up Secretary Perkins and repeated the conversation to her. After comparing notes, Taylor, a very rich man himself, mused that Sloan seemed strangely preoccupied with this fortune: "It must be that that's in his mind all the time. That idea must be in the back of his mind all the time."[51]

For her part, Perkins, though quite upset, was able to refrain from calling the president and telling him of Sloan's change of mind (which, after all, did not reflect well on her judgment). By this time, the president had already told her that he thought Sloan to be nothing more than "a low comedy figure."[52] While Perkins probably called no one that evening—she really did try to leave work behind her when she was at home with her family—the next day, or soon after, she leaked her conversation with Sloan so that, directly or indirectly, the leading newspaper columnists of the day, Drew Pearson and Robert Allen, got wind of it.[53]

Alfred Sloan had spent a great deal of time and money working on GM's public image and on his own place in American society. The limits to his success in this regard were made painfully clear to him in the climactic days of the Flint strike. Specifically, he learned how little his efforts had affected several of the key media pundits of the New Deal Era. On the day of Sloan's phone conversation with Secretary Perkins, Walter Lippman, doyen of American pundits, chided Sloan in his nationally syndicated daily column for his "bungling" and accused him of "making a bad situation worse." Lippman wrote:

> [T]he power of dealing with the sit-down strike is beyond the power of a private corporation, and the responsibility must be placed upon the Government, it is too big, too grave, too momentous a problem for private business men to resolve. Not Mr. Sloan but Mr. Roosevelt is the man who must take that problem in hand, and the greatest mistake of all Mr. Sloan's mistakes had been that he did not see this. . . . Why on earth should Mr. Sloan then feel that destiny had appointed him to solve the problem of the new American labor movement, when he can turn that grave responsibility over to Mr. Roosevelt?[54]

Lippman was lecturing Sloan like he was an imbecile, telling him that the American government through its elected leader, not he, the board-appointed president of the corporation that paid each and every worker, had the right and the responsibility to manage the labor force of General Motors. Sloan undoubtedly read Lippman's generally well-respected column. Sloan was known to bang his fists on his desk and yell, quite loudly, when he was angry; it is hard to believe that Lippman's column was not cause for one of those rare eruptions.

The newspapers gave Alfred Sloan much worse treatment a few days later. Some of what he had said to Frances Perkins out of anger and frustration appeared in print, though it was distorted and accompanied by outright lies about his career and his accomplishments. Drew Pearson and Robert Allen, in their widely syndicated column "Washington Merry-Go-Round," mercilessly ridiculed Sloan for his sit-down strike performance. First they claimed that he had been born "with a silver spoon in his mouth," and that his fortune was almost entirely due to an inheritance that he received from his father (who had died, remember, less than five years earlier). They then patronized his accomplishments by blandly and inaccurately asserting that his rise to the head of GM was based on nothing more than having been born rich and of having made the acquaintance of the du Ponts at MIT. He kept his job, they informed readers, by serving "primarily as a watchman for the du Pont interests." Then they asserted that he knew little about automobiles and less about life: "He would never put you to sleep, nor would he keep you awake. . . . You can't help being a little sorry for him." And then as a topper, they "quoted" Sloan crying out, "Why should I be bothered with all this? I'm worth $50,000,000 in my own right. My doctor tells me it's suicide to work like this. I should have quit long ago." Poor Mr. Sloan, they reported, "gives the impression of being riled and nervous, almost in a state of jitters."[55] Pearson and Allen had taken away $20 million of Sloan's fortune, just to give him one more insult to swallow.

After the Perkins' fiasco, Sloan withdrew publicly from the fray. He had Donaldson Brown, the finance man who had an interest in politics, formally take over the chore of representing the corporate office. Knudsen continued to carry the brunt of the negotiating responsibilities. Behind the scenes, though, Sloan continued to play a role. In his New York apartment, he met with key corporate officers as well as with Walter Chrysler and Chrysler's legal counsel, Nicholas Kelley, to discuss strategy. Sloan must have taken some comfort in having Chrysler there with him, in his home, as the bad news kept unfolding.[56]

In the last month of 1936, GM had manufactured about fifty thousand autos. In the first week of February, crippled by the sit-down strikes, they turned out 125.[57] On February 1, the UAW had escalated the battle by seizing another key GM production facility in Flint, Chevrolet No. 4 Engine plant. John L. Lewis made it clear that the workers would not back down. He taunted Governor Murphy, who was trying to move the negotiations along by threatening to use force to evacuate GM's plants. Lewis stated:

> I am not going to withdraw those sit-downers under any circumstances except a settlement. What are you going to do? You can get them out in just one way, by bayonets. You have the bayonets. Which kind do you prefer to use—the broad double blade or the four-sided French style? I believe the square style makes a bigger hole and you can turn it around inside a man. Which kind of bayonets, Governor Murphy, are you going to turn around inside our boys?[58]

Sloan, as he had promised, had gotten an injunction against the sit-down strike from a Michigan judge. But on February 3, with the injunction in effect, the governor chose not to use force against the strikers. That same day, William Knudsen agreed to met with Lewis. Knudsen had agreed to the meeting only after he secured word, via Frances Perkins, that the president of the United States requested his participation. Knudsen, in a face-saving gesture, formally stated to Governor Murphy that he was meeting only because "[t]he wish of the of the President of the United States leaves no alternative except compliance."[59] Sloan was silent.

On February 11, 1937, General Motors signed an agreement with the UAW ending the sit-down strikes. While the UAW negotiators did not get everything they wanted, they got more than enough. GM agreed to bargain exclusively, if only for a set period of time, with the UAW. By October of 1937, the once fragile union had some four hundred thousand dues-paying members. The UAW had spearheaded a wave of labor militancy that would shatter the nature of industrial relations in the United States. Sit-down strikes in other major industries followed those in Flint by the hundreds. Organized labor gained victory after victory leading to an era of unprecedented—if still limited—power in American history. None of the labor victories would have been even remotely possible without the militant actions and dedication of the workers themselves. But as Alfred P. Sloan knew too well, labor's numerous victories would not have occurred without New Deal legislation and the support of liberal Democratic politicians, judges, and administrators throughout the nation. While Sloan and GM would learn to live with the labor unions, the Flint sit-down strike was Sloan's most bitter defeat and it would haunt him.

* * *

Sloan's misery did not end with the signing of the UAW agreement. Beginning on February 15, 1937, just four days after the strike ended, Senator Robert La Follette Jr. of Wisconsin led a special Senate subcommittee investigation into antilabor activities at General Motors. These were the exact hearings that John L. Lewis had called for a month earlier. Sloan was not personally attacked by the senator or his investigators but that was only small relief. In headline-making news, the hearings lambasted General Motors for employing labor spies and engaging in a series of dastardly deeds against GM unionists. The hearings were almost completely one-sided. As the hearings-sympathetic historian Jerold S. Auerbach notes, "The committee's report on industrial espionage read like a UAW brief against General Motors."[60]

The New Dealers were not done with Alfred Sloan. In June, Sloan and his wife were publicly charged by the Treasury Department, before a congressional committee, with "moral fraud" for having avoided paying $1,921,587 in federal income taxes between 1934 and 1936. The Rene Corporation, the holding company that Sloan had set up to buy and maintain his yacht, was targeted by the Treasury Department as a tax loophole scam. In support of the investigation, President Roosevelt sent a message to Congress excoriating the methods wealthy Americans, Sloan included, used to avoid their fair share of taxes: "All are alike in that failure to pay results in shifting the tax load to the shoulders of others less able to pay and in mulcting the Treasury of the Government's just due." Sloan's travails were headline news. Furious, he fought back. In a prepared statement, he informed the press that he paid 60 percent of his 1936 income in state and federal taxes. Of the dollars he had left, he gave half to charity (which, though he did not state it, would have included donations to political causes and the like). While his statement was reported, even the usually Sloan-friendly *New York Times* put in its headline the fact that in 1936 Sloan reported earning $2,876,310 ($34,882,895 in year 2000 dollars). No follow-up stories appeared stating that Sloan was never charged with having done anything illegal.[61]

During and immediately after this onslaught, Sloan showed no signs of emotional weakness or distress. After the sit-down debacle, he seemed to have steeled himself to a new public role in American life. If he could not be the model leader of a new corporate society, as he had been in the 1920s, then he would be a behind-the-scenes champion of economic rationalism. He would find ways to use his money and his talent to teach Americans what the modern private enterprise system did to make American life better. Sloan was not defeated by what he had endured in 1937, though he had become embittered and defensive.

Rather than concede to the New Dealers, Sloan fought back in late 1937 with one of his most enduring contributions to American public life. Shortly after his public humiliation by the Treasury Department, Sloan turned over $10 million to the Alfred P. Sloan Foundation (in 2000 dollars adjusted for inflation, that would be $120,080,000). In his public statement he announced, "This particular foundation proposes to concentrate to an important degree on a single objective, i.e., the promotion of a wider knowledge of basic economic truths generally accepted by authorities of recognized standing and as demonstrated by experience."[62] In a private letter to Irénée du Pont, he spoke more plainly:

> You appreciate, Irénée, that I am not thinking of developing a research organization. What I am trying to do is to encourage the many movements that have been, and are about to be started, to do a better job so that the attack [on the New Deal] can be widened along a broader front. If we could get across to the people of the United States, the fact that they can not get something for nothing, to my mind, it would be a great accomplishment. Too many people believe that that is possible, and there are too many people in high places, telling them that it is possible.[63]

For the next two decades, Sloan devoted his foundation almost exclusively (with one major exception to be discussed later), to "American economic education and research." Akin to the public relations work of the National Association of Manufacturers with which he had become involved, the Sloan Foundation's public education projects focused on "new enterprises" of an "experimental character." Sloan was particularly interested in exploring the utility of film in spreading the free-enterprise gospel. Through a large grant to New York University, Sloan hoped to create "a measurement program" to evaluate the efficacy of the economic education films his foundation generously funded. "Such a program," he wrote, "will supply a constant fund of information which, when applied to the production of subsequent films, will make each one increasingly effective for the purpose for which is it intended and for the audience for which it is designed." Sloan had never been happy with the public relations work he had overseen at General Motors, NAM, and other allied organizations. As he wrote Charles Kettering in the spring of 1938, "[O]ur attention has been so concentrated on building up business that [we] have not given sufficient thought to simultaneous development of our relations with the public."[64] Perhaps, he thought, he could use the foundation's grants to bring the kind of analytic precision to this area as he had to other critical corporate functions like finance and inventory control.

In addition, Sloan began giving large amounts of money to institutions of higher education, mainly his alma mater, the Massachusetts Institute of Technology. During the first years of his grant making, his largest sums went to creating an "industrial leadership" program at MIT. Sloan believed his own narrow education—and as already stated, Sloan seems to have exaggerated, in his own mind, the limits of his educational opportunities at MIT in the 1890s—contributed to his difficulties in preparing GM for the political realities of the 1930s. Many corporate executives, at all levels, he believed, were similarly ill prepared for managing social externalities. In the 1940 report of the Sloan Foundation, the major grants to MIT for fellowships in industrial leadership, begun in 1938, were explained:

> The increasing participation of government in the economic life of the nation, labor's newly created privileges, the growing public consciousness of the prerogatives and obligations of consumers suggest the need for a type of education for industrial leadership that will expand the notion of managerial skill to include the broader implications of social and economic understanding.

For the rest of his life, Sloan pondered the kind of management training it would take to best prepare corporate executives for the technical, political, and economic problems that would invariably impinge on their primary responsibility: running a profitable enterprise.

For the next two decades, Sloan spent an increasing amount of time running his foundation. He ran it quite differently from the way he oversaw the running of GM. Rather than rely on committees and consultation, Sloan surrounded himself with "yes men," including his much less successful younger brother (a Twentieth Century Fund retrospective report on "the big foundations" noted that Harold Sloan, up until that time an associate professor of economics at Montclair College, the New Jersey state teachers college, "brought unstinted enthusiasm, if not much else, to his new position"). Alfred personally picked every project and allocated each grant.[65] Though he saw little clear success in his efforts to change the public's perception of the free enterprise system, he nevertheless must have believed that the effort was worth making.

Even as Sloan took on yet another responsibility, he by no means shirked his primary duties at General Motors. But beginning in the spring of 1937 those duties did begin to evolve. Sloan turned sixty-two years old that May. His hearing had gotten much worse, making committee meetings less productive than they had once been. While he was not ready to retire, he had begun to think about the process of succession at General Motors. Ironically, given what columnists Pearson and Allen had said about him being a mere "watchman" for the du Ponts, Sloan wanted to make sure that the men who followed him would be men dedicated above all else to General Motors. He did not want the du Pont interests, despite their immense and long-standing investment in GM stock, to determine key corporate policies. He wanted men like himself, corporate managers who understood industry, to control General Motors' destiny. He feared that when he retired no one within General Motors had the necessary power and authority, as he had, to lead the company forward in its own best interests. In writing about the 1937 reorganization struggle from the perspective of the du Pont interests, the business historian Charles Cheape not unfairly states:

> From the time of his successful bouts with Pierre [du Pont] in the 1920s, Sloan had strongly felt that the needs of the business, not the owners, should determine organization and policy. In an extraordinary demonstration of the hubris of the professional manager, he later wrote [Donaldson] Brown that the organization ought to be set up on the basis of what is best for the business. The representation of the stockholders should be a second consideration.[66]

Sloan used his peerless administrative capacity to reorganize the corporation on several fronts at the same time. As a key first step, he returned to the organizational chart he had created. Sloan insisted that the two key committees that had been set up by the du Ponts at the end of Billy Durant's reign, the executive and finance committees, be refashioned into one far-reaching committee: the policy committee. He argued that the bifurcation of authority between executive and finance committees had proven to be an artificial device—all executive decisions had financial implications and vice versa. Better to have one committee that could study the most pressing issues from all perspectives and then make sound business decisions.

Such logic was compelling, but it hid Sloan's major motive. The finance committee, since the deposing of Billy Durant, had been the du Pont interest's power base in General Motors. Under Sloan's reorganization plan, the du Pont's hold was weakened, as he placed six GM men on the new committee, one Morgan banker, and but two men to represent du Pont's major investment in the corporation. The new committee not only weakened the du Pont hold but it provided his hand-picked men with invaluable experience. Sloan wanted key GM executives to have the kind of broad-based corporate decision-making experiences that would prepare them to run the entire business. Not surprisingly, given what Sloan had long said about picking the right man for the job, three of the GM men Sloan selected for the new policy committee would become heads of the corporation.

Sloan did want to step back from his corporate responsibilities—at least somewhat. He wanted William Knudsen to become president of GM and to take over much of the day-to-day decision making at the corporate level. What Sloan wanted for himself was to be chairman of the board of General Motors. Lammont du Pont, who was the GM chairman at the time, told Walter Carpenter, a high-ranking Du Pont executive and GM board member, "that Alfred intended to, and wanted it known that he was lightening his burden." But, he continued, Sloan did not want to step aside completely, nor did he want to be viewed as some kind of corporate figurehead. Sloan was quite worried, according to Lammont du Pont, that "the public would get the impression that he thought was undesirable . . . that he had been 'kicked upstairs.' "[67] The sit-down strike debacle and the embarrassing La Follette hearings (the Treasury Department business was just ahead) weighed heavily on Sloan's self-esteem.

Sloan got his way. By this time, whatever outside difficulties had transpired, no one on GM's board of directors outright opposed anything

Alfred P. Sloan wanted.[68] He had earned the right to make the big decisions. William Knudsen took over as GM president. Lammont du Pont stepped down as chairman and Sloan took his place. In fact, Sloan gave himself a new position: chief executive officer. He intended to hold the position for only a short period of time—long enough to make it clear that he, and no one else, decided what role he would play at GM, but not so long as to impede Knudsen's authority. Events—the coming of war—would conspire against that projected time line. Still, Sloan was stepping back, at least somewhat, from his grueling responsibilities as leader of General Motors.

* * *

Ironically, Sloan's worst year also turned out to be Franklin Roosevelt's nadir. Not long after the sit-down strike was resolved, President Roosevelt saw his support from both Congress and the American people plummet. Both angrily rejected Roosevelt's ill-considered Supreme Court "packing" legislation (FDR hoped to reverse a string of Supreme Court rulings against the New Deal by adding additional justices to the Court; he was only hoping to help, he said, the "aged and infirm" justices with their heavy burden of work). New Deal historian William Leuchtenburg argues: "In attempting to alter the Court, Roosevelt had attacked one of the symbols which many believed the nation needed for its sense of unity as a body politic. . . . The greater the insecurity of the times, the more people clung to the few institutions which seemed changeless."[69] The great politician, by overreaching, had taken a grievous misstep.

Even worse, for Roosevelt and the American people, the recession that GM's men had warned against right after FDR's reelection struck at the end of the summer of 1937, though not for the reasons the executives had predicted. In December of 1936, Roosevelt's advisors had divided over economic policy. Federal Reserve chairman Marriner Eccles urged Roosevelt to continue large-scale federal spending to stimulate the economy. Secretary of the Treasury Henry Morgenthau Jr. argued that the federal government needed a balanced budget to bolster private sector confidence in the recovery. Roosevelt, exhibiting shades of the "sound" conservative economic thinking that had mollified Sloan's opinion of Roosevelt in 1932 and 1933, sided with Morgenthau. The federal budget was cut from $10.3 billion to $9.6 billion in 1937. At the same time, social security taxes began to be collected and the Federal Reserve Board imposed higher interest rates. These measures combined to throw the fragile economy into the "Roosevelt recession." Some 5 million Americans lost their jobs. Roosevelt and the New Deal were in trouble.[70]

Conservatives, in government and out, took advantage of the misery to take the political offensive. The uneasy congressional coalition of conservative southern Democrats (recall Sloan's cash contribution to Georgia governor Eugene Talmadge in 1936) and liberal northern Democrats began to come apart. Roosevelt's own vice president, the former Texas congressman and Speaker of the House, John Nance Garner, who had been particularly disgusted by Roosevelt's sympathies for the sit-down strikers, helped to lead the revolt. While a few key pieces of legislation would be passed over the next year, the era of New Deal reform was coming to a close.

Sloan could take no immediate solace in the president's predicament. The most liberal New Dealers, rather than concede Roosevelt's mistaken fiscal policies, were blaming Big Business for the recession. New Deal historian Alan Brinkley writes that these liberals insisted "that the recession was a result of unregulated monopoly power in the marketplace. Corporate interests, they believed, had colluded to suppress competition and create what liberals liked to call 'administered prices,' choking off what had otherwise been a healthy recovery."[71]

Assistant Attorney General Robert Jackson, head of the antitrust division and a Roosevelt confidant, took the lead. He accused "monopolists" of deliberately causing the recession, stating that a "strike of capital" by business was behind the economic slowdown. He lambasted "the percentage advance that big business has given to its own darlings," singling out Alfred Sloan's impressive salary as evidence of industry's misdeeds. "Certain groups of big business," Jackson intoned, "have now seized upon a recession in our prosperity to 'liquidate the New Deal' and to throw off all government interference with their incorporated initiative." The ever-acerbic Interior Secretary Harold Ickes, a New Deal heavyweight, joined the attack. On December 30, 1937 he spoke on NBC radio, warning the American people of a "big business fascist America—an enslaved America." He concluded that an "irreconcilable conflict" existed between "the power of money and the power of the democratic instinct."[72] Key New Dealers, with the president's sympathies, fought the political fallout of the economic downturn by raising that old progressive banner: the evils of monopoly. General Motors was an obvious target.

In May 1938, the Department of Justice secured an antitrust criminal indictment against General Motors, as well as against Ford and Chrysler. The government charged that each of the car manufacturers illegally restrained trade by requiring their respective dealers to only use the company-associated finance company (GMAC in the case of GM). Chrysler and Ford quickly signed consent agreements with the Justice Department. Sloan, believing the government action to be a form of "legal blackmail," decided to fight. In various forms, the antitrust suit would drag on for some fourteen years.[73]

The antitrust action was unpleasant, especially as Sloan was personally charged with criminal activity. Sloan was, however, found innocent on the charges—even if General Motors was not. Far more worrisome was the government's larger intent. With reason, Sloan feared that the Justice Department might come after the corporation as a whole. Sloan had long been concerned about federal antitrust action. As the smaller auto manufacturers fell by the wayside, and as General Motors' share of the market approached 50 percent, Sloan deliberately sought to keep GM's market share down. He told *Fortune* magazine in late 1938: "Our bogie is 45 per cent of each price class . . . we don't want any more than that."[74] Sloan had almost certainly been driven to making this public statement of his concerns by the New Deal administration's spring 1938 offensive.

On April 29, 1938, President Roosevelt sent a message to Congress titled "Recommendations to the Congress to Curb Monopolies and the Concentration of Economic Power." In it, he warned:

> The first truth is that the liberty of democracy is not safe if the people tolerate the growth of private power to a point where it becomes stronger than the democratic state itself. That, in its essence, is Fascism—ownership of Government by an individual, by a group, or by any other controlling private power. The second truth is that the liberty of a democracy is not safe if its business system does not provide employment and produce and distribute goods in such a way as to sustain an acceptable standard of living.[75]

Out of this heated message came the "Investigation of Concentration of Economic Power" by the Temporary National Economic Committee (TNEC), a public body composed equally of representatives of federal agencies and of members of Congress. The TNEC had broad investigative powers. In 1938 Sloan felt the need to respond to it and the rest of the antitrust activities of the New Deal. He launched a public relations blitz defending corporate bigness, while ensuring that GM's market share did not increase that year.

The TNEC appeared at first to be the ax blade Sloan had long feared the New Deal was preparing for Big Business. But by the time the TNEC went to work, it had become something very different: the death rattle of the anti–Big Business wing of the New Deal. The political force that had fostered its radical guise in the spring of 1938 was, shockingly, gone in just a few months time.

In the early summer of 1938, Roosevelt made another major political blunder. He attacked what he called Democratic Party "Copperheads" (referencing the northern Democrats who had opposed the Civil War). FDR took to the road, campaigning to replace incumbent conservative Democratic congressmen with more liberal candidates. Overwhelmingly, his attempt to create a national liberal Democratic Party failed when almost all of the conservative Democrats Roosevelt opposed won their reelection bids. Moreover, Republicans won eight Senate seats and picked up eighty-one House seats. Roosevelt had lost a working majority for almost all new major government reforms.

Not only was the political wind changing. By mid-1938 the economy had recovered from the federal fiscal policies of the previous year. And, more long lastingly, key New Dealers were by 1939 beginning to make their own separate peace with the kind of economic system Alfred Sloan championed. Thurman Arnold, who took over as head of the antitrust division of the Justice Department in 1938, could write by 1942: "There can be no greater nonsense . . . than the idea that a mechanized age can get along without big business—its research, its technicians, its production managers."[76] After some five years of economic policy experimentation, in which everything from the National Recovery Administration's voluntary industrial cartelization to "Kingfish" Huey Long's campaign for a radical redistribution of income had been on the political table, a new détente between Big Business and the government was being sorted out. Business would face government regulation and a policing of its competitive practices; organized labor would be protected by the state; and federal fiscal policy would be used to stimulate consumer demand and investment practices. The basic structure of the market economy, however, would be left untouched. No major New Dealers were advocating the dismantling of Big Business. New Deal economist Alvin Hansen explained the underlying premise motivating the new thinking: "Let us now turn to a high-consumption economy and develop that as the great frontier of the future."[77] Alfred P. Sloan Jr. would have happily made the exact same statement.

As a result of these political, economic, and ideological changes, by 1939 both the political will and economic justification for New Deal challenges to Big Business had largely dissipated. This new, more accommodating spirit was in evidence when Sloan testified before the TNEC in May 1939. He was cordially received. He was allowed to present a blizzard of facts demonstrating GM's fairly achieved success. He concluded his lengthy testimony by noting: "I am speaking purely in the interest of economy; that is everything to me. The personal point is inconsequential, but I do think that we have to have more profit in industry." The acting chairman of the committee, Utah senator William King, politely asked him: "The profit motive, then, stimulates investment?" Sloan cheerfully replied: "As long as we have the profit motive, we have to respect it."[78]

Despite this taming of the New Deal reform impulse, as the shadow of war began to reach America Alfred Sloan remained disgusted with the federal government. As he saw it, the damage New Dealers had inflicted on his corporation and on economically productive men had been done. His America, he believed, in which business leaders had the basic right to run their enterprises as they saw fit, with support from their government, had been destroyed. Instead, he and his peers had to manage their businesses while confronting confiscatory taxes and a range of distrustful government bureaucrats who were ever ready to take them to task through a range of agencies, departments, and legal statutes. Sloan saw the new political order as antagonistic. In response he increased GM's defensive capacity. In July 1938 he gave the go-ahead to Donaldson Brown to set up a special subcommittee on "Social and Economic Trends." GM would have its own experts report on the large-scale political and economic trends that affected the corporation.[79]

Sloan shared his frustrations with Walter Carpenter, who had become president of Du Pont in May 1940. Sloan wrote: "In industry today, the labor leader determines the economics, the public relations department the policies, and the politicians get whatever is left over. Really, there is not much use for anybody else in the picture, so far as I am beginning to see."[80] While several recent histories have concluded that, in the end, the New Deal deliberately did little to challenge the fundamental tenets and practices of Big Business, Alfred Sloan would surely have sided with more traditional accounts that picture the New Deal as a counter to the corporate freedoms Sloan and his peers had taken as their due in the 1920s. While the "profit motive" was, indeed, left untouched by the New Deal, aggressive government economic regulation, increased taxes (corporate, personal, and social security), and government protection of organized labor had changed how Alfred Sloan and his peers managed America's great corporations. Business had acquired a partner—a junior partner—in the federal government. While some corporate leaders embraced government's stabilization of the economy, provision of basic social welfare measures, and even intervention in labor relations, Sloan, along with most of his peers, did not.[81]

To Sloan, the New Deal was a raw deal. Personally, it was not the worst blow he took in the late 1930s. On May 26, 1938, Walter Chrysler had a stroke. As he convalesced at his estate on Long Island, his wife Della suffered a cerebral hemorrhage, on August 8, and died a few hours later. Walter Chrysler, grief stricken, never recovered from the stroke, though he did have good days as well as bad. Wheelchair-bound, his health deteriorated; his closest friends watched "the light . . . go out of him."[82] He had another stroke and then died on August 18, 1940. Sloan's dearest friend was dead and he never would have another like him. It was a rotten way to end a terrible decade.

SLOAN RULES

The manager was very placid, he had no vital anxieties now, he took us both in with a comprehensive and satisfied glance: the "affair" had come off as well as could be wished.

—**Joseph Conrad, *Heart of Darkness***

Alfred Sloan watched the coming of world war with dread. His antipathy for the Roosevelt administration and concern for General Motors, far more than any dread of human carnage, drove his anxieties. Some twenty years earlier, the writer Randolph Bourne had warned: "War is the health of the State."[1] Sloan worried that war mobilization would give the Roosevelt administration the power to control the economy; New Dealers would have the legal authority to rob GM of personnel, profit, and managerial autonomy. He feared that federal wartime mandates, even after victory was attained, could leave General Motors ill prepared for the eventual return to its core consumer businesses.

But as America prepared for and then entered the war, Sloan came to understand that the war would actually benefit General Motors specifically and the free enterprise system in general. Victory would come down to which nation performed best in the industrial realm. World war meant that the politicians were, once again, dependent on men like Sloan, men who know how to produce. Throughout the war, Sloan remained remarkably—even shockingly—indifferent to its emotional vicissitudes and even to its outcomes. He was, however, disgusted by the sheer destructiveness of the war and by the inability of humans to work more productively toward useful ends.

Personally, the war did affect Sloan's choices, principally his decision to stay on as CEO at GM for longer than he had intended. As a result, instead of leaving GM at a point of political and economic uncertainty, he left feeling that victory had been won—not over the fascist threat to democracy, as most Americans would say—but over the government that had challenged General Motors and the free enterprise system. Soon after the war ended, he stepped down from his executive position—though he remained chairman of the board for another ten years—confident that General Motors and the United States were headed in the right direction. He was at that time seventy-one years old. In Sloan's long twilight years he remained active in the world, further weaving his vision into the fabric of American society.

* * *

Predictably, Sloan viewed the growing belligerency in Europe during the 1930s and early 1940s through the GM corporate lens. All the rest—ideology, civilian deaths, military conquest, race hatred, national subjugation—none of it touched him or his analyses. He had always believed that corporate investments and practices overseas should be judged only by their impact on corporate profitability. He was constantly annoyed by government efforts to limit his overseas business based on some official's notions of national interest or statesmen-like claims about international justice.

As early as December 1934, American government concerns about German rearmament following the Nazi takeover of Germany began to impinge on General Motors' freedom to act. Executives with I. G. Farben, the German chemical company, approached GM to discuss the possibilities of setting up a tetraethyl lead plant. Such a plant would be quite useful for German gasoline refining which, in turn, would be quite helpful to Germany's military preparations. Irénée du Pont, still GM chairman, personally urged Sloan not to proceed: "Of course, we in the Du Pont Company have always recognized the propriety and desirability of closely cooperating with the War Department of the United States. . . . In any case, I know that word has gone to the War Department and have the impression that they would be adverse to disclosure of knowledge which would aid Germany in preparing that chemical."[2] The fact that the du Ponts had just gone through a humiliating Senate investigation of their

World War I munitions business (a contemporary popular book had labeled them "Merchants of Death") undoubtedly added to du Pont's concerns about GM's involvement with any possible German rearmament efforts. Sloan rejected du Pont's worries: "I do not agree with your reasoning to this question. . . . I will make it my business to go over it with you in person, the next time you are available."[3] He followed up a few days later: "I intended to convey [in the first letter] the idea that the subject, as I saw it, was far more fundamental . . . than the question of making a little money out of lead in Germany."[4] General Motors and Standard Oil of New Jersey, in collaboration, went ahead with the German tetraethyl lead venture. As war broke out in Europe, Sloan's position became clearer and more public.

By early 1939, General Motors began receiving flak from a variety of people, including stockholders, over its German operations. By this time, a powerfully rearmed Germany had already expanded into Austria and Czechoslovakia and was threatening to move on Poland. The Nazis were openly and virulently anti-Semitic. And, from a strictly corporate viewpoint, they were not good for business: the Nazi regime had made it impossible for GM to take any profits out of its extensive German operations (Opel). In response to at least one stockholder's concerns, Sloan personally wrote a comprehensive, private answer explaining GM's position:

> General Motors Corporation is an international organization. It operates in practically every country in the world where motors cars are used. . . . Its export activities have been quite an outstanding achievement of its development and represent an evolution of something like twenty years of aggressive, and I believe in the main, intelligent effort. . . . The profits which the stockholders have received as a result of its overseas activities have been outstanding.
>
> . . . Now I believe that if an international business, such as General Motors, engages in the commercial activity of any country with the idea of making a profit . . . that it has an obligation to that country, both in an economic sense as well perhaps as in a social sense. It should attempt to attune itself to the general business of the community; make itself a part of the same; conduct its operations in relation to the customs. . . . I believe further, that that should be its position, even if, as is likely to happen and particularly as was the case during the past few years, the management of the Corporation might not wholly agree with many things that are done in certain of these countries. In other words, to put the proposition rather bluntly, such matters should not be considered the business of the management of General Motors.[5]

Sloan was unbending in this belief. He had put himself on a collision course with the American government.

Sloan's antagonism toward the New Deal transferred without diminution to the Roosevelt administration's war mobilization efforts. His antipathy was only intensified by the government's treatment of his friend and colleague John Pratt in the late summer of 1939. Just before war broke out in Europe, President Roosevelt quietly began planning—or perhaps preplanning—for war. The public was still overwhelmingly opposed to American intervention abroad and Roosevelt felt he had to proceed with the utmost caution. He created an extragovernmental advisory board to consider how government and industry might best organize for war mobilization. Not surprisingly, Roosevelt needed major industrialists to oversee the process. The president asked Edward Stettinius to chair what came to be called the War Resources Board (WRB). Stettinius had left General Motors in 1934 and by 1938 had become the largely ornamental chairman of the board of U.S. Steel. His remarkable charm and his graceful service in Washington, D.C. had served him extraordinarily well. Stettinius had remained close friends with his GM mentor John Pratt, and his first move on accepting Roosevelt's invitation was to ask Pratt to work with him on the WRB. Pratt provided the know-how to produce the report Roosevelt had requested.

Pratt had stepped down from his executive position with GM after Sloan's 1937 reorganization, though he had stayed on as a member of the board (a position he would hold until 1968). In late September, Pratt wrote Sloan a full account of his frustrating government service, capped by Roosevelt's rejection of his WRB report—not because of any fault with Pratt's analysis but for reasons that were solely political.[6] Sloan immediately wrote him back: "What I do not understand is with the perfectly obvious record of the past six years, that distinguished industrialists of experience and accomplishment, like yourself, seem to like to go down to Washington, one after another, knowing that there is just one outcome; viz, the eventual 'kick in the pants.' "[7] Politicians, Sloan believed, could not be trusted; facts meant nothing to them. They dealt in votes, backroom deals, and power plays, not objective analyses. Over the next couple of years, Sloan would have several opportunities to repeat these sentiments to other GM executives as they chose to leave GM for patriotic reasons.

Most famously, in May 1940 William Knudsen stepped down for the presidency of GM to serve his adopted country. His native Denmark had fallen to the Nazis during the German blitzkrieg that had also rolled over Norway, Luxembourg, Holland, Belgium, and France. Knudsen had spoken out at the time, urging the United States to prepare "like the government prepared for the gangsters so that if anybody tries to get us involved they will know they have somebody to deal with who can handle himself in a scrap."[8]

President Roosevelt personally called Knudsen, the nation's best known production man, and asked him to come to Washington and help oversee industrial war mobilization. Before agreeing, Knudsen told Roosevelt he would need to discuss the matter with Alfred Sloan. The next day, Knudsen met with Sloan in New York. According to Knudsen's account of the conversation in his 1947 biography, Sloan told him not to accept Roosevelt's request: "They'll make a monkey out of you, down there in Washington."

Knudsen replied: "That isn't important, Mr. Sloan. I came to this country with nothing. It has been good to me. Rightly or wrongly, I feel I must go."

"That's a quixotic way of looking at it."

"Perhaps you are right, Mr. Sloan. Nevertheless, I am going."

"What do they want you to do?"

"I don't know exactly, what the President has in mind. . . ."

"And still you go?"

"Yes. As I said, the President asked me to come. I feel I ought to answer his calls. Besides, if I do not go it will look bad for the corporation."

According to Knudsen, at that Sloan was silent "for a full minute." He then angrily responded, "Very well." They shook hands without another word and Knudsen left the company, never to return as an executive (though he was made a member of the board after the war).[9]

Knudsen told this story, at the time, to one of his subordinates, Fred Horner, who soon after made the same trip to Sloan's office to request a leave of absence to work in Washington. He, too, was harshly interrogated. Horner concluded that Sloan hated to see GM executives work for the government, even after the nation was directly involved in the war. "Primarily, I always thought," he wrote later, "because he hated the Franklin D. Roosevelt regime here in Washington, so that even though we were at war, he still sort of put everybody that went to Washington, under Roosevelt."[10]

War or no war, Sloan expected the New Dealers to maul any industrialist who was foolish enough to work for them. It had happened to John Pratt in 1939.[11] It happened to Knudsen in January 1942 when he learned through a news ticker announcement that the president had removed him from his post. No one, especially including the president, had bothered to tell him. Knudsen, some say, was reduced to tears (Knudsen swallowed his humiliation and patriotically went on to serve as a troubleshooter for the Army with the rank of general).[12] But Sloan had warned the man.

Sloan dispassionately watched the Nazis take Europe. Immediately following the 1940 blitzkreig he received a letter from John Pratt in which he urged Sloan to cooperate fully with the government preparedness program. Pratt asked that Sloan not begin retooling GM's auto plants for the 1941 year models, but to wait and see if the government needed to contract with GM to use them for war production. Sloan dismissed Pratt's concerns. It was too late anyway, Sloan wrote, and probably not necessary:

> It looks as if the war in Europe is rapidly moving toward a conclusion. Probably I am wrong about that but I can't see how it can be otherwise. It seems clear that the Allies are outclassed on mechanical equipment and it is foolish to talk about modernizing their Armies in times like these, they ought to have thought of that five years ago. There is no excuse for them not thinking of that except for the unintelligent, in fact, stupid, narrow-minded and selfish leadership which the democracies of the world are cursed with.
>
> It is all very well as long as everybody is in the same position, but when some other system develops stronger leadership, works hard and long, and intelligently and aggressively—which are good traits—and, superimposed upon that, develops the instinct of a racketeer, there is nothing for the democracies to do but fold up. And that is about what it looks as if they are going to do.[13]

Clearly Secretary of Labor Frances Perkins had been wrong when she said Sloan never thought about "what's democratic and undemocratic." By 1940, he had thought a fair amount about how democracies work: he found them wanting.

* * *

Sloan had planned to step away from management responsibilities in 1940. That year he would be sixty-five years old and GM would produce its twenty-five millionth car. He had been working on his life story (in collaboration with the professional writer Boyden Sparkes). Wonderfully titled *Adventures of a White Collar Man,* it was published early in 1941. The book was primarily a soft-sell celebration of American industry with long passages extolling the free market system. The material on General

Motors was long on the virtues of "bigness" and short on actual decision making, controversies, and colorful anecdotes. The Flint sit-down strike, Sloan's interest in politics, his foundation, and his adult personal life are not mentioned. Almost certainly the book was planned as a public relations event marking the end of Sloan's corporate leadership. (Sloan was probably influenced by Walter Chrysler, who died in 1940; he had collaborated on a biography of his life titled *Life of An American Workman,* published in 1937). Sloan's book, given world events at the time, as much as its droning prose on the greatness of the free market and American industrial enterprise, made little impact on the reading public. That seems not to have disturbed Sloan. He, too, had much more on his mind.

With Knudsen's abdication from GM's presidency, Sloan had positioned Charles E. Wilson, a trusted GM man, to become president of the corporation. The Du Pont interests were dubious about Wilson's capacities and wanted Sloan to stay on as CEO.[14] Sloan had long believed that a man should step down from his GM responsibilities no later than his sixty-fifth birthday. But he understood the uncertainties that plagued the corporation, both internally and externally. With some reluctance, he agreed to continue—though he further reduced his day-to-day corporate responsibilities. He had no idea that he had committed himself to nearly six more years as CEO.

Franklin Roosevelt, too, seemed to be less than enthusiastic about holding onto the presidency in 1940. Right up to the July 1940 Democratic presidential nominating convention, not even his closest advisors knew exactly what Roosevelt wanted. In part, he was exhausted by the political strife. He also was not sure what the American people might make of his bid for a third presidential term. But the European war and no obvious successor to sustain the New Deal orientation of his presidency left him uncertain about how he could step aside. To demonstrate that he did not seek a third term on his own behalf, he refused to campaign for the Democratic nomination—though he also pointedly refused to endorse any other Democratic candidate. When he was drafted by the Democratic Party at the July 1940 convention in Chicago, he accepted their call.

After Roosevelt's renomination, Sloan gave several speeches highly critical of FDR and the New Deal. The New Deal, he argued, had determined that "accomplishment is a crime." He warned that the economic upswing in 1940 was illusory, based as it was on government military spending: "Defense material is wealth having no permanent benefit." It was a game effort on his part, but he doubted that his speeches would sway many voters. By the fall of 1940 Sloan had come to believe that Americans were "an economically illiterate people," incapable of responding intelligently to his rational appeals.[15] Sloan supported Republican presidential candidate Wendell Wilkie, an anti–New Deal businessman and political neophyte, with a donation of some $36,000. But he expended far less energy than he had during the 1936 campaign.[16] He was not surprised to see Roosevelt easily win his third term in office.

Regardless of the outcome of the election, Sloan knew that the New Deal, as a growth industry, had reached its limits. With the federal government focused on war production, the tables were turned. Immediately before the election, with Roosevelt's victory almost certain, Sloan began a new rhetorical tack with an address carried nationally over the radio. "The nation that is able to produce the most effectively," he told the American people, "is the one less vulnerable from attack." In a rare public display of ironic humor, he said that his only concern for the United States was that "we haven't got enough 'economic royalists' among us to do this job for national defense."[17] Despite Roosevelt's personal popularity, Sloan was beginning to see how to claim an advantage.

A few months later, on May 21, 1941, after Roosevelt had been—yet again—sworn into the nation's highest office, Sloan spoke at length, privately, to a gathering of top GM executives in Detroit. In a rush of words, he laid out his perspective on what was to come:

> I am sure we all realize that this struggle that is going on through the World is really nothing more or less than a conflict between two opposing technocracies manifesting itself to the capitalization of economic resources and products and all that sort of thing. . . . [T]he materials that we use are the materials that are needed the most and the things that count the most and the technical skills that we have, likewise, is needed the most in the things that count the most, and likewise the fact that most of the things that are needed in such prodigious quantities that it needs a type of organization that is used to doing things in a very big way in order to meet the demands that are upon us.[18]

By the time Sloan described the war as "really nothing more or less than a conflict between two opposing technocracies," the Nazis had conquered almost all of the European continent. London was under air attack and England was imperiled. The United States, while narrowly maintaining its nonbelligerent status, was committed to the support of Great Britain. Sloan—like a great many other Americans, it should be emphasized—still was morally and emotionally indifferent to the spread of Nazism.

Sloan was, however, concerned that the growing frenzy of the war mobilization effort (in May 1941 Sloan still did not expect direct American involvement) would demand sacrifices from General Motors. He knew that war work, for public relations reasons and because of government demands, would likely not be as profitable as GM's consumer operations. He worried that if the government forced GM to stop making autos, consumers' brand loyalty could be diminished. And he also knew that converting GM's manufacturing facilities from the production of consumer goods to war material would be a massive, potentially costly, time-consuming effort.

Even so, Sloan saw an overriding advantage. Industrial mobilization would reveal the unbeatable productive power of GM, the greatest corporation created within the private enterprise system. It would force the government—Roosevelt's government—to turn to industry and acknowledge its key role. The American people would see the strength of America's industrial corporate system.[19]

By mid-1941, the war reached deep into the operations of General Motors. War contracts were consuming a great deal of GM's productive capacity, even as Sloan and his men pushed on with new car production. Of less direct impact—but for Sloan, still quite irksome—was the fact that GM's global operations were coming increasingly under the scrutiny of American government officials.

By this time, GM's position in Germany had caused Sloan a good deal of trouble. Since the mid-1930s, the corporation's vice president of overseas operations, James D. Mooney, had been trying to manage the constraints the German government had placed on Opel. Mooney, following Sloan's dictum about respecting the customs of GM's host country, had tried to maintain amiable relations with the Nazi government. Mooney, it should be emphasized, especially given the controversies then and now surrounding GM's German operations, had no particular sympathy for the Nazi government. He had no particular antipathy to it, either.[20] He worked with the Nazis in maintaining GM's German operations in accord with Nazi needs. His work was much appreciated by the Nazi government, so much so that on August 10, 1938, Adolf Hitler bestowed upon him the Merit Cross of the German Eagle, First-Class, which Mr. Mooney graciously accepted. (The aviation hero and Nazi sympathizer Charles Lindbergh, as well as the boisterously anti-Semitic Henry Ford also received the medal.) The United States and Germany were not at war; it was just business.[21]

Mooney's efforts to keep GM's operations viable in Germany under

Nazi rule took a variety of twists and turns. At the end of 1939, at the personal request of Field Marshal Hermann Goering, Mooney found himself in the odd position of acting as a back channel between the Nazis and the British government. This secret mission soon involved American leaders, including President Roosevelt, whom Mooney briefed in the White House in December and then again in January 1940. By the early summer of 1940, presidential advisor Harry Hopkins believed Mooney to be a Nazi appeaser and cut off his contact with the White House.[22]

Sloan probably knew the basic drift of Mooney's activities. He certainly did not disapprove of Mooney's work with the Germans. On June 18, 1940, however, Sloan personally reassigned Mooney from his overseas duties—Opel was by that time being run under the direction of the Nazi economic ministry led by Goering.[23] Somewhat ironically, at least from the perspective of some anti-Nazi Americans, Sloan reassigned the talented Mooney to be executive assistant to GM president Charles Wilson. Mooney's new job was to take "full charge of all negotiations involving defense equipment and of such liaison activities as may be necessary in connection with the engineering and production of such material."[24] At least one major anti-Nazi group, the Non-Sectarian Anti-Nazi League, took offense—and perhaps, fright—at Sloan's decision and wrote privately to President Roosevelt warning him of Mooney's record: "[H]ow should we interpret the placing of a Hitler sympathizer and a Hitler servant (one must render service to the Reich to deserve such a medal) at the throttle of our defense program? Doesn't that appear suspiciously similar to the planting of Nazi sympathizers in key positions in the European democracies?"[25] Someone at the White House sent the letter to FBI director J. Edgar Hoover, who had already received other documents decrying Mooney's role in Nazi Germany. Hoover, not having received specific instructions as to how he was to proceed, chose not to begin a formal FBI investigation.[26]

Over the next year, Sloan found himself increasingly annoyed by government interference in GM's business. Men who knew little or nothing about industry were prying into corporate affairs. Operationally, Sloan had hardly anything to do with the conversion to war work, a process that was accelerating rapidly. In fact, he had decided, well before the United States actually entered the war, to concentrate his attention not on war mobilization but on postwar reconversion. He wanted to make sure that as soon as the hostilities concluded and America's emergency war buildup stopped, General Motors would be capable of quickly restoring its domestic and international consumer-oriented businesses. In May 1941, Sloan lectured GM's top men in Detroit:

> It is all very well to talk to some of these people down in Washington who say, "Never mind what is going to happen afterwards, let's take care of the problems as they stand today." The problem of today has got to be taken care of. At the same time, with all the resources and all the ability in this country, and all the ability we have in General Motors, certainly we can give some thought to what is going to happen after this thing is over, because even if we are fortunate enough to win the War and do our part in helping it to be won, we won't accomplish much if we lose what we have gained. That is just as important in my mind as winning the War.
>
> I wouldn't want you to think, by what I have said, that I am particularly discouraged about the long pull position. . . . The only reservations I have, the only thing I am concerned about, perhaps unduly because we all think along certain lines, what appalls me is the terrible stupid way we go at things and the complete lack of intelligence in meeting the great issues of the day, and it is discouraging when we see that this great country of ours which has risen to such great heights and all that, to my mind, has degenerated to a country of rackets of one kind or another.[27]

Sloan's sense that, under Roosevelt, the United States "had degenerated to a country of rackets of one kind or another" (less than a year earlier, he had described Nazi Germany in almost exactly the same way) had been exacerbated by the recent demands of officials at the State Department. Starting in December 1940, a young Nelson Rockefeller (scion of the Rockefeller dynasty and future New York governor), who had only recently begun working in Washington as White House coordinator of inter-American affairs, began insisting that Sloan sever GM's relationship with a number of its Latin American auto dealers. Rockefeller claimed they were pro-Nazi or profascist. When Sloan refused to do as he asked, Rockefeller turned to the State Department and convinced them to make the same demand.

Sloan was furious. In April 1941, he wrote to Walter Carpenter at Du Pont looking for support:

> I told those who have been dealing with me on this matter, that I thought rather than pick on some of these things which are more or less inconsequential in relation to the total in South America, that somebody might get busy putting in jail, or exporting, some of the Communists who are causing

> the many labor troubles in this country. But, of course, naturally, a dealer in Santiago has no vote, whereas a lot of Communists in this country have many votes. I have flatly declined to cancel dealers, irrespective of what the circumstances may be on the political charge.[28]

Gently, Carpenter suggested that Sloan was wrong. He sent him the Du Pont Company policy on dealing with Germany, Italy, Japan, and their agents in other countries, which had been adopted October 23,1940. It left a lot of maneuvering room. But Carpenter than forcefully explained his own position:

> I think that General Motors has to consider this problem from three standpoints; first, from the commercial, second, the patriotic and, third, the public relations standpoint. . . . We are definitely a part of the nation here and our future is very definitely mingled with the future of this country. The country today seems to be pretty well committed to a policy opposite to Germany and Italy. . . . It is true, as you say, that we have many bad actors in this country who are working against the interests of industry, perhaps, against the interests of the country itself. The fact that we don't move up on those faster in this country does not seem to me to offer a very good excuse why we should not do our part in connection with this program of agents if it seems a wise one. . . . If we don't listen to the urgings of the State Department in this connection it seems to me just a question of time when there will be a blast of some form from Washington. The effect of this will be to associate the General Motors with Nazi or Fascist propaganda against the interests of the United States. . . . [T]he effect on the General Motors Corporation might be a very serious matter and the feeling might last for years.[29]

Carpenter urged Sloan to listen to the State Department.

Sloan politely demurred. Somewhat oddly, given his long record of concern over GM's public image, he was unmoved by Carpenter's worry that GM could be branded by the government as sympathetic to the Nazi cause. Perhaps after years of antagonism between the Roosevelt administration and GM, Sloan believed his managerial freedom was more important than potentially negative public relations spawned by hostile government acts. He did respond directly to Carpenter's overall argument. He told Carpenter: "I do not think it is up to General Motors to police the political sympathies or activities of people in these various countries. We have enough trouble on our hands without undertaking that phase of it."[30] Sloan said much the same thing to Nelson Rockefeller and to the man in charge of national security issues in Latin America, Assistant Secretary of State Adolph Berle.

Berle basically was in charge of overseeing collective security in the Western Hemisphere. But, as Sloan knew, he was much more than a second-tier State Department official. Brilliant, immodest, difficult, and cunning, his biographer wrote that Berle "wanted to be Marx *and* Machiavelli."[31] He was one of three original New Deal brain-trusters (the other two were Raymond Moley and Rexford Tugwell). An expert on corporate finance, Berle had become well known in intellectual and public policy circles for coauthoring *The Modern Corporation and Private Property,* published in 1932. In 1933, *Time* magazine called it "the economic Bible of the Roosevelt Administration."[32] The book was a sophisticated attack on the giant corporations to which Alfred Sloan and his peers had dedicated their lives. Its logic helped to underwrite early New Deal interventions in the market economy.

Berle and his coauthor, Gardiner C. Means, wrote: "It is conceivable—indeed it seems almost essential if the corporate system is to survive—that the 'control' of the great corporations should develop into a purely neutral technocracy, balancing a variety of claims by various groups in the community and assigning to each a portion of the income stream on the basis of public policy rather than private cupidity."[33] Berle, as much as any man, had given intellectual justification to the political decisions made in the early New Deal years to reign in and regulate the power of Big Business. In May 1941, at a State Department meeting, he told GM officials who reported directly to Alfred Sloan that the government had the right to make General Motors fire people of whom it did not approve. The GM officials did not agree.[34]

Berle was incensed at the attitude displayed by the GM executives. He fully believed their foot-dragging and hostility to his requests came directly from orders given by Sloan. After the meeting, Berle spoke with his State Department people and concluded "that certain officials of General Motors were sympathetic to or aligned with some pro-Axis groups. . . . That this is 'real Fifth Column' and is much more sinister than many other things which are going on at the present time." Berle ordered the FBI to begin a full and thorough investigation of the loyalty of James D. Mooney, Graeme K. Howard, who had taken over as head of the export division of GM, and Alfred P. Sloan Jr.[35]

For the next several months, the FBI investigated the GM executives. Sloan must have known about the investigation as several of his colleagues in Detroit and in New York were interviewed. All the GM men interviewed, not surprisingly, attested to Sloan's patriotism. Most also underlined a possible government motive in the investigation by pointing out Sloan's outspoken criticism of New Deal economic policy. While both Mooney and Howard were found by the FBI to have been "soft" on Nazi Germany and even supportive of Nazi economic policy on past occasions, no evidence indicated any allegiance to Nazi ideology, let alone any "Fifth Column" activity or acts of disloyalty on the part of either man. As for Sloan, the FBI agent in charge of the investigation, in his final report to J. Edgar Hoover on September 5, 1941, stated: "No derogatory information of any kind was developed with respect to Alfred Pritchard Sloan, Jr."[36] Sloan made no public comments and did not indicate in extant correspondence how he felt about the New Deal-sponsored investigation. One can only guess.

By early December, any remaining questions about GM's international operations were made moot by America's entry into the war. Opel was formally taken over by the Reich Minister for the Treatment of Enemy Property. GM cooperated with State Department demands regarding its overseas operations. Domestically, the corporation became the key industry in the "arsenal of democracy."

Between 1942 and 1945, GM produced little for the consumer marketplace. This was not wholly voluntary; GM president Charles Wilson lobbied, even after Pearl Harbor, to manufacture more new cars but he was personally turned down by William Knudsen at the Office of Production Management. Over 90 percent of all GM production was of war material. Since the near bankruptcy of GM in 1920, Sloan and his colleagues had made the corporation an extraordinarily productive and efficient manufacturer. During World War II, GM performed for the American people. It continued to make money, with sales of $13.4 billion and net profits of $673 million; but for GM those were slim profit figures and deliberately so.[37]

War conversion was a monumental task for General Motors, the auto industry as a whole, and American industry in general. Donald Nelson, the Sears executive who took over from William Knudsen the job of coordinating war production, wanted the auto industry to manufacture about one-fifth of all American war material.[38] Such a commitment was a risky business for GM and other manufacturers, who feared that after the war they would be unprepared to produce for the consumer marketplace. Early on in the war effort in particular, auto executives worried that their competitors would take what advantage they could of any laxity in the government's oversight and gain a leg up on preparing for the postwar consumer marketplace. One exasperated government official wrote his superior: "The dread of what a better-prepared competitor may do to them in the postwar market dies hard in many of the boys."[39]

To assuage such concerns and, in fact, meet automakers' demands, the federal government paid almost all the auto industry's massively expensive wartime conversion costs. Thus, when General Motors built some $900 million worth of plants between 1940 and 1944 to produce for the war effort, the government footed almost the entire bill. In addition, the federal government provided industry numerous other incentives, including tax breaks, guaranteed profits through "cost-plus" contracts, and regulatory relief. Secretary of War Henry Stimpson wrote in his diary (later published) a remark often quoted: "If you are going to try to go to war or prepare for war in a capitalist country, you have got to let business make money out of the process, or business won't work."[40]

Stimpson was right, which prompts a moral question: At a time of war, when hundreds of thousands of American men sacrifice their lives for the nation, how harshly should one judge the cupidity of corporate executives who demand that they and their businesses face minimal risk and maximum financial reward? Sloan, of course, would have reformulated the issue, approaching the problem from another side: the profit motive had created the world's most productive industrial system, managed by the world's most talented executives; without such a system and such people, the war could not have been won, regardless of any number of individual sacrifices.[41]

General Lucius Clay, the supremely capable Director of War Material during World War II, saw it Sloan's way. Clay stated: "I had to put into production schedule the largest procurement program the world had ever seen. Where would I find somebody to do that? I went to General Motors."[42] The decentralized corporate structure that Sloan had cooperatively created and staffed to efficiently and economically produce massive amounts of manufactured goods in an innovative and flexible manner, whatever the political wrangling and the moral debate, met the fundamental challenge of world war.[43]

Though largely out of the limelight during the war, Sloan was far from done. While he took no role in the war production, as stated above, he charged himself with preparing GM for the war's end. He created and chaired the Post-War Planning Committee (it was the only policy group he chose to chair). He studied all aspects of GM's wartime conversion and he worked with men throughout the corporation to plan how to reverse that process while making use of GM's wartime plant expansions and retoolings. It was an incredibly complex, detailed task. Sloan pursued the effort throughout the war.[44]

Sloan also took particular interest in GM's public relations campaign during the war. GM, like many major corporations, had to find a way to keep consumers' brand conscious, even if they had no brand-name products to sell. Paul Garrett, head of the public relations policy group, told Sloan, Charles Wilson, and other top men that his first priority was "interpreting to the public what General Motors is doing in the war in ways that will build a strong public position for the future."[45] Throughout the war, GM produced wave after wave of advertising that demonstrated the massive job General Motors had successfully undertaken for the American people. The ads gave GM the opportunity to explain its accomplishments and also to express a powerful political message:

> "KNOW-HOW" SAVES MANPOWER, MATERIALS AND MONEY—AND GETS THE JOB DONE! Fortunately for all of us, American Industry has this "Know-How."
>
> They said that American was unprepared for war and could not arm in time. But they overlooked our "secret weapon"—industrial "know-how." They forgot that in America free enterprise had for years been encouraging—stimulating—urging men to learn how to make things better and better—in greater volume—at constantly lower prices. Now that the needs of peace have given way to the demands of war—now that "Victory is our business"—our training in this mass production is making itself felt.

In ad after ad, GM reminded Americans of the productive capacities of the free enterprise system and gave detailed accounts of how GM made everything from machine guns to military trucks. The new GM slogan, "Victory is our business," closed each ad.[46] Sloan personally contributed to the effort, detailing GM's role on "the production front" in his quarterly messages to stockholders. Sloan took care to link GM's free-market corporate productivity with the nation's war-time success.[47]

During the war, Sloan remained chairman of the Policy Committee, to which each policy group reported. All major strategic corporate decisions passed through him. While Sloan continued to work long hours for GM, he remained highly active in related affairs: the National Association of Manufacturers, the National Highway Users Conference, the Automobile Safety Foundation, his own philanthropic foundation, and, somewhat more quietly, anti–New Deal politics.

Sloan pursued his whirlwind of tasks even as he first felt the fingers of old age reaching for him. At the end of 1943, he wrote Charles Kettering, with whom he had developed a friendship: "You and I have reached the point where we cannot help but realize that the opportunities for the future, as measured by time, are narrowing down." A year later, he wrote Kettering again: "I wish you could do something about these passing years. It would be a great accomplishment for some of us who have seen too many come and go."[48] Despite his growing sense that his best years were behind him and the fact that his hearing was not good at all, Sloan still believed he had work to do. He intended to make himself useful.

During the last half of 1944, with victory over the Axis powers certain, Sloan made a series of speeches envisioning a postwar American economic boom; these speeches would be among the last major addresses of his life. In them he outlined a new high-employment, high-consumption society based on industrial productivity. Sloan, better than many economists, understood that the war had produced a huge pent-up consumer demand and the purchasing power to satisfy it. He believed that if government kept out of the way, industry could successfully fuel a new and dramatic rise in the nation's economy. General Motors, he promised, would invest hundreds of millions of dollars to meet the consumer demand—as yet unproven—of the immediate postwar era. This huge investment would not only profit General Motors, but the nation as a whole; corporate action would stimulate the economy, creating an upward-spiraling era of good times:

> Out of this situation that I speak of, this tremendous aggregation of purchasing power, the tremendous demand for all kinds of goods, arises, according to my way of thinking, a question and a very important question. . . . That question is this: Would it be possible, if American industry stepped forward and planned boldly and dramatically with courage, and expanded its operations, expanded its capacity, to take care of this postwar demand, to capitalize this purchasing power? Would it be possible to raise the national income and, of course, hence the standard of living to an amount far in excess of what we have ever had before?

Sloan was sure that industry's time had come. If corporate leaders simply measured "the elasticity of demand of the various things they make," they would see that tremendous opportunities both for profit and for private-sector-driven national economic stimulus lay before them. General Motors, Sloan promised his fellow industrialists, was going to take the calculated risk and meet the challenge: "I have recommended, and our directors have approved, an expenditure that involves something like five hundred million dollars. We propose to expand our production something like 40 or 50 percent."

Sloan's public promise of massive investment in GM's productive capacity was made in the face of conventional wisdom. In the aftermath of the 1937–38 recession, Harvard economist Alvin Hansen had used his presidential address to the American Economic Association to lay out a "stagnationist analysis" of the United States. He had warned that the nation had reached economic maturity and that no likely increase in demand was foreseeable. Hansen insisted that the only way out of "secular stagnation" was through massive federal spending engineered by government planning. As the war drew to an end, and with it the government's unprecedented deficit spending, most economists and policy makers feared that the massive unemployment of the prewar depression era would return. To fight this specter, many influential congressional liberals were championing a Full Employment Bill. This legislation was based on the premise that the private sector, in the postwar years, would not be able to supply enough Americans with jobs; hence the federal government would be mandated to provide every American who wanted a job with some kind of employment.[49]

Sloan utterly rejected this logic. He feared, not unreasonably, that the Full Employment Bill was one more stalking horse for a massive federal intervention in the market economy. On behalf of the corporation, Don Brown, who was by 1945 GM's vice chairman, took a key role (along with most Republicans and almost the entire organized business community) in successfully fighting this proposed legislation.[50]

As mentioned above, unlike numerous economists and government officials, Sloan believed that the economy would boom in the postwar years, spurred on by wartime personal savings and the pent-up demand for consumer products. That no new cars had been manufactured in nearly four years certainly bolstered Sloan's confidence in the accuracy of his demand projections for his particular industry. Still, the impressive dollar amount Sloan announced GM would invest in meeting that demand powerfully demonstrated his belief that the private sector, not the government, would deliver the American people into a new era of economic prosperity and corporate America into an age of august profitability.

* * *

As World War II came to a close, Sloan was confident that industry had proven itself, once again, to the American people. It was America's productive capacity that had won the war, he believed, and that fact must be obvious to all. At the moment of victory—a victory won in large part by American industry—industry was positioned to again take the lead in American life. Speaking before an enthusiastic assembly of manufacturers in New Jersey, the state where he had run his first business, Sloan predicted the end of American industry's subordination to government planners and antibusiness politicians:

> We think the attitude of the American public is completely changed with respect to industry and industry's problem as the result of their experience in the war. We believe that the rabbit-out-of-the-hat business, the something-for-nothing, the destroying of wealth on the philosophy that by doing so we increase wealth, the idea that money is value in itself without regard to what it is exchanged for—all that and a lot of other panaceas that I might mention were characteristics of the New Deal in the 1930s, are finished, and will not be carried into the postwar period.[51]

Sloan had prepared General Motors well for the postwar world.[52] He had made it his responsibility, his last great task at GM, to supervise the entire reconversion process and to plan GM's corporate investment strategy. He succeeded. By September 1945, GM was producing automobiles, and the American people could not get enough of them. As Sloan had predicted, pent-up consumer demand exploded. The economy boomed. General Motors led the way. Sloan had met the challenge.

When the war ended, Alfred P. Sloan was seventy years old. He had continued in place at GM far longer than he had intended. The time had come to step down from management. But once more, circumstances intervened. Immediately after the war's end, labor troubles again threatened GM's stability. The United Auto Workers (UAW), flush with members but also suffering from mass layoffs in the immediate aftermath of the war, demanded substantial wage increases. Far more troubling, from Sloan's perspective, the UAW leadership insisted that GM pay its workers a 30 percent wage increase without increasing the price of cars. When GM's president Charles Wilson balked, arguing that the corporation could not afford such an arrangement, the union's head, Walter Reuther, promptly asked him to prove it by opening up GM's books to the UAW.[53]

Wilson was in charge of the negotiation but Sloan stood behind him. Sloan understood the stakes involved. Reuther believed the UAW could take partial control of corporate decision making. He wanted some kind of co-management in which organized labor, through access to corporate records, had a say in how the corporation spent its money. As Reuther told the GM negotiating team: "Unless we get a more realistic distribution of America's wealth, we won't get enough to keep this machine going." When the GM negotiator accused Reuther of being some kind of socialist, Reuther calmly responded: "If fighting for a more equal and equitable distribution of the wealth of this country is socialistic, I stand guilty of being a Socialist."

Sloan would not have it. He wrote Walter Carpenter at Du Pont: "General Motors has taken the position that it will not bargain for wages with an operating statement in its hands."[54] With Sloan's strong support, GM bought space in newspapers around the country to make its case: "America is at the crossroads! It must preserve the freedom of each unit of Americans business to determine its own destiny. . . . The idea of ability to pay, whatever its validity may be, is not applicable to an individual business within an industry as a basis for raising its wages beyond the going rate."[55] Free enterprise, in any definition Sloan could credit, meant that management, on behalf of the shareholders—*not* labor and *not* the government—decided how best to run a corporation.

Both Reuther and Sloan understood the stakes involved. The UAW struck. And after a long and bitter strike, they gained a substantial wage increase. But Walter Reuther and the UAW did not win any access to GM's records. The corporation made no deal about the price of its automobiles. GM's executives refused to give organized labor a voice in its decision-making processes. Sloan had won.

Arguably, Sloan's victory was shared in by GM's many unionized hourly wage earners. GM's management-led postwar success produced an economic boon for GM's workers. Between 1946 and 1949, the corporation pursued smooth production and labor peace by providing workers' with health insurance and pensions. In 1950, in the famous "Treaty of Detroit," as *Fortune* magazine dubbed it, GM and the UAW amiably agreed to a five-year, billion-dollar contract. GM gained a stable workforce and predictable labor costs. Workers were guaranteed regular wage increases and an annual pay raise based on improvements in corporate productivity.

Labor historian Nelson Lichtenstein mournfully concluded that the UAW had "virtually accepted the principle that advances in real wages would be pegged to increased productivity, thus acquiring a stake in the maintenance of stable, efficient industrial relations with the giant corporation."[56] Labor radicals who had challenged the right of corporate managers and corporate board members to determine overarching corporate policy, work-place rules, and corporate distribution of profits had, for all practical purposes, lost the political fight. Sloan, who had long insisted that workers had to trust the corporation to make the money that would provide them with good-paying jobs, had triumphed. But as he would have emphasized, his ideological triumph produced for his workers incomes that allowed them to live out consumer dreams that would be the envy of people around the world.

In 1946, Sloan finally stepped down from his management role. But he stayed on as chairman of the board for ten more years, in what was more than a mere token role. He was not overwhelmed with how Charles Wilson ran GM between 1946 and early 1953, and he made sure that Wilson knew his limits. Sloan in fact was not displeased to see Wilson resign to become secretary of defense under President Eisenhower (whom Sloan lukewarmly supported; Sloan preferred Eisenhower's opponent for the Republican presidential nomination, the more conservative, antilabor Ohio senator Robert Taft).[57]

Sloan's last major public role on behalf of both General Motors and the free enterprise system came at the very end of 1955. A Wyoming senator named Joseph O'Mahoney, a populist of the old school, was leading a Senate investigation into monopolistic corporate practices. Sloan came before him to defend General Motors. Sloan, in the last months of his chairmanship, was eighty years old.

O'Mahoney believed that any corporation as large as General Motors was an inefficient behemoth that used its size not for scales of economy but to squash its competition. The senator began: "Mr. Sloan . . . is there any limit to the number of activities which your corporation can enter, before you would say that the growth would not be economically justified?" Sloan, after some difficulties with his hearing aid, fired back:

> If your question is centered around the question of efficiency relative to size, if that is in the back of your mind, let me say that efficiency and size have nothing to do with one another. Where size comes in, it simply requires a certain type of administration technique, that is where the difference is. . . . I think the efficiency depends upon the administrative technique and the people who comprise General Motors.

Sloan answered every question with precision and the certainty that he was right. Supported by Republican members of the committee, he ended the session unfazed. When Sloan stood up, the entire delegation of General Motors men in attendance stood with him and applauded their champion.[58]

Sloan's last years as chairman of the board were far from uneventful. Beginning in 1948, and not fully concluded until fourteen years later, the Department of Justice pursued a comprehensive antitrust action against the Du Pont Corporation's investment in General Motors. The government charged Du Pont with using its influence to unfairly gain contracts with GM and so restrain trade. Du Pont executives believed the Department of Justice action to be a politically motivated attack, payback for the du Ponts' massive contributions to anti–New Deal causes. They were wrong; the antitrust actions were a calculated attempt by liberals in the New Deal and then by President Harry Truman's administration to regulate industry so as not to have to intervene more directly in the national economy. Sloan was much involved in the case, testifying at length. For him, it was a point of honor—and fact—to demonstrate that decisions at GM were made not on the basis of human relationships, let alone through illegal conduct, but through a rational, decision-making process. In 1954, Sloan triumphed when the federal district court judge Walter LaBuy ruled that General Motors—Sloan—"exercised complete freedom" in its contracting practices.[59] (That Du Pont was later forced, by a 1957 Supreme Court decision, to disinvest from GM, was of far less consequence to Sloan; the decision was based not on past wrong-doing but on "a present-day probability of restraint of trade.")[60]

Even as Sloan continued to invest time and energy overseeing GM's strategic turns, he began to spend more time on his philanthropic work. At the end of 1945, he donated more than $2.56 million to the Memorial Hospital in New York City to establish the Sloan-Kettering Institute for Cancer Research (later the Memorial Sloan-Kettering Cancer Center), along with substantial sums to fund ongoing research. Sloan had not been motivated by some personal encounter with cancer. Charles Kettering (whose interest was both scientific and personal) had, on an intellectual basis, interested Sloan in cancer research. For that reason, Sloan placed Kettering's name alongside his own on the new center.

In funding the fight against cancer so generously, Sloan was making a humanitarian gesture. But Sloan also saw cancer research as an organizational challenge. He believed that if cancer—what he called the "greatest curse nature has leveled against man"—could be attacked "just like industry attacks a problem," it could be defeated. His model of technical, organizational problem solving, Sloan believed, could and should be widely applied throughout society. Kettering, whom Sloan allowed to take center stage at the press conference announcing the new center, made the comparison explicit: "Mr. Sloan and I over the years have worked together on many apparently hopeless industrial problems which today seem so simple that I am inclined to feel we can apply some of these time-tried techniques to this age-old problem." Defeating cancer through such methods would further validate the corporate system Sloan had done so much to create and develop.[61]

In more direct support of his corporate vision, Sloan donated tens of millions of dollars to his alma mater, the Massachusetts Institute of Technology. In 1950, Sloan, through his foundation, gave MIT $5.25 million to create the MIT School of Industrial Management. (In 1964, the MIT trustees chose to honor their benefactor by renaming the school the MIT Sloan School of Management.) Sloan believed that MIT's programs in science and engineering could be tailored to produce corporate managers. Management, he explained, should be taught at the university level as "a phase of scientific education." Sloan's school would offer degrees of Bachelor of Science in Management Science, Master of Science in Management, Master of Science in the Management of Technology, and Doctor of Philosophy. MIT, he hoped, would be an exemplar, showing other major universities how to produce the men needed to manage American prosperity.

Sloan believed that it was imperative to link American higher education more closely to the needs of business. In 1954 he told a radio interviewer that business leaders had to support universities, and not just with money, but through active involvement. If business failed to take on this responsibility, he warned, "the control of our educational institutions moves over to the government. The political factor becomes more important than the business factor." Such politicization, Sloan feared, would gravely retard American development. As usual, he did not acknowledge in any way that corporate involvement in and of itself might be political.[62]

Sloan wished, before he died, to make one more fundamental statement on his life's work: managing General Motors. In 1954, he gathered a team to help him produce a book explaining how he and the men around him had worked to run GM. He was not interested in producing a trite personal account or a public relations-driven sham. Sloan wanted to make a scientific study of management that would stand the test of time. To undertake the actual writing, never Sloan's specialty, he hired John McDonald, whom Sloan knew through his work at *Fortune* magazine. McDonald was one of the nation's premier business journalists and an acclaimed writer. Sloan hired a professional research team and a variety of editorial consultants The lead researcher was a young professor named Alfred Chandler, who would become the nation's leading expert on the history of corporate management. Sloan knew how to select talented men.

In early 1959 the book was nearing completion, scheduled for publication in the fall by Doubleday. On March 4, 1959, the eighty-three-year-old Sloan met with his writer, John McDonald. As McDonald tells the story, Sloan reported that the book could not be published. GM's lawyers had decided that the book was too risky a proposition. The antitrust actions of the previous few years, along with ongoing federal actions against GM, made the corporation too vulnerable. Sloan's accounts of GM's expansion strategy (buying profitable operations, rather than starting up its own manufacturing concerns), his outline of the original attack on the Ford Motor Company—all could fuel the political fires. A senior partner in Cravath, Swaine & Moore, GM's outside legal counsel, told Sloan personally that he agreed with the decision. Sloan was most unhappy but he would not, of course, endanger the corporation. The man who had spent more than forty years managing General Motors in one way or another was now being managed by it.

McDonald, whose arrangement with Sloan provided for a book royalty share of 50 percent, was incensed. Sloan, however, had final word on the decision to publish. McDonald refused to accept Sloan's decision—and its financial consequences—and began legal action against GM for suppressing the manuscript. Sloan watched with interest. And when GM offered to allow publication of a heavily rewritten version—a sequel to *Adventures of a White Collar Man*—Sloan met with McDonald and the various lawyers and said he would not trade in his manuscript for a fake: "It's a masterpiece," roared the eighty-seven-year-old honorary chairman of the board of General Motors. A deal was made and in 1964, shortly before Sloan's eighty-ninth birthday, his book arrived. Early in the twenty-first century, *My Life with General Motors* is still in print—now, with a testimonial from Microsoft CEO and chairman of the board Bill Gates on the cover. It takes a certain kind of person to appreciate the book: the kind of person who wants to understand how to rationally manage men, money, markets, and machines. More than a million copies have been sold.[63]

Two years after his "masterpiece" reached the American people, Alfred P. Sloan Jr.'s heart stopped.

Afterword

They know only the rules of a generation of self-seekers. They have no vision, and when there is no vision the people perish.

—Franklin Delano Roosevelt,
inaugural address, March 4, 1933

After Alfred Sloan's death in early 1966, GM chairman of the board Frederick Donner had reason to ponder Sloan's legacy. The corporation was having a very bad year, not in terms of revenues, which were quite good, but in regard to public image and government relations. Mr. Donner—indirectly—blamed Alfred Sloan for GM's predicament.

The public image troubles had begun on February 13, 1966, exactly four days before Alfred Sloan died. That day, the *Washington Post* ran a story about a young lawyer named Ralph Nader. The newspaper reported that Nader was a consultant to a Senate subcommittee investigating auto safety. The previous year Nader had published *Unsafe at Any Speed,* a scathing attack on the safety record of the Chevrolet Corvair. That was the background; the article had a news "hook." A guard at the Senate office building in which Nader worked discovered that Nader was being surveilled by two men. These men, it turned out, had been hired by General Motors as part of an effort—an unsuccessful effort—to smear Nader's public reputation in order to destroy the credibility of his attack on GM's safety record.

The mass media jumped on the "David and Goliath" story and on March 8, 1966 the chair of the Senate subcommittee, Connecticut senator Abraham Ribikoff, blasted GM on the Senate floor for its underhanded attempt to interfere in his investigation. In a no-win situation, GM president James Roche stepped forward and publicly apologized to the Ribikoff subcommittee, which was by then holding a special investigation into GM's behavior. Ribikoff, his committee, and the issue of auto safety all were headline news. Largely because of Nader's muckraking work and GM's dismal handling of the exposé, Congress passed the 1966 National Traffic and Motor Vehicle Safety Act. The act created federal standards for auto safety and gave the government power to force automakers to recall car models that had safety-related defects.[1]

In the aftermath of the incident, GM chairman Fred Donner tried to explain what had gone wrong to a sympathetic *Fortune* magazine writer. Donner claimed that GM just did not know how to operate in the public realm or to navigate the shoals of Washington politics. GM, he said, was merely a car company trying to make the best vehicles it could for the American people. That tight focus, he said, was the legacy of Alfred Sloan: "[T]the degree to which his generation had to deal with the things we're talking about [the social and political challenges] was very small." *Fortune*'s writer agreed, noting that GM had always before been able largely to avoid politics and public issues of all kinds. Alfred Sloan and his men, the article sagely observed, had been fortunate that they could concentrate on corporate growth and nothing else.[2]

History still was not a hot topic at GM. In 1935, almost exactly thirty years before Nader's harrowing account of the Corvair, the young muckraker Joseph Furnas had published his "blood-curdling" exposé of death and destruction on the nation's roadways. Sloan had instantly responded, not by investigating Furnas, but by creating the immensely successful Automobile Safety Foundation. (In the previously quoted words of the *Detroit News:* "Let the industry which has given us cars—so necessary in American life—establish the rules by which those same useful cars will cease to be weapons of death and injury.") The idea that Alfred Sloan, through the Great Depression and the New Deal, and then during the era of World War II—sixteen years out of the twenty-three that Sloan held the corporation's highest executive position—could simply ignore the public and political realms is not substantiated, as Sloan himself might have said, by the facts.

How then to explain the seemingly genuine conviction of Fred Donner and *Fortune* magazine that GM's leaders, before the mid-1960s onslaught of Great Society liberal policy makers and radical activists, had been able to safely ignore the world outside of its industrial operations? A partial explanation might be that Sloan's efforts in weathering the storm of the 1929–46 period had been so successful that most of his work outside the narrow confines of the corporation had become largely invisible, at least invisible as political work, to the GM men who followed him and to the public itself. This, even though in 1966 the Auto Safety Foundation, for example, was still operating, as were the National Highway Users Conference, auto industry lobbying groups in Washington, and myriad other GM-related or sponsored associations and corporate public-relations efforts.

Donner was either a very good salesman or he had really come to believe what Sloan's hand-picked successor, Charles Wilson, had told the Senate committee holding hearings on his nomination as Dwight Eisenhower's secretary of defense: "I thought what was good for our country was good for General Motors—and vice versa. The difference did not exist."[3] By this logic GM was not involved in politics because GM was above the partisan fray. Its mission of meeting and making a mass consumer marketplace based on corporate productivity and the incentive of corporate profitability was at the heart of American life. GM's economic power was not a problem but proof of America's economic strength. This twining of corporate power and national good was Sloan's dream come true.

Sloan's dream has never been an uncontested vision of American life. The business corporation, from its emergence in the mid-nineteenth century through its global reach in the early years of the twenty-first century, has always had legions of critics, whether angry Populist farmers, militant labor unionists, social gospel ministers, small business owners, black-clad anarchists, whole communities destroyed by corporations that have moved their factories in pursuit of cheaper labor, or human-rights activists appalled at corporations' cooperation with brutal regimes around the world. In the 1930s Franklin Roosevelt's New Deal, while no enemy of corporate capitalism or the free market in general, did take seriously some of these concerns about corporate capitalism. That is why New Dealers used government power to protect workers' rights to unionize, to create public works jobs at a time of high unemployment, to regulate financial markets in the name of the public good, to legislate a social security system to protect those financially unprotected by the private sector, and to raise taxes on corporate profits and the wealthy to pay for additional government services.

Sloan and the men and women who follow in his corporate footsteps are extremely good at what they do. Better than any other elite, they have delivered economic growth and widespread prosperity. But as Sloan's life demonstrates, at least some of them can envision a world—they can believe in a world—in which corporate profits alone demonstrate human success.[4] Alfred Sloan did not recognize that Adolph Hitler or Josef Stalin were evil men and that cooperating with them and their regimes was not a moral activity. Sloan did not find racists and anti-Semites uncomfortable political bedfellows. He did not seem to care if people were maimed or killed by the products he manufactured. He saw nothing unjust about safeguarding executives' bonuses and salaries during the Great Depression, even as tens of thousands of GM hourly workers were laid off without even benefit of a national system of social provision.

In part, Sloan failed to recognize these issues as problematic because he was an unusual man, "a narrow man," in his own words. Sloan was not much ruled by moral vision or a sense of compassion for others. President Roosevelt might well have been thinking about Alfred Sloan when he thundered: "They know only the rules of a generation of self-seekers." At stake, however, in Sloan's decision making and in Franklin Roosevelt's condemnatory words are not just issues of personality quirks.

Sloan, in ignoring the moral concerns and questions of social justice for which Franklin Roosevelt condemned him, was doing his job. Sloan's ability to put aside almost all issues that did not directly affect GM's profitability is a part of what made him so extraordinarily good at his job. And General Motors, in so many ways, I believe, was (even accounting for accompanying social problems) good for America: producing marvelous machines at reasonable cost that extended people's individuality and sense of freedom (and helped the nation to win World War II); employing hundreds of thousands of people at high wages that brought them good lives (even noting the failures of the Great Depression and the mixed blessings of consumer society); and serving as a model of corporate productivity that helped the U.S. economy, as a whole, prosper and become a model for much of the world.

But Sloan's genius also made him a dangerous kind of citizen of the United States. When business leaders like Sloan face a difficult, morally charged business decision, they have an obligation—they should have an obligation—to give the benefit of the moral doubt to their enterprise. Sloan certainly gave every moral benefit of the doubt, if he ever had such doubts, to GM's profitability. Somebody, however, has to have the moral vision and, more importantly, the countervailing power to tell corporate leaders like Sloan that profit and economic exploitation are not the sole values that make the United States or any society just and good.

In the United States, a powerful tension has long existed between those who single-mindedly champion the market freedoms that help to produce both general prosperity and unequal individual economic reward and those who protect the republican virtues that safeguard the social justice that ensures the moral legitimacy of American society.[5] Alfred Sloan's battles with Franklin Roosevelt and the New Deal were a critical chapter in that tense war. We do well to remember that striking the balance in this struggle—muddling through, often enough—not enduring victory by one side or the other, marks the many successful encounters Americans have had with the nation's great historical crises. Sloan, and those who have followed him in the corporate world, rule the marketplace. In the 1930s, at least, Sloan's rules as they applied to wider society were tempered by the power a democratic people gave their government to seek broad social justice. Where the balance between private-sector market values and government-protected social justice resides in the future is the national and, increasingly, international history we will continue to write.

Acknowledgments

My work on this book has taken me around the country and I have piled up debts to archivists and librarians at many of the nation's greatest repositories of American history: Franklin D. Roosevelt Library, Herbert Hoover Presidential Library, Library of Congress, Hagley Museum and Library, Butler Library at Columbia University, Columbia University Oral History Research Office, Bentley Library at the University of Michigan, Richard P. Scharchburg Archives/Kettering University GMI Alumni Foundation Collection of Industrial History, Bancroft Library at the University of California, Berkeley, Alderman Library at the University of Virginia, and Zimmerman Library at the University of New Mexico. I want to single out Michael Nash at the Hagley for his mastery of business history with which he is so generous. I owe special thanks to the family of auto industry lobbyist and automobile safety leader Pyke Johnson for sharing privately held documents. I also thank the late Frederick Horner, a New Deal Democrat who worked for GM and donated his unexpurgated papers to the Library of Congress.

Jeff Roche worked for several months as my research assistant on this project. Besides successfully prowling around in government documents, it was his idea to obtain the FBI file on Sloan, which turned out to be full of good stuff. I would not have been able to hire Jeff without a generous grant from the Aspen Foundation Nonprofit Research Sector Fund in 1998, which also provided me with a summer stipend and some expense money. The National Endowment for the Humanities (NEH) funded my participation in the 1994 NEH seminar on biography at the University of California, Berkeley, which got me going on this thing. Thanks as well to University of New Mexico history chairs Richard Robbins and Jane Slaughter for providing me with small grants to assist in the final manuscript preparation.

A number of scholars contributed to this project in diverse ways. Alfred Chandler, at the beginning, shared his memories of Alfred Sloan with me and helped give me the confidence I needed to see the work through. Charles Cheape, years ago, in the best public talk I have ever heard given by a historian, showed me—and a large group of retired Du Pont executives—how to think critically and fairly about a corporate giant (and his biography of Walter Carpenter was inspirational). I was helped a great deal on this project by the late James Breslin, who led the NEH seminar on biography; thanks, too, to the rest of the seminar participants who put up with a grumpy historian. Ron Edsforth, who refereed the manuscript for the University of Chicago Press, while not always in agreement with my account of Sloan and the auto industry, gave this book a thorough and brilliant critical read. My special thanks, too, to the anonymous reader used by the University of Chicago Press; his incisive comments encouraged me to write more clearly about Sloan's business genius as well as his limitations. That reader's praise was awfully nice to hear at the end of this long process.

Doug Mitchell, at the University of Chicago Press, has coaxed me, inspired me, fed me (very well), and listened to me talk. A book on Alfred Sloan is not his usual fare but he has maintained his enthusiasm for this project for half a dozen years and I appreciate everything he has done for me over the many years, from *Chicago '68* to *Sloan Rules.*

A major intellectual debt resides—still—with Barry Karl. His intellectual approach to managers, planners, administrators, elites, and bureaucrats figures throughout this work. Every now and then I take his short but not small book, *The Uneasy State,* off the shelf and use it to think about modern society.

For too many years a number of colleagues have supported my work by writing letters of recommendation, reading proposals, and generally doing me favors. In particular, my thanks to Stan Katz, Linda Kerber, Bill Tuttle, and Richard Immerman. In completely different ways, Tuttle and Immerman are my professional role models—and they are both my friends.

A couple of other friends, Bill Katovsky and Dan Frank, made all the difference when this project and one or two other things almost got derailed. This book is for you, my brothers.

Thanks as always to my parents who opened doors and gave me choices.

Max Warsaw Bailey/Farber is taller than me. I'm glad that he gets a kick out of the fact that his mother and I write books. I look forward to reading one of his down the road.

Beth Bailey read every word. Again. She has painstakingly taught me how to write. And she makes sure that I think harder, live better, and take trips to strange places. Arm-in-arm into the next adventure.

Notes

PROLOGUE

1. Much of the personal accounts about Sloan is pieced together from scraps of information. For a sense of Sloan's life, aside from the more conventional sources cited in the notes that follow, I wish to thank Alfred Chandler, the preeminent business historian, for speaking with me for a couple of hours in his Harvard Business School office about his recollections of Sloan. Also useful are the oral history transcripts of both Nicholas Kelley and Warren Weaver, Columbia Oral History Collection, Butler Library, Columbia University, New York City; Warren Weaver, *Alfred P. Sloan, Jr., Philanthropist* (New York: Sloan Foundation, n.d.); Peter Drucker's fascinating, if problematic, recollections of Sloan, sketched in his illuminating introduction to the 1990 edition of Alfred P. Sloan Jr., *My Years with General Motors* (New York: Currency Doubleday, 1990), v–xii; and Drucker's *Adventures of a Bystander* (New York: Harper and Row, 1979), 256–93. Other insights were gained—extrapolated?—from reading thousands of pages of documents written by Sloan and his business associates.

2. Sloan, *My Years with General Motors*, xxiii.

3. The quoted material comes from two linked articles, "A Calm Philanthropist: Alfred Pritchard Sloan, Jr." *New York Times,* 19 May 1965, 44; and Eric Pace, "Sloan Is Honored for Cancer Work," *New York Times,* 19 May 1965, 44.

CHAPTER ONE

1. For the life of boys in the turn-of-the-century city see, David Nasaw, *Children of the City* (Garden City: Doubleday, 1985).

2. Sloan's speech is remarked upon by many who knew him. The business historian Alfred Chandler, who worked for Sloan as a researcher for *My Years with General Motors* (New York: Currency Doubleday, 1990), mentioned it to me in a conversation we had about Sloan. His voice is preserved in "Spotlight on Alfred Sloan," an audiotaped interview with Edward Stanley (Tucson: Learning Plan, Inc., 1969). This twenty-eight-minute interview of Sloan was originally aired on NBC radio, probably sometime in 1952. The earliest surviving recording of Sloan, I believe, is Alfred P. Sloan, [Industrial Recovery], Speech to the Illinois Manufacturers Association in Chicago, 11 December 1934, Brander Matthews Dramatic Museum Collection, Library of Congress, Washington, D.C. Details of Sloan's boyhood are presented in Alfred P. Sloan Jr., in collaboration with Boyden Sparkes, *Adventures of a White Collar Man* (New York: Doubleday, 1941), pt. 1. The photo appears in "Alfred P. Sloan, Jr.: Chairman," *Fortune,* April 1938, 73. It was also included in the first edition of Sloan's *Adventures of a White Collar Man* with a more generic caption. My source for the Columbia bicycle is

David A. Hounshell, *From the American System to Mass Production 1800–1932* (Baltimore: Johns Hopkins University Press, 1984), 191 (photo), 200.

3. Rich detail on Sloan's early years is provided in *Alfred P. Sloan Jr., Fifteenth Hoover Medalist* (New York: Hoover Medal Board of Award, 1954). It appears that Sloan provided the detail as it is not the usual biographical information supplied by GM's public relations. Other details are from his parents' obituaries, "Alfred P. Sloan, Sr., Dies at Plandome," *New York Times,* 31 August 1932, 17; and "Mrs. Alfred P. Sloan Dies Suddenly at 80," *New York Times,* 25 December 1932, 13.

4. Quoted in David Noble, *America by Design* (New York: Oxford University Press, 1977), 25.

5. Sloan, *Adventures of a White Collar Man,* 5.

6. Transcript for Alfred Pritchard Sloan Jr., 218–19, Office of the Registrar, Massachusetts Institute of Technology, Cambridge, Massachusetts. Peter Drucker, in *Adventures of a Bystander* (New York: Harper and Row, 1979), states that at MIT "[Sloan] had graduated with the highest grades anyone ever earned there" (260). Based on Drucker's statement preceding the claim—"Sloan himself was proud of his record at M.I.T."—I gather that it was Sloan who led Drucker into this claim. In fact, using his actual transcript as evidence, Sloan's overall grade average is quite mediocre. That so careful an observer and researcher as Drucker made such a mistake indicates the difficulty of getting the facts straight on Sloan, who was not a perfectly reliable source of biographical information about himself.

7. The quoted remarks are supplied by Warren Weaver, long-time president of the Sloan Foundation; Warren Weaver, Columbia Oral History Collection, Butler Library, Columbia University, New York City, 733. The "narrow man" phrase seems to be a clear and compelling self-portrayal, but I wonder what Sloan really meant and how far to take it (and I have to wonder how accurately Weaver recollected Sloan's remarks). Sloan was speaking in response to Weaver's request that Sloan donate money to the Lincoln Center for the Performing Arts. Sloan, long hard of hearing, was completely uninterested in music and was mainly indicating his uninterest in attending, let alone subsidizing, cultural performances of any kind. Like so much of the evidence about Sloan's character, especially as reported by others, one must move cautiously. I have concluded that Sloan, a brilliant manager of men, often said what was most useful in communicating his perspective and in drawing out a discussion he found of interest. Not that he lied (though his comments about his education at MIT, if accurately reported, seem to be a deliberate shading of the truth), he simply emphasized what was useful for the occasion, leaving his listener to fill in and extrapolate a picture of Sloan that was only simulated for the particular interlocutor. This simulation was not necessarily an accurate portrait (see note 6 for an example). I do believe that explains why Sloan comes across so differently, say, in the portraits drawn of him by two exceptionally astute men who know him in his last years: Peter Drucker and Warren Weaver.

8. Noble, *America by Design,* 30.

9. Weaver, oral history, 733; Warren Weaver, *Alfred P. Sloan, Jr., Philanthropist* (New York: Sloan Foundation, n.d.), 7.

10. Facts on the study of electrical engineering at MIT are in Noble, *America by Design,* 136.

11. Paul F. Douglas, *Six upon the World: Toward an American Culture for an Industrial Age* (Boston: Little, Brown, 1954), 130. Seemingly, Sloan told Douglas of his memories of these events—alas, providing no real sense for how he felt about them. I have

characterized his feelings based on the scraps of evidence offered by Douglas and on what I have extrapolated from other material.

12. Carlos Schwantes, *Coxey's Army* (Lincoln: University of Nebraska Press, 1985); for context see Robert Wiebe, *The Search for Order 1877–1920* (New York: Hill and Wang, 1967), 90–91; John Whiteclay Chamber II, *The Tyranny of Change* (New York: St. Martins, 1992), 3–6; Sidney Fine, *Laissez Faire and the General Welfare State* (Ann Arbor: University of Michigan Press, 1964), 325–26.

13. Sloan, *Adventures of a White Collar Man,* 5.

14. "Spotlight on Alfred Sloan."

15. Ibid.

16. Sloan, *Adventures of a White Collar Man,* 5.

17. Sloan transcript, MIT. I should note, to be fair, that before December 1951, an F was not the lowest possible grade, that would have been an FF. A single F meant, "Failed conditionally. Entitled to a re-examination." Sloan retook the exam the next semester and received a P, for "passed."

18. For the Hyatt roller bearing, see John T. Cunningham, *Newark* (Newark: New Jersey Historical Society, 1966), 181.

19. I am following closely the account given in ibid., 180.

20. Sloan, *Adventures of a White Collar Man,* 14.

21. Ibid., 19.

22. Some confusion exists over the marriage date. This lack of certainty in the published sources is a small indicator of the veil that surrounds much of Sloan's private life. Sloan says he married in the summer of 1898. The Hoover Medal profile of Sloan gives the date as September 28, 1898. The date of September 27, 1897 (not 1898), is given by Alfred Chandler, "Sloan, Alfred Pritchard, Jr.," *Dictionary of American Biography,* supp. 8 (New York: Scribner's Sons, 1988), 598. I think the date given in the Chandler bio is a misprint. The Chandler piece is the single best biographical sketch of Sloan. I had the opportunity, some years back, to write the Sloan biography for the all-new *DAB,* and decided not to undertake the assignment in homage to Chandler's gem.

23. The photo appears in *Adventures of a White Collar Man* and in the 1964 edition of *My Years with General Motors.*

24. Weaver, *Alfred P. Sloan, Jr., Philanthropist,* 6–7.

25. Drucker, *Adventures of a Bystander,* 284–85.

26. Douglas, *Six upon the World,* 131.

27. The list of French words comes from an astute analysis made by Vincent Curcio, *Chrysler: The Life and Times of an Automotive Genius* (New York: Oxford University Press, 2000), 134.

28. My horse facts come from Clay McShane, *Down the Asphalt Path: The Automobile and the American City* (New York: Columbia University Press, 1994), chap. 3. See also Mark Foster, *From Streetcar to Superhighway* (Philadelphia: Temple University Press, 1981), 10. James J. Flink, *Car Culture* (Cambridge: MIT Press, 1975), 34, argues that 2.5 million pounds of manure fell each day in New York and adds that sixty thousand gallons of urine perfumed the air. On this critical fact, McShane had the richer citation so I went with the lower figure.

29. The auto industry has earned a rich literature. For general guidance on the early years I put my trust in James Flink, *The Automobile Age* (Cambridge: MIT Press, 1988); James Flink, *America Adopts the Automobile, 1870–1910* (Cambridge: MIT Press, 1970); Hounshell, *From the American System to Mass Production 1800–1932,* chaps. 5–7;

Ronald Edsforth, *Class Conflict and Cultural Consensus: The Making of a Mass Consumer Society in Flint, Michigan* (New Brunswick, N.J.: Rutgers University Press, 1987); and McShane, *Down the Asphalt Path.*

30. Sloan's account of Haynes appears in *Adventures of a White Collar Man,* 24–26, with the quoted remark appearing on 25. For another take on Haynes that focuses instead on his technical sophistication, see Curcio, *Chrysler,* 143–44.

31. Sloan, *Adventures of a White Collar Man,* 39. The story is also recounted in Leland's fascinating biography by Mrs. Wilfred C. Leland with Minnie Dubbs Millbrook, *Master of Precision* (Detroit: Wayne State University Press, 1966), 91–92.

32. Sloan, *My Years with General Motors,* 20.

33. Flink, *America Adopts the Automobile,* 48–49.

34. The bearing and the copy appear in illustration 6, following page 44 in the first edition of *My Years with General Motor* (1964). The picture is not included in the 1990 edition.

35. Sloan, *Adventures of a White Collar Man,* 41–42.

36. Quoted in Olivier Zunz, *Making America Corporate* (Chicago: University of Chicago Press, 1990), 181. "Drummers and Salesman," chapter 7 of *Making America Corporate* is a superb account of the new corporate salesman.

37. Stated by George W. Stark and quoted in Norman Beasley, *Knudsen* (New York: McGraw-Hill, 1947), 59.

38. Ibid., 81–83.

39. Quoted in Roland Marchand, *Creating the Corporate Soul: The Rise of Public Relations and Corporate Imagery in American Big Business* (Berkeley: University of California Press, 1998), 42.

40. This description of Leland's political adventures comes from the superb history of General Motors by Ed Cray, *Chrome Colossus: General Motors and Its Times* (New York: McGraw-Hill, 1980), 105; and from Leland, *Master of Precision,* 167–68.

41. Hounshell, *From the American System to Mass Production,* 224.

42. Henry Ford, "Ford Recalls His Accomplishments," in *Giant Enterprise,* ed. Alfred Chandler (New York: Harcourt, Brace, and World, 1964), 35.

43. Quoted in Stephen Meyer III, *The Five Dollar Day* (Albany: SUNY Press, 1981), 9. I am following the debate about "Taylorism" and Ford made by Hounshell, *From the American System to Mass Production,* 249–53.

44. Hounshell, *From the American System to Mass Production,* chap. 6.

45. *Giant Enterprise,* 122.

46. Quoted in James Michaels, "Get Paranoid!" *Forbes* 158, no. 8 (1996): 132.

47. Sloan, *Adventures of a White Color Man,* 91–93.

48. Bernard Weisberger, *The Dream Maker* (Boston: Little, Brown, 1979), 27.

49. Ibid., 28.

50. The main source for the Durant biography and the beginning of General Motors is Weisberger, *The Dream Maker;* also useful is Cray, *Chrome Colossus,* pt. 1; and Edsforth, *Class Conflict and Cultural Consensus,* chap. 3. Edsforth offers a provocative revisionist history of Durant's management of GM; I have, however, followed the more traditional—and more critical—accounts of Durant's tenure as GM's head.

51. Rich detail on Sloan's physical characteristics is given in "Alfred P. Sloan, Jr.: Chairman," *Fortune,* April 1938, 73.

52. Sloan, *Adventures of a White Collar Man,* 96.

53. I am following Sloan's own account in *My Years with General Motors,* 22–23.

54. Sloan, *Adventures of a White Collar Man,* 98–99.

55. "Alfred P. Sloan, Jr.: Chairman," 110.

56. See Joan Hoff Wilson, *Herbert Hoover: Forgotten Progressive* (Boston: Little Brown, 1975), chap. 1.

CHAPTER TWO

1. Alfred D. Chandler Jr. and Stephen Salisbury, *Pierre S. Du Pont and the Making of the Modern Corporation* (New York: Harper and Row, 1971), 443; the stock purchase information is found on 455.

2. I follow the conclusions drawn in the tour de force essay by James Flink with Glenn Niemeyer, "Billy Durant and the Bull Market," included as chapter 5 in James Flink, *Car Culture* (Cambridge: MIT Press, 1975), 113–39.

3. Alfred P. Sloan Jr., in collaboration with Boyden Sparks, *Adventures of a White Collar Man* (New York: Doubleday, 1941), 119; Walter Chrysler, *Life of an American Workman* (New York: Dodd, Mead, 1937), 156.

4. Chrysler, *Life of an American Workman,* 156–57.

5. Sloan, *Adventures of a White Collar Man,* 114–15.

6. Alfred P. Sloan Jr., *My Years with General Motors* (New York: Currency Doubleday, 1990), 27.

7. Quoted in Alfred Chandler, *Strategy and Structure* (Cambridge: MIT Press, 1962), 127. The GM and Du Pont corporate organization material is basically drawn from Chandler's work. For more on Pratt and Durant, see Bernard Weisberger, *The Miracle Worker* (Boston: Little, Brown, 1979), 247–48.

8. For those noting the historic dollar equivalent conversions, remember that inflation had picked up dramatically between 1916 and 1920; thus, in 1916 the ratio between then and "now" was over 15 to 1 and by 1920 it was just over 9 to 1.

9. Chrysler, *Life of an American Workman,* 161.

10. Sloan, *My Years with General Motors,* 31.

11. Ibid., 11.

12. No purchase was made due to Chrysler's compelling objections; Chrysler, *Life of An American Workman,* 162–63.

13. Ibid., 12.

14. Ibid., 50.

15. For Chrysler's womanizing and his relationship with Della, see Vincent Curcio, *Chrysler: The Life and Times of an Automotive Genius* (New York: Oxford University Press, 2000), 639–41.

16. The friendship is noted by both Sloan and Chrysler in their respective writings cited above but is detailed nowhere—here I am piecing the scraps. Irene's feelings are extrapolated from the only letter by her I found. It is a gem: Irene Sloan to John Raskob, n.d. [summer 1921], John Raskob Papers (JR), Box 2109, Hagley Library, Wilmington, Delaware.

17. Sloan, *My Years with General Motors,* 51.

18. I draw again on the letter from Irene Sloan to John Raskob letter, note 16 above. Alfred Sloan states that he never discussed business with his wife. See Sloan, *Adventures of a White Collar Man,* 99–100.

19. As scholars know, Durant angrily denied that GM's massive, ill-timed expansion was his idea; he blamed Raskob and the du Ponts. A nice set of documents exploring the controversy is collected in *Giant Enterprise,* ed. Alfred Chandler Jr. (New York: Harcourt, Brace, and the World, 1964), 71–86.

20. The 894 stockholder figure is based on a GMC Press Release, 6 June 1930,

listing stockholders over time, in Kettering Archives (KA), Box 114, 87–11.5, Alumni Collection of Industrial History, GMI, Flint, Michigan.

21. The interesting relationship between Raskob and Sloan, about which more will soon be said, is hinted at in JR, Box 2109, which contains information on Raskob's social life in the 1918 to 1921 period; particularly useful is a letter from Alfred Sloan to John Raskob, 23 December 1918.

22. Harold Livesay, *American Made: The Men Who Shaped the American Economy* (Boston: Little, Brown, 1979), 239. Livesay's chapter, "The Organization Man: Alfred P. Sloan," is a brilliant explanation of Sloan's organizational genius. In praising Sloan's corporate achievements I am much influenced by his interpretation.

23. An edited version appears in *Giant Enterprise*, 114–15.

24. For a compelling account of the blast, see Paul Avrich, *Sacco and Vanzetti* (Princeton: Princeton University Press, 1991), 204–7; see also Ron Chernow, *The House of Morgan* (New York: Simon and Schuster, 1990), 212–14.

25. I am following du Pont's version which is given in its entirety in a letter from Pierre du Pont to Irénée du Pont, 26 November 1920, reprinted in *Giant Enterprise*, 81–86; the quoted remark appears on p. 83. This same letter, supplied probably by Sloan's research assistant, Alfred Chandler, appears in its entirety, albeit without Chandler's useful notes, in Sloan, *My Years with General Motors*, 32–38. Its inclusion indicates Sloan's desire to demonstrate objectively, so to speak, Durant's problematic character and manner of running GM.

26. The last days of Durant are compiled from several sources, most importantly: Weisberger, *The Dream Maker*, 275–363; James Flink, *The Automobile Age* (Cambridge: MIT Press, 1988), 87–111; Flink, *Car Culture*, 113–39; Chandler and Salisbury, *Pierre S. Du Pont and the Making of the Modern Corporation*, 482–89; Ed Cray, *Chrome Colossus: General Motors and Its Times* (New York: McGraw-Hill, 1980), 163–82.

27. Sloan, *My Years with General Motors*, 43–44. Personal sensitivity disclosure and potential analytic bias: the author is five feet seven inches tall.

28. Pieced from documents in JR, Box 2109, especially the letter from Alfred Sloan to John Raskob, 23 December 1918.

29. Sloan, *My Years with General Motors*, 72.

30. Ibid., 53.

31. For more, much more, on the engineer as problem-solver consultant, see Walter G. Vincenti, *What Engineers Know and How They Know It* (Baltimore: Johns Hopkins University Press, 1990), esp. 254–57. Vincenti's historically minded work has been very useful in helping me to understand Sloan's problem-solving processes.

32. The "Organization Study" is, in the main, laid out in *My Years* on 53–54; a better place to find it detailed might be Chandler, *Strategy and Structure*, 134; see generally Chandler's incomparable discussion of Sloan's creation in ibid., 133–42. Ed Cray, in *Chrome Colossus*, ever the genial iconoclast, dismisses "Organization Study" as "neither original nor very complicated. It depended essentially on the staff-line division of effort developed by the German army in the last quarter of the nineteenth century" (192). Of course, Sloan knew nothing of the German army, and while the notion of staff-line division of effort is in general terms not a hugely complicated mental construct, I think Cray is being a bit too cavalier about Sloan's concrete achievement.

CHAPTER THREE

1. Alfred Sloan deposition, 28 April–9 May 1952, *United States v. E. I. du Pont de Nemours, General Motors Co. et al.*, Civil Action No. 49c-1071, District Court for

Northern Illinois, at 28. This material is available at the Hagley Library, Wilmington, Delaware, under the source abbreviation "GM Case."

2. Alfred P. Sloan Jr., *My Years with General Motors* (New York: Currency Doubleday, 1990), 56.

3. This version of the hard-work adage is taken from a speech by Sloan, "The Principles and Policies behind General Motors," 28 September 1927, GM Proving Grounds, Milford, Michigan, Frederick Horner Papers (FH), Box 37:149, Library of Congress, Washington, D.C. The sandwich story is recounted by Ed Cray, *Chrome Colossus: General Motors and Its Times* (New York: McGraw-Hill, 1980), 194; and Warren Weaver, *Alfred P. Sloan, Jr., Philanthropist* (New York: Sloan Foundation, n.d.), 7. Sloan's hard work is recounted in many sources; for a contemporary account, see B. C. Forbes, "Open Mind—How He Gets Executive Teamwork," *Forbes,* 29 March 1924, 774; and the slightly later version in "Alfred P. Sloan, Jr.: Chairman," *Fortune,* April 1938, 112.

4. Weaver, *Alfred P. Sloan, Jr.,* 33.

5. "Spotlight on Alfred Sloan," audiotaped interview with Edward Stanley, aired originally on NBC radio probably in 1952 (Tucson: Learning Plan, Inc., 1969).

6. Ibid.

7. Wendy Hall Maloney, "Pratt, John Lee," *Dictionary of American Biography,* supp. 9 (New York: Charles Scribner's Sons, 1994), 622.

8. Corporate executives' faith in their methods and scorn for politicians' less quantifiable approaches is a twentieth-century constant seen in aspects of key Progressive Era reform and the quixotic 1992 presidential bid of billionaire businessman Ross Perot.

9. As noted by Oliver Zunz, *Making America Corporate* (Chicago: University of Chicago Press, 1990), 73–74, 90, the Hotel McAlpin was as scientifically managed as Pratt hoped to make GM.

10. The John Lee Pratt Papers (JLPa), General Motors Executive Alumni Archive, GMI, Flint, Michigan, convey little of his personal life, though the *John Lee Pratt Register* has a useful chronology of his life. The best source material on Pratt's personal life appears in the Edward Stettinius Papers (ES), Box 376, Special Collections, Alderman Library, University of Virginia, Charlottesville, Virginia, which contains a series of rich correspondence between Lilian Pratt to Edward Stettinius and from John Pratt to Stettinius from 1933 to 1935. The Lilian Pratt quote is from Lilian Pratt to Edward Stettinius, 27 December 1933, ES, Box 376. Very useful is an untitled clipping in Box 376 from the *Richmond News Leader,* 3 December 1935, which supplies key biographical information on Pratt. Also useful are the letters collected in Box 5, "Personal Correspondence, 1931–1939" (which actually have letters through 1943) the John Lee Pratt Papers (JLPb), Special Collections, Alderman Library, University of Virginia, Charlottesville, Virginia. The ulcer problem is recounted in John Pratt to Fred Shibley, 6 February 1943, JLPb, Box 5. I have also fudged the chronology a bit in this sketch; Chatham was not bought until 1931 and I am not sure if Lilian lived in Virginia or in New York before 1931.

11. Peter Drucker, *Adventures of a Bystander* (New York: Harper and Row, 1979), 264.

12. Donaldson Brown, *Some Reminiscences of an Industrialist* (Easton, Penn.: Hive Publishing, 1977), 11.

13. Ibid., 11–16.

14. Much of what follows is drawn from three critical sources: Richard Tedlow, *New and Improved* (New York: Basic Books, 1990), chap. 3; James Flink, *The Automobile Age*

(Cambridge: MIT Press, 1988), chaps. 3–4; and Sloan, *My Years with General Motors,* chap. 4. Also informing this part of the text is the provocative article by Anthony Patrick O'Brien, "How to Succeed in Business: Lessons from the Struggle between Ford and General Motors during the 1920s and 1930s," *Business and Economic History,* 2d ser., 18 (1989): 79–87; and Clarence H. Young and William A. Quinn, *Foundation for Living: The Story of Charles Stewart Mott and Flint* (New York: McGraw-Hill, 1963), 81–99.

15. Sloan discusses the "Transformation of the Automobile Market" in chapter 9 of *My Years with General Motors.*

16. Durant-Dort is insightfully discussed in Ronald Edsforth, *Class Conflict and Cultural Consensus: The Making of a Mass Consumer Society in Flint, Michigan* (New Brunswick, N.J.: Rutgers University Press, 1987), 41–43; I have also benefited here from Ron Edsforth's comments on the manuscript for this part of the book.

17. Sloan, *My Years with General Motors,* 64.

18. Young and Quinn, *Foundation for Living,* 83.

19. Ibid., 46.

20. Ibid., 51.

21. Ibid., 55.

22. Ibid., 65.

23. Sloan, *My Years with General Motors,* 150.

24. Ibid., 77.

25. Ibid., 78.

26. Ibid., 79.

27. Ibid., 81.

28. Ibid., 325, 329.

29. Drucker, *Adventures of a Bystander,* 284.

30. Sloan's dress during visits to dealers is described in "Alfred P. Sloan, Jr., Dead at 90," *New York Times,* 18 February 1966, 30.

31. Sloan's meeting style is described in "Alfred P. Sloan, Jr.: Chairman," *Fortune,* April 1938, 73.

32. Here I rely on the absence of concern shown in letters and the lack of mention by friends, associates and reporters—perhaps not the best of evidence, but it is all I found.

33. The remark is quoted by Roland Marchand, *Creating the Corporate Soul* (Berkeley: University of California Press, 1998), 131. Marchand's book is a masterpiece and I rely on it for the next several paragraphs of the text.

34. Sloan, *My Years with General Motors,* 102–4.

35. Ibid., 133.

36. Ibid., 132–33.

37. The Barton biographical material comes from T. J. Jackson Lears, "From Salvation to Self-Realization: Advertising and the Therapeutic Roots of the Consumer Culture, 1880–1930," in *The Culture of Consumption,* ed. Richard Wightman Fox and T. J. Jackson Lears (New York: Pantheon, 1983), 30–38; the quote, "the founder of modern business," appears on 31.

38. Marchand, *Creating the Corporate Soul,* 134–35.

39. Quoted in ibid., 136.

40. "Alfred P. Sloan, Jr., Dead at 90," *New York Times,* 30.

41. Alfred P. Sloan Jr., in collaboration with Boyden Sparks, *Adventures of a White Collar Man* (New York: Doubleday, 1941), 133.

42. Sloan, *My Years with General Motors,* 98.

CHAPTER FOUR

1. Alfred P. Sloan Jr., *My Years with General Motors* (New York: Currency Doubleday, 1990), 98.

2. Stuart Leslie, *Boss Kettering* (New York: Columbia University Press, 1983), 15. I rely throughout my discussion of Kettering on Leslie's scrupulously researched and sure-handed account. Also of use in understanding Kettering is the biography by his onetime colleague, Thomas A. Boyd, *Professional Amateur: The Biography of Charles Franklin Kettering* (New York: Dutton, 1957).

3. Leslie, *Boss Kettering,* 1.

4. Ibid., 14.

5. Thomas Hughes, *American Genesis: A Century of Invention and Technological Enthusiasm, 1870–1970* (New York: Penguin, 1989), brilliantly explores the making of American technology in the late nineteenth century and early twentieth century. The best critical history of the industrial lab is by David Noble, *America by Design: Science, Technology and the Rise of Corporate Capitalism* (New York: Oxford University Press, 1979), see esp. chap. 7.

6. Leslie, *Boss Kettering,* 36.

7. From a memo from Sloan to Pierre du Pont in December 1921, in Sloan, *My Years with General Motors,* 80.

8. Quoted in "The Saga of the Copper-Cooled Engine," ed. Thomas Bonsall, avail. at the website <www.rideanddrive.com>.

9. Quoted in Norman Beasley, *Knudsen* (New York: McGraw-Hill, 1947), 127–28.

10. Sloan, *My Years with General Motors,* 86.

11. Ibid., 87.

12. Ibid., 88.

13. Ibid., 90–91.

14. Leslie, *Boss Kettering,* 144.

15. Ibid.

16. Again, I have closely followed the account in Leslie's tour de force chapter "The Copper-Cooled Engine," in *Boss Kettering,* 145–48.

17. Ibid., 184.

18. The richest treatment of this project comes from a recent, harshly critical exposé by Jamie Lincoln Kitman in "The Secret History of Lead," *Nation,* 20 March 2000, 11–44. I generally follow Kitman's account and also draw on material from Leslie, *Boss Kettering,* 149–80; also useful is Sloan's cleaned-up account in *My Years with General Motors,* 221–26, and an insightful overview by Hughes, *American Genesis,* 223–35.

19. Kitman, "The Secret History of Lead," 16.

20. Ibid., 22.

21. Ibid., 25.

22. Ibid.

23. Here I am following the account given by Ed Cray in *Chrome Colossus: General Motors and Its Times* (New York: McGraw-Hill, 1980), 239. Cray's account is based on a letter from Sloan to Irénée du Pont dated 8 August 1926. It is possible Sloan's letter reveals his attempt to explain to du Pont how Standard got a contract that du Pont expected, rather than a straightforward indication of Sloan's feelings in 1924.

24. Both quotes are from the superbly researched account in Kitman, "The Secret of Lead," 26.

25. The Court's majority decision in *Lochner* is discussed in Nancy Woloch, *Muller v. Oregon: A Brief History with Documents* (New York: Bedford Books, 1996), 101.

26. Irving Bernstein, *The Lean Years* (Baltimore: Pelican, 1966), 166–67.

27. Christian Warren, "Toxic Purity: The Progressive Era Origins of America's Lead Paint Poisoning Epidemic," *Business History Review* 73, no. 4 (winter 1999): 726.

28. New Jersey worker compensation law is outlined by Edward Berkowitz and Kim McQuaid, *Creating the Welfare State* (Lawrence: University Press of Kansas, 1992), 48–49.

29. From a *New York Times* story, quoted by Kitman, "The Secret History of Lead," 28.

30. From the ironic prose master Frederick Lewis Allen, *Only Yesterday* (New York: Harper and Row, 1962), 162. The book was originally published in 1931.

31. I am relying on Kitman's account and my own researches into the Coolidge presidency as summarized in David Farber, "Calvin Coolidge and the Politics of Presidential Silence," in *The Reader's Companion to the American Presidency*, ed. Alan Brinkley (Boston: Houghton Mifflin, 2000), 345–53.

32. Kitman, "The Secret History of Lead," 31–37.

33. Cray, *Chrome Colossus*, 242.

34. See "The Ballyhoo Years," chap. 8 in Allen, *Only Yesterday.*

35. As reported in "Alfred P. Sloan," *Wall Street Journal* newspaper clipping, dated August 1926 (no specific date on clipping and no page number), in Frederick Horner Papers (FH), Box 72:3, Library of Congress, Washington, D.C.

36. Ibid.

37. William Cronon, *Nature's Metropolis: Chicago and the Great West* (New York: Norton, 1991), 35.

38. James Flink, *The Automobile Age* (Cambridge: MIT Press, 1988), 115.

39. Ibid., 114.

40. Ibid., 112–13.

41. Nancy MacLean, *The Mask of Chivalry* (New York: Oxford University Press, 1994), 135–37. For Klan membership numbers, see ibid. at xi; the Klan claimed to have 5 million members.

42. For Ford's wisdom and celebrity, see the juicy account by Robert Lacey, *Ford: The Man and the Machine* (New York: Ballantine, 1986), 217–49; see also Robert Higham, *Strangers in the Land* (New York: Atheneum, 1966), 277–86. On May 3, 1925, President Coolidge took a public stand against anti-Semitism by laying the cornerstone for the Jewish Community Center in Washington, D.C.; see the photo in "Prosperity and Thrift: The Coolidge Era and the Consumer Economy, 1921–1929," avail. at <http://www.memory.loc.gov/ammem/cool.html>, digital Id Cph3c1645.

43. B. C. Forbes, "Open Mind—How He Gets Executive Teamwork," *Forbes,* March 29, 1924, 759.

44. A mid-nineteenth-century description of frontiersman Kit Carson by Charles Averill, *Life in California* (Boston: George Williams, 1849), preface.

45. Forbes, "Open Mind," 774.

46. A characterization of the era, quoted by Virginia Scharff, *Taking the Wheel: Women and the Coming of the Motor Age* (New York: Free Press, 1991), 113. In chapter 7, "Corporate Masculinity and the 'Feminine' Market," Scharff presents a pathbreaking history of how men and women related the auto to their concepts of gender in the 1920s.

47. Joseph Schumpeter, *Capitalism, Socialism, and Democracy* (New York: Harper and Brothers, 1947 [1942]), 127–28.

48. Sinclair Lewis, *Dodsworth* (New York: Modern Library, 1947), 19.

49. "Alfred P. Sloan," *Wall Street Journal,* note 35 above.

50. The quote is used by Flink, *The Automobile Age,* 125.

51. Forbes, "Open Mind," 774.

52. "Cylinder Battlers Square Off! FORD VS. SLOAN," *New York Journal,* newspaper clipping, dated December 1927, in Pierre du Pont Papers (PDP), Box 624, Folder 7, Hagley Library, Wilmington, Delaware.

53. The quote is from Alfred P. Sloan to Charles Kettering, 1 August 1934, Charles Kettering Papers (CK), 87–11.5–11, Alumni Collection of Industrial History, GMI, Flint, Michigan. For vacation plans, friendship, and housing, see also John Raskob Papers (JR), Box 2109, Hagley Library, Wilmington, Delaware; Walter P. Chrysler, *Life of an American Working Man* (New York: Dodd, Mead, 1937), 162; Richard D. Wyskoff, *Wall Street Ventures and Adventures* (New York: Harper and Brothers, 1930), 285; and "Alfred P. Sloan Jr.: Chairman," *Fortune,* April 1938, 110.

54. Quoted in a profile of GM, "General Motors IV: A Unit in Society," *Fortune,* March 1939, 45. The conversation he had with Secretary of Labor Frances Perkins in 1937, recounted in chapter 8, makes me think he was not being completely honest about his disregard for making money.

55. Quoted in Arthur Schlesinger, *The Crisis of the Old Order* (Boston: Houghton Mifflin, 1957), 56.

56. Lynn Dumenil, *The Modern Temper: American Culture and Society in the 1920s* (New York: Hill and Wang, 1995), 87.

57. These facts are drawn from Ronald Edsforth, *The New Deal* (Boston: Blackwell, 1999), 12.

58. Ronald Edsforth, "Made in the USA: Mass Culture and the Americanization of Working Class Ethnics in the Coolidge Era," unpublished paper in the author's possession.

59. Quoted in "Calvin Coolidge," avail. at <http://www.whitehouse.gov/WH/glimpse/presidents/html/cc30>.

60. Calvin Coolidge, *Foundations of the Republic* (1926), quoted in Arthur Shenfield, "Against the Creation of Wealth: The Threatening Tide," *The Freeman,* avail. at <http://www.self-gov.org/freeman/8901shen.html>.

61. Ibid.

62. Beasley, *Knudsen,* 15.

63. Ibid., 109. The other biographical material also comes from *Knudsen.*

64. The quotes and the analysis come directly from David Hounshell, *From the American System to Mass Production 1800–1932* (Baltimore: Johns Hopkins University Press, 1984), 265; see generally ibid., chap. 7.

65. Peter Drucker, *Adventures of a Bystander* (New York: Harper and Row, 1979), 281.

66. The material on Grant comes from "G.M. III: How to Sell Automobiles," *Fortune,* February 1939, 74–78. For a pithy overview, see Richard Tedlow, *New and Improved* (New York: Basic Books, 1990), 172–73.

67. Beasley, *Knudsen,* 131; and on Sloan's personnel work, see Drucker, *Adventures of a Bystander,* 280–81.

68. Beasley, *Knudsen,* 132.

69. Sloan, *My Years with General Motors,* 156–59.

70. Alfred P. Sloan Jr., *Adventures of a White Collar Man* (New York: Doubleday, 1941), 184.

71. Scharff, *Taking the Wheel,* 113.

72. Ibid.

73. For Sloan's attitude toward styling and marketing, see Sloan, *My Years with General Motors,* chap. 15; Sloan, *Adventures of a White Collar Man,* 184–85; Tedlow, *New and Improved,* 164–73.

74. This part of the text is based on several sources: Stephen Bayley, *Harley Earl* (New York: Taplinger, 1990), 36–47; David Halberstam, *The Fifties* (New York: Ballantine, 1993), 123–25; Sloan, *My Years with General Motors,* 266–70; Cray, *Chrome Colossus,* 243–45; David Gartman, *Auto Opium* (New York: Routledge, 1994), 68–92; and Vincent Curcio, *Chrysler: The Life and Times of an Automotive Genius* (New York: Oxford University Press, 2000), 350–53. The Earl quote on "oblongs" is from Halberstam, *The Fifties,* 124.

75. See "General Motors II: Chevrolet," *Fortune,* January 1939, 46, 103; and Cray, *Chrome Colossus,* 245. The quote is from Sloan, *My Years with General Motors,* 273.

76. Sloan, *My Years with General Motors,* 270.

77. Ibid., 272.

78. Ibid., 271.

79. For the Wanamaker quote, see William Leach, *Land of Desire* (New York: Vintage Books, 1994), 43; the statistics are from ibid., 42.

80. Ronald Edsforth, *Class Conflict and Cultural Consensus: The Makings of a Mass Consumer Society in Flint, Michigan* (New Brunswick, N.J.: Rutgers University Press, 1987), 21.

81. Quoted in Roland Marchand, *Advertising the American Dream* (Berkeley: University of California Press, 1985), 157.

82. A vast historical and sociological literature on the subject of advertising and marketing exists, much of it highly critical. Many of the key works appear throughout my notes for this chapter. Other useful books include Susan Strasser, *Satisfaction Guaranteed* (New York: Pantheon, 1989), a thoroughly researched, sophisticated analysis of the pre–World War I consumer marketplace; Stewart Ewen, *Captains of Consciousness* (New York: Basic Books, 2001), first published in 1976, an influential polemic against corporate advertisers; and Jackson Lears, *Fables of Abundance* (New York: Basic Books, 1994), a multifaceted, brilliant history that looks at advertising as a seminal part of consumer culture—"a new way of ordering the existing balance of tensions between control and release" (11).

83. Marchand, *Advertising the American Dream,* 157.

84. The auto statistics are from *Giant Enterprise,* ed. Alfred Chandler (New York: Harcourt, Brace and World, 1964), 3–7; the stock figures are from GMC, press release, 12 June 1930, CK, 87–11, 5–1.

85. Flink, *The Automobile Age,* 229–31.

86. Ibid., 229.

87. Sloan, *My Years with General Motors,* 162.

CHAPTER FIVE

1. William Leach, *Land of Desire* (New York: Vintage, 1993), 341.

2. Sloan's foreign travels in the 1920s and 1930s are detailed in Sloan's FBI file that I received through a Freedom of Information Act request: Subject: Alfred P. Sloan Jr., File No. 100–25806. The file was created to assess Sloan's patriotism and to investigate his ties to the Nazi regime. The 1940–41 activities of James Mooney, who had run GM's overseas business and who was sympathetic to Germany before war between the United States and the Axis powers broke out, triggered the investigation of Sloan.

The specific document on Sloan's foreign travels is: Alfred Pritchard Sloan Jr., File No. 100–3230, 7/9/41, Federal Bureau of Investigation (APS-FBI).

3. Here I have drawn mainly from the portrait given in Matthew Josephson and Hannah Josephson, *Al Smith: Hero of the Cities* (Boston: Houghton Mifflin, 1969), 356–57.

4. John Raskob to Steward Prosser, 16 June 1926, John Raskob Papers (JR), Box 2109, Hagley Library, Wilmington, Delaware.

5. Information on the New York Yacht Club, including the Morgan quote, is drawn from the club's website at <www.nyyc.org>.

6. Ron Chernow, *The House of Morgan* (New York: Simon and Schuster, 1990), 151.

7. Ibid., 53, 80.

8. See Senate Banking and Currency Committee, *Stock Exchange Practices: Hearing,* 73d Cong., 1st Sess. (1933), 880.

9. Ibid.

10. Ibid., 882, 896.

11. For a general look at Kettering on education, see Stuart Leslie, *Boss Kettering* (New York: Columbia University Press, 1983), 286; the specific story of Kettering and GMI, including the quoted passages, are in Richard Scharchburg, "Charles Kettering: Doing the Right Thing at the Right Time," Kettering Institute website at <www.gmi.edu>.

12. Alfred P. Sloan Jr., "General Motors Institute of Technology: Conception Purposes and Program," n.d. (1926?), Kettering Archives, 87–11.4.1, Alumni Collection of Industrial History, GMI, Flint, Michigan. A rich treatment of cooperative education for industry is provided by David Noble, *America by Design: Science, Technology and the Rise of Corporate Capitalism* (New York: Oxford University Press, 1979), chap. 8.

13. Sloan discusses GMI almost not at all. Aside from the remarks made on the institute's reopening—see note 12—I base this part of the text on Peter Drucker, *Adventures of a Bystander* (New York: Harper and Row, 1979), 260–61, 290–91. Given Sloan's powerful interest in MIT, I think Drucker is right to emphasize how much Sloan cared about GMI; still, I wonder if Sloan did not give Drucker the impression that he cared a good deal about GMI because he know that Drucker was a college professor. Sloan, as I have suggested before, often presented himself and his interests to people in ways he thought useful rather than simply as a reflection of some core beliefs. For Dougherty's notions, see the seven-page memo, N. F. Dougherty, "Memo to Top Executives for Comment on Subject of Education," 3 July 1928, KA, 87–11.4–2.

14. Noble, *America by Design,* 313. I am closely following Noble's breakthrough account of the course and of the careful interlinking of engineering, corporate enterprise, and higher education by Sloan and many other industrial leaders.

15. Again I am drawing heavily on Nobel, *American by Design,* 313–15. Sloan's feelings are not revealed but his increasing connections and then large financial gifts to MIT support the conclusions drawn in the text.

16. This story is reported by GM executive Frederick Horner, unpublished memoir, 122, Frederick Horner Papers (FH), Box 70, Folder 3, Library of Congress, Washington, D.C. He says he was told the story, dialogue included, by Sloan's executive secretary Alfred Brant.

17. Vincent Curcio, *Chrysler: The Life and Times of an Automotive Genius* (New York: Oxford University Press, 2000), 639–40.

18. John Raskob to Alfred P. Sloan, 21 July 1922, JR, Box 2109.

19. Josephson and Josephson, *Al Smith,* 356.

20. Morton Keller, *Regulating A New Economy* (Cambridge: Harvard University Press, 1990), 217–19.

21. Robert S. McElvaine, *The Great Depression* (New York: Times Books, 1984), 23–24.

22. For the quoted phrase and more on Raskob and du Pont's role in anti-Prohibition efforts and the Smith campaign, see the incisive account by Robert F. Burk, *The Corporate State and the Broker State* (Cambridge: Harvard University Press, 1990), chap. 3.

23. Pierre du Pont to Alfred P. Sloan Jr., 26 February 1931, Pierre du Pont Papers (PDP), Box 1023, Folder 17, Hagley Library, Wilmington, Delaware.

24. The letter is quoted by Curcio, *Chrysler,* 642.

25. William L. Riordon, *Plunkitt of Tammany Hall* (New York: Signet, 1995), 7.

26. Josephson and Josephson, *Al Smith,* 353–58.

27. Burk, *The Corporate State and the Broker State,* 53.

28. Josephson and Josephson, *Al Smith,* 372.

29. Burk, *The Corporate State and the Broker State,* 54.

30. W. Parnell to John Raskob c/o General Motors, 11 July 1928, PDP, Box 624.

31. Alfred P. Sloan to W. Parnell, 20 July 1928, PDP, Box 624.

32. Alfred P. Sloan, Direct Testimony, *United States v. E. I. du Pont de Nemours, General Motors Co. et al.*, Civil Action No. 49c-1071, District Court for Northern Illinois, trial transcript at 2847–48. This material is available at the Hagley Library, Wilmington, Delaware, under the source abbreviation "GM Case."

33. Charles Cheape, *Strictly Business: Walter Carpenter at du Pont and General Motors* (Baltimore: Johns Hopkins University Press, 1995), 121.

34. Quoted in Allen J. Lichtman, *Prejudice and Politics: The Election of 1928* (Chapel Hill: University of North Carolina Press, 1979), 181.

35. Arthur M. Schlesinger, *The Crisis of the Old Order, 1919–1933* (Boston: Houghton Mifflin, 1957), 127.

36. John J. Raskob to Alfred P. Sloan Jr., 17 July 1928, JR, Box 2109.

37. "The Raskob Resignation," clipping, Boston News Bureau, Irénée du Pont Papers (IP), Box 42, File 208, Hagley Library, Wilmington, Delaware. No date, but evidence indicates it was published on July 25, 1928. See also Alfred P. Sloan Jr. to Pierre du Pont, 25 July 1928, PDP, Box 624, Folder 9; and Alfred P. Sloan Jr. to Irénée du Pont, 25 July 1928, IP, Box 42, Folder 208.

38. Burk, *The Corporate State and the Broker State,* 54.

39. Alfred P. Sloan Jr. to Irénée du Pont, 25 July 1928.

40. "Du Pont Gets Leave from Motors Post to Fight Dry Law," *New York Times,* 10 August 1928, 1. Note that the story made the *Times'* front page.

41. "Dupont Granted Leave as Head of Motor Board," clipping, *Mobile Daily Register,* 10 August 1928, 1, PDP, Box 624, Folder 7. The GM decision was headline news around the nation.

42. *New York Times,* 10 August 1928, 1.

43. Ibid., 3.

44. Burk, *The Corporate State and the Broker State,* 54.

45. Sloan first appears in the 1924 edition. *Who's Who in America,* vol. 13, ed. Albert Nelson Marquis (Chicago: A. N. Marquis, 1924), 2938.

46. Alfred Sloan to Roy Chapin, 27 July 1928, Roy Chapin Papers (RC), Box 17, Bentley Library, Ann Arbor, Michigan; and Roy Chapin to Alfred P. Sloan, 23 July 1928, RC, Box 17. A copy in the folder of Chapin's form letter to the twenty-six auto executives lists each of their contributions.

47. Coleman du Pont to Pierre du Pont, 15 August 1928, Defendants' Trial Exhibit No. GM-19, Box 9, GM Antitrust Suit, Hagley Library, Wilmington, Delaware.

48. Josephson and Josephson, *Al Smith,* 372.

49. "Sloan, General Motors Head, Backs Hoover," *New York Herald Tribune,* 4 September 1928, clipping, JR, Box 2109.

50. *United States. v. Du Pont, GM, et al.,* trial transcript, 2848.

51. Burk, *The Corporate State and the Broker State,* 55.

52. Frederick Lewis Allen, *Only Yesterday* (New York: Harper and Row, 1962), 252.

53. McElvaine, *The Great Depression,* 55.

54. Pete Daniel, *Deep'n As It Come: The 1927 Mississippi River Flood* (New York: Oxford University Press, 1977), 10.

55. James Flink, *The Automobile Age* (Cambridge: MIT Press, 1988), 71. Hoover was not in charge of this particular standardization effort, which had complex causes; it is, however similar to the efforts he championed in many other industries.

56. McElvaine, *The Great Depression,* 58.

57. Irving Bernstein, *The Lean Years* (New York: Penguin, 1966), 250.

CHAPTER SIX

1. Frederick Lewis Allen, *Only Yesterday* (New York: Harper and Row, 1962), 252.

2. Ibid., 264

3. Ron Chernow, *The House of Morgan* (New York: Simon and Schuster, 1990), 313.

4. Ibid., 317.

5. Arthur M. Schlesinger, *The Crisis of the Old Order, 1919–1933* (Boston: Houghton Mifflin, 1957), 158.

6. John Kenneth Galbraith, *The Great Crash* (Boston: Houghton Mifflin, 1961), 126.

7. For this overview of the crash of 1929, I have relied in particular on Chernow, *House of Morgan,* chap. 16; Allen, *Only Yesterday,* chaps. 12–13; Schlesinger, *The Crisis of the Old Order,* chap. 19; Galbraith, *The Great Crash,* chap. 8.

8. "Spotlight on Alfred Sloan," an audiotaped interview with Edward Stanley (Tucson: Learning Plan, Inc., 1969), which originally aired on NBC radio, probably sometime in 1952.

9. Schlesinger, *The Crisis of the Old Order,* 162.

10. Ibid.

11. I am here closely following the account given by Ronald Edsforth, *The New Deal* (Boston: Blackwell, 2000), 20–22.

12. Alfred P. Sloan Jr., *My Years with General Motors* (New York: Currency Doubleday, 1990), 172.

13. Ibid., 173.

14. Sloan's words and those of O'Brien are from, Anthony Patrick O'Brien, "How to Succeed in Business: Lessons from the Struggle between Ford and General Motors during the 1920s and 1930s," *Business and Economic History,* 2d ser., 18 (1989): 82.

15. Sidney Fine, *The Automobile under the Blue Eagle* (Ann Arbor: University of Michigan Press, 1963), 4.

16. Paul F. Douglas, *Six upon the World: Toward an American Culture for an Industrial Age* (Boston: Little, Brown, 1954), 165.

17. Ibid., 164.

18. This part of the text relies on E. D. Kennedy, *The Automobile Industry* (Clifton, N.J.: Kelley Publishers, 1972), 221–223.

19. See "James E. Watson," avail. at <http://www.indianahistory.org/watson.html>.

20. Douglas, *Six upon the World,* 165.

21. Schlesinger, *The Crisis of the Old Order,* 164.

22. Douglas, *Six upon the World,* 170.

23. Quoted in a long report on Sloan's public statements and their reception made by Ralph Hayes to Edward L. Bernays, 7 December 1932, Edward Bernays Papers (EB), Box 177, Library of Congress, Washington, D.C.

24. Galbraith, *The Great Crash,* 144–45.

25. The information about Sloan's yacht is from Douglas, *Six upon the World,* 171; see also "Power Yachts Here for Finishing," *New York Times,* 30 January 1930, 47; and "Mr. and Mrs. Alfred Sloan at Launching of Their Yacht 'Rene,' " 19 September 1929, Pusey and Jones Photo, 72.350.3810, Hagley Library, Wilmington, Delaware.

26. I am not certain that Sloan was sipping martinis during Prohibition but I do know that at least later in life he regularly enjoyed them (learned in conversation with Alfred Chandler). The photo appears in Vincent Curcio, *Chrysler: The Life and Times of an Automotive Genius* (New York: Oxford University Press, 2000), 341.

27. Alfred Sloan to John Raskob, 19 August 1930, John Raskob Papers (JR), Box 2109, Hagley Library, Wilmington, Delaware.

28. Alfred P. Sloan to Charles Kettering, 11 August 1930, Kettering Archives (KA), 87–11.4–4, Alumni Collection of Industrial History, GMI, Flint, Michigan..

29. The meeting was memorialized in a picture booklet, "GM Executive Conference," 19–21 September 1930, White Sulphur Springs, West Virginia, Edward Stettinius Papers (ES), Box 551, University of Virginia, Charlottesville, Virginia.

30. See Alfred P. Sloan Jr. to Roy Chapin, 28 July 1917; and Roy Chapin to Alfred P. Sloan Jr., 13 August 1917, Roy Chapin Papers (RC), Box 4, Bentley Library, Ann Arbor, Michigan.

31. Alfred P. Sloan Jr. to Roy Chapin, 16 August 1932, RC, Box 23.

32. J. D. Mooney to Alfred P. Sloan Jr., 20 October 1930, 1–2, 13–14, enclosure from Mooney to Sloan dated 10 November 1930, Walter Carpenter Papers (WC), Box 821, Hagley Library, Wilmington, Delaware.

33. Thomas Hughes, *American Genesis: A Century of Invention and Technological Enthusiasm, 1870–1970* (New York: Penguin, 1989), 268. Hughes provides a rich portrait of Hugh Cooper and the Soviet project at 261–69. A picture of Cooper and Stalin sharing a meal appears on 269.

34. Julian Barnes to Ivy Lee, 4 July 1927, "Julian Barnes," Commerce Papers, Herbert Hoover Presidential Library, West branch, Iowa.

35. I have no record of Sloan and Cooper discussing the matter on Cooper's return from the Soviet Union. Dining and drinking with Stalin is described by Milovan Djilas, *Conversations with Stalin,* trans. Michale B. Petrovich (New York: Harcourt, Brace and World, 1962), 151–61. Special thanks to Russian historian Richard Robbins for information on Stalin's favorite beverages.

36. For a thoughtful history of American attitudes toward the Soviet Union between the world wars, see Peter G. Filene, *Americans and the Soviet Experience, 1917–1933* (Cambridge: Harvard University Press, 1967). For business approaches, see ibid., chaps. 4 and 8; the RFC cotton deal is mentioned on 237.

37. Sloan to Chapin, 16 August 1932.

38. John T. Blossom to Roy Chapin, September 19, 1932, Box 22, RC.

39. James J. Flink, *The Automobile Age* (Cambridge: MIT Press, 1988), 51–55.

40. Edsel Ford to Roy Chapin, 7 January 1932, RC, Box 21.

41. Johnson took it upon himself to educate Sloan and the other members of the NACC taxation committee on the mechanics of political pressure. At the very beginning of the antitax campaign, he felt it necessary to write: "Nothing that can be done in Washington by paid representatives can ever be so effective as the voice of the constituent." He asked each of the chief executives to urge their dealers, suppliers, and manufacturers around the country to explain to their congressmen and senators the negative effect the new tax would have on their businesses. Pyke Johnson to Roy Chapin, 1 January 1932, RC, Box 21. While I am not certain, I believe this general letter was sent to all members of the committee or was passed on by Chapin to the others. It is worth restating that Sloan's communications with the NACC are only available by looking at extant collections of the men with whom he corresponded. The Chapin Papers are extremely rich in this regard from 1930 through 1934.

42. Mark H. Rose, *Interstate: Express Highway Politics, 1941–1956* (Lawrence: University Press of Kansas, 1979), 4. For the federal gas tax, also see John C. Burnham, "The Gasoline Tax and the Automobile Revolution," *Journal of American History* 48 (December 1961): 453–59.

43. Pyke Johnson to Roy Chapin, 1 June 1932, RC, Box 22.

44. Chandler, *Giant Enterprise*, 6–7.

45. Excellent inside information on the early years of the NHUC is found in Boxes 41, 42, 44, 48, and 59 of the Frederick Horner Papers (FH), Library of Congress, Washington, D.C. Horner was a second-tier GM executive who played a major role in national transportation issues. That Horner was an ardent supporter of the New Deal makes his notes on a variety of GM-related issues particularly fascinating. Also vital is Box 22 of RC.

46. Pyke Johnson to Alfred Sloan, 26 November 1932, FH, Box 41, Folder 191. For general information on Pyke Johnson, the most important auto lobbyist from the 1920s through the 1950s, I thank his son, Tom Johnson of Littleton, Colorado, phone conversation, 19 December 1998.

47. Minutes of a Special Meeting of National Highway Users Conference, 1775 Broadway [the GM building in New York City], 23 January 1933, 1, FH, Box 44, Folder 228. The minutes reveal Sloan as a master of the pithy statement that moves the proceedings exactly where he wants them to go. Clearly, GM was willing to compromise on truck size to ensure the railroad interests would back off on the gas tax. Still, in August 1935, when the New Deal Congress passed the Motor Carrier Act, which did regulate buses and trucks engaged in interstate commerce, GM was not pleased. A memo from GM's executive in charge of the issue to Alfred Sloan complains, "Today highway transportation is over-regulated and over-taxed." Frederick Horner to Alfred Sloan, 5 February 1936, part 3, 2, FH, Box 48, Folder 274.

48. As clearly stated privately in Alfred P. Sloan to Roy Chapin, 23 June 1932, RC, Box 22. Sloan states that "trucks and buses" are of primary concern to many in the group but that he would focus on the "passenger car problem."

49. Press release, 29 January 1933, Joint Committee of Railroad and Highway Users, FH, Box 41, Folder 191.

50. Excerpt of National Transportation Committee Report of 1933, n.d., FH, Box 48, Folder 274.

51. The NHUC continued to be a major presence at both the state and federal level for the next several decades. Its major function was to safeguard gas taxes, at all levels of government, against any encroachment by any other interest for any other purpose. It was remarkably successful and Sloan would continue to enjoy a key role

in the group for years to come. NHUC is discussed in the very useful, Rose, *Interstate: Express Highway Politics, 1941–1956.*

52. Alfred Sloan, 30 October 1930, "GMC Correspondence 1930–1933," ES, Box 550.

53. Edward Bernays, General Motors Corporation Notes, n.p., n.d., EB, Box 177.

54. "Alfred P. Sloan, Sr., Dies at Plandome," *New York Times,* 31 August 1932, 17.

55. "Mrs. Alfred P. Sloan, Sr., Dies Suddenly at 80," *New York Times,* 25 December 1932, 13.

CHAPTER SEVEN

1. N. W. MacChesney to Roy Chapin, 20 September 1932, Roy Chapin Papers (RC), Box 23, Bentley Library, Ann Arbor, Michigan. MacChesney, director of the National Hoover–Curtis Committee noted that Sloan and Chapin were the leaders of the effort to "organize the motor industry" for Hoover in 1932.

2. Roy Chapin to Walter Teagle, 27 September 1932, RC, Box 23. Chapin discusses a private White House visit that day.

3. Vincent Curcio, *Chrysler: The Life and Times of an Automotive Genius* (New York: Oxford University Press, 2000), 644.

4. John Pratt to Walter Carpenter, 21 May 1931, Walter Carpenter Papers (WC), Box 542, Hagley Library, Wilmington, Delaware.

5. A. Bradley to Edward Stettinius, 24 February 1933, Edward Stettinius Papers (ES), Box 10, University of Virginia Library, Charlottesville, Virginia; see also Sidney Fine, *The Automobile under the Blue Eagle* (Ann Arbor: University of Michigan Press, 1963), 19–20.

6. For a detailed and lucid account see Charles Cheape, *Strictly Business: Walter Carpenter at du Pont and General Motors* (Baltimore: Johns Hopkins University Press, 1995), 140–53.

7. Here I am influenced in language and concept by Robert Putnam, *Bowling Alone* (New York: Simon and Schuster, 2000).

8. Alfred P. Sloan Jr. to Roy Chapin, 25 January 1932, RC, Box 21.

9. Pyke Johnson to Roy Chapin, 15 February 1932, RC, Box 21.

10. Cheape, *Strictly Business,* 124.

11. Quoted in Roy Chapin to E. Hunt, 20 November 1932, RC, Box 24.

12. Roy Chapin to General R. E. Wood, 25 June 1932, RC, Box 22.

13. Ibid.

14. Ron Chernow, *The House of Morgan* (New York: Simon and Schuster, 1990), 354.

15. Alvan Macauley to Roy Chapin, 15 November 1932, RC, Box 24.

16. Alfred P. Sloan Jr. to Alvan Macauley, 16 January 1933, RC, Box 25.

17. For Sloan and the FDR message, see Alfred P. Sloan Jr. to E. R. Stettinius, 25 November 1932; and for more on the share the work program, see the rest of the material in the Share the Work Movement folder, (ES), Box 5. On the Special Conference Committee and Share the Work Movement, see "Extracts from the Minutes of the Meeting of the Special Conference Committee," New York, Special Conference Committee, 7 December 1932, Charles Kettering Papers (CK), Box 114, GMI, Flint, Michigan.

18. "The Institutional Objective" and "The Competitive Buying Attitude Objective," n.d. [late 1932?], (ES), Box 19, Folder: J. David Hauser.

19. See Edward L. Bernays, *biography of an idea: memoirs of public relations counsel* (New York: Simon and Schuster, 1965), chap. 43. Not surprisingly, Bernays puts quite a spin on the story and completely leaves out Sloan's disgust for some of Bernays's operations. This disgust, as I see it, costs Bernays the GM contract, which he does not report. For an outstanding analysis of the relationship between Sloan and Bernays, see William L. Bird Jr., *"Better Living": Advertising, Media, and the New Vocabulary of Business Leadership, 1935–1955* (Evanston, Ill.: Northwestern University Press, 1999), 36–40.

20. Edward Bernays, General Motors Corporation Notes, n.p., n.d., Edward Bernays Papers (EB), Box 177, Library of Congress, Washington, D.C. In his published memoir, Bernays moderates his tone and descriptions.

21. Bernays, *biography of an idea,* 543.

22. J. David Hauser, "The Public, the Automobile and the General Motors Corporation," 1932, ES, Box 19. The quote appears on page 6 of the seventy-six-page document.

23. Paul Garrett to Alfred P. Sloan Jr., 11 November 1931, ES, Box 550. Garrett promotes the idea that will become Arthur Pound's, *The Turning Wheel* (Garden City, N.J.: Doubleday, 1934). Garrett writes: "Being written by a recognized historian . . . it would command the respect of intelligent readers. . . . [T]here is a vast difference between putting out an unbiased history of the character I describe and sponsored by a recognized publishing house and putting out something that clearly is propaganda through an arrangement with some private printer and easily recognized as such."

24. Sloan describes the program and reproduces the remarkable conversation he held in 1925 with other key GM men on the subject in *My Years with General Motors* (New York: Currency Doubleday, 1990), 165–68.

25. In Box 175, Folder GM 1933 of the Bernays Papers are dozens of newspaper clippings about the Better Transportation Ventilation Committee. In the same box is an untitled, undated memo with a marginal note, "a short capsule of ELB's services," that outlines the "technique" and what is later called "the technique of propaganda" employed in the ventilation and composite body campaigns.

26. Thomas G. Estop to Charles Kettering, 15 December 1933; Thomas Parran to Alfred P. Sloan Jr., 19 December 1933 (the tone of the letter indicates Parran knew Sloan); and Alfred P. Sloan Jr. to Paul W. Garrett, 27 December 1933; EB, Box 177.

27. For the record, Bernays states in his memoir, *biography of an idea,* 556, that his contract was not renewed because of jealousy over one of his successes by a couple of GM vice presidents. He does not at all mention the fiasco. The June 1934 *Journal of the American Medical Association* had a column condemning public-relations-driven associations and testimonials by doctors: "There is no legitimate excuse for imposing on the public, either professional or lay, in this manner." The good Dr. Goodchild was blasted in the piece and he, in turn, demanded that Bernays somehow help him to restore his reputation. All this is collected in EB, Box 177.

28. Drawn from "Summary of letters from Hayes to ELB," 12 December 1932, and Ralph Hayes to Edward Bernays, 12 December 1932, EB, Box 177.

29. "Militant Leadership Argued by Sloan," *New York Times,* 31 December 1932, 21.

30. "Roosevelt Works with House Chieftains for Federal Cuts," *New York Times,* 31 December 1932, 1.

31. "Leaders Put Faith in the Machine Age to End Depression," *New York Times,* 9 January 1933, 1.

32. William E. Leuchtenburg, *Franklin D. Roosevelt and the New Deal* (New York: Harper and Row, 1963), 22.

33. Paul Garrett to Edward L. Bernays, 30 January 1933, EB, Box 176.

34. For Woodlock, see George Melloan, "Journal Editorials and the Common Man," *Wall Street Journal* Centennial Edition, 23 June 1989, avail. at <http://www.opinionjournal.com/about/com.html>.

35. For the Detroit bank fiasco, see Curcio, *Chrysler*, 503–17, with the Ford quote on 508. See also Arthur Schlesinger, *The Crisis of the Old Order: 1919–1933* (Boston: Houghton Mifflin, 1957), 475–76.

36. Alfred P. Sloan Jr. to Roy Chapin, 21 September 1932, RC, Box 23.

37. Alfred P. Sloan Jr. to Franklin D. Roosevelt, 11 March 1933, President's Personal Files (PPF), Box 144, Franklin D. Roosevelt Library, Hyde Park, New York.

38. Alfred P. Sloan Jr., "A Statement to the People of Detroit," 24 March 1933, RC, Box 25.

39. Bernays, *biography of an idea*, 548–49.

40. "Inaugural Address," 4 March 1933, in *The Public Papers and Addresses of Franklin D. Roosevelt*, vol. 2 (New York: Random House, 1938 [1933]), 12.

41. Quoted in Leuchtenburg, *Franklin D. Roosevelt and the New Deal*, 44.

42. For Pyke Johnson's bulletins, see the February, March, and April folders in RC, Box 25; the quote on Roosevelt is from Pyke Johnson to Roy Chapin, 19 April 1933, RC, Box 25. At the top of the letter and almost all the other Washington correspondence from Johnson to Chapin in 1933 is the note "identical letter to Alfred P. Sloan, Jr." Sloan's public works strategy is recorded in Pyke Johnson to Alfred Reeves, 17 April 1933, RC, Box 25.

43. "Thirty-Hour Week Bill," Hearings before the Committee on Labor, House of Representatives, 73d Cong., 1st Sess., on S. 158 and H.R. 4557 and Proposals Offered by the Secretary of Labor, 25–28 April and 1–5 May 1933 (Washington, D.C.: Government Printing Office, 1933), 790. Sloan met with Senator Vandenberg and told him that he was "chiefly anxious to be sure that officers, executives, etc. were clearly exempted" from the maximum hours restrictions. Arthur H. Vandenberg to Roy Chapin, 6 April 1933, RC, Box 35.

44. "Thirty-Hour Week Bill," 783–84.

45. In discussing the National Recovery Administration I draw on the superbly researched work by Sidney Fine, *The Automobile under the Blue Eagle: Labor, Management and the Automobile Manufacturing Code* (Ann Arbor: University of Michigan Press, 1963).

46. Pyke Johnson to Alfred P. Sloan, Roy Chapin, and Edward Stettinius, April 19, 1933, Box 25, RC.

47. David Noble, *America by Design: Science, Technology and the Rise of Corporate Capitalism* (New York: Oxford University Press, 1979), 279–80.

48. Robert Collins, *The Business Response to Keynes, 1929–1964* (New York: Columbia University Press, 1981), 27.

49. I am drawing specifically here on Joseph Huthmacher, *Senator Robert F. Wagner and the Rise of Urban Liberalism* (New York: Atheneum, 1968), 144–47.

50. For Pyke Johnson's reports, see the May 1933 folder, RC, Box 25; the quote is from "An Analysis of the Position of the NACC under the NRA," 23 May 1933, RC, Box 25.

51. Minutes, Special Conference Committee, 18 May 1933, Kettering Archives (KA), 87–11.5–7, Alumni Collection of Industrial History, GMI, Flint, Michigan.

52. Taken from Fine, *The Automobile under the Blue Eagle,* 21.

53. General Bulletin, NACC, 6 June 1933, RC, Box 25. Pyke Johnson reported, "The new provision on collective bargaining is much more satisfactory than the old." Pyke Johnson to Roy Chapin, 6 June 1933, RC, Box 25.

54. McQuaid, *Big Business and Presidential Power,* 30.

55. Sloan's hopes for the NRA were still alive but fast fading at the end of 1933, as he states in a letter to his friend and respected peer Pierre du Pont. See Alfred P. Sloan Jr. to Pierre du Pont, 15 December 1933, Pierre du Pont Papers (PDP), Box 1173, Folder 5, Hagley Library, Wilmington, Delaware. The Pratt quote is from John Pratt to Congressman Walter Pierce, 31 October 1933, KA, P76–5.11. Sidney Fine has produced numerous scholarly works on the NRA and the auto industry; the most thorough is Fine, *The Automobile under the Blue Eagle.* See ibid., 44–47, for Sloan's views.

56. Alfred P. Sloan Jr. to Edward R. Stettinius, 21 November 1933 (two letters are sent that day), ES, Box 24.

57. Alfred P. Sloan Jr. to Louis A. Kirstein, 14 November 1933, ES, Box 24.

58. Sloan was not, however, a man to let his agitation get in the way of practicalities, at least usually. So, as long the NRA existed, he attempted to get out of it what use he could. For example, he supported the NRA Auto Code attempt to systematize car dealer practice; dealer relations were long a problem for all the major auto manufacturers. See Fine, *The Automobile under the Blue Eagle,* 135–37.

59. Minutes, Special Meeting of N.A.C.C. with General Johnson Held in General Motors Building, Detroit, 28 July 1933, 7, RC, Box 26.

60. Alfred P. Sloan Jr. to Pierre du Pont, 15 December 1933, 2.

61. Walter Carpenter to Donaldson Brown, 9 January 1941, Government Trial Exhibit No. 139, *United States v. E. I. du Pont de Nemours, General Motors Co. et al.,* Civil Action No. 49c-1071, District Court for Northern Illinois.

62. This matter came to public light in the antitrust action taken against General Motors and Du Pont by the federal government in the 1950s. I am following the account and taking the quote from Ed Cray, *Chrome Colossus: General Motors and Its Times* (New York: McGraw-Hill, 1980), 270.

63. The quote is an indirect one taken from the summary of Alfred Reeves of the NACC. Alfred Reeves to Roy Chapin, 22 June 1933, RC, Box 26. For Pyke's entreaty, see Pyke Johnson to Alfred P. Sloan Jr., 12 May 1933, RC, Box 25.

64. For Hoffman's early efforts, see Paul Hoffman to Roy Chapin, 25 January 1934, RC, Box 27. And for more on Hoffman and events in 1933–34, see Donald Critchlow, *Studebaker* (Bloomington: Indiana University Press, 1996), 108–10.

65. Sloan, *My Years with General Motors,* 446–47.

66. Sloan was not on the NACC Committee on Labor Relations; Knudsen was. And at least by December 1934, though probably earlier, Don Brown was in charge of handling labor issues for GM in regard to the NRA and the Automobile Labor Board; see NACC Committee on Labor Relations, 25–26 January 1934, RC, Box 27; and "Notes of Discussion of Regularization of Employment," Washington, D.C., RC, Box 28.

67. See, for example, Sloan's statement, General Motors Press Release, 2 April 1934, CK, 87–11.5–10.

68. Bird, *"Better Living,"* 27.

69. Alfred P. Sloan Jr., "Address before the Poor Richard Club of Philadelphia," 17 January 1936, 7, 83–12.16, Alumni Collection of Industrial History, GMI, Flint, Michigan.

70. By the mid-1930s, Kettering had become a good friend and trusted ally of Sloan's, Charles Kettering to H. G. Weaver, 5 June 1942, CK, Box 111. The late date indicated the continuity of concern felt by GM leadership, even into the war years, on this matter.

71. Paul Garrett to Alfred P. Sloan Jr. and Charles Kettering, 25 June 1934, CK, Box 110. Sloan's stockholder messages are available in the pamphlet collection at the Hagley Library. For a good example, see Sloan, "Business Bigness," 11 July 1935.

72. Franklin D. Roosevelt telegram to Alfred P. Sloan Jr., 26 May 1934, CK, 87–11.5–12.

73. Clipping from *New York American,* 5 December 1935, ES, Box 578.

74. Samuel Grafton, "Propaganda from the Right," *American Mercury* 34, no. 135 (March 1935): 264.

75. "Attack," *Newsweek,* 14 December 1935, 10–11.

76. This material is drawn from "NAM through the Ages," *New Republic,* 22 December 1937, 184.

77. NIIC, "The Origins and Objectives of the National Industrial Information Committee," *Annual Report 1943,* 2–3, National Association of Manufacturers Papers (NAM), Box 842, Hagley Library, Wilmington, Delaware.

78. NIIC, "Telling Industry's Story," 1938, NAM, Box 843. The quotes and story synopsis are from Bird, *"Better Living,"* 54–58.

79. NIIC, "Telling Industry's Story."

80. NIIC, "Report of the Industrial Information Council," 1941, NAM, Box 842.

81. NIIC, "*Confidential:* Certain Recommendations in Connection with NAM's Public Information Program in 1941," n.d., 1, NAM, Box 843.

82. See Elizabeth A. Fones-Wolf, *Selling Free Enterprise: The Business Assault on Labor and Liberalism, 1945–60* (Urbana: University of Illinois Press, 1994), 25.

83. The Furnas article is discussed in Joel W. Eastman, *Styling vs. Safety: The American Automobile Industry and the Development of Automotive Safety, 1900–1966* (Lanham, Md.: University Press of America, 1984), 137–38.

84. Hoffman, unlike Sloan, saw auto safety features as a major selling point and made his Studebaker cars the industry leader. See Alan R. Raucher, *Paul G. Hoffman* (Lexington: University Press of Kentucky, 1985), 28.

85. Ibid., 143.

86. Tom Johnson, son of Pyke Johnson (Pyke Johnson managed the foundation from 1942 to 1953), provided me with several pamphlets created by the ASF. All the quoted material and statistics come from the *Silver Anniversary Automotive Safety Foundation Booklet 1937–1962* (1962). The ASF clearly accomplished a great deal in improving road safety and its officers and trustees rightfully earned praise in the *Congressional Record* and recognition by a number of professional organizations. Its first grants went to developing a program in traffic engineering at Harvard (and then Yale) and for a college program for traffic police at Northwestern. In 1938, grants were made to study and reform traffic courts and to develop course material for high school driver training, as well as to aid the International Association of Chiefs of Police in developing standards for police traffic control functions. ASF leaders like Johnson and Paul Hoffman were genuinely committed to safety issues; for a rich treatment of the progressive role of traffic engineers, see Clay McShane, "The Origins and Globalization of Traffic Control Signals," *Journal of Urban History* 25, no. 3 (March 1999): 379–404. No one would argue, however, that part of the ASF's purpose was to ensure that safety costs were not borne by the auto industry. This perspective was certainly held by Sloan. As noted earlier in the text, Sloan was aware that the use of safety glass in car windows

would reduce injuries but the cost of such an improvement was relatively high and Sloan believed that people would not pay extra for it, especially at a time of reduced car sales. So safety glass was not introduced into GM cars as standard equipment until several years later. See Alfred P. Sloan Jr., direct testimony, trial transcript, *United States v. Dupont, GM, et al.*, 193–94.

87. "Sloan in Attack on New Deal Says 'It Retards Revival,' " *New York Times*, 30 April 1936, 1.

88. Irénée du Pont to Pierre du Pont, 10 July 1934, Irénée du Pont Papers (IDP), Box 63, Hagley Library, Wilmington, Delaware.

89. Alfred P. Sloan to Pierre du Pont, 14 June 1935, PDP, Box 771.

90. I am relying on the standard work on the Liberty League, George Wolfskill, *The Revolt of the Conservatives: A History of the American Liberty League, 1933–40* (Boston: Houghton Mifflin, 1962). Also of great use is Robert F. Burk, *The Corporate State and the Broker State* (Cambridge: Harvard University Press, 1991), chaps. 8, 10. The information on contributions and budget is from Wolfskill, *The Revolt of the Conservatives*, 62–63. In George Seldes, *You Can't Do That!* (New York: Modern Age Books, 1938), 252, Sloan is reported to have given five thousand dollars and loaned twice that amount to the American Liberty League in 1935. John Pratt gave the same amount.

91. General Motors executives, not just Sloan, were quite careful about their record-keeping habits. Many documents are just not in the archives. A hint of the culling practices emerges in the papers of Frederick C. Horner, a rare pro–New Deal GM executive. He kept things in his collected papers he was not supposed to keep. A letter Horner sent to his boss, E. R. Breech, dated July 23, 1935, which reveals an inappropriate business relationship between du Pont and GM, has scrawled across it in pencil, "Destroy this letter and your file copy, ERB." See Frederick Horner Papers (FH), Box 59, File 13, Library of Congress, Washington, D.C.

92. *New York Times*, 18 April 1936, 1. Later, after adverse publicity about the organization's anti-Semitism, and Sloan's donation, came out—and it is very possible that Sloan knew little about the group—he apologized for his donation. He stated: "Under no circumstances will I further knowingly support the Sentinels of the Republic." Rather disingenuously, he concluded: "I have no desire to enter into any questions involving religious or political considerations." The quote appears in Paul F. Douglas, *Six upon the World: Toward an American Culture for an Industrial Age* (Boston: Little, Brown, 1954), 176.

93. Here I am relying on Wolfskill, *The Revolt of the Conservatives*, which details Sloan's limited role; see 175–78, 231–34, 239–42. For other groups supported by the League and Sloan, see ibid., chapter 9. See also Arthur Schlesinger, *The Politics of Upheaval* (Boston: Houghton Mifflin, 1960), 521–23.

94. Franklin D. Roosevelt, "Address at Madison Square Garden, New York City," 31 October 1936, in *The Public Papers and Addresses of Franklin D. Roosevelt*, vol. 5 (New York: Random House, 1938 [1936]), 568–69.

CHAPTER EIGHT

1. "The World Isn't Finished," 25 October 1936, Kettering Archives (KA), 87–11.5–16, Alumni Collection of Industrial History, GMI, Flint, Michigan. For more on the address and others Sloan gave in 1936, see Paul Garrett to Charles Kettering, 19 May 1936; and Alfred P. Sloan Jr. to Charles Kettering, 28 July 1936, KA, 87–11.5–15.

2. President's Personal Files (PPF), Box 92, Franklin D. Roosevelt Library, Hyde Park, New York.

3. American Liberty League, "Some Reasons Why the Present Administration Can and Will Be Defeated," 11 May 1936, Pierre du Pont Papers (PDP), Box 771, Hagley Library, Wilmington, Delaware.

4. Arthur Schlesinger, *The Politics of Upheaval* (Boston: Houghton Mifflin, 1960), 594.

5. Ibid., 623–25, 639 (for the poll data).

6. George Wolfskill, *The Revolt of the Conservatives: A History of the American Liberty League* (Boston: Houghton Mifflin, 1962), 207, 220. Of that amount, $32,500 was made in Mrs. Sloan's name.

7. For an excellent treatment of New Deal political realignment in general, and the source for the 1936 results, see Anthony J. Badger, *The New Deal* (New York: Noonday Press, 1989), chap. 6.

8. "General Motors Corporation Unit Sales of Total Cars and Trucks—By Division," in Alfred P. Sloan Jr., *My Years with General Motors* (New York: Currency Doubleday, 1990), 446–47.

9. W. H. Swartz, Lehman Corp. confidential office memo, 4 November 1936, Alexander Sachs Papers (AS), Box 92, FDR.

10. W. H. Swartz, Report of 8 December 1936, AS, Box 92.

11. Sidney Fine, *Sit-Down* (Ann Arbor: University of Michigan Press, 1969), 25–27. Fine's brilliantly researched and written work plays a fundamental role in this part of the text.

12. Joseph J. Huthmacher, *Senator Robert Wagner and the Rise of Urban Liberalism* (New York: Atheneum, 1968), 170.

13. Jerold S. Auerbach, *Labor and Liberty: The La Follette Committee and the New Deal* (Indianapolis: Bobbs-Merrill, 1966), 112. Sloan never saw any need to comment on such unpleasantness in his own writings and, not surprisingly, the paper collections of General Motors men like Charles Kettering, Pierre du Pont, and John Pratt similarly provide no evidence of responsibility for anti-union activities by the corporation in general or by a particular executive.

14. Fine, *Sit-Down,* 28–29.

15. Ronald Edsforth, *Class Conflict and Cultural Consensus* (New Brunswick, N.J.: Rutgers University Press, 1987), chap. 7. The prior quote by Lenz is in ibid., 164.

16. Ed Cray, *Chrome Colossus: General Motors and Its Times* (New York: McGraw-Hill, 1980), 424–26.

17. Irving Bernstein, *Turbulent Years* (Boston: Houghton Mifflin, 1970), 516.

18. I am relying on the solid summary in ibid., 516–17. The papers of GM executives available in noncorporate archives are almost completely stripped bare of documents relating to the labor troubles of the 1930s.

19. Fine, *Sit-Down,* 100.

20. Ibid., 96. The UAW quote is in Sidney Fine, *Frank Murphy: The New Deal Years* (Chicago: University of Chicago Press, 1979), 291.

21. Besides *Sit-Down,* I am also following the account given by Sidney Fine, "The General Motors Sit-Down Strike: A Re-examination," *American Historical Review* 70 (April 1965): 691–713; and Melvin Dubofsky and Warren Van Tine, *John L. Lewis* (New York: Quadrangle, 1977), 254–57. For much of what follows in the account of the strikes, I also rely on Frances Perkins, oral history transcript, Columbia University Oral History, Butler Library, New York City, esp. 113–23, 176–218.

22. Quoted in Ronald Edsforth and Robert Asher, with the assistance of Raymond Boryczka, "The Speedup: The Focal Point of Workers' Grievances, 1919–1941," in *Autowork,* ed. Robert Asher and Ronald Edsforth, with the assistance of Stephen Mer-

lino (Albany: SUNY Press, 1995), 70. I rely on this compelling essay for analysis of auto workers' grievances against GM.

23. Edsforth, *Class Conflict and Cultural Consensus,* 139.

24. Edsforth and Asher, "The Speedup," 77.

25. Alfred P. Sloan Jr., "General Motors and Its Labor Policy," 5 January 1937, Frederick Horner Papers (FH), Box 48, Library of Congress, Washington, D.C.

26. Fine, *Frank Murphy,* 299.

27. Frances Perkins, oral history transcript, 118.

28. Fine, *Sit-Down,* 163.

29. Niccolò Machiavelli, *The Prince,* trans. Harvey C. Mansfield (Chicago: University of Chicago Press, 1985), 66.

30. Fine, *Frank Murphy,* 297

31. I am relying on the powerfully told first chapter of Fine, *Sit-Down,* as well as the detailed coverage of the events in the *New York Times,* 12 January 1937, 1, 12.

32. *New York Times,* 13 January 1937, 3.

33. Frances Perkins, oral history transcript, 113–14.

34. "A 'Labor Democracy,' " *New York Times,* 17 January 1937, 7E.

35. Harrison George, "Column Left!" *Daily Worker,* 25 January 1937, clipping, Edward Stettinius Papers (ES), Box 565, University of Virginia Library, Charlottesville, Virginia.

36. Samuel Romer, "Profile of General Motors," *Nation,* 23 January 1937, 96–98.

37. Here I am following Fine, *Sit-Down,* 242–54; also useful is Norman Beasley, *Knudsen* (New York: McGraw-Hill, 1947), 172.

38. George Martin, *Madame Secretary: Frances Perkins* (Boston: Houghton Mifflin, 1976).

39. Schlesinger, *The Coming of the New Deal* (Boston: Houghton Mifflin, 1958), 300.

40. Fine, *Sit-Down,* 254.

41. Frances Perkins, oral history transcript, 123.

42. Quoted in Bernstein, *Turbulent Years,* 535–36.

43. Fine, *Sit-Down,* 257.

44. C. L. Sulzberger, *A Long Row of Candles* (New York: Macmillan, 1969), 17.

45. "The Three Hundred and Thirty-eighth Press Conference," 22 January 1937, *The Public Papers and Addresses of Franklin D. Roosevelt: The Constitution Prevails, 1937,* vol. 6 (*PPAFDR-6*) (New York: Russell and Russell, 1941), 7.

46. Bernstein, *Turbulent Years,* 536.

47. "The Three Hundred and Thirty-ninth Press Conference," 26 January 1937, *PPAFDR-6,* 20–21.

48. Again I rely on Fine, *Sit-Down,* 258.

49. Frances Perkins, oral history transcript, 204–6. Sloan left no version of this phone conversation; one wonders if Perkins has not rewritten, somewhat, their respective lines.

50. Ibid., 209, 214.

51. Ibid., 216–18.

52. Ibid., 208.

53. Based on the nationally syndicated column, Drew Pearson and Robert Allen, "Washington Merry-Go-Around," 8 February 1937, newspaper clipping, Stewart Mott Papers (SM), Box 77, GMI, Flint, Michigan.

54. Walter Lippman, "The Sit-Down Strike, Whose Problem Is It?" *Detroit Free Press,* 29 January 1937, clipping, SM, 77–7.4–1.33–2.

55. Pearson and Allen, "Washington Merry-Go-Round," 8 February 1937. Pearson

was willing to go after just about anyone; FDR called him "a chronic liar" and Senator Kenneth McKellar spoke for many congressmen when he called Pearson "an infamous liar, a revolting liar, a pusillanimous liar." For more on Pearson and these quotes, see David Brinkley, *Washington Goes to War* (New York: Knopf, 1988), 186–87.

56. Vincent Curcio, *Chrysler: The Life and Times of an Automotive Genius* (New York: Oxford University Press, 2000), 583.

57. Dubofsky and Van Tine, *John L. Lewis,* 268.

58. Ibid., 269.

59. Fine, *Sit-Down,* 286.

60. Jerold S. Auerbach, *Labor and Liberty: The La Follette Committee and the New Deal* (Indianapolis: Bobbs-Merrill, 1966), 113. For the convoluted and confusing testimony of GM's industrial relations man Merle C. Hale and other GM officials, see "Violations of Free Speech and Rights of Labor," *Hearings before a Subcommittee of the Committee on Education and Labor United States Senate,* 75th Cong., 1st Sess., pt. 6, Labor Espionage General Motors Corporation, 15–19 February 1937 (Washington, D.C.: Government Printing Office, 1937).

61. The income dollar amount is reported in "Tax of 10 More Cut by Company Device," *New York Times,* 30 June 1937, 10. Sloan's response: "Sloan Says He Paid 60% of His Income," *New York Times,* 1 July 1938, 8. For Sloan and the tax charges, see *Hearings before the Joint Committee on Tax Evasion and Avoidance,* 75th Cong., 1st Sess. (1937), 226–30.

62. Quoted in Horace Coon, *Money to Burn* (New York: Longmans, Green, 1938), 198. Coons is among the very first to explore the vexing question of what the wealthy thought they were doing when they expended great sums of money publicly promoting a probusiness, procapitalist viewpoint during the New Deal years. The statement was reported in the *New York Times,* 17 December 1937. Sloan had set up the foundation in 1934 by donating five hundred thousand dollars in GM stock, but he had not cashed in the stock or made any grants prior to 1937.

63. Alfred P. Sloan Jr. to Irénée du Pont, 13 January 1938, Irénée du Pont Papers (IDP), Box 280, Hagley Library, Wilmington, Delaware.

64. Alfred P. Sloan Jr. to Charles Kettering, 14 May 1938, KA, 87-11.5-20.

65. The quoted passages are from "History and Field of Activity," *Report Alfred P. Sloan Foundation 1940* (New York: Alfred P. Sloan Foundation, 1941), 39. For Sloan's handling of the foundation, see Warren Weaver, oral history transcript, Columbia Oral History Collection, Butler Library, Columbia University, New York, 702–35.

66. Charles Cheape, *Strictly Business: Walter Carpenter at du Pont and General Motors* (Baltimore: Johns Hopkins University Press, 1995), 161. I follow Cheape's astute analysis of the reorganization as outlined on pages 158–68.

67. Lammont du Pont to Walter Carpenter, 23 April 23 1937, Government Trial Exhibit No. 196, *United States v. E. I. du Pont de Nemours, General Motors Co. et al.,* Civil Action No. 49c-1071, District Court for Northern Illinois.

68. As Charles Cheape demonstrates in *Strictly Business,* 161–64. Walter Carpenter at Du Pont was not in favor of much of Sloan's reorganization and did make his objections clear. But, in the end, he did not stand in Sloan's way, even as he continued to argue for a rethinking of aspects of the plan.

69. William Leuchtenburg, *Franklin Roosevelt and the New Deal,* 235–36.

70. Based on Anthony J. Badger, *The New Deal* (New York: Hill and Wang, 1989), 111–12.

71. Alan Brinkley, *The End of Reform* (New York: Knopf, 1995), 56.

72. For the Sloan aspect, see Leuchtenburg, *Franklin Roosevelt and the New Deal,* 247. For the other quotes, see Brinkley, *The End of Reform,* 57–58.

73. "G.M. III" How To Sell Automobiles," *Fortune,* February 1939, 109. Sloan discusses the issue and its resolution in 1952 in *My Years with General Motors,* 309.

74. "General Motors," *Fortune,* December 1938, 158.

75. *PPAFDR-*6, 305–6.

76. Brinkley, *The End of Reform,* 114.

77. Ibid., 135.

78. "Investigation of Concentration of Economic Power," *Hearings before the Temporary National Economic Committee,* 75th Cong., 1st Sess., pt. 9 (Washington, D.C.: Government Printing Office, 1940), 3668.

79. Donaldson Brown to Alfred P. Sloan Jr., 15 July 1938, Walter S. Carpenter Papers (WSC), Hagley Library, Wilmington, Delaware, Box 821.

80. Alfred P. Sloan Jr. to Walter S. Carpenter Jr., 24 April 24 1941, WSC, Box 837, Folder 33A.

81. For the most cogent, if still-not-convincing version of the New Deal as a champion of business, see Colin Gordon, *New Deals* (New York: Cambridge University Press, 1994).

82. Curcio, *Chrysler,* 647.

CHAPTER NINE

1. Randolph S. Bourne, *War and the Intellectuals* (New York: Harper, 1964), 71.

2. Irénée du Pont to Alfred P. Sloan Jr., 28 December 1934, Irénée du Pont Papers (IDP), Box 42, Hagley Library, Wilmington, Delaware.

3. Alfred P. Sloan Jr. to Irénée du Pont, 21 December 1934, IDP, Box 42. This letter actually precedes the previous letter quoted, but it is clearly responsive to the same problem.

4. Alfred P. Sloan Jr. to Irénée du Pont, 3 January 1935, IDP, Box 42.

5. Alfred P. Sloan, Jr., to Helen Lewis, April 6, 1939, FBI Report, August 8, 1941, File No. 100–3230, p. 21; FBI-FOIA Subject: Alfred P. Sloan, Jr., File No. 100–25806 (APS-FBI). The letter is about 1500 words long and is in direct response to Mrs. Lewis's specific concerns. Sloan always took the time to do a job right that he felt needed doing.

6. On the inner workings of the Roosevelt administration's war mobilization efforts, I rely on Alan Brinkley, *The End of Reform* (New York: Knopf, 1995), chap. 8.

7. Alfred P. Sloan Jr. to John Pratt, 29 September 1939 (JP), Box 76.

8. Norman Beasley, *Knudsen* (New York: McGraw-Hill, 1947), 226.

9. Ibid., 235.

10. Frederick Horner, unpublished memoir, 78, Frederick Horner Papers (FH), Box 70, Library of Congress, Washington, D.C.

11. Despite the early unpleasantness, Pratt and Stettinius continued in government war work; Stettinius, who was mockingly called "Junior" by Washington insiders, ended the war as secretary of state. Bruce Catton, *The War Lords of Washington* (New York: Harcourt, Brace, 1948), 8.

12. Catton, *The War Lords,* 71; see also Brinkley, *The End of Reform,* 183.

13. Alfred P. Sloan Jr. to John Pratt, 12 June 1940, JP, Box 76.

14. Charles Cheape, *Strictly Business: Walter Carpenter at Du Pont and General Motors* (Baltimore: Johns Hopkins University Press, 1995), 164.

15. All quotes are from Alfred P. Sloan Jr., "Economic State of the Nation," 24

September 1940, Pittsburgh, Pennsylvania, printed as a pamphlet by General Motors, Kettering Archives (KA), 83–12.17, Alumni Collection of Industrial History, GMI, Flint, Michigan.

16. Robert F. Burk, *The Corporate State and the Broker State* (Cambridge: Harvard University Press, 1990), 274–77.

17. I take this quote from Ed Cray, *Chrome Colossus: General Motors and Its Times* (New York: McGraw-Hill, 1980), 316–17. Cray quotes an AP dispatch on the radio broadcast sent to the *Los Angeles Times,* 19 October 1940.

18. Alfred P. Sloan Jr., Minutes of Meeting Held at the D.A.C., 21 May 1941, 2, KA, 87–11.4–18.

19. I found the following article quite helpful in laying out key economic mobilization issues: Brian Waddell, "Economic Mobilization for World War II and the Transformation of the U.S. State," *Politics and Society* 22, no. 2 (June 1994): 165–94.

20. As late as June 1940, Mooney still saw the Nazis and the British as more or less equally responsible for the horrible events in Europe, and he expressed no moral reservations—or moral approval—of the Nazis. James D. Mooney, "War or Peace in America?" Address at the Fifty-fifth Alumni Reunion Banquet, Case Alumni Association, Case School of Applied Science, University Club, Cleveland, Ohio, 1 June 1940, in Alfred Pritchard Sloan Jr., File No. 100–3230, Federal Bureau of Investigation (APS-FBI).

21. The issue is summarized by J. Edgar Hoover, Director, FBI to Lawrence M. C. Smith, Chief, Neutrality Laws Unit, 24 September 1940 (APS-FBI). An interesting perspective on Mooney's feelings about Germany and the Nazi government are revealed by his friend, the journalist Louis Lochner, in his memoir. Louis P. Lochner, *Always the Unexpected* (New York: Macmillan, 1956), 262–72.

22. Based on Lochner, *Always the Unexpected,* 262–72.

23. GM's relationship with Opel from 1939 through 1945 is an immensely controversial subject. GM's official position on this matter was most recently stated by John F. Smith Jr., CEO and president of General Motors on December 14, 1998 in response to a *Washington Post* story of November 30, 1998 alleging that GM collaborated with the Nazis during World War II. Smith denies the charge, stating that in 1939 GM withdrew its executives in charge of Opel operations and that the last American employee assigned to Opel left in March 1941, and further that the relationship was completely severed when war was declared by Germany on the United States on December 11, 1941. John F. Smith, "General Motors and World War II," press release by Corpwatch: Holding Corporations Accountable, avail. at <http://www.corpwatch.org/trac/feature/humanrts/history/gm.html>. Bradford C. Snell has alleged that GM collaborated with the Nazis. See Snell, "American Ground Transport: A Proposal for Restructuring the Automobile, Truck, Bus, and Railroad Industries. Report presented to the Committee of the Judiciary, Subcommittee on Antitrust and Monopoly, U.S. Senate, 26 February 1974 (Washington, D.C.: Government Printing Office, 1974), 16–24. He has continued to make such statements and is writing a book based on German documents, as well as American sources, that will explore this issue in depth.

24. Sloan gave a routine press release on the reassignment, quoted in Hoover to Smith memo, 24 September 1940.

25. B. Dubovsky to President Franklin D. Roosevelt, 28 August 1940 (APS-FBI).

26. John Edgar Hoover to Lawrence Smith, 14 October 1940 (APS-FBI).

27. Sloan, Minutes of the Meeting Held at the D.A.C., 11.

60. Cheape, *Strictly Business,* 240.

61. The Sloan quotes are from "Spotlight on Alfred Sloan." The donation information comes from "Alfred P. Sloan, Jr., Dead at 90," *New York Times,* 18 February 1966, 30. The Kettering material is from Stuart Leslie, *Boss Kettering* (New York: Columbia University Press, 1983), 319–21.

62. Sloan's remarks are from "Spotlight on Alfred Sloan." Information on the Sloan School is from the MIT Sloan School of Management website at <http://mitsloan.mit.edu> and from "Alfred P. Sloan, Jr., Dead at 90," *New York Times.*

63. My account of the publication of *My Life with General Motors* is based on Dan Seligman, "Prior Restraint," *Forbes,* 19 October 1998, avail. at <http://www.forbes.com/forbes/98/1019/620907a.htm>. Peter Drucker, in *Adventures of a Bystander* (New York: Harper and Row 1979), offers a completely different version of this story. He states that Sloan wrote the book between 1947 and 1952 and that he did not publish the book until much later because he did not want to offend any of the GM executives mentioned in the book. He also states that Sloan wrote the book in response to a book Drucker had published on GM in 1946; Drucker, *Adventures of a Bystander,* 282, 288. Drucker suggests that he was told this version of events by someone at GM. Based on coauthor McDonald's account, as told to Dan Seligman, I think someone at GM—possibly including Sloan, with whom Drucker spoke many times throughout the 1950s—deliberately misled Drucker.

AFTERWORD

1. My account is based on Ed Cray, *Chrome Colossus: General Motors and Its Times* (New York: McGraw-Hill, 1980), 423–27.

2. Dan Cordtiz, "The Face in the Mirror at General Motors," *Fortune,* August 1966, 117–19, 206–10. The quoted passage appears on p. 118.

3. Cray, *Chrome Colossus,* 7.

4. For a brilliant contemporary account of free market zealotry, captured by the phrase "market populism," see Thomas Frank, *One Market under God* (New York: Doubleday, 2000).

5. I am much influenced here by Barry Karl, *The Uneasy State* (Chicago: University of Chicago Press, 1983).

Index